THE FORMATION OF
CHRISTIANITY IN ANTIOCH

One of the major puzzles of Western civilisation is how early second-century Christianity was transformed into a non-Jewish, Gentile religion, when Christianity began as one of many Jewish factions in the diverse Judaism of the period.

Magnus Zetterholm uses theoretical insights from the social sciences to deal with the complex issues raised by the parting of Judaism and Christianity and the accompanying rise of Christian anti-Semitism in ancient Antioch. He argues that the separation arose both from the socio-political situation in the Roman Empire, and from ideological elements within the Jewish faction of the Jesus movement, primarily concerning the status of Gentiles within the movement.

The study shows that separation was mainly between Jews and Gentiles *within* the Jesus movement. Gentile adherents to the Jesus movement strove to become a legally-recognised voluntary association completely separated from Judaism, and the anti-Judaism of early Christianity was used as a resource in this struggle of independence.

This novel approach to a much-debated subject will be valuable reading for both advanced students and academics, as well as the general reader with an interest in Jewish-Christian relations in antiquity.

Magnus Zetterholm is Research Fellow at the Centre for Theology and Religious Studies, Lund University, and was awarded the 2002 Clio Prize for best historical work, all categories.

THE FORMATION OF CHRISTIANITY IN ANTIOCH

A social-scientific approach to the
separation between Judaism
and Christianity

Magnus Zetterholm

Routledge
Taylor & Francis Group

LONDON AND NEW YORK

First published 2003
by Routledge
2 Park Square, Milton Park, Abingdon, Oxon, OX14 4RN

Simultaneously published in the USA and Canada
by Routledge
270 Madison Ave, New York, NY 10016

Reprinted in 2005

Routledge is an imprint of the Taylor & Francis Group

The author can be contacted directly at Magnus.Zetterholm@teol.lu.se

Typeset in Garamond by
BOOK NOW Ltd
Printed and bound in Great Britain by
Antony Rowe Ltd, Wiltshire

British Library Cataloguing in Publication Data
A catalogue record for this book is available from the British Library

Library of Congress Cataloging in Publication Data
Zetterholm, Magnus, 1958–
The formation of Christianity in Antioch : a social-scientific approach to the
separation between Judaism and Christianity / Magnus Zetterholm.
p. cm.
Includes bibliographical references and indexes.
1. Jewish Christians–Turkey–Antioch–History–Early church, ca. 30–600. 2.
Religion and sociology–Turkey–Antioch–History. 3. Christianity and other
religions–Judaism–History. 4. Judaism–Relations–Christianity–History. 5.
Antioch (Turkey)–Church history. I. Title.
BR195.J8 Z48 2003
275.64'01–dc21   2002033316

ISBN 0-415-29896-2 (hbk)
ISBN 0-415-35959-7 (pbk)

TO KARIN, ANNA,
MICHAEL, LINDA, SOFIA

CONTENTS

CONTENTS

FIGURES

ABBREVIATIONS

ʿAbod. Zar.	ʿAbodah Zarah (Mishnah, Tosefta, Talmud)
ʾAbot	ʾAbot (Mishnah, Tosefta, Talmud)
Add. Esth.	Additions to Esther (Apocrypha and Septuagint)
A.J.	Antiquitates judaicae (Josephus)
Ann.	Annales (Tacitus)
Aug.	Divus Augustus (Suetonius)
B.J.	Bellum judaicum (Josephus)
Bar.	Baruch (Apocrypha and Septuagint)
C. Ap.	Contra Apionem (Josephus)
Chron.	Chronographia (John Malalas)
CIJ	Corpus inscriptionum judaicarum (Epigraphica)
CIL	Corpus inscriptionum latinarum (Epigraphica)
Civ.	De civitate Dei (Augustinus)
CPJ	Corpus papyrorum judaicarum (Papyri, Ostraka)
Diogn.	Diognetus (Apostolic Fathers)
Dom.	Domitianus (Suetonius)
Ebr.	De ebrietate (Philo)
1 En.	1 Enoch (OT Pseudepigrapha)
Ep.	Epistulae (Pliny the Younger)
Ep.	Epistulae morales (Seneca)
Eph.	Ignatius, To the Ephesians (Apostolic Fathers)
Ḥal.	Ḥallah (Mishnah, Tosefta, Talmud)
Hist. eccl.	Historia ecclesiastica (Eusebius)
Hist.	Historiae (Tacitus)
Jdt	Judith (Apocrypha and Septuagint)
Jos. Asen.	Joseph and Aseneth (OT Pseudepigrapha)
Jub.	Jubilees (OT Pseudepigrapha)
Leg.	De legibus (Cicero)
Legat.	Legatio ad Gaium (Philo)
Let. Aris.	Letter of Aristeas (OT Pseudepigrapha)

Lev. Rab.	*Leviticus Rabbah* (Midrash)
LXX	Septuagint (Greek translation of the Hebrew Bible)
1–4 Macc.	1–4 Maccabees (Apocrypha and Septuagint)
Magn.	Ignatius, *To the Magnesians* (Apostolic Fathers)
MAMA	*Monumenta Asiae Minoris Antiqua* (Epigraphica)
Med.	*De Medicina* (Celsus)
Menaḥ.	*Menaḥot* (Mishnah, Tosefta, Talmud)
Nero	*Nero* (Suetonius)
Or.	*Orationes* (Libanius)
Phld.	Ignatius, *To the Philadelphians* (Apostolic Fathers)
Pol.	Ignatius, *To Polycarp* (Apostolic Fathers)
Pss. Sol.	*Psalms of Solomon* (OT Pseudepigrapha)
1QM	*Milḥamah* (Qumran)
Rom.	Ignatius, *To the Romans* (Apostolic Fathers)
Sanh.	*Sanhedrin* (Mishnah, Tosefta, Talmud)
Šeqal.	*Šeqalim* (Mishnah, Tosefta, Talmud)
Sib. Or.	*Sibylline Oracles* (OT Pseudepigrapha)
Smyrn.	Ignatius, *To the Smyrnaeans* (Apostolic Fathers)
Spec.	*De specialibus legibus* (Philo)
T. Levi	*Testament of Levi* (OT Pseudepigrapha)
T. Mos.	*Testament of Moses* (OT Pseudepigrapha)
Tob.	Tobit (Apocrypha and Septuagint)
Verr.	*In Verrem* (Cicero)
Vita	*Vita* (Josephus)
Yebam.	*Yebamot* (Mishnah, Tosefta, Talmud)
Yoma	*Yoma* (Mishnah, Tosefta, Talmud)

ACKNOWLEDGMENTS

This book constitutes a revised version of my doctoral dissertation, which was publicly defended at Lund University in November 2001. It is one of several studies within the multidisciplinary project *The Ancient Synagogue: Birthplace of Two World Religions* at Lund University, sponsored by the Bank of Sweden Tercentenary Foundation, to which I am especially grateful, since their sponsorship has enabled me to do this research. For additional financial support I wish to thank Crafoordska stiftelsen, Knut och Alice Wallenbergs stiftelse, and various minor funds at Lund University.

I wish to express my thanks to Professor Birger Olsson for inviting me to participate in this project and for giving me and other doctoral students at the Department of Theology and Religious Studies at Lund University the intellectual freedom to develop new perspectives and experiment in matters of methodology. While Birger Olsson was my advisor in the beginning of my Ph.D. studies, my real thesis advisor has been Professor Bengt Holmberg. I wish to express my deepest thanks to him for our numerous and lively discussions, which have been of enormous help in defining my position, and for his indefatigable work of reading and commenting on the manifold versions of this book. I owe a debt of gratitude to the members of the New Testament Seminar Group for their critical reading of this study at various stages. I am especially indebted to Dr. Mikael Tellbe, who read the whole manuscript for a final seminar and suggested several corrections.

Among my colleagues, my deepest gratitude goes to my wife, Karin. Her profound knowledge of Jewish studies in general and rabbinic Judaism in particular, as well as her interest in Jewish–Christian relations, made her the perfect partner for thorough and stimulating discussions. The value of having almost instant access to an initiated debating partner round the clock cannot be overrated. Our numerous exchanges have constituted many of the real pleasures in life during the last few years, and Karin's encouragement and support have been of immeasurable value to me.

Many other people have taken a keen interest in my work, and I am especially grateful to two of my colleagues, Dr. Dieter Mitternacht and Dr. Anders Runesson, with whom I have been involved in an ongoing discussion during the last decade. I wish to express my deepest thanks to my friends and colleagues from the section of Sociology of Religion, Professor Curt Dahlgren, Professor Göran Gustafsson and Professor Eva Hamberg, for numerous fruitful discussions and for having read and commented on the whole manuscript.

I am also indebted to Professor Fredrik Lindström for having gone through and commented on the whole manuscript; to Dr. Mark D. Nanos for stimulating discussions on various subjects connected to this study; to Dr. Jan Hermanson for comments on chapter 1; to Professor Eva Österberg for having talked about methodological issues with me; to Dr. Eva-Maria Jansson at the Royal Library in Copenhagen for having assisted me on numerous occasions to find books and articles; to Dr. Lars Dahlin for a long friendship and for having helped me with some medical evaluations; to Dr. Carole Gillis for having improved my English; and, finally, to M. F. A. Jonas Bjurström, for having never exchanged views on anything connected to my dissertation, but for being a good and supportive friend for many years. Any remaining mistakes of any kind are, of course, all my own and it should also be pointed out that I have agreed to disagree with some of my readers and discussion partners.

Scripture quotations are from the New Revised Standard Version of the Bible, copyright © 1989 by the Division of Christian Education of the Council of the Churches of Christ in the United States of America, and are used by permission. Quotations from various Classical authors (see bibliography) are from the Loeb Classical Library, Cambridge: Harvard University Press. The Loeb Classical Library® is a registered trademark of the President and Fellows of Harvard College. I would like to express my thanks for their kind permission to reprint brief excerpts from the works used in this book.

Finally, I would like to express my warmest gratitude to my family, especially to Karin, not only as partner in profession but also in life, for her constant encouragement and love; to Sofia, who was born during the completion of my dissertation, for having slept well at night; to Linda and Michael for long nights of beating up the Zerg in Starcraft™ or conquering evil in the world of Diablo II™; and to Anna for occasionally taking her weary father to some café.

Magnus Zetterholm
Lund, July 2002

1

AIM, METHOD AND PERSPECTIVES

Πᾶ βῶ, καὶ; χαριστίωνι τὰν γὰν κινήσω πᾶσαν.
("If I have somewhere to stand, I will move the whole earth
with my *charistion*.")

Archimedes

The aim of the study

The basic problem—from Jesus to Ignatius

Undoubtedly, most Jews and Christians of today consider that they
belong to different religions. For modern people this division between
Judaism and Christianity seems normal because, in Christian tradition,
Judaism has often been pictured as the ultimate contradiction of
Christianity. As J. D. G. Dunn has put it, "[i]t would hardly be
surprising if someone brought up in Protestant Christianity thought
of Judaism as the antithesis of Christianity."[1] G. Boccaccini, however, has suggested that we should understand Judaism as denoting
"the whole family of monotheistic systems that sprang forth from the
same Middle Eastern roots."[2] Seen in this way Judaism includes
Rabbinism, Karaism, Samaritanism—and Christianity. In Boccaccini's
model Judaism denotes the *genus*, while the branches, such as
Christianity, denote the *species*.

To picture the relation between different religious expressions in
this way has its obvious advantage, especially over previous confes-
sionally oriented models, and it certainly emphasizes the aspect of
continuity. Boccaccini is undeniably right in drawing attention to
biases that have led to a confessional terminology. His choice of an
all-inclusive extreme, however, can lead to other problems. One
must, for instance, reflect upon the meaningfulness of a terminology
that for many Jews and Christians might even be considered

1

offensive. Boccaccini admits that his statement "may be shocking."[3] I would, however, go further—it is simply incorrect.[4]

For the majority of Christian conceptions, Christian identity is not consistent with a Jewish life. In most Christian ideologies, Christ is considered to have *invalidated* the torah. This process is operative from the other side of the divide as well. According to secular Israeli legislation, a Jew who has converted to Christianity (or any other religion) loses the right to immigrate to Israel according to the Law of Return, which applies to Jews only. Thus, according to this definition, a Jew who converts to Christianity ceases to be Jewish. G. G. Stroumsa has summarized the fact of the matter in the following way:

> From the second to the fourth centuries, we can follow the birth out of the traditional faith of Israel, of not one, but at least two religions. Rabbinic Judaism, which emerged at Yavneh before the end of the first century, grew into a full-fledged religion with the development of the Talmudic culture, during the same centuries in which Christianity developed into a new religion with a structure and an identity that were quite different from those of its genitor.[5]

Christianity certainly was a variety of Judaism but definitely ceased to be so. Already at the beginning of the second century we find the first signs of the *Adversus Iudaeos* literature, which can be taken as early evidence of a development that resulted in Judaism being considered as heretical. Henceforth, Judaism and Christianity are best understood as two different religions.[6] One early and rather clear indication of the emergence of Christianity as a new religion is to be found in the writings of Ignatius of Antioch.

Probably during the end of Emperor Trajan's rule (98–117 CE), Ignatius, the bishop of Antioch, was sent to Rome to be executed.[7] During the journey he wrote several letters to various churches in Asia Minor, addressing local problems he knew either from personal visits or from delegations sent to him from local churches. In two letters, to the Magnesians and to the Philadelphians, the local situation led Ignatius to comment on Judaism. It is clear from these comments that Ignatius understood Judaism to be *something profoundly different from Christianity*. In *Magn.* 8:1, for instance, he warns against Jewish influences:

> Be not led astray by strange doctrines or by old fables which are profitless. For if we are living until now according to

2

Judaism [εἰ γὰρ μέχρι νῦν κατὰ Ἰουδαϊσμὸν ζῶμεν], we confess that we have not received grace.

In this text it is evident that Ignatius sees a clear contradiction between Christianity and Judaism. To some extent he probably draws from popular prejudice of Judaism: dependency on fables or myths were common accusations against Judaism.[8] While the text seems to echo Paul in Galatians 5:4, the context of the situation is completely different. As J. Lieu has noted, Ignatius opposes not law and grace but *Judaism and grace*.[9] While Paul addressed the question of how Gentile adherents to the Jesus movement should relate to Judaism from a position *within Judaism*, Ignatius argues from a position *outside Judaism* in order to nullify the whole Jewish religious system. As he states in *Magn.* 10:3:

It is monstrous to talk of Jesus Christ and to practise Judaism [ἰουδαΐζειν]. For Christianity did not base its faith on Judaism, but Judaism on Christianity [ὁ γὰρ Χριστιανισμός οὐκ εἰς Ἰουδαϊσμὸν ἐπίστευσεν, ἀλλ᾿ Ἰουδαϊσμὸς εἰς Χριστιανισμόν], and every tongue believing on God was brought together in it.

We may conclude that, less than a century after the execution of Jesus, we find in many respects one part of the Jesus movement that had turned into something profoundly different. For instance, it seems clear that Jesus directed his mission predominantly, if not completely, to the people of Israel and that, while it cannot be ruled out that in some ways he may have represented a novel interpretation of Jewish traditions, he was deeply rooted within the Judaism of the period. The same, I venture to say, is true for Paul, who most certainly lived and died as a torah-obedient Jew, convinced that the god of Israel intended to fulfill his covenantal promise to the people of Israel, at the same time extending his grace to include also the Gentiles.

We have thus identified the main problem of this study: namely, *if the Jesus movement started out as a Jewish messianic faction, how can it be explained that a representative of the same movement, about eighty years later, finds the basic religious outlook of Judaism to be incompatible with the movement he represents?* What mechanisms lie behind a development that makes Christianity an anti-Jewish religion, entirely separated from Judaism?

3

J. D. G. Dunn and the partings of the ways

These questions have certainly been dealt with before.[10] One modern work of vital importance is Dunn's *The Partings of the Ways: Between Christianity and Judaism and their Significance for the Character of Christianity* (1991). Dunn claims that, during the end of the first century, two new religions emerged: rabbinic Judaism and Christianity. He states that the fact that they emerged from the same matrix makes relevant the question of why they split and became distinct.[11] Despite the obvious merits of Dunn's work, there are reasons for taking a fresh look at the separation between Judaism and Christianity.

Firstly, *Dunn's theoretical outlook and analytical tools are almost exclusively focused on ideological aspects*. He identifies what he considers to be the four pillars of second temple Judaism, namely, mono-theism, election, the covenant focused in the torah, and land focused in the temple. His basic hypothesis is that the partings of the ways was a result of the new movement's questioning and the redefinition "of these four axioms in greater or less degree—at any rate, to a degree unacceptable to mainstream Judaism."[12] While ideological aspects certainly played a vital part in the process, it seems more correct to assume that what Dunn understands to be *the cause* of the separation process actually represents *the result* of the separation defined in ideological terms. The reason for this assumption is that *concrete cultural resources* (e.g., church architecture, symbolic practices, liturgical forms) are more likely to be the object of contention, while *abstract resources* (e.g., ideas, ideologies, values) are easier to manipu-late and often function as strategically mobilized resources in con-flicts over other kind of resources.[13] A full historical analysis of the separation between Judaism and Christianity has to take into consideration the role of social mechanisms as well as the function of ideological aspects in a social conflict perspective. In this study I intend consequently to focus on the sociological aspects of the sepa-ration process: while naturally I will not disregard the ideological aspects, these will be treated within a sociological framework.

Secondly, while Dunn takes into account the extensive reappraisal of the character of Judaism and even refutes what he views as too simplistic a dichotomy between gospel and torah,[14] he reiterates the old dichotomy in a new way. Paul does not attack the torah or the covenant, Dunn, states, but "*a covenantal nomism which insisted on treating the law as a boundary round Israel, marking off Jew from Gentile, with only those inside as heirs of God's promise to Abraham.*"[15]

4

However, when it comes to the relation between the torah and the covenant, it becomes evident that Dunn believes that Paul replaced the torah with faith in Christ for both Jews and Gentiles. Since entry into the covenant is by faith, Dunn argues, circumcision is no longer necessary, and membership in the covenant should not be tied to specific rules but rest solely on faith.

> Faith in Christ *is* the climax of *Jewish* faith, but it is no longer to be perceived as a specifically *Jewish* faith; *faith should not be made to depend in any degree on the believer living as a Jew (judaizing).*[16]

In the wake of K. Stendahl's important collection of essays *Paul Among Jews and Gentiles* (1976), there has been an increasing awareness of Paul's Jewish context that in important areas moves beyond Dunn's understanding of Paul's relation to the torah and Judaism. This new way of looking at Paul and his relation to the torah, the Jewish people, and the Gentiles represents something of a paradigm shift. It is now possible to speak of an independent tradition made up of several well-established and highly respected scholars who offer an alternative solution to the problem of Paul, the torah, and Jewish and Gentile adherents to the Jesus movement.

J. G. Gager has made a very useful summary of the problems associated with the traditional view of Paul and the advantage of a reconstruction of Paul that allows him to be firmly rooted within the diversified Judaism of the first century. The present study agrees with the basic elements of the new view as presented by Gager.[17] Thus, it is assumed that the audience addressed in Paul's letters are Gentiles. Consequently, discourses where the contradiction between the torah and belief in Christ are salient are not applicable to the situation of the Jewish believers at all but are part of a rhetorical discourse aimed at preventing Gentiles from becoming Jews.[18] Thus, it can no longer be assumed that Paul considered the torah to have ceased to have relevance for Jesus-believing Jews. As P. Lapide puts it: "[f]or Jews and for Jewish proselytes the Mosaic Law, as Paul sees it, retains its full and unaltered validity."[19] It is the point of departure of this study that Paul meant Jesus-believing Jews to remain Jews and Jesus-believing Gentiles to remain Gentiles and that the torah had continued validity for Jews.

It must be emphasized that it is not my intention to make any contribution of my own to the problem of Paul's relation to the torah. In these matters I will base my reconstruction exclusively on the works of others, who in my opinion have showed the reasonability of a new view of Paul to a sufficient degree. While there are certainly several more problems to deal with in this field, the focus of this study is a different one. This means that I, as anyone who engages in issues where the relation between the torah and Paul is relevant, side with a specific scholarly tradition whose results are used as a point of departure. This new understanding of Paul is sufficient by itself to motivate a new study of the separation process.

Thirdly, Dunn's view of Paul and the torah implies that the original Jewish and Gentile identities of the adherents to the Jesus movement are transformed *into a common new Christian identity*. Without dealing with the specific theological implications of this, from a social-psychological point of view such a development is highly unlikely. A Jew who came to embrace belief in Jesus as the Messiah could not be said to change one symbolic universe for another. To become a Messiah-believing Jew would rather represent *a new orientation within the same symbolic universe*. The social consequences for a Jew who in an urban environment became attached to a messianic synagogue probably did not initially affect the individual's social and religious identity in any profound way. It was more likely a much greater step to become a member of the strict, monastic Qumran sect.

The social and cognitive consequences for a Gentile who became an adherent of the Jesus movement would be far more serious. It seems clear that it was not consistent with belief in Christ to worship simultaneously other deities.[20] Because of the socio-political system in the Greco-Roman world, reluctance to maintain a Gentile religious identity could have severe effects on the individual's social identity. In this case we may speak of a conversion in the meaning of leaving one religion for another. Such a process would involve the individual's complete repudiation of his or her original social and religious context and a corresponding resocialization into a new. This implies that to a higher degree we must take into consideration that Jews and Gentiles became "Christians" from rather different points of departure. Hence, when dealing with the situation in the first century we cannot speak of "Christians" as if they constituted a homogeneous group. It is of utmost importance that this insight is evidenced in and affects the analytical work. Thus, in the present study I will use the designations "Jesus-believing Jew" and "Jesus-believing Gentile" to describe the followers of the "Jesus movement."[21]

The aim specified

this is an theological separation which you can make because it is not a "social" definition

Since it cannot be assumed that the separation between Judaism and Christianity occurred simultaneously everywhere and was caused by the same circumstances, *a sensible strategy seems to be to restrict an initial study to one location* and only in a second step to examine whether results from such a study are applicable also to other locations. This strategy is also preferable if one considers the amount of available sources. The likelihood of being able to reconstruct the whole process of separation between Judaism and Christianity from the few available texts is almost nil. Even if we confine ourselves to study only one location, the task is an extremely complicated one. However, there is one location that is dealt with or at least touched upon to a greater extent than others: namely Antioch-on-the-Orontes. As already mentioned, Ignatius was the bishop of Antioch and has written several letters that may have a bearing on the Antiochean situation. Paul's letter to the Galatians deals with one specific incident at Antioch that is of utmost importance for our understanding of the relations between Jews and Gentiles. The Gospel of Matthew may have originated in Antioch and almost certainly played an important role in the community of Ignatius. The traditions of the Maccabean martyrs in 4 Maccabees may also be connected to Antioch, and Josephus specifically mentions circumstances concerning the Jewish community in Antioch.

Thus, the present study will be restricted to an investigation of the separation between Judaism and Christianity in an Antiochean context, from the period from the introduction of the Jesus movement in Antioch up to the death of Ignatius. *The main aim is to provide an understanding of how the Jewish Jesus movement turned into a new non- and even anti-Jewish Gentile religion, completely separated from Judaism.* In my analysis, which will focus upon the social aspects of the process without neglecting ideological elements, I will emphasize the different conditions for Jewish and Gentile adherents to the Jesus movement.

Even with the limitations of time and space, the task is a complicated one. The main problem is the paucity of relevant sources and the tendentious character of those available. This implies the need to use other tools and an innovative and even experimental approach regarding the methodology. We will therefore turn to questions about method and perspectives.

The method and perspectives of the study

Theories, perspectives and the question of verification

"The truth is out there"—textuality and meaning

There are several basic problems involved in a study such as this one. Firstly, the separation between Christianity and Judaism is a process of immense complexity. Given the amount and character of the sources, together with the distance in time, we must admit that no reconstruction of the process can ever capture the fullness of the course of events. What we can possibly aim at is to understand different aspects involved in the process. This implies that, whatever the outcome of this study, it is only a partial explanation that emphasizes some aspects, while neglecting others.

The reason for this is our total dependence on different kinds of source material. In the case of the problem of the separation between Judaism and Christianity, we are almost entirely dependent on *ancient literary texts*. Having stated this, an enormous number of problems arise. Are the sources reliable? Are they suitable for answering our questions? Is there enough material to create a complete picture? The answer is that the sources are usually biased and frequently part of a rhetorical discourse, that they were not written to give answer to our specific questions, and that they are always too few. This implies that in addition to the general problems of textual interpretation, we face severe difficulties in relating the sources to the specific problem on which we are focusing.

The increasing awareness of the problems involved in determining how texts create meaning and the role of the readers in constructing meaning make it impossible not to comment upon such issues. One does not have to go as far as S. Fish who states that there is *nothing* in the text since everything is in the interpretation, to realize that reading texts is connected with certain interpretative difficulties.[22] A more pragmatically oriented approach is the one suggested by W. Iser. Unlike Fish, Iser does not question the existence of stable constraints in texts but rather emphasizes their *indeterminate status*.[23] During the reading process the reader fills in "gaps" in the text through an act of interpretation. Here it becomes clear that *the "meaning" arrived at through the reading process is dependent on what the gaps in the text are being filled with*. Thus, different readers may arrive at different "meanings" since their interpretations are made from different points of departure.

What is true on the level of interpretation of one single text is, of course, also true when it comes to the reconstruction of a complex historical process that is dependent on the interpretation of texts, archaeological remains, or any other artefact. In our effort to understand what happened in the past, we are compelled to fill in gaps when the sources are few, corrupt, tendentious, or even lacking. It is important that we understand that, as every reading process is a *meaning-constructing process*, so is the work of every historian. Perhaps this is true to such an extent that we should think of "reconstructions" rather in terms of "constructions" that may involve as much artistic creativity as the modern interpretation of a pavane by L. Milán, played from the original tablature.[24]

The "truth" may be out there, but its appearance is almost completely dependent on a construction based on the interpretation of sources from certain perspectives and points of departure.

Theories and perspectives

The insight that every historian is doomed to perceive the past not only through ancient sources but through their *interpretation*, makes the use of modern theories or models urgent. As P. F. Esler has rightly noted, everyone uses "models," even though we should perhaps refer to our subjective pre-understanding with some other term.[25] Nevertheless, it is true that the totality of assumptions, beliefs, prejudgments, and experiences that can be said to constitute our symbolic universe obviously affects the interpretation of ancient sources.[26] In this respect it is not possible to choose whether a given problem shall be viewed with or without subjective points of view. We may become conscious of the subjectivity of our analysis, but we can never disconnect from it. What, however, may be affected is the choice of *specific* theories or models.

There are two main problems in using ancient literary sources. The first problem relates to how information in texts is to be valued. Some texts relate events that cannot possibly have happened: people walking on water or corpses coming alive, etc. Furthermore, texts may be part of rhetorical discourses that are hard for us to decode, since the communicative situation is no longer known. The other main problem, however, is the paucity of relevant sources. This is, of course, a general problem, but in the case of the separation between Judaism and Christianity it becomes especially urgent. The study of this part of history therefore requires a special methodological strategy.

In dealing with the problem of using sociological analyses in New Testament exegesis, R. Scroggs has proposed that, if the available data

> evidence some *parts* of the gestalt of a known model, while being silent about others, we *may* cautiously be able to conclude that the absence of the missing part is accidental and that the entire model was actually a reality in the early church.[27]

In commenting on this, B. Holmberg raises the question of the legitimacy of such a methodology. Holmberg finds that Scroggs's use of sociological models is based on a misunderstanding of the concept. He states:

> [Sociological models] are simply abstractions, constructed types that do not depict any reality exactly. It is illegitimate to use them as prescriptions or prognoses about what must have happened or been there when there is no evidence to say so.[28]

Holmberg is of course right in stating that sociological models or theories are abstractions without any possibility of depicting reality exactly. The sad thing is that they share this fate with *every other way of depicting a historical reality, such as spoken language, written texts, and archaeological remains.* In my opinion, the use of specific theories may help us tackle some of the problems with ancient literary sources. They may help us evaluate information given in texts and infer information not given. In both cases, in fact, they act as gap-fillers. For instance, a theory of gravitation may help us evaluate texts about people walking on water. In such a case we may have to be open to the possibility that a model or theory can perform the function of correcting an ancient source. However, when we possess no sources about a process we may assume was operative in antiquity, we may perhaps be able to use models applied to similar processes elsewhere.

Thus, I would ascribe a somewhat more salient function to theories and models as providers of information. They can certainly function as merely heuristic tools, and by using them we may be able ask new questions of the texts, but, when the texts are unable to answer any questions, a specific theory about reality may.[29] To some extent, in the absence of sources, specific theories can actually be used in order to speculate about what may have happened. The ideal situation is, of course, when we have literary or other remains that can be interpreted with help from theories about reality. With regard to scientific generalization R. Stark has stated that "it is precisely the abstract generality of science that makes it possible for social science to contribute anything to our understanding from social scientific theories."[30]

If the theories seem to be good theories, based on empirical studies of humanity, there is no reason why we should not use them, *if the alternative is to say nothing.* "Need," Stark continues, "is the only justification for the application of social science to fill in historical blanks."[31] The problem of why Judaism and Christianity became separated seems to be precisely such a case. This leads us to the problem of verification.

How do we know when we know?

One of the main problems with (re)constructions of complex scenarios in antiquity is how to verify our suggestions. It is often possible to verify individual data: we know, for instance, with reasonable certainty that Jesus existed, that Julius Caesar was assassinated in 44 BCE, and that Titus besieged Jerusalem in 70 CE. Other historical assertions are more uncertain, and the scholarly community may be divided into two or several parties.

For instance, what relation did Paul have to the torah? Could Jews eat with Gentiles? Do Galatians 2 and Acts 15 relate the same story? Was Judaism a legalistic religion? Unfortunately, there is no single answer to these questions, and the scholarly community has been involved in numerous discussions about these problems. One problem of extreme complexity is when an analysis of a process in antiquity must relate to other conditions in the environment that are not completely known to us or when different or even contradictory opinions exist regarding a certain question. How do we verify a reconstruction of a course of events that is based on conditions that are not fully known to us? These questions relate to the overarching problem of verification of knowledge.

There are basically two ways of approaching the problem of how to verify a statement. We may, on the one hand, assume that a statement is true *if it corresponds to reality.* There are, of course, several difficulties involved in such a definition of scientific truth: what do we mean by "correspondence," for instance? However, on a pragmatic level it is fairly evident what is hinted at. We "know" that the Roman Empire existed, since we have an overwhelming amount of evidence that indicates this. We can thus say that the statement "the Roman Empire existed 2000 years ago" is true because it corresponds to the reality indicated by different and numerous sources. When we begin to pose questions about the function of different aspects in the empire, how different institutions related to each other, how authority was administered, what the social conditions were, etc., we may, however, find it difficult to determine whether a statement corresponds to reality, *since we do not know what this reality looked like.*

When we are forced to use assumptions about reality in constructing plausible models of what Roman ancient reality may have looked like, we may find that "coherence" is a more useful criterion for historical truth. According to J. Hospers, a body of beliefs is coherent when none of them is inconsistent with any other and when they mutually support one another.[32] This way of verification takes into account that several elements are related to each other and that the validity of one single element is dependent on its place within the whole system.

It is obvious that using this kind of verification system is problematic. The risk of circular reasoning, for instance, is obvious. However, this is a risk we must take: in fact, *the state of things leaves us no alternative.* If one single piece of evidence can be given several interpretations, we may be justified in choosing one that seems to fit into the system as a whole. W. V. Quine and J. S. Ullian have compared this state of affairs to an engine:

> Often in assessing beliefs we do best to assess several in combination. A very accomplished mechanic might be able to tell something about an automobile's engine by examining its parts one by one, each in complete isolation from the others, but it would surely serve his purpose better to see the engine as a whole with all the parts functioning together. So with what we believe. It is in the light of the full body of beliefs that candidates gain acceptance or rejection; any independent merits of a candidate tend to be less decisive.[33]

To sum up: the sources are few and to some extent inadequate, the interpretation of texts and other sources requires an interpretative act, and, furthermore, some elements upon which we base our argumentation are themselves based on assumptions and non-verifiable elements. We must conclude that it may be the case that our reconstructions correspond in some degree to reality, but we have little chance of knowing when we have reached such correspondence. *The "truth" may be out there, but we will never know when we have found it.*

12

What we may aim at is to create a coherent, plausible system based on the interpretation of all available sources from certain carefully chosen perspectives. We will now turn to how this task is carried out in the present study.

The method of the study

A hermeneutical model of interpretation   *Project*

In creating such a plausible reconstruction of the process of separation of Christianity from Judaism in Antioch, we must obviously adopt a methodological strategy that takes into consideration the difficulties involved in historical reconstructions. We must be able to show that our reconstruction is not only possible, but also a plausible suggestion of how things may have developed. The available sources must be given a reasonable interpretation within the system, and the perspectives that underlie the interpretation of them should be accounted for.

The primary source material in this study is literary. In order to create as plausible a reconstruction as possible when interpreting the sources, I intend to use the combination of 1) a basic, general theoretical perspective regarding society, 2) specific social-scientific theories used in empirical studies of modern societies, and 3) comparative material from antiquity. Through the reciprocity between these elements, we should be able to construct an interpretative frame that will help us understand literary and other sources that are related to the subject under discussion. When such material is scanty or even lacking, the model may help us to fill the gaps and create a plausible and testable reconstruction of history.

As the most basic theoretical concept I will use the phenomeno-logically oriented approach of P. L. Berger and T. Luckmann, as presented in the classic *The Social Construction of Reality: A Treatise in the Sociology of Knowledge* (1966). The fundamental presumption about humanity and society that permeates this study is contained in the statement *"[s]ociety is a human product. Society is an objective reality. Man is a social product."*[34]

Using the perspective of sociology of knowledge makes it possible for us to make some important assumptions about peoples' relation to each other and to the world surrounding them. According to Berger and Luckmann, it is the *biological constitution* that compels mankind to create a social world that is eventually perceived as objective. *Homo sapiens* is also *homo socius*, and this is the reason why it can be assumed that some basic mechanisms regarding human social life are operative in all human societies.[35]

In addition to this I will draw on some specific theories from different social-scientific traditions in order to make suggestions that go beyond what is stated in the literary sources. It is important to note that my intention is not to test these theories. The empirical material used in building them up is from my point of view considered to be sufficient. Rather, I aim to employ these specific theories as propositions about reality.

Finally, I will use comparative material from antiquity. As far as possible I intend to draw from the works of other scholars in trying to find ancient parallels to phenomena that concern the present study.

Thus, if we find something in texts about the local situation in Antioch that makes sense from an underlying social-scientific perspective, and if this text can be analyzed with modern theories in order to extract more information from it, and if we also find expressions of the same phenomenon in other ancient texts dealing with other locations, I would say we have a case. Admittedly, it will not always be possible to use this hermeneutical strategy consistently, but it is my ambition to increase the validity of the reconstruction by letting the sources interact with these three elements.

The theoretical approach is most clear in chapters 3 and 5. In chapter 2, I deal with some introductory issues such as the history of Antioch and its Jewish community, as well as the social and religious life in general. This chapter gives some important information about the religious and political situation in a Greek city under the dominance of Rome. In chapter 3, I analyze the religious differentiation of the Jewish community of Antioch using modern theories about international migration and assimilation. This chapter tries to differentiate between religious groups within the Jewish community. In chapter 4, I focus on the interaction between Jews and Gentiles in Antioch. How were Jews generally looked upon in the Roman Empire and what expressions did this take in Antioch? A large part of the chapter deals with how Jews and Gentiles interacted within the Jesus movement. Chapter 5, finally, integrates the results of the previous chapters in suggesting how and why the separation took place by using theories about collective action. In the Epilogue there is a short summary of the main results of the study, as well as a discussion of their relevance for explaining the separation between Judaism and Christianity in general.

Summary and conclusion

The present study aims to contribute an understanding of how the Jewish Jesus movement in Antioch turned into a Gentile religion and became separated from Judaism. The problems involved in interpreting literary texts in general and ancient sources in particular is dealt with from a theoretical point of view. It is suggested that it may be possible to construct a picture of the separation process using text interpretation in combination with theoretical models and ancient comparative material. As much as possible, the assumptions of the study are brought to the surface.

Such an approach of openly accounting for the assumptions leaves the present study exposed to criticism on several levels. This, of course, is an important part of scholarly discourse. One may, for instance, discuss the interpretation of individual texts from the suggested perspectives. Furthermore, the choice and application of the specific theories are open for discussion and the relevance of the ancient comparative material may be questioned. Finally, it is perhaps the coherence of the complete picture, including its assumptions and theoretical presuppositions, as well as the relation between the different elements, that will determine the plausibility of what is here suggested. *The "truth" is out there—the present study is but one attempt to grasp some of its elusiveness.*

Notes

1 Dunn, "Against the Law," 455.
2 Boccaccini, *Middle Judaism*, 20.
3 Ibid., 15.
4 Charlesworth, who has written the foreword to Boccaccini's book, seems to agree. He refers to a number of objections to defining Christianity as a Judaism and puts the question: "[a]re not the differences today between Christianity and Judaism obvious and indeed essentially attractive?" See "Refreshing Developments," xviii.
5 Stroumsa, "Anti-Judaism," 10.
6 To comprehend Judaism and Christianity as two separate religions is scarcely controversial, see e.g., Segal, *Rebecca's Children*, 1: "[t]he time of Jesus marks the beginning of not one but two great religions of the West," and Dunn, *Partings*, 1, who states that "two of the world's great religions, emerged from the same matrix." Borgen, *Early Christianity*, 16, finds that Christianity *first* existed within a Jewish context but *then* "grew into the Graeco-Roman world with an identity of its own." Sigal and Sigal, *Judaism*, 80, discusses how "Christianity ceased to be Jewish," and Cohen, *Maccabees*, 168, discusses in a similar way how "Christianity

ceased to be a Jewish sect," and states that Christianity is no longer "a Jewish phenomenon but a separate religion." Sanders, *Judaism*, 5, calls first-century Palestine "the cradle of two of the West's three major religions: rabbinic Judaism and Christianity." Finally, Alexander, "Parting," 1, deals with the question of "how we have reached the present situation in which Christianity and Judaism are manifestly separate religions." Alexander also points at the Jewish and Christian self-definition respectively as being different from the other. Judaism understands itself *as not being* Christianity and vice versa (see pp. 1–2).

7　Lieu, *Image*, 25, suggests c. 114; Trevett, *Study*, 9, suggests 107. Generally the date is disputed: for overviews of the general discussions of dating and authenticity, see Schoedel, *Ignatius*, 5–6, Hübner, "Thesen"; Trevett, *Study*, 3–15; Koester, *Introduction 2*, 57–9; and Legarth, *Guds tempel*, 103–9.

8　Lieu, *Image*, 28.

9　Ibid., 29.

10　See, e.g., Dunn, *Partings*, 1–15, for an overview of different ways of picturing the relation between Judaism and Christianity, from the beginning of the nineteenth century (F. C. Baur) to the late 1970s (E. P. Sanders).

11　Dunn, *Partings*, 17.

12　Ibid., 35.

13　Kniss, "Ideas," 8–9.

14　Dunn, *Partings*, 120.

15　Ibid., 138.

16　Ibid., 133.

17　See Gager, *Reinventing Paul*, 3–75, for an extensive overview of the basic problem involved in the traditional view of Paul and a summary of the fundamental assumptions underlying the new way of understanding Paul's relation to the torah, Judaism, Gentiles, and the Jewish people.

18　See, e.g., Gal. 3:10–11; Rom. 3:20, 9:31; 2 Cor. 3:4–18.

19　Lapide and Stuhlmacher, *Paul*, 42.

20　See, e.g., 1 Cor. 10:1–22.

21　In commenting on my article about the incident at Antioch (Zetterholm, "Covenant"), Holmberg objects to terminology he considers to be "unwieldy," even to represent a "misnomer." He argues that the "first-century believers" did not simply believe in Jesus but in "something much more specific and notable." Holmberg concludes: "if 'Christian' is a term used about a specific group of people and their specific faith and ethos by others and themselves already in the first century, it is hard to understand why modern anxieties about how the term might be misunderstood should prevent its use in historical investigation of this very phenomenon" (see "Life" 226–8). This terminology can indeed be cumbersome, but that is arguably a small price to pay for a higher degree of analytical precision. It is likely that Jewish adherents to the Jesus movement thought of Jesus as "the promised Messiah of Israel." A Gentile person, however, who was primarily socialized within the Greco-Roman religious system, had to form an understanding of the concept of "the promised Messiah of Israel" from a completely different angle. This is true even if we assume Gentile participation in the life of the synagogues. Thus, the implications are not as clear, or as free of circular reasoning, as Holmberg suggests. For instance, we cannot assume from the beginning that Jesus-believing Jews and Jesus-believing Gentiles formed a group that was separate from Jewish communal life, or that the term "Christian" was already in use by others and themselves before the end of the first century. The references in Acts to which Holmberg appeals arguably refer to historical developments by the time of Luke's writing, usually dated to late in the first century, but these designations are not found in Paul's letters. It could even be the case, as will be suggested, that the term—if at all used in the middle of the first century—was an intra-Jewish designation for a Jewish messianic synagogue in Antioch. Moreover, the use of the term "Christian" obscures the situation, if, as will also be argued, Gentile adherents to the Jesus movement had to subordinate themselves to the synagogue authorities, and may even have pretended to be Jews in order to gain acceptance in the political system of the Greco-Roman *poleis*. Thus, it is hard to know exactly who was referred to by the designation "Christian" in these earliest references. Finally, the long and varied use of terms such as "Christian" and "Christianity" to refer to people and institutional entities clearly distinguished from—even opposed to—Jewish people and communal life after the first century certainly limits their descriptive value. On this see also Esler, *Galatians*, 3–5; Nanos, *Irony*, 20, n. 5.

22 See Fish, *Text*, 1–17.
23 Iser, *Act of Reading*.
24 Milán's *Libro de musica de vihuela de mano intitulado El Maestro* was originally published in Valencia in 1535, and is presumably the earliest Spanish tablature. The music is written without using ordinary notes; the tablature indicates where on the fingerboard the musician should press the string. The performance of this music is to an even higher degree an act of interpretation compared to music written with modern notes. Since the possibility for the composer to specify, e.g., the duration of a particular voice and its interaction with other voices is rather limited, these decisions are almost entirely left to the interpreter.
25 Esler, *First Christians*, 12. Horrell, "Models," 85, has rightly objected to the labeling of presuppositions, assumptions etc. as "models." On the use of models in New Testament interpretation, see also Esler, *Community*, 9, and "Models."
26 On "symbolic universe," see Berger and Luckmann, *Social Construction*, 113–14.
27 Scroggs, "Sociological Interpretation," 166.
28 Holmberg, *Sociology*, 15.
29 Consequently, I do not completely agree with Esler, *First Christians*, 13, who states that "[t]he texts must supply the answers, not the model." Models or specific theories can actually do more than that.
30 Stark, *Rise of Christianity*, 23.
31 Ibid., 26.
32 Hospers, *Introduction*, 183–4.
33 Quine and Ullian, *Web of Belief*, 16.
34 Berger and Luckmann, *Social Construction*, 79.
35 Ibid., 69.

2

THE SETTING

Antioch-on-the-Orontes

Il existe certains coins comme ça
dans les villes si stupidement laids
qu'on y est presque toujours seul . . .
Louis-Ferdinand Céline, *Voyage au bout de la nuit*

Introduction

There are several events in the history of Antioch that may help us
understand why the relations between Jews and Gentiles developed
as they did. The purpose of this chapter is to provide a general understanding of what it was like to live in the city and to emphasize certain
aspects of the conditions that had a bearing on our overarching
question.

After a short overview of the general history of Antioch, ranging
from the foundation of the city in 300 BCE to the outbreak of the
Jewish War in 66 CE, we will focus on the *polis* of Antioch and its
religious and political institutions. We will see how the different
religious institutions acted together in creating a pan-Hellenic religious system, and what religious duties the individual inhabitants of
the city had. The focus will then shift towards the basic social
conditions that determined life in the city. We will deal with issues
of population density, sanitary conditions, mortality rates and social
networks in order to see how these factors affected human life,
biologically as well as socially.

We will then turn specifically to the Jewish population in its
attempt to establish its position in the religious world of Antioch.
How was the Jewish community organized, internally as well as in
relation to the city and to Rome? How was the problem of the refusal
to worship deities other than the god of Israel dealt with in the
context of the religious pluralism of Antioch? What legal status did

18

Jewish communities have in antiquity and how was this reflected in the case of Antioch? Finally we will try to determine the degree of Jewish influence on the Antiochean society and the social function of the synagogues in the rather complex milieu of ancient Antioch.

A short history of Antioch

The foundation and early development of the city

In May 300 BCE, after having defeated Antigonus at Ipsus in 301, Seleucus I Nicator (312–281 BCE) founded Antioch by the Orontes River. His aim was to make Antioch one of four "sister cities" that were involved in the strategic process of the colonization of the area, perhaps as a way of linking seaports with inland cities: from Antioch it was only one day's sail to the Mediterranean Sea.[1] Seleucus named the city after his father Antiochus and erected a temple dedicated to Zeus Bottios,[2] who together with Apollo was of special importance for the Seleucid dynasty.[3]

The city appears to have been modeled on other Hellenistic cities, if one considers the arrangements of the streets, the size of the *insulae*, and the presence of surrounding walls. Since the sources are meagre for this period, the existence of some public buildings which are not mentioned in literary sources or revealed by excavations must be conjectured by analogy with other Hellenistic cities. Public buildings, including the temple of Zeus, would consequently have been located around the *agora*. It may, accordingly, be assumed that, at the least, Seleucus planned other public buildings such as temples, a theater, and military and administrative installations.[4] There is no evidence of a stadium, apart from one in Daphne which was in existence in 195 BCE, but it is generally assumed that Antioch had a stadium or a hippodrome.[5]

The city was adorned with different statues. The best-known is a bronze statue of Tyche sitting on a rock representing Mount Silpius. She is wearing a turreted crown, representing the city wall, and at her feet is the body of a youth as a symbol of Orontes.[6] In this way the goddess became a personification of the city as well as its protector. Seleucus also erected a statue of Zeus, a stone figure outside the city in honor of Zeus's eagle, and a marble statue of the priest Amphion, who had been involved in the ceremonies connected with the foundation of the city. As a gesture of triumph and as a symbol of friendship, a statue of Tyche of Antigonia was erected for the original inhabitants of the city. The people from Antigonia erected in their turn a statue of Seleucus. There was also a statue of Athena that Seleucus had brought from Antigonia for the Athenians in Antioch.[7] During the reigns of the immediate successors of Seleucus I Nicator, the most important event was that the capital of the Seleucid Kingdom was transferred from Seleucia Pieria to Antioch, an event of great importance for the further development of the latter.[8] During the reign of Antiochus II Theos (261–247/46 BCE), a period of Egyptian influence began, due to the fact that the king married Berenice, the daughter of the Egyptian Pharaoh Ptolemy Philadelphius. One can also notice the introduction of Cypriot cults during this period,[9] which may have been followed by the cults of Isis and Sarapis during the reign of Seleucus II Callinius (246–226 BCE).[10]

The last Greek immigrants seem to have settled in Antioch during the reign of Antiochus III (223–187 BCE), who may have wanted to improve the noble stock of the city. The king completed an area, originally founded by his father, for these new settlers on the island of the city. Antiochus III is also said to have adorned the city, and when he built a temple to Olympian Zeus, he had a statue of the god made after his own likeness.[11]

From Antiochus IV Epiphanes to Titus

It is during the reign of Antiochus IV Epiphanes (175–163 BCE) that Antioch became one of the foremost cities of antiquity. The motivating factor for Antiochus' political program arose from a desire to unify the people through cultural resources. The reason for this was the increasing power of the Roman Empire. As a consequence of the defeat of Antiochus III by the Romans in the Battle of Magnesia in 190 BCE, the Seleucid Kingdom had lost much of its military power and a heavy tribute had been imposed on it by the Romans. One aspect of Antiochus' political program was the reinforcement of the ruler cult and, closely connected to this, the cult of Zeus Olympius with whom Antiochus identified himself.[12] It was also during this period that the Jewish population became divided into two camps— one faction who attempted to dissolve Judaism completely into Greek culture, and one who very strongly opposed any such attempt, as is evident from 1 Macc. 1:11–15:[13]

> In those days certain renegades came out from Israel and misled many, saying "Let us go and make a covenant with the Gentiles around us, for since we separated from them many disasters have come upon us." This proposal pleased

them, and some of the people eagerly went to the king, who authorized them to observe the ordinances of the Gentiles. So they built a gymnasium in Jerusalem, according to Gentile custom, and removed the marks of circumcision, and abandoned the holy covenant. They joined with the Gentiles and sold themselves to do evil.

It is reasonable to assume, as G. Downey does, that the Jewish population in Antioch was affected by the Maccabean revolt that followed as a result of the king's having plundered the temple in Jerusalem.[14] This may have influenced the tradition of the Maccabean martyrs in 2 and 4 Maccabees, to which we will return later. The plundering of the temple seems also to have had some explicit consequences for the Jews of Antioch, since Josephus in *B.J.* 7.44 mentions that the Seleucid rulers who succeeded Antiochus IV Epiphanes "restored to the Jews of Antioch all such votive offerings as were made of brass, to be laid up in their synagogue."[15] This may indicate that the Seleucid rulers considered the Jews of Antioch to be closely tied to Palestinian Jewry.[16]

As for Antioch in general, Antiochus' greatest grant to the city was the foundation of a new quarter called Epiphania. With the construction of this area, the city had taken definite physical shape, and this can also be taken as evidence of an increased population. One of the features of Epiphania seems to have been a new *agora*, which thus made two *agoras* at Antioch. This may reveal a shift in the relation between the king and municipal authorities. It seems that Antiochus erected a *bouleuterion* at this new *agora*, which could imply that this *agora* was "free," devoted to political and educational activities. It has been suggested that the construction of the *bouleuterion* implies that Antiochus was willing to share some of his power with other officials. Another sign of this is the municipal coinage, which bore both his portrait and the name of the city.[17]

After the death of Antiochus IV Epiphanes, the aspects of most historical-social significance were the rise of Rome and the fall of the Seleucid Kingdom, culminating in the conquest of the area by the Romans in 64 BCE. Furthermore, this period was characterized in general by political turbulence, revolts and warfare, on account of constant rivalry battles for political power. This meant that Antioch, itself became the scene of important events, and her different rulers did not fail to contribute to her embellishment. Restorations were sometimes necessary, since the area suffered from numerous severe earthquakes.[18]

The political turbulence resulted from time to time in situations of special relevance for the Jewish population. First Maccabees 11:20–52 and *A.J.* 13.137–42 describe how Demetrios II (145–139 BCE), with help from Jewish troops, managed to cope with civil war. After having outmaneuvered Alexander I Balas and been established in power with the help of a force of Cretan mercenaries, Demetrios, trying to diminish his expenses, dismissed his native troops, thus leaving them without means of support. He retained only the Cretan mercenaries. These became unpopular both among the people in Antioch from which the native soldiers were recruited, and among the followers of Alexander Balas. Demetrios, who probably feared the outbreak of a riot, ordered the foreign troops to disarm the native and now dismissed troops. Unfortunately it was precisely this precautionary measure that led to a state of civil war. In this situation Demetrios appealed for help to Jonathan, the Hasmonean ruler, who sent 3,000 soldiers to the aid of the king. Josephus describes the events in *A.J.* 13.138–9:

> Now when the Jews saw the Antiochians getting the upper hand, they went up to the roofs of the palace buildings, and from there hurled missiles at the Antiochians; and while they themselves, being high above their opponents, were too far away to be hurt by them, they could inflict much damage on them by fighting from above; and so they drove them out of the adjoining houses, which they quickly set on fire; and as the houses were closely together and mostly built of wood, the flames spread over the whole city and entirely consumed it.

First Maccabees 11:47–8 continues to describe how the Jewish troops pillaged the city and massacred its inhabitants:

> So the king called the Jews to his aid, and they all rallied around him and then spread out through the city; and they killed on that day about one hundred thousand. They set fire to the city and seized a large amount of spoil on that day, and saved the king.

The numbers given here are certainly exaggerations, but it seems clear that Jewish soldiers were involved in plundering the city. There can be no doubt that such an incident had immediate consequences for the Jewish community in Antioch at this specific time. It is furthermore highly probable that it influenced the formation of a generally negative attitude towards Jews.[19]

During the period up to the occupation of the area by the Romans, the sources do not reveal much about Antioch: thus, not until the beginning of the Roman period can one speak of a new epoch in the history of the city. It is clear that Antioch held a position of honor and that no other city could serve as the capital of the Roman province of Syria. The social and economic consequences of this were, of course, of major importance for the continued development of the city. Many important developments on several levels occurred during the reign of Julius Caesar (49–44 BCE). One of his most famous buildings was called *Kaisarion*, in front of which statues of himself and of Tyche of Rome were erected. It seems that Caesar attached great political and religious importance to this edifice and that he combined elements from the Hellenistic ruler cult and the cult of *Dea Roma*, which was later developed further by Augustus.[20] He was also responsible for the rebuilding of the Pantheon and the construction of an amphitheater and a public bath. More than his predecessors Caesar introduced a Roman way of life into Antioch. The amphitheater is a good illustration of this, since it was built in a typically Roman way, one which was almost unknown in the Greek East.[21]

During the political turbulence that followed the assassination of Caesar in March 44 BCE, Cassius found support from the Syrian population, and in order to finance his military plan he seized property from the Jews. There may have been a connection between this and the fact that Cassius had succeeded in winning the support of the people of Antioch. Josephus mentions in *A.J.* 14.272 that, when he arrived at the Syrian cities, Cassius "collected arms and soldiers from them, and imposed heavy tribute upon them. Worst of all was his treatment of Judaea, from which he exacted seven hundred talents of silver." From this account we infer that, although the Jews were not the only ones taxed, they had to contribute proportionately more, probably not only in Judaea but also in the Syrian cities. It may be that the confiscation of Jewish property was related to negative attitudes towards Jews. It might have been easier for the people of Antioch to endure the heavy tax burden if they knew that the despised Jews had to contribute even more. After Anthony defeated Cassius, he went to Syria and restored to the Jews of Antioch and other cities the property that had been seized by Cassius.[22]

The reconciliation of East and West during the Augustan Empire, and the golden age that resulted from the *Pax Augusta* allowed a long period of material prosperity for Antioch. Syria, because of its strategic importance, was made an imperial province, governed by a *legatus Augusti* who was responsible directly to the emperor. The provincial administration had its headquarters in Antioch, which meant that the city came to play a role in international affairs: one of the major events in the history of Antioch under Augustus was the foundation of what eventually became the famous Olympic Games of Antioch. During the reign of Augustus (30 BCE–14 CE) and Tiberius (14–37 CE) the city was enlarged as a result of the increase in the population and further beautified. The great colonnaded street which ran through the city was built. In addition, several temples, baths,[23] and statues were erected and the theater was enlarged.[24]

From the reign of Gaius (37–41 CE) the Jewish community was involved in several incidents which eventually culminated in the outbreak of the Jewish War, and during the reign of Nero (54–68 CE) a number of major events in Antioch were connected to Jewish rebellion. The outbreak of the Jewish War in 66 CE resulted in a corresponding eruption of anti-Jewish feelings in Syria, and Josephus describes several conflicts between the Jews and Gentiles from this period. From the same time we also possess evidence of Gentile conversions to Judaism.[25]

The social and religious life of Antioch

Antioch as a Greco-Roman polis

While the population of Antioch had different ethnic origins, the heart of the city was Greek.[26] This meant that it was organized as a Greek *polis*,[27] with elected magistrates, a council and an assembly of citizens.[28] Even during the Roman period this assembly was comprised of members of the local aristocracy, in accordance with Rome's policy of relying on the co-operation of the local elite to handle local affairs and to govern in the name of Rome.[29] Usually, and as long as this did not interfere with Roman rule, each city was permitted to keep its own customs and laws.[30]

At the center of the concept of *polis* stood the people, not the territory. The *polis* was thought of as a community of individuals,[31] but a high proportion of the population of a city were not citizens but rather free foreigners or slaves.[32] It was thus not possible to equate the citizens of a *polis* with the people who inhabited a certain area, and we must thus distinguish, as the Greeks did, between an *inhabitant* of a city and a *citizen*. The *polis* was nevertheless thought of as comprising all its inhabitants. M. H. Hansen explains:

24

As a setting for human production and reproduction the *polis* is a society, not a state; the term *polis* designates a conurbation (sometimes including the hinterland) rather than a political community, and all inhabitants are members of the *polis*. But as a political community the *polis* is a state rather than a society, and the term *polis* designates the adult male citizens only, united by their political institutions, in which the citizens participate completely isolated from women, metics[,] foreigners and slaves.[33]

It was within this framework that Greek religion operated. In fact, religion was imbedded in every aspect of life in such a way that no separate private, political or religious sphere could be discerned.[34]

Public and private worship

Each *polis* formed one specific part in a pan-Hellenic religious system, which basically constituted one religious ideal,[35] and religion was perceived as "the facet of *polis* ideology that all citizens should respect most; thus a sign of disrespect towards religion is a sign of disloyalty towards the *polis* and the *politeia*."[36]

Within each *polis*, religion operated on different levels. On one level we find the cult of those divinities that were connected to the identity and protection of the actual *polis*.[37] As mentioned above, Zeus and Apollo had a special status in Antioch since they were considered the protectors and founders of the Seleucid dynasty, and when the city was founded Seleucus I erected a temple for Zeus and a statue of Apollo. While the Greek pantheon basically consisted of the twelve pan-Hellenic Olympian deities, on a local level various gods had different traits and characteristics.

One way of dealing with the multiplicity of gods was through a firm structure of calendars of festivals.[38] The culmination of such festivals was the animal sacrifice in the temple of the god, with the ensuing civic banquet through which the participants constantly reactivated their relation to the gods—and to the *polis*.[39] "[I]t is in the context of the practices connected with 'eating and drinking together under the eyes of the gods,'" P. Schmitt-Pantel states, "that the ties necessary for social cohesion in the city are reinforced."[40] Sacrifices, which in every aspect constituted one of the major foundations of Greek religion, could also be initiated by an individual for a number of occasions unconnected with official festivals.[41] As was the case with the sacrificial cult in Jerusalem, parts of the animal were offered to the deity, while other parts were distributed by the participants or sacerdotal functionaries for immediate consumption.[42] The meat that was sold commercially in shops in the marketplace had usually been involved in some sacrificial ceremony.[43] It could either have been allotted to the priests and resold by them, or the animal could have been consecrated by a first-fruit offering, which meant that some hairs cut from the animal's head were thrown at the altar-fire.[44]

In Antioch, as in every other major city, the gods of the Greek pantheon were well represented through temples and statues, but, as F. Miller has pointed out, the Greek city of the Roman imperial period would be more correctly described as "Greco-Roman," on account of its "fusion or mélange of languages and constitutions, types of public entertainment, architectural forms, and religious institutions."[45] As for religion, this is reflected in the presence of several other influences, such as Syrian, Cypriot, Egyptian, Persian and Roman.[46]

While there were certainly differences between Greek and Roman religions,[47] the systems seem to have been rather compatible. Roman emperors who visited Greek cities gladly participated in local festivals and sacrifices and helped to repair temples damaged in earthquakes, and also financed the erection of new temples.[48] At the same time, during the first century CE, the cult was principally under Roman control. However, since Roman rule generally supported Greek religious practices, this had few practical consequences, and Greek cults were generally admired due to their antiquity.[49]

One aspect of public religion was the cult of the emperor.[50] Emperor-worship had existed in the Hellenistic world since Alexander and his successors,[51] but during Roman time it had been "the accepted way of acknowledging the authority of a suzerain,"[52] and the cult of Augustus and members of his family spread rapidly through the empire during the first century CE.[53] When Greek cities came under Roman dominance they simply established cults of the foreign rulers modeled on existing cults of the gods,[54] so that the religious recognition of the emperor suggests that "the 'Greek-city' of the Empire embodied at every level an explicit recognition of the distant presence of the Emperor."[55] As noted above, there is evidence from Antioch of Roman ruler cult dating from Julius Caesar, and Augustus appears on a series of coins presenting the emperor as high priest of his own cult, which suggests both the existence and importance of the ruler cult in Antioch.[56] The position of high priest in the imperial cult was a very prestigious office, since it could be a point of entry to the Roman Senate and was also often occupied by members *locals could participate* ⟶ *elite city established* *out of empire* ⟶ *Satisfied Emperor* *of loyalty & honor*

(collegia) established + forbidden ⟶

of the local aristocracy.[57] Participation in the emperor cult was, of course, indispensable for anyone having an official function in the *polis* or belonging to the upper social strata. While there was probably no enforceable obligation for private individuals to take part in the emperor cult, "*the strong presence and influence of the cult in its many various forms in the provinces put a considerable social pressure on individuals to participate.*"[58]

On another level, *polis* religion found expression in the *collegia*, the voluntary associations that characterized much of civic life in the urban centers of the Hellenistic period.[59] The *collegia*, which are usually divided up into *religious clubs* and *professional associations*, and in the case of Roman *collegia* also into *funeral associations*,[60] were all in a sense "religious," since religion permeated every aspect of civic life.[61] Foreign cults were organized as *collegia*, and the introduction of new cults required the approval of the authorities,[62] which during the imperial period, meant principally the emperor.[63] The decision was, however, usually left to the local authorities.[64] There is evidence which suggests that imperial supervision extended well beyond the city of Rome.[65] This has to do with the fact that voluntary associations were not unequivocally supported.[66] During the republic the *collegia* had developed rather freely, but during the civil wars it became clear that some *collegia* had masked revolutionary activities. For that reason the senate dissolved all suspect *collegia* in 64 BCE,[67] and we hear of several subsequent restrictions of the activities of different voluntary associations: "in times of factionalism and strife," P. Richardson states, "collegia tended to be permitted, but in times when reconstruction and consolidation were important, collegia were restricted."[68]

The religious activities of the *collegia* were one expression of *polis* religion in addition to participation in the official cult: it is believed that as many as one-third of the male population were involved in the *collegia* during the second century CE.[69] Normally, there was little risk that they would conflict with each other: the *collegia* did not represent a sectarian way of life but, rather, confirmed the social order. *This means that a member of a certain collegium could in no way disregard his or her obligation to participate in the public worship, sacrifices and festivals.*[70] To fail in duties related to the official *polis* religion, even for an adherent of a foreign cult, was considered *impiety* and could result in exile or even death.[71] For the individual, *piety* meant participation in the official cult, including worship of the emperor, sacrifices and festivals, as well as financial support.[72] On the family level, *piety* meant showing respect for dead relatives, devotion of the family deities, and the carrying out of necessary cultic activities connected with the beginning and end of life.[73] In short, to be *pious* was "to believe in the efficacy of the symbolic system that the city had established for the purpose of managing relations between gods and men, and to participate in it, moreover, in the most vigorously active manner possible."[74]

Collegia thus existed on the condition that they did not violate public law.[75] If they did, they were brutally suppressed.[76] We have already noted that the Senate prohibited all *collegia* in 64 BCE. In 58 BCE they were all permitted again but two years later political clubs were prohibited, and sometime between 49 and 44 BCE Julius Caesar prohibited all *collegia* empire-wide with the exception of the most ancient ones.[77] It is reasonable to assume that the different *collegia* were anxious to maintain their privileges, which also has a bearing on the social function of voluntary associations. It seems as if the *collegia* provided status, community and security, as well as "fictive kinship" among the lower classes,[78] who had been uprooted from their original families.[79] This becomes more intelligible when we consider the social conditions in Antioch.

Social conditions in Antioch

Most accounts of ancient cities discuss the statues and buildings different rulers erected and provide overviews of the political situation, but seldom take up what it was like to live in a city such as Antioch during antiquity. First, ancient cities had an extremely high population density. In the first century CE, Antioch may have had 300,000–400,000 inhabitants,[80] and the population density was probably as high as 195 persons per acre. (This may be compared to Chicago, where there are twenty-one inhabitants per acre, or New York, which overall has thirty-seven per acre. In modern Mumbai the density is 183 persons per acre and in Calcutta it is 122.)[81] This, together with the fact that the overwhelming majority lived in tiny cubicles in tall tenements that occasionally collapsed, gives some idea of the crowded life most inhabitants had to endure.

The basic conditions imply sanitation problems. Water was supplied via aqueducts, but all of the larger cities had to store water in cisterns, which affected its quality. There are no references discussing the water supply for the original foundation of Antioch, but there were springs on the side of Mount Silpius where cisterns may have been constructed, and it is likely that an aqueduct was erected from Daphne to the city.[82] The earliest extant evidence of a water system, an aqueduct running along the mountain above the city, dates from the second century BCE; Julius Caesar later initiated the construction of an aqueduct and a public bath to serve those people who lived on the upper part of the mountain.[83] The majority of the population, however, had to bring home water in jugs, so in reality the water supply was very limited and water was usually contaminated.[84]

According to Downey a sewage system existed in Antioch from the foundation of the city.[85] Many ancient cities had underground sewers, but their capacity is exaggerated. In Rome, for instance, the sewers carried water from the baths and the public latrines out of the city, but for the overwhelming majority of residents the chamber pot and pit latrine were what was available. These were emptied in open ditches on the streets.

With such conditions, there can be no doubt that most deaths in Antioch were caused by infectious diseases. There is a direct correlation between the size of a community and the effects of infectious diseases. If the size of a community falls below 250,000 inhabitants, acute viral infections such as measles and smallpox will not gain a permanent foothold. Instead, the infection will either kill individuals or create immunity, and every new outbreak will occur as a result of the virus having been introduced from outside. In larger communities, however, the infection will be carried dormant by humans and cause recurrent major outbreaks.[86] As noted above, Antioch probably had a population above this critical level, and we can consequently assume the existence of recurring major outbreaks of measles, influenza and smallpox, causing high mortality in infancy and childhood.

Another infection which is highly dependent on population density is tuberculosis.[87] Human primary gastrointestinal tuberculosis is predominantly rural,[88] since it is related to the consumption of milk.[89] It may, however, have had an impact even in urban environments through dairy products such as fresh or soft cheese, which was sold at least at the Athenian market.[90]

It is, however, the pulmonary, airborne form of tuberculosis that was normally found in the cities of antiquity. While the other infections mentioned usually affected children and suggest that infant mortality was very high, up to at least 200 deaths in the first year of life per thousand live births,[91] tuberculosis, while certainly infecting children, kills first in early adulthood.[92] Open sewers and water cisterns also suggest recurrent outbreaks of cholera and typhoid fever.[93]

Apart from more or less epidemic diseases, rather harmless infections could have severe consequences.[94] It is likely that primary infections of the tonsils, middle-ear cavity and bronchial tree were as frequent during antiquity as today,[95] and were responsible for frequent and often lethal secondary bone infections, as well as septicemia and pneumonia, which could also lead to death.[96] Maxillary sinusitis, which can cause severe secondary infections, may have been very frequent due to the fact that the apartments were smoky and ill ventilated.[97] "Such an environment," C. Roberts and K. Manchester state, "would favour the production and stagnation of pus within the sinuses and so create the chances of inflammation."[98]

Childbirth, of course, posed certain risks both for the mother and for the child, and there is evidence that suggests, not surprisingly, that mortality rates were higher for women of childbearing age than for men. While epidemic childbed fever seems to have been a result of the unsanitary conditions in the early modern hospital, women in antiquity nevertheless suffered and died from puerperal infections.[99] Other serious risks to pregnant women were malaria and tuberculosis.[100]

This, of course, seriously affected the average life expectation. We can safely assume that mortality rates were very high and that the average life expectation was accordingly low—that at birth (e_0) was between twenty and thirty years.[101] Based on UN model life-tables, K. Hopkins reaches the conclusion that, if the average life expectation at birth among the *aristocracy* in the late republic was twenty-five years ($e_0 = 25$), about one-third of twenty-year-old males would have died before the age of forty and c. 59 percent of forty-year olds would have died before the age of sixty.[102] There are reasons to assume an even more pessimistic scenario for the female population, and one still worse for the poor.[103]

Due to this very high mortality rate—which in itself implies that the health of the living was very poor—ancient cities were dependent on a constant influx of people just to maintain their populations. The obvious consequence of this was that Greco-Roman cities were to a high degree populated by recent newcomers, who were strangers to each other. Since it is personal attachments that bind people to the moral order, a milieu where interpersonal attachments are few would result in high crime rates.[104] Finally, earthquakes and fires contributed to making Antioch a place on the verge of social chaos. There are reports of two earthquakes at Antioch during the first century CE, one on the morning of March 23, 37, and one about ten years later.[105] R. Stark summarizes the situation:

Any accurate portrait of Antioch in New Testament times must depict a city filled with misery, danger, fear, despair, and hatred. A city where the average family lived a squalid life in filthy and cramped quarters, where at least half of the children died at birth or during infancy, and where most of the children who lived lost at least one parent before reaching maturity. A city filled with hatred and fear rooted in intense ethnic antagonisms and exacerbated by a constant stream of strangers. A city so lacking in stable networks of attachments that petty incidents could prompt mob violence. A city where crime flourished and the streets were dangerous at night. And, perhaps above all, a city repeatedly smashed by cataclysmic catastrophes: where a resident could expect literally to be homeless from time to time, providing that he or she was among the survivors.[106]

It is obvious that *collegia* provided stability and order in an environment that was otherwise characterized by a certain amount of social chaos. Since the organization of the *collegia* often mirrored the social and municipal organization of the *polis*,[107] the individual, who otherwise was without any real influence on a macrocosmic level, could in the microcosm of the *collegium* be in control at least over the destiny of this limited part of reality.[108] In this respect, the synagogue, which must be regarded principally as a *collegium*, would have functioned in exactly the same way. We will now turn to the origin, legal status, organization and social function of the Jewish community in Antioch.

The Jewish community in Antioch up to 66 CE

The origin of Jewish presence in Antioch

According to Josephus, Jews were among the original settlers of Antioch. In two references, *C. Ap.* 2.39 and *A.J.* 12.119, he claims that Seleucus I Nicator, the founder of the city, granted them some privileges. There is no reason to doubt this information even if one must be aware of, as C. H. Kraeling puts it, "the tendency to lay a prior claim to places, persons and ideas important to pagan antiquity."[109] These Jews were probably retired soldiers,[110] from Babylon,[111] who had been enlisted in Seleucus' army,[112] and there may have been Jews among the native Syrians.[113] Josephus, in reporting about their rights, states in *A.J.* 12.119 that the Jews "received

31

honour from the kings of Asia when they served with them in the war" (Ἔτυχον δὲ καὶ τῆς παρὰ τῶν βασιλέων τῆς Ἀσίας τιμῆς, ἐπειδὴ συνεστράτευσαν αὐτοῖς).

According to Kraeling these Jews probably did not constitute a separate identifiable group in the beginning, but were part of the non-Macedonian inhabitants.[114] As we will see, there are reasons to doubt this. According to Josephus (B.J. 7.43) it was from the reign of Antiochus I that Antioch had become a safe place for Jews to live in. This could imply that they had by then become a discernible group who enjoyed some basic protection.[115]

The legal status of the Jews of Antioch

There are reasons to assume that the Jewish communities in the Diaspora were considered one of many collegia,[116] although with privileges going far beyond those of other collegia. Richardson has referred to the attitudes of Julius Caesar and Augustus towards the Jews as evidence of this: when Julius Caesar prohibited all collegia in the empire, sometime between 49 and 44 BCE, he excluded some of the most ancient ones, among them Judaism.[117] When Augustus took action against collegia, the synagogues were again exempted, which indicates that the synagogue was treated as a kind of collegium.[118] However, as L. V. Rutgers has shown, regarding the situation in the city of Rome, protection and privileges could easily be abolished and were given on condition that law and order were maintained. In 19 CE and during the reign of Claudius, legal and administrative actions were taken against the Jews of Rome.[119]

Another, far more complicated aspect of the relation between the Jewish community and the polis of Antioch is the question of whether Jews had attained citizenship. We have already noted that only some of the inhabitants of a Greco-Roman polis were citizens, the rest being either slaves or free foreigners. In three texts, however, Josephus seems to claim that the Jews of Antioch were also citizens of the polis. First, in C. Ap. 2.39, he states that "[o]ur Jewish residents in Antioch are called Antiochenes, having been granted rights of citizenship (τὴν γὰρ πολιτείαν αὐτοῖς ἔδωκεν) by its founder, Seleucus." Here Josephus states that the Jews of Antioch were among the original settlers and that Seleucus, in connection with the foundation of Antioch, granted them πολιτεία, here translated as "citizenship." As has been stated earlier there is no reason to doubt the information about early Jewish presence in Antioch, but it is more uncertain what Josephus meant by the term πολιτεία.

THE SETTING: ANTIOCH-ON-THE-ORONTES

In the following text, from *A.J.* 12.119, Josephus emphasizes that the Jews were given πολιτεία *equal to the one given to Macedonians and Greeks* and that this πολιτεία of theirs "remains to this very day":

> They also received honour from the kings of Asia when they served with him in war. For example, Seleucus Nicator granted them citizenship in the cities which he founded in Asia and Lower Syria and in his capital, Antioch, itself, and declared them to have equal privileges with the Macedonians and Greeks (πολιτείας αὐτοὺς ἠξίωσε καὶ τοῖς ἐνοικισθεῖσιν ἰσοτίμους ἀπέφηνε Μακεδόσιν καὶ ῞Ελλησιν) who were settled in these cities, so that this citizenship of theirs remains to this very day (τὴν πολιτείαν ταύτην ἔτι καὶ νῦν διαμένειν).

In the next text, from *B.J.* 7.44, we find the same accentuation of equality, though now only with Greeks, but here it is said that these privileges were given to the Jews by the successors of Antiochus IV Epiphanes:

> For, although Antiochus surnamed Epiphanes sacked Jerusalem and plundered the temple, his successors on the throne restored to the Jews of Antioch all such votive offerings as were made of brass, to be laid up in their synagogue, and, moreover, granted them citizen rights on an equality with the Greeks (συνεχώρησαν αὐτοῖς ἐξ ἴσου τῆς πόλεως τοῖς ῞Ελλησι μετέχειν).

There are several problems associated with these texts. Firstly, there is an evident confusion in the sources concerning *when* and *by whom* the πολιτεία was conferred to the Jews. According to *C. Ap.* 2.39 and *A.J.* 12.119, it was in connection with the foundation of the city in 300 BCE that Seleucus I Nicator granted πολιτεία to the Jews, while *B.J.* 7.44 states that kings succeeding Antiochus IV Epiphanes, from 163 BCE and onwards, gave to the Jews the right to "share the city." Secondly, one cannot, as noted above, unequivocally determine what Josephus meant by the wordings. Is Josephus, for instance, expressing different aspects when using πολιτεία and τῆς πόλεως μετέχειν?

There have been several suggestions as to how this should be resolved.[120] Kraeling concludes that *certain* individual Jews could possibly have held citizenship privileges from the days of Seleucus I

Nicator and that it was possible to apply for full citizenship. Thus, for him, the Jewish community did not belong as a whole to the δημός of Antioch.[121] From the middle of the second century BCE, Kraeling notes, however, that "a special place was found for Jews as such in the constitution of the polis."[122] Downey believes that Josephus' statement in *C. Ap.* 2.39 is an exaggeration and considers it more likely that ex-soldiers were enrolled in the citizen lists. According to Downey, the reason why full citizenship would not be an option for the majority of the Jews is that this would have included worship of the city gods.[123] This statement seems to be in accordance with our general knowledge of the Greek *polis*.

W. A. Meeks and R. L. Wilken believe that the Jews were being "recognized as a distinct group within the city, free to follow their own customs."[124] They consider the statement in *A.J.* 12.119 to refer to formal citizenship and mention the scholarly debate which doubts the accuracy of Josephus regarding this matter.[125] D. D. Binder also understands Josephus as referring to the "rights as Greek citizens," and states that these privileges were attested only to some prominent individual Jews.[126] Similarly, J. M. G. Barclay finds that some but not all Jews may have acquired such rights, which were not given to the majority of the Jewish community. However, he does not deny the possibility that the Jews as a group may have had some rights. He furthermore finds that Josephus makes "multiple and not entirely consistent claims concerning the settlement and rights of Antiochene Jews," and labels Josephus' statements as "suspect and inconsistent."[127]

Thus, it seems that there is consensus concerning *what* Josephus is referring to, namely citizenship, but that he was consciously or unconsciously mistaken concerning the applicability of this term to the specific Jewish conditions in Antioch. The existence of certain Jewish privileges is, however, not denied.

Generally speaking, it would most certainly have been an anomaly if the Jewish population in its entirety had been granted formal citizenship.[128] As noted at the beginning of this chapter, the majority of the inhabitants of a Greek *polis* would not normally have been citizens but rather slaves or free foreigners. After having performed an extensive analysis of how Josephus uses different terms in connection with the legal status of the Jewish community in the Diaspora, S. Applebaum reaches the conclusion that regardless of whether or not Josephus may have thought so, the Jews of Antioch were not citizens in any formal way.[129] He indicates, furthermore, that what we know of Jewish rights during the first part of the first century relates mainly to internal privileges and not to citizenship.[130]

H. Strathmann has pointed out that πολιτεία in 2 and 4 Maccabees never carries the meaning of "civil rights" or "constitution" but refers rather to "the pious order of life which, ordained by the Law of Moses, is inherited from the fathers, and which Judas Maccabaeus fights to preserve."[131] This implies that πολιτεία in fact could refer to *the right of the Jewish community to practice its own religion and to live governed by its own legislation*,[132] and that the emphasis on "equality" expressed by the phrases ἰσοτίμους ἀπέφηνε Μακεδόσιν καὶ Ἕλλησιν and ἐξ ἴσου τῆς πόλεως τοῖς Ἕλλησι μετέχειν stresses that the Jews were part, not of the *same* πολιτεία, but of another one of the *same kind*.[133] The Jews were consequently citizens in the "socio-political entity" formed by the *Jewish community* in Antioch, not the *polis* of Antioch.[134]

This is the view of A. K. Kasher, who maintains that Josephus uses πολιτεία with reference to the rights to organize as a πολίτευμα with certain privileges.[135] He deals primarily with the conditions in Alexandria, but part of the discussion is of relevance also to the conditions in Antioch. Regarding Alexandria, Kasher reaches several important conclusions. The Jews there were organized as separate, independent bodies with the πολίτευμα as the basic organizational form, and were not citizens of the Greek *polis*.[136] Their rights and political status had been bestowed upon them by the central power. This led to friction between the real citizens in the *polis* and the Jewish πολίτευμα, since the Greek *polis* desired to establish only one single πολιτεία, connected to the cult.[137]

When dealing with Antioch in a comparative study, Kasher takes as his point of departure the observation that most scholars, as we have seen, suspect Josephus of apologetics or falsification and assume that his statements refer to citizenship in the *polis* of Antioch. He points to the fact that Josephus, for instance, makes a distinction between the Jews of Antioch[138] and the δῆμος of the Antiocheans,[139] an observation which definitely supports his view.[140] According to Kasher, this right to be organized as a separate πολιτεία was, as in Alexandria, derived not from the *polis* but from the central government.[141] We recall from the texts cited above that it was *Seleucus I Nicator* who granted the Jews πολιτεία and that *Antiochus IV Epiphanes' successors* were involved in giving the Jews permission to participate in the city on equal terms with the Greeks (ἐξ ἴσου τῆς πόλεως τοῖς Ἕλλησι μετέχειν).[142] Josephus (*B.J.* 7.100–11) also attests that, when the people of Antioch wanted the Jews expelled from the city, Titus did not comply with their request but instead *confirmed* the right of the Jews to enjoy the same privileges as before. The

35

implications this had for the relations between Jews and Gentiles are not to be underrated and will be returned to later. The expression ἐξ ἴσου τῆς πόλεως τοῖς "Ελλησι μετέχειν, which most probably is synonymous with the others, makes perfect sense only if we presuppose that πολιτεία refers to the right of the Jews to follow their own laws, since it *was exactly this privilege Antiochus IV Epiphanes annulled.*[143]

Generally speaking, examples of the phenomenon of parallel communities are found in Heraclea Pontica, for instance, where both Roman and Greek inhabitants resided, constituting two communities. In Antioch-in-Pisidia, Roman *magistrates* appeared alongside Greek *gymnasiarchs*.[144] This would be in perfect accordance with both Greek and Roman practice since the general rule was to use the defeated people's existing structures of organization.[145] The main results of Kasher's study (that is, the Jews being citizens of their own πολίτευμα and not in the *polis*) can also be said to constitute the present scholarly consensus. G. Lüderitz has, however, questioned the accuracy of the Jews being organized as a πολίτευμα in Alexandria. Lüderitz shows, quite convincingly, that there are reasons to revise this assumption, since the only unambiguous reference to a Jewish organization designated πολίτευμα, from Berenice in Cyrenaica, might be "a local peculiarity of the Jewish diaspora in Cyrenaica."[146] His analysis also reveals that it is not possible to make a clear differentiation between πολιτεύματα and other associations such as κοινόν or σύνοδος.[147]

As a consequence, Barclay has suggested a more complex scenario with regard to the situation in Alexandria: even though the majority of Alexandrian Jews were not, technically speaking, citizens but enjoyed the status of being "privileged residents," which included self-government to a certain extent, as well as the right to practice their "ancestral laws," Barclay finds sufficient evidence "that at the peak of the Jewish social pyramid were a minority of families, mostly still loyal to the Jewish community, who had attained citizen status, or at least considered they were entitled to it."[148] It may well be, Barclay argues, that it was precisely at this point that the question of citizenship became a source of dissension between Jews and Gentiles in Alexandria, since it thus could be possible for Jews to become *citizens without worshiping the gods of the city*.[149] This is, of course, at the heart of Apion's complaint in *C. Ap.* 2.65. Irrespective of the fact that the term πολίτευμα might not be useful in describing the organizational status of the Jewish community, it seems as if they nevertheless constituted, as Barclay puts it, "a community with powerful mechanisms of self-regulation and a strong sense of its own identity, almost a state within the state."[150] That, not the nomenclature, is the important issue here.

If we are to sum up these discussions in trying to find a solution to the question of the legal status of the Jews in Antioch, it seems plausible that Josephus, through his use of πολιτεία and τῆς πόλεως μετέχειν, was referring to the privileges of the Jewish community and not to the right of the Jews as formal citizens. These privileges seem to have comprised the right to assemble, to observe the Sabbath and festivals, to collect and send the temple tax, to observe dietary laws, and to be exempted from military service and from participation in the imperial cult.[151] It is clear that these privileges were confirmed by the central administration—that is, Rome. The Jewish community was considered by the authorities, by the Gentile population, and probably even by themselves as one *collegium* among many others, and as such it enjoyed protection on the condition that law and order were maintained. Furthermore, it cannot be ruled out that some prominent Jews really had attained formal citizenship in the *polis* of Antioch, and that they could maintain this status and still be loyal to the Jewish community.

One community—several congregations

Above, we reached the conclusion that the Jews of Antioch had been recognized as an identifiable entity since the foundation of the city. The basic Jewish institution during the first century CE was, of course, the synagogue. From literary sources it is possible to identify three synagogues during the first century CE,[152] but the exact numbers are unknown, since there were no specific Jewish remains found in the excavations of the city.[153] If we were to follow Meeks and Wilken, assuming a Jewish population of about 22,000,[154] it seems reasonable to presume the existence of several more synagogues.

The situation in Rome and Alexandria could perhaps provide us with comparative material. In Rome we know of at least eleven congregations, and perhaps as many as thirteen.[155] Binder, who estimates the Jewish population of Rome as about 40,000, states that "the number of synagogues in the city must have been quite high," and concludes that "a large number of synagogues existed in Rome."[156] In Alexandria, the situation seems to have been similar. Binder states that, since the Jews in Alexandria were so numerous, dozens of synagogues must have been required.[157]

It is reasonable to assume a similar situation in Antioch. M. Hengel allows for a considerable number of synagogues, something that does not exclude a main synagogue, as was the case in Alexandria.[158] If we follow Binder in his conclusion of the main functions of the synagogue in the Diaspora, namely that they functioned as places for prayers, study and the teaching of scripture on the Sabbath,[159] and, moreover, postulate a Jewish population of 22,000, of which 50 percent ought to be male, this would leave us with about 11,000 men, of whom c. 50 percent had attained religious maturity. If we, furthermore, assume that one synagogue can accommodate 300 individuals,[160] eighteen synagogues would be required.[161] The source of error in this kind of speculation is of course considerable. I have, for instance, not taken into consideration the role of women, which might have been substantial, at least in the Diaspora.[162] Further, I have assumed that all Jews always attended all the services. In sum however, I believe there is enough substance in the reasoning to support the view of the existence, during the first century CE of twenty to thirty synagogues in Antioch.

The internal organization of the Jewish community

As for the internal organization of the Jews of Antioch, there is almost a complete lack of relevant evidence for our period.[163] The only functionary known to us is the ἄρχων, mentioned by Josephus in *B.J.* 7.47. Our understanding of the structure of the Jewish community must hence rest on well-founded conjectures related to our knowledge of the situation elsewhere. A key to how to treat this delicate matter may, however, be provided by our understanding of the concept of the synagogue in general.

In one of the most recent discussions of the synagogue during the second temple, Binder reaches the conclusion that there was a strong connection between the temple of Jerusalem and the synagogue institution, and that the latter was modeled on the former. He concludes:

> On the basis of the evidence examined in the preceding chapters, it is reasonable to suggest that the synagogues of the Second Temple period functioned de facto, if not necessarily by design, as vehicles that transported the ancient worshipers closer to the center; that they served in effect as distant courts of the Temple, wherein a congregation had some sense of being near to the *axis mundi*.[164]

If Binder is right in his conclusion about the connection between synagogue and temple, we may,[165] consequently, dare to draw specific

38

conclusions from a more general knowledge of the synagogue institution *since the same underlying ideology would permeate the synagogue
institution as a whole.*[166]

Having evaluated the available pre-70 literary and epigraphic
material, Binder finds that the synagogues were generally "highly
institutionalized organizations with several echelons of functionaries."[167] At the top of this hierarchic structure he finds the ἄρχων[168]
and the ἀρχισυνάγωγος,[169] with the former principally responsible for
the judicial and legislative affairs and the latter mainly in charge of
the religious services. A college of elders representing the people
surrounded these functionaries, and also served as advisors.[170] Binder
points furthermore to the fact that the title ἄρχων occurs frequently
in Greco-Roman literature, where it denotes a magistrate of a city or
region. Since ἄρχοντες often served as benefactors, personal wealth
was a prerequisite for being elected to the office. Binder also emphasizes the significance of the *gerousia* or *synedrion*, which surrounded
the high priest, as a possible pattern for the organization of the
synagogue.[171] According to Binder, this system seems to have been
operative in Alexandria and he believes that the same was true for
Antioch.[172] In fact, Binder finds evidence for the same organizational
pattern in all Jewish communities in the eastern Mediterranean.[173]
He states that synagogues "in the east were frequently organized
within the framework of a politeuma, where civic authority was
placed firmly upon the shoulders of the local Jewish authorities."[174]

So, to sum up our results so far, it seems reasonable to take for
granted the existence of a fairly large number of synagogues in
Antioch. The term ἄρχων is attested, and some sort of council could
perhaps cautiously be inferred if we take into consideration both the
situation in the eastern Mediterranean area and Binder's general
theory about the modeling of the synagogue institution.[175] I have
previously stated that from the foundation of the city the Jews of
Antioch had been recognized as an identifiable entity. Since
privileges were bestowed on this group, known as "the Jews," the
existence of such a council in charge of the judicial and legislative
relations with the *polis* of Antioch, as well as Rome, seems very
reasonable.

The synagogue as a community center

Finally, a few words should be said about the social function of the
synagogue. L. I. Levine has pointed to the communal, "non-worship"
dimension of the synagogue and emphasized its role as a community

center.[176] "[T]he synagogue," Levine states, "functioned first and foremost as a community center with a broad and varied agenda."[177] Levine cites a passage from Josephus that gives us an idea of the activities in the synagogues of the first century CE. Josephus tells us in *A.J.* 14.235 about how Jews had pointed out for him that, from earliest times, they "have had an association [σύνοδον] of their own in accordance with their native laws and a place of their own, in which they decide their affairs and controversies with one another." This text implies that the Jewish community was organized as a *collegium*, and had achieved the right to follow certain laws and also had a special place to gather. The text refers to one vital aspect of the synagogue institution: namely, to serve as a place for administering justice. There are several indications that sentences were meted out in the synagogues,[178] and trials were probably also conducted there.

Josephus also mentions that people met in the synagogue to "decide their affairs," which could be taken as evidence that different sub-groups within the community used the synagogue as a meeting place. There is evidence that a burial society met in a synagogue in Egypt, and one association in Apollonopolis that organized a series of banquets may have used the local synagogue.[179] That communal meals took place in the synagogue is indicated in *A.J.* 14.214–16, where Josephus refers to an edict by Julius Caesar in which the rights of the Jews to assemble according to tradition and to collect money for communal meals are acknowledged. The nature of these meals is unfortunately not known to us, but they may have been holiday meals, communal gatherings on the Sabbath, meals for visitors, etc. One very interesting issue is the role of Gentiles at such meals. It is generally accepted that Gentiles interested in Judaism, often called "god-fearers," existed in close connection to Jewish communities. It cannot be ruled out that such Gentiles, at least in some synagogues, may have participated in communal meals held in the synagogues. Generally speaking, the connection between meals and religious cult is well attested in the Hellenistic world. Meals were often held in association with sacrificial rites in a temple,[180] and in different *collegia* shared cultic meals had a prominent position.[181] Furthermore, the synagogue seems to have taken care of visitors and transients,[182] and there is evidence of a wide range of charitable activities, which taken together with the other evidence strongly suggests that the communal aspects of the synagogue "constituted the very essence of the institution at this time."[183]

Summary and conclusion

Founded in 300 BCE, Antioch eventually developed into one of the most important cities in the ancient world. Famous for its beauty and wealth, the city represented an amalgamation of different peoples, religions and traditions that made it in many ways comparable to a modern urban melting pot. During the Roman period, it served as the capital of the imperial province of Syria and thus constituted an important center of Roman power in the East.

Originally founded by Seleucus I Nicator as a Greek *polis*, Antioch kept much of its Greek character even during the Roman period. The city remained organized as a Greek *polis*, which, among other things, meant that only a part of the inhabitants were real citizens of the *polis*, while the rest were free foreigners or slaves. One obligation that was incumbent upon all inhabitants, with the exception of the Jewish community, was to pay respect to the gods of the city. This usually meant participating in the frequent pan-Hellenic festivals and sacrifices, but also to acknowledge the Roman emperors as deities.

Many Greeks and people from other ethnic groups combined participation in the religion on an official level with membership in a *collegium*, a kind of *voluntary association* founded around a deity or a common interest, for instance, drinking or as a professional guild. Foreign cults, that is, Cypriot or Egyptian cults as well as the different mystery religions, were all organized as *collegia* and had to be authorized by the state. This was true also for the Jewish community.

Jews were probably among the original inhabitants of the city. According to Josephus, the Seleucid rulers granted the Jews certain rights—for instance, to practice their own religion without worshiping the gods of the city and to live governed by their own legislation. At least this is the interpretation of Josephus that makes most sense. This means that the Jewish community in Antioch was considered to be one of many *collegia*, but at the same time a *collegium* with rights in many ways beyond those of other *collegia*. This, together with the fact that these rights were bestowed upon the Jewish community by Rome and not by the *polis* of Antioch, may have been one reason for the strained relations between Jews and Gentiles in Antioch, for which there is certainly evidence. We may notice that the only way of being exempted from the official cult would have been formally to convert to Judaism, since only the Jews had the right to practice their own religion without worshiping the gods of the city including the deified emperors.

41

ANTIOCH

This interest in Judaism may be related to the general social situation in the city. Because of an extremely high population density, in combination with a population of possibly over 300,000 inhabitants in the first century CE, which implies severe sanitation problems, the average life expectancy was very low, somewhere in the range of twenty to thirty years of age. To keep the population constant, the city had to rely on a constant influx of people, which in turn implies that Antioch was populated largely by newcomers. In this situation, characterized to a rather high degree by social chaos, with people who had few interpersonal attachments, the institutions of the different *collegia* provided exactly what was lacking, namely, social stability and interpersonal attachments. The Jewish community, which may have constituted between 5 and 10 percent of the population, with as many as thirty synagogues, must have made up an easily identifiable element in the city. It may be hypothesized that the character of the synagogue also contributed to attracting Gentiles to the community of the Jews. Besides being the religious center of Diaspora Judaism, the synagogue functioned as a community center for the Jewish population, and a wide range of charitable activities took place within it. It is reasonable to assume that an institution with a well-developed social network, even between different cities of the empire, and with both the ideology to provide for the less fortunate and the means to realize such an ideology, would exercise a considerable influence in a milieu where bronchitis could lead to death from septicemia.

This raises, of course, a series of questions about the Jewish community and its relation to the Gentile society. To what extent did Jews and Gentiles interact? What was the status of those Gentiles— usually referred to as god-fearers—who did not formally convert to Judaism, but lived between two religious worlds? Did all Jews, and all synagogues, welcome Gentile sympathizers in their midst, or is it possible to identify a difference in attitude towards Gentiles? In the following chapters we seek answers to these and several other questions, in order to find a solution to the overarching problem of the separation between Judaism and Christianity. In chapter 3 we will study in more detail how the Jewish community at Antioch was ideologically stratified.

Notes

1 Kondoleon, "City," 3.
2 Takács, "Pagan Cults," 198; Downey, *Antioch in Syria*, 67–8. Downey's

work is hitherto the most extensive presentation of the history of Antioch and draws from several kinds of sources. The excavations of ancient Antioch began in 1932 and continued annually up to the outbreak of the Second World War in 1939, and four volumes of excavation reports have been published (see Kondoleon, "City," 5–8 for a short excavation history). However, the major sources for the history of Antioch are literary; most important are the sixth century chronicler John Malalas and the writings of the orator and teacher Libanius, who was born in Antioch in 314 CE. One important source of information is coins—for the Augustan period these are the main source (for an overview of the mint of Antioch, see Metcalf, "Mint"). For an exhaustive discussion and account of the sources, see Downey, *Antioch in Syria*, 24–45. There has recently been published a beautiful catalogue on the occasion of an exhibition on Antioch in Worcester, Cleveland and Baltimore including several essays and many illustrations, to some extent dependent on Downey's work, see Kondoleon, *Antioch: The Lost Ancient City*.

3 Norris, "Religious Center," 2329, 2335, 2337.
4 Downey, *Antioch in Syria*, 72.
5 An area for horse and chariot racing probably existed in Daphne from the late third century BCE, while the first hippodrome was probably constructed in 67 BCE; see Humphrey, *Roman Circuses*, 457.
6 Norris, "Religious Center," 2342–3. See Descamps, "Tyche," 118, for an illustration of a replica of the original statue.
7 Downey, *Antioch in Syria*, 73–7; Takács, "Pagan Cults," 198.
8 Downey, *Antioch in Syria*, 87. Cf. Haddad, *Aspects*, 10–11, who states that Antioch was the real centre of Seleucid rule even earlier.
9 Norris, "Religious Center," 2357; Downey, *Antioch in Syria*, 89.
10 Norris, "Religious Center," 2361–2; Norris, "Isis," 205–6. It is possible, however, that Libanius, *Or.* 11.114, may have placed the introduction of the Egyptian cult too early. Isis first appears on coins during the reign of Antiochus IV (175–163 BCE), and since Isis and Sarapis were closely connected with the Ptolemies it is possible that a Seleucid ruler hesitated to introduce the cult of a rival dynasty; see Takács, "Pagan Cults," 199.
11 Norris, "Religious Center," 2332; Downey, *Antioch in Syria*, 93.
12 Ibid., 95–6.
13 See also Hengel, *Judaism: 1*, 267–309, and Schäfer, *History*, 35–44.
14 Downey, *Antioch in Syria*, 109.
15 Cf. Downey, *Antioch in Syria*, 190, n. 106, who expresses doubt about the historicity of this statement. In general, however, Josephus is considered to be reliable as a historian, see Bilde, *Flavius Josephus*, 191–200.
16 Brooten, "Jews," 31.
17 Downey, *Antioch in Syria*, 96–102.
18 As, for instance, in 148 and 65 BCE, see Guidoboni, Comastri and Traina, *Catalogue*, 152, 164–8.
19 Kraeling, "Jewish Community," 147.
20 Norris, "Religious Center," 2360.
21 Downey, *Antioch in Syria*, 155–6.

22 *A.J.* 14.319–23.
23 Yegül, "Baths," 148.
24 Downey, *Antioch in Syria*, 169–84.
25 *B.J.* 7.45.
26 A good part of the population was of Greco-Macedonian origin, as names and language also attest to Syrian influence, and a certain part of the population was of Latin origin; Haddad, *Aspects*, 117.
27 Ibid., 13. This was the normal form of organization within the empire (see Walker-Ramisch, "Graeco-Roman," 132), and it is an "adequate description both of the formal public status and constitutions and of the social character of the major urban centres of northern Syria in the Roman period"; Millar, *Near East*, 241. See also Wallace and Williams, *Three Worlds*, 85, who point to the fact that Rome was actually even more active in establishing Greek *poleis* than the Macedonian kings had been. Cf. Downey, who states that Antioch was originally organized not as a Greek *polis* but according to Macedonian standard. However, this concerns primarily the internal organization, and not the fundamental division of the residents into formal citizens and foreigners, and by the time of Augustus there are indications that Antioch was organized as a Greek *polis*; see Downey, *Antioch in Syria*, 114–15.
28 On the *polis* institution during Roman rule, see Wallace and Williams, *Three Worlds*, 111–16.
29 It should be noted, however, that the conditions are only partially known for the Roman province of Syria, among other places; see Millar, "Greek City," 243.
30 Maas, "People," 16; Wallace and Williams, *Three Worlds*, 85.
31 Tcherikover, *Hellenistic*, 23, 24; Millar, "Greek City," 246.
32 Hansen, "Citizen-State," 8; Applebaum, "Organization," 464; Wallace and Williams, *Three Worlds*, 95–6. There were usually four categories of foreigners in Greek cities: a) permanent residents, called metics, b) more or less permanent residents who had yet to become recognized as metics, c) temporary visitors, and d) slaves; see Grant, *Social History*, 123.
33 Hansen, "Citizen-State," 17.
34 Price, *Ancient Greeks*, 3; Walker-Ramisch, "Graeco-Roman," 135; Schmitt-Pantel, "Collective Activities," 200.
35 According to Price, *Ancient Greeks*, 7, the religious system of the Greeks was fairly stable during the period ranging from the Archaic era to the second and third centuries CE.
36 Sourvinou-Inwood, "*Polis* Religion," 305.
37 Ibid., 307.
38 Price, *Ancient Greeks*, 24–5.
39 See Ekroth, *Sacrificial Rituals*, 247–58, for an overview of the significance and meaning of animal sacrifice ending with a meal in different contexts. See also Burkert, "Meaning," 36–9, for the use of temples in the cult, and pp. 39–44 on the relation between temples and the *polis*.
40 Schmitt-Pantel, "Collective Activities," 207.
41 Rosivach, *System*, 3.
42 See Bruit-Zaidman and Schmitt-Pantel, *Religion*, 28–41, for an overview of sacrifice in Archaic and Classical Greek cities.

43 Stambaugh and Balch, *Social World*, 129; Wallace and Williams, *Three Worlds*, 103.
44 Bruit-Zaidman and Schmitt-Pantel, *Religion*, 34–5. See also Seland, *Paulus*, 83.
45 Millar, "Greek City," 238.
46 See Norris, "Isis," and "Religious Center," and Takács, "Pagan Cults," for overviews of Greek religion, as well as other religious influences known to have existed in Antioch.
47 See Price, *Ancient Greeks*, 148–58, for a comparison of Greek and Roman religions.
48 Both Gaius and Claudius are reported to have contributed to the repair of the city after earthquakes; see Malalas, *Chron.* 243, 246.
49 Price, *Ancient Greeks*, 156–7.
50 Tellbe, *Synagogue and State*, 31, points to the fact that the ruler cult is not only to be perceived as a political phenomenon, but was also designed to express piety.
51 Cf. Price, *Ancient Greeks*, 155–6, who states that "[t]he religious articulation of imperial power at Rome itself paraded its roots in Roman practices (for example, the apotheosis of Romulus) and was distinguished from whatever religious honours the Greek subjects saw fit to offer the Roman emperor."
52 Wallace and Williams, *Three Worlds*, 115.
53 Winter, "Imperial Cult," 93–7.
54 Price, *Ancient Greeks*, 7, 158.
55 Millar, "Greek City," 246.
56 Downey, *Antioch in Syria*, 167; Norris, "Religious Center," 2361.
57 Maas, "People," 16.
58 Tellbe, *Synagogue and State*, 35.
59 See Stambaugh and Balch, *Social World*, 124–7, for a brief overview of *collegia* in the Roman period.
60 The existence of a specific *collegia funeraticia* is, however, a matter of dispute, since it could be argued that funeral was only one element among others in the *collegia*. Patterson, "Patronage," 20, states that "*fabri* and *centonarii* were often involved in burying their members, as were *collegia* with religious names, and we even find that the *convictores* at Fanum had their own burial place." On Roman funeral associations in general, see also Hopkins, *Death*, 211–17.
61 Kloppenborg, "Collegia," 18. Another way of classifying *collegia* is on the basis of membership, and results in three groupings: a) those associated with a household, b) those formed around a common trade, and c) those formed around the cult of a deity; see "Collegia," 26.
62 Cicero, *Leg.* 2.8.19.
63 When the senate bestowed upon Augustus the title *Pontifex Maximus*, he took this prerogative upon himself; Cotter, "Collegia," 79.
64 Koester, *Introduction 1*, 365.
65 Cotter, "Collegia," 79.
66 "[T]heir existence was tolerated rather than encouraged"; Kloppenborg, "Collegia," 16. Augustus seems, however, to have encouraged the formation in Rome of *compitalia*, neighbourhood cults, which he associated with the imperial house, see Patterson, "Patronage," 19

(referring to Suetonius, *Aug*. 31). Burial clubs seems also to have been allowed; see Hopkins, *Death*, 212.

67 Cotter, "Collegia," 76.

68 Richardson, "Early Synagogues," 93.

69 MacMullen, *Enemies*, 174.

70 Walker-Ramisch, "Graeco-Roman," 134; Tellbe, *Synagogue and State*, 41.

71 See Price, *Ancient Greeks*, 82–8, on responses to religious threats in Classical Athens.

72 Participation in festivals, for instance, was not only a privilege but a duty; see Tcherikover, *Hellenistic*, 28.

73 Bruit-Zaidman and Schmitt-Pantel, *Religion*, 13; Price, *Ancient Greeks*, 89–101, 108. There are two examples of household shrines from Antioch "with figures mounted in small groups on miniature bronze semicircular platforms with four steps at the center, probably intended to simulate the entrance to a temple"; see Russell, "Household," 88.

74 Bruit-Zaidman and Schmitt-Pantel, *Religion*, 15.

75 Walker-Ramisch, "Graeco-Roman," 133.

76 For examples of Roman suppression of foreign cults, see Tellbe, *Synagogue and State*, 27–8, or Koester, *Introduction 1*, 364–5.

77 Richardson, "Augustan-Era," 18; Richardson, "Early Synagogues," 93. One exception was the *symphoniaci*, who played music at public sacrifices; Patterson, "Patronage," 19, referring to *CIL* 6.4416.

78 *Collegia* were constituted mainly by urban poor, i.e., freedmen, slaves and resident aliens, see Kloppenborg, "Collegia," 16, 17.

79 Walker-Ramisch, "Graeco-Roman," 134; Seland, "Philo," 112. According to Patterson, "Patronage," 23, "[t]he collegia can be seen as a means of 'humanizing the city,' by providing an opportunity for social interaction within groups identified by their location within the city, their devotion to a particular deity, their professional activities, their love of feasting—or all four." See also MacMullen, *Enemies*, 174, who states that the function of the *collegia* can be summed up in the phrase "social security."

80 The question of the size of the population of Antioch, Gentile as well as Jewish, during the first century CE is a complicated matter. Generally speaking, Antioch was, as Haddad, *Aspects*, 67, states, "one of the most populous cities in the Hellenistic-Roman period." He estimates the population as 200,000 free inhabitants, which, in turn would give us a total of 400,000 inhabitants including slaves (pp. 70–1). See also his discussion of different views on this matter on pp. 68–9. Downey, "Population," 86, suggests about 300,000 free inhabitants in the first century CE and states that it is not possible to calculate the number of slaves and non-citizen inhabitants. See also Nixon and Price, "Size," 160, and Roberts and Manchester, *Archaeology*, 20–1.

81 Stark, *Rise of Christianity*, 150.

82 Downey, *Antioch in Syria*, 72.

83 Ibid., 103, 155. The baths of Trajan were the first to be connected to a major aqueduct; see Yegül, "Baths," 148.

84 Stark, *Rise of Christianity*, 150–4.

85 Downey, *Antioch in Syria*, 72.

86 Roberts and Manchester, *Archaeology*, 18–19.
87 Ibid., 141; Manchester, "Palaeopathology," 11.
88 Ibid.
89 Roberts and Manchester, *Archaeology*, 137; Aufderheide and Rodríguez-Martín, *Encyclopedia*, 125.
90 Dalby, *Siren Feasts*, 66.
91 Hopkins, *Death*, 72.
92 Petersen, *Population*, 366.
93 Manchester, "Palaeopathology," 12; Aufderheide and Rodríguez-Martín, *Encyclopedia*, 198.
94 Common complications of influenza, are, for instance, hemorrhagic bronchitis, pneumonia, sinusitis, otitis and bronchitis; see Aufderheide and Rodríguez-Martín, *Encyclopedia*, 211.
95 Roberts and Manchester, *Archaeology*, 127.
96 Ibid., 126–8.
97 Stark, *Rise of Christianity*, 151.
98 Roberts and Manchester, *Archaeology*, 131.
99 Demand, *Birth*, 8, 75, but cf. Roberts and Manchester, *Archaeology*, 25, who states that, while childbirth was undoubtedly a contributing factor to more males surviving into old age, as is indicated by archaeological remains, there may be a problem with the accuracy of sex attribution, since "older people develop skeletal structures which are more robust, and a skeleton may be attributed mistakenly for a male rather than a female."
100 The evidence is from Classical Greece but may have been relevant also for the situation in Antioch, see Demand, *Birth*, 81–6.
101 Petersen, *Population*, 343; Hopkins, "Graveyards," 116, and *Death*, 71–2; Stark, *Rise of Christianity*, 155. These high levels of mortality are generally accepted by Roman social historians and are also now supported by empirical evidence, see Frier, "More," 150, and Scheidel, "Progress," 24–5.
102 Hopkins, *Death*, 72. See also Hopkins, "Graveyards," 115–16.
103 Kajanto, *Problem*, 23.
104 Stark, *Rise of Christianity*, 156–7. In the Classical Greek city there was usually no standing force to carry out police functions; Morris, "Early Polis," 44. In Roman Antioch there may, however, have existed a locally recruited police force, and order could also be maintained via the Roman legions; see Stambaugh and Balch, *Social World*, 34.
105 Malalas, *Chron.* 243, 246. See also Guidoboni, Comastri and Traina, *Catalogue*, 187–8.
106 Stark, *Rise of Christianity*, 160–1.
107 Walker-Ramisch, "Graeco-Roman," 134; Rajak and Noy, "Archisynagogoi," 84. The same was true for the synagogue, see Rajak, "Synagogue," 164–5.
108 Kloppenborg, "Collegia," 26; Seland, "Philo," 112.
109 Kraeling, "Jewish Community," 132.
110 Downey, *Antioch in Syria*, 79–80.
111 Haddad, *Aspects*, 51; Kasher, *Jews*, 301.
112 That the Jewish population in Babylon was considered a good source from which military settlers could be recruited is recorded from the

time of Antiochus III, since Josephus, in *A.J.* 12.148–53, describes how 2,000 Jewish families from Babylon and Mesopotamia settled in Phrygia and Lydia. The Jews of these settlements, and of similar ones in Syria, were probably organized in κατοικίαι; see Applebaum, "Legal Status," 432.

113 Brooten, "Jews," 30.
114 Kraeling, "Jewish Community," 145.
115 Ibid., 146.
116 Richardson, "Augustan-Era," 18, 19; "Early Synagogues"; "Architectural Case"; Rajak, "Synagogue," 164–6; Meeks, *First Urban*, 32. Cf., however, Levine, "First-Century," 27–8, who has pointed out that, while there are certainly similarities between the institution of the synagogue and that of the *collegia*, one must not disregard the differences. One major difference is that the synagogue had a wider range of both activities and privileges than the ordinary *collegia*. The privileges are given some attention by Richardson, see "Augustan-Era," 18, and "Early Synagogues," 103. Levine also mentions that one may question whether participation in the activities of the synagogue could be labelled "voluntary," since Jews were more or less forced to associate with the institution that provided the legal framework. As Walker-Ramisch, "Graeco-Roman," 131, has pointed out, this is true even for modern associations such as churches and trade unions. Religious affiliation is often a result of the process of socialization, and membership in trade unions can be a condition of employment. Principally, these associations are voluntary, and the same must have been true for the ancient synagogue: it was possible to break with the Jewish community. Levine's remark is still important: if the synagogue is to be defined as a *collegium*, we must remember that it constituted a special kind of association. See also Binder, *Temple Courts*, 229–32, 338–9, who generally agrees with Richardson but also suggests some points where he finds that Richardson's proposal needs refinement.
117 Richardson, "Early Synagogues," 93.
118 Cotter, "Collegia," 78–9. See also Philo, *Legat.* 156–8. Richardson, "Early Synagogues," 93.
119 Rutgers, "Roman Policy," 115.
120 See Levinskaya, *Diaspora Setting*, 128–9, for an overview of the scholarly debate and further references.
121 Kraeling, "Jewish Community," 137–8.
122 Ibid., 138.
123 Downey, *Antioch in Syria*, 80.
124 Meeks and Wilken, *Jews and Christians*, 2.
125 Ibid., 2, n. 5.
126 Binder, *Temple Courts*, 265.
127 Barclay, *Mediterranean Diaspora*, 244, 245.
128 As for the situation in Alexandria, Barclay, *Mediterranean Diaspora*, 63, labels the opinion that all Jews of Alexandria were also citizens in the city as "universally abandoned."
129 Applebaum, "Legal Status," 440.
130 Ibid., 452.
131 Strathmann, "πολιτεία," 526, referring to 2 Macc. 8:17. The same

meaning of πολιτεία is, according to Strathmann, evident also in 2 Macc. 8:17, and 4 Macc. 4:19, 8:7, 17:19. He concludes by stating that the word here refers to "a religious and moral concept rather than a political concept." Only in 3 Macc. 3:21, 23, does Strathmann find πολιτεία used in the sense of "civil rights."
132 Applebaum, "Legal Status," 452. Cf. also Hoenig, "Oil," 69, who regards "citizenship" and "equal privileges" as referring to the freedom from worshiping the gods of the city.
133 See Troiani, "Πολιτεία of Israel," 13, who draws attention to the fact that whenever Josephus touches on the subject of πολιτεία "he usually speaks of 'equal citizenship' (ἰσοπολιτεία), not of 'citizenship.'" Kasher, *Jews*, 309, notes the same and states that "Josephus does not give the slightest hint of Jews having rights as citizens of the *polis*."
134 On a *polis* level there existed similar arrangements from the Classical period, but more frequently in the Hellenistic period, namely treaties of *isopoliteia* or *sympoliteia*. These treaties meant that people living in one *polis* could exercise citizen rights in another *polis*, as an exception to the principle that citizenship was limited only to those who belonged to a *polis* and could not be acquired as a right by those who settled in another *polis*; see Rhodes, "Greek *Poleis*," 174–5, and Applebaum, "Legal Status," 436.
135 Kasher, *Jews*, 305.
136 See Smallwood, *Jews*, 360, who considers the situation in Antioch to have been exactly like the one in Alexandria.
137 Kasher, *Jews*, 356–7.
138 *B.J.* 7.44, 47, 54, 111.
139 *B.J.* 7.47, 100, 107.
140 Kasher, *Jews*, 305–6.
141 Ibid., 308.
142 Regarding the situation in Antioch, Barclay, *Mediterranean Diaspora*, 245, n. 30, rejects Kasher's suggestion that Josephus here refers to "the right of the Jewish *politeuma* to exist alongside the Greek citizen body." He continues: "if Josephus meant this, his language is, at the very least, disingenuous." He is right, of course, in that there is nothing to support the view that the Jews in Antioch were constituted as a πολίτευμα, but I can find no evidence to support that Josephus did not mean to refer to the legal rights of the Jewish community. In fact, if Josephus by the terms πολιτεία and τῆς πόλεως μετέχειν intended to refer to formal citizenship, his writing appears even more curious. That he consciously intended to give the impression that the Jews were citizens of Antioch would have lowered his credibility, since everybody would know him to be wrong. That he himself would be unaware of the state of the matters is perhaps even more improbable, since he had been residing in Jerusalem and moreover was involved in the political struggle for independence.
143 1 Macc. 1:41–53; *A.J.* 12.253–6.
144 Applebaum, "Legal Status," 452–3. See also Applebaum, "Organization," 473, and Meeks, *First Urban*, 13.
145 Applebaum, "Legal Status," 420. See also Applebaum, "Organization," 464: "However non-Greek elements might be formally incorporated

into the new citizen body, there normally remained within the
settlement non-citizen populations, often of native origin, organized
after their own fashion."

146 Lüderitz, "Politeuma," 222.
147 Ibid., 202–3.
148 Barclay, *Mediterranean Diaspora*, 67. See pp. 67–9 for Barclay's
arguments. In, for instance, commenting on *C. Ap.*, he definitely has a
point in drawing attention to the fact that "it is hard to see how Apion
and his delegation could have complained about Jewish citizens if they
had lost their Jewish identity in becoming citizens" (pp. 69–70). See
also Seland, *Paulus*, 134.
149 Barclay, *Mediterranean Diaspora*, 69.
150 Ibid., 43.
151 See Tellbe, *Synagogue and State*, 37–51, for a thorough discussion of
Jewish rights and privileges.
152 Kraeling, "Jewish Community," 143. He mentions one inside the city,
one near Daphne and one east of the city. The existence of the last one is,
however, called into question by Meeks and Wilken, *Jews and Christians*,
9.
153 Barclay, *Mediterranean Diaspora*, 243.
154 Meeks and Wilken, *Jews and Christians*, 8. Cf. Kraeling, "Jewish
Community," 136, who assumes a Jewish population of 45,000 in the
first century CE. Binder, *Temple Courts*, 264, and Levinskaya, *Diaspora
Setting*, 134, however, believe the lower figure of Meeks and Wilken to
be the more accurate. The situation for Rome is about the same, with
different estimations varying from 20,000 to 60,000; see Hedner-
Zetterholm, "Jewish Communities," 132.
155 Ibid., 137.
156 Binder, *Temple Courts*, 320, 321.
157 Ibid., 251–2.
158 Hengel and Schwemer, *Between Damascus*, 186.
159 Binder, *Temple Courts*, 449.
160 Most *collegia* ranged from between fifteen and 100 members, but there
is evidence from Rome and Ostia of professional *collegia* with two to 300
members; see Kloppenborg, "Collegia," 25, and Meeks, *First Urban*, 31.
161 The existence of several synagogues is taken for granted by other
scholars as, for instance, Applebaum, "Organization," 485, who states
that "at least three are recorded and there must have been more."
Levinskaya, *Diaspora Setting*, 134, claims that there "is no doubt that in
the Roman period there existed more than one," and Meeks and
Wilken, *Jews and Christians*, 8, allege that the main synagogue "was
surely not the only synagogue within the city." As for the general
situation in the Diaspora, Levine, *Ancient Synagogue*, 272, states that
"[l]arger communities undoubtedly boasted many more than one
synagogue," and more specifically of Antioch he suggests that there was
probably a number of synagogues (see p. 20).
162 For overviews of the role of women in the synagogue, see Binder, *Temple
Courts*, 372–9, or Horbury, "Women," 375–88.
163 See Levinskaya, *Diaspora Setting*, 133–4, for an overview of all, including
later, references. Applebaum, "Organization," 485, however, believes

that the information which refers primarily to the fourth-century situation reveals an organization which "was of long standing and can be related to the first century of the present era."
164 Binder, *Temple Courts*, 478.
165 Cf. Cohen, "Temple and Synagogue," 321, who notes that most synagogues which have been discovered "do not imitate the temple's orientation; they face not east but the temple, thereby indicating that they are not mirror images of the temple but remote outposts of the sacredness of the centre."
166 The idea that the synagogue institution is modeled after the temple of Jerusalem is rather harshly refuted by Levine, "First-Century," 26–7, who finds Binder's claim "speculative and forced, at best," and furthermore that Binder is "unable to substantiate his sweeping and all-inclusive theories." Levine's critique seems unnecessarily austere, and it is hard to dismiss Binder's proposal so categorically. It may be right, as Levine states, that there is no explicit halakhic or exegetical evidence in favour of Binder's suggestion, but, having taken into consideration the evidence Binder actually puts forward (see *Temple Courts*, 479–93), I find it hard to rule out the possibility of a connection between the temple in Jerusalem and the synagogue institution on a (social psychological-level.) The synagogue may have functioned in the way Binder suggests without this having left any explicit marks in the surviving sources, and there may even have existed theological reasons to tone down such an ideological connection.
167 Binder, *Temple Courts*, 371.
168 Cf. Levine, *Ancient Synagogue*, 402, who finds the evidence for the office of ἄρχων in a synagogue setting "spotty and uncertain."
169 Cf. Rajak and Noy, "*Archisynagogoi*," 78, 84–9, who have shown from inscriptions that the title ἀρχισυνάγωγος was used for functionaries in *Gentile collegia*, and was also used for purely honorific reasons, and could be attributed to non-Jews. See also Levine, *Ancient Synagogue*, 399, who draws attention to the fact that this must not be interpreted as if it was the only function of the title. In addition, there is evidence from inscriptions mainly from the second to the sixth centuries CE that the title ἀρχισυνάγωγος was attributed to women, see Horbury, "Women," 388–9.
170 Binder, *Temple Courts*, 371.
171 Ibid., 346. Sanders has criticized the prevalent scholarly consensus about the existence of a *synedrion* in Jerusalem, see Sanders, *Judaism*, 472–88. Binder, while certainly acknowledging some of Sanders's critique, states that Sanders "seems to be overstating the matter" in that he regards the *synedrion* to be only an *ad hoc* body; see Binder, *Temple Courts*, 345, n. 3. Cf. also the traditional consensus; see Safrai, "Self-Government," 379–400.
172 Binder, *Temple Courts*, 265, 347. So does Walker-Ramisch, "Graeco-Roman," 138, who states that "[t]he clearest evidence for this type of Jewish federative organization is to be found in the literary and epigraphical sources for the large Jewish populations of Alexandria and Syrian Antioch."
173 This does not imply that there must have been identical organizations.

In drawing attention to the possibility of a more diversified situation in Rome, Williams, "Structure," 137, has pointed to a certain variation in the use of titles in the Diaspora synagogues. These are not to be regarded as contradictory statements. There is, of course, the obvious possibility of a similar overarching organization with local variations. Cf. also Kraeling, "Jewish Community," 137, who finds no reason "to suppose that the organization in Syria differed radically from that of other parts of the diaspora."

174 Binder, *Temple Courts*, 338.

175 Cf. also Kraabel, "Unity," 26, who finds that "the Greek-speaking Jews in the cities of the Roman world . . . developed a new form of organization which was fairly uniform from one Diaspora city to the next."

176 Levine, *Ancient Synagogue*, 128–34.

177 Ibid., 134; but cf. Binder, *Temple Courts*, 450, who stresses the role of the synagogue as a "sacred" rather than a "profane" building.

178 Matt. 10:17–18; Mark 13:9; Luke 21:12; Acts 22:19; 2 Cor. 11:24.

179 Levine, *Ancient Synagogue*, 129, referring to *CPJ* 138–9.

180 Burkert, "Meaning," 36–7; Price, *Ancient Greeks*, 33–6.

181 As, for instance, in Mithraism, see Beck, "Mysteries," 182.

182 As evident from the Theodotos inscription, see *CIJ* 1404, and Levine, "Second Temple," 17.

183 Ibid., 134. See also Rajak, "Synagogue," 170, who points to the variety of activities going on in the synagogue.

3

THE CULTURAL AND RELIGIOUS DIFFERENTIATION

> They teased and vilified the Radzymin Chassidim—who made no effort to defend themselves. Why argue with enemies? In the Radzymin study house, no one dared ask questions. Their Radzymin Rabbi, nevertheless, remained constant in his beliefs . . .
>
> Isaac Bashevis Singer, *In my Fathers' Court*

Introduction

It is a sad fact that our knowledge of the Judaism of the first century CE is rather limited. It is true that we know quite a lot about the *ideology* of different Jewish groups. The pioneering works of C. G. Montefiore, G. F. Moore, R. T. Herford, J. Parkes, and W. D. Davies, for instance, culminating in that of E. P. Sanders,[1] have been of tremendous importance in showing that ancient Judaism was not a legalistic religion in which salvation was earned by merit, but a living religion of grace and forgiveness.

Now, ideology as expressed in literary texts reflects mainly the view of the cultural elite and not that of ordinary people. The connection between these levels is not self-evident. One additional problem is that, when we do find information about how ideology was being transformed into action, namely, in the Tannaitic literature, this is also a product of the religious elite. The conclusion to be drawn is that we possess almost no sources that can provide us with information about how ordinary Jews in Palestine and in the Diaspora gave a concrete form to torah obedience. What is lacking is information about how religiousness may have varied between different groups and places. Can we, for instance, assume that all Jews related to the torah in the same way, or is it reasonable that the halakhic process differed from place to place? Is it possible that different groups followed different halakhic standards?

This extremely interesting and complex problem lies well beyond the scope of the present study but one aspect that could serve as a point of departure for a continued study of torah obedience and the halakhic process in first-century Judaism relates to the issue of the distribution of religious preferences within the Jewish population. This chapter focuses on the religious differentiation of the Jewish population in Antioch and aims to discern different entities or religiously defined groups within the Jewish community in Antioch up to 66 CE.

This attempt exemplifies very well the problem of trying to gain an understanding of historical conditions with all too few sources at our disposal. In one of the most recent books on the synagogue, *The Ancient Synagogue: The First Thousand Years* (2000), L. I. Levine states that, "despite its large size and relatively long history, the Jewish community of Syria generally, and of Antioch in particular, is only partially known."[2] D. D. Binder, in his study *Into the Temple Courts: The Place of the Synagogue in the Second Temple Period* (1999), finds, when evaluating the evidence of the synagogues of the Diaspora, that "we are best informed about the synagogues of Egypt."[3] J. M. G. Barclay, who in *Jews in the Mediterranean Diaspora: From Alexander to Trajan (323 BCE–117 CE)* (1996), has analyzed the degree of assimilation among the Jews of Egypt, and considers it impossible to make a similar analysis on other Diaspora locations. "Unfortunately," he states,

> we lack the breadth of evidence to provide an analysis of this sort for any single Diaspora location outside Egypt during our period. Our evidence from the individual sites we have surveyed is simply too scanty, too piecemeal or too obscure to fill even our rough categories with meaningful examples.[4]

He is of course right. The sources *are* scanty, piecemeal and even obscure. Levine is quite correct in stating that, for the pre-70 period, we "must rely almost exclusively on Josephus and several traditions preserved by the sixth-century chronicler Malalas."[5] Consequently, underlying almost every interpretation of the Jewish community of Antioch we find Josephus and Malalas, mainly in the interpretations of S. Krauss ("Antioche" [1902]) and C. H. Kraeling ("The Jewish Community at Antioch" [1932]), referred to in the previous chapter.[6] To my knowledge there has been no attempt to make a comprehensive analysis of the Jewish community of Antioch that essentially reaches beyond these early studies.

Thus, the task I have set for myself in this chapter requires the methodological approach I argued for in the introduction to this study: namely, the combination of 1) a basic, general theoretical perspective regarding society, 2) specific social scientific theories used in empirical studies of modern societies, 3) comparative material from antiquity, and 4) primary sources. Through the reciprocity among the first three of these we should be able to construct an interpretative frame that will help us both to understand literary and other sources and, when such material is scanty or even lacking, to fill the gaps and create a plausible and inter-subjectively testable reconstruction of history.

Apart from the general perspective from the sociology of knowledge, I will here make use of a theory of religious change derived from studies of international migration in a Western European context. I will argue that effects operational in connection with international migration such as value changes can help us interpret the situation in Antioch. Since changes of religion or religiousness always involve a social aspect, I will use in addition a theory of assimilation in order to say something about the relation between the Jewish community and the surrounding society. Since Diaspora Judaism had to adapt itself quite considerably to Hellenistic society, this task must focus to some extent on the relation between Hellenism and Judaism in general. One major aspect of being Jewish in the Diaspora would consequently relate to the degree of adaptation to, or dissociation from, Hellenistic influences. I will, finally, make comparisons with the situation in other locations in antiquity. Barclay's thorough study of the Jews in Egypt will serve as excellent material.

To begin, let us turn to the question of the possibility of value-changing processes.

Constructing analytical tools

A theory of religious differentiation

Religion and value-changing processes

It is generally accepted that the Judaism of the first century CE was not homogeneous but a complex, diversified phenomenon. At the same time these somewhat different realizations of Jewish life had something in common. E. P. Sanders has referred to what he calls "common Judaism" as "what the priests and the people agreed on."[7] In a more recent article we find a summary of what he is aiming at:

> There was, in other words, something that we may call 'common Judaism'. It was based on general acceptance of the Bible, especially the law of Moses, and on a common self-perception: the Jews knew themselves to be Jews and not Gentiles, and to some degree or other they stood apart from other people.[8]

Sanders mentions monotheism, the refusal to worship statues, circumcision, Sabbath rest, food laws, the formation of associations, and a general study and observance of the law of Moses as vital components of common Judaism.[9] A decade earlier, J. D. G. Dunn defined the "unifying core for second Temple Judaism" as monotheism, election, torah and temple.[10]

When trying to get a picture of how the Jewish community in Antioch looked, it is tempting to start with one of the most obvious diversifying aspects of Judaism, namely, the religious parties. Different historical circumstances gave rise to three main factions known from both Josephus and the New Testament: Pharisees, Sadducees and Essenes.[11] These and other institutionalized religious factions are probably what scholars usually have in mind when using descriptions such as "complex" or "diversified."[12] People who belonged to these parties would all agree on the importance of the above-mentioned institutions but would have different views of the temple, the torah or purity regulations. This shows that it was possible to hold different beliefs and still belong to the same religious community.[13]

The main body of people, however, did not belong to any religious party; in addition,[14] the sources do not provide us with any direct evidence of the presence of any of these parties in Antioch.[15] Most likely they were all represented in one way or another, but to take religious parties as the point of departure for a study of Judaism in Antioch does not seem to be adequate. It is thus not the different religious factions but rather the group of common people on whom we focus, a group who, according to Sanders, "accepted widespread and common religious practices, especially as taught and administered by the priesthood, with no denominational tag and no membership in a group other than the people of Israel."[16]

Within this "common Judaism" there were at the same time different conceptions of how Jewish institutions should be realized in everyday life. To some extent we could speak of a geographically determined dispersion, since a major dividing line seems to have existed between Jews in the Diaspora and in Palestine, which A. T. Kraabel has summarized in describing Roman Diaspora Judaism:

> The shift to minority status in places outside the Homeland led to the abandonment of many elements of the ancestral religion, and a new emphasis on others, and the adoption of the new environment's iconography, architecture, and organizational form.[17]

Here it seems as if the Diaspora situation itself led to changes in the religiousness of the Diaspora Jews. What is suggested is in fact *that the shift from majority to minority status promotes changes in the individual's value system.*

The existence of such changes in an individual's value system or worldview once that person has reached adulthood has been the subject of a substantial scholarly debate during recent years.[18] In a study of Hungarian immigrants to Sweden, E. M. Hamberg finds indications of considerable changes in the individual's value system in connection with international migration. Since Hamberg is able to compare interview data from the Hungarian immigrants to Sweden with data from both Swedes and Hungarians in their home countries, changes in values and worldviews become evident. Two general tendencies are discernible: either the values of the Swedish-Hungarians are more similar to those of the Swedes, or they represent a kind of intermediary stage between those of Hungarians and Swedes.[19] Both these tendencies indicate the possibility of value-changing processes in connection with migration situations. Hamberg concludes:

> [I]t is possible that the migration process, by influencing plausibility structures, may create conditions which are especially favourable to value changes. If this should be true, value changes may conceivably occur in connection with international migration, even *if* they should not be common under more ordinary circumstances.[20]

Hamberg's study thus speaks in favor of the possibility of value changes in connection with international migration, a situation which is usually accompanied by a shift to minority status.

Similar effects would most probably have been operative in ancient Antioch. We noted in the previous chapter that ancient cities were dependent on a constant inflow of people, and we know that the

Roman road system, in combination with efforts to maintain law and order, facilitated travelling, which resulted in a high degree of general mobility in the Roman Empire.[21] There is every reason to assume that this applied also to the Jewish population.

We do know of Jewish migrations, voluntary as well as involuntary. In *A.J.* 12.149, Josephus mentions how 2,000 Jewish families from Mesopotamia and Babylonia were forced to move to Phrygia and Lydia during the reign of Antiochus III. In *Let. Aris.* 12–13, the author mentions the deportation of some 100,000 Jews to Egypt, during the reign of Ptolemy I Soter (367/6–282 BCE).[22] In addition to this, there is specific evidence of immigration to Antioch. In *B.J.* 7.43, Josephus reveals the following about the situation in Syria and Antioch:

> The Jewish race, densely interspersed among the native populations of every portion of the world, is particularly numerous in Syria, where intermingling is due to the proximity of the two countries. But it was at Antioch that they specially congregated, partly owing to the greatness of that city, but mainly because the successors of King Antiochus had enabled them to live there in security.

Josephus here emphasizes the greatness of the city and the proximity between Palestine and Syria, and Antioch must indeed have been an attractive settlement for anyone interested in business and trading.[23] Kraeling, referring to Josephus' *A.J.* 13.135–42, mentions political reasons as supplementary causes of the migration to Antioch: Jewish dependence upon the Seleucid kings involved, during certain periods, "the furnishing of auxiliary troops levied or hired from the Palestinian communities."[24]

We can thus conclude that there is every reason to assume rather extensive immigration of Jews to Antioch from Syria, from Palestine, and, following M. Stern, "from Babylonia and other parts of the Parthian Empire."[25] This implies that effects noticed in connection with international migration might be used in interpreting the religiousness of the Antiochean Jews. In order to gain an understanding of such effects, let us now turn to some recent studies on religious change in connection with migration in Western Europe.

Muslims and religious change in modern Europe

In a study of the institutionalization of Islam in a Dutch context, J. Waardenburg distinguishes between several ways of interpreting "being Muslim" or having a "Muslim identity." Waardenburg suggests that Muslims in Dutch society could choose between certain options. The "secular option" would mean the total assimilation to Dutch models, including conversion to Christianity, conscious agnosticism or atheism, while the "cooperation option" implies the downplaying of specific Muslim features while engaging together with non-Muslims in social or political activities. The "cultural option" for Waardenburg means that the religious aspects of Islam are neglected while the cultural features are retained. The opposite of this is the "religious option," which would result in a reinforcement of the religious aspects of a Muslim identity at the expense of its cultural aspects. Religious and cultural aspects combined with specific ethnic components would constitute the "ethnic-religious option."[26] These "options" represent a kind of diversity different from adherence to a certain religious faction, since they are alterations brought about by the migration process and concern the religious commitment.

What additional effects this may have on the religious commit-ment of the individual is the question at issue in a comparison between the religiousness of peasants of Subay in Turkey and that of migrants from that village now living in modern Germany. In this study W. Schiffauer found that religious commitment could find diametrically opposed expressions. In the Turkish village, religion is very closely related to society in general. This means that during sacred times the society changes into a religious community and participation in religious rituals is always a collective matter related to the society as a whole. Many of these religious obligations are, in fact, considered to be a burden.[27] In the new society, the close connection between secular and religious structures is altered so that the religious community stands in opposition to the social one. Instead of being a way of demonstrating affiliation with the society as a whole, ritual practice expresses membership in the minority group. This could dissociate members of the minority group from German society.[28] This practice encourages the development of a purely religious motivation for participation in religious activities and also of more individualistic and therefore more pluralistic tendencies. Schiffauer states that, "in terms of religious practice, the migrants vary much more among themselves than do the peasants in their native village. Some heads of households are negligent to an extent that would never occur back in the village."[29]

What we see here is presumably what Waardenburg called the "secular option." As we recall, Waardenburg also reckons with the possibility of a "religious option." In Schiffauer's study we find that as a result of the individualizing of religious practice, the "decision to embrace Islam becomes an existential question."[30] This process of a deepening religious commitment Schiffauer calls "Islamization of one's self."[31]

With reference to the relation between migration and religious change in a modern Western European context, J. Rex has pointed to another aspect of how to direct religious commitment. Rex suggests that we must expect what he calls "religious and ethnic traditionalists" to strive to bring religion back to what it was in the place of origin, but also with "new creative forms which seek to adapt to their new situation and handle the new problems which that situation presents."[32]

In an article that evaluates different empirical studies on the relation between religion and migration,[33] Hamberg finds the same tendencies, with the addition of one group where religious beliefs and practices remain unchanged. She concludes:

> [I]nternational migration may affect the religious beliefs and religious practices of migrants in different ways. Sometimes religious beliefs and practices appear to remain more or less unchanged by migration. In some instances, religious beliefs and/or practices are weakened during the immigrant's life in the new country, in other instances religious beliefs and/or practices are strengthened. Sometimes immigrants drastically change their religious beliefs and practices as well as their religious affiliation, for example by converting to religious sects.[34]

Here we have the various possible responses to a migration situation well formulated. In the studies dealing with empirical material we have seen that a migration situation can lead to changes in the individual's set of values and worldviews. We have seen the effect of migration in contemporary situations, with special attention to changes in the specific set of values represented by religion and how religion in a migration situation may become optional. In a pluralistic milieu, the individual can direct his or her religious commitment to a higher degree,[35] which results in religion becoming more of a personal choice, something which can basically express itself in *traditionalistic, secular* or *innovative tendencies.* We have also seen how a person's religious commitment may not undergo any changes at all. All studies have dealt with religious change in connection with a migration situation, and a common denominator seems to be the contrast between a religiously homogeneous and a religiously pluralistic society. It is the changes in the plausibility structure brought about by the migration situation that appear to create conditions which can result in value changes.[36] In the following I will try to show that it is plausible to apply such empirical material to an ancient situation by an explication of the function and nature of "plausibility structures" connected to a discussion of pluralism in the Hellenistic society.

Pluralism and religious differentiation

According to Berger and Luckmann, a *plausibility structure* is the social base each *symbolic universe* requires for its continuing existence. A symbolic universe is defined as "bodies of theoretical tradition that integrate different provinces of meaning and encompass the institutional order in a symbolic totality."[37] It integrates all sectors of the institutional order so that all human experience occurs within it. Symbolic universes order and give meaning to all aspects of life; they are "sheltering canopies over the institutional order as well as over individual biography."[38] The plausibility structure functions by constantly legitimizing the existence of a certain symbolic universe:[39]

> Subjective reality is thus always dependent upon specific plausibility structures, that is, the specific social base and social processes required for its maintenance. One can maintain one's self-identification as a man of importance only in a milieu that confirms this identity; one can maintain one's Catholic faith only if one retains one's significant relationship with the Catholic community; and so forth.[40]

The more stable this plausibility structure, the firmer the individual's symbolic universe which is based upon it. These *reality-maintenance* processes function mainly through language.

It is primarily through *conversation* that the reality of the world is confirmed, and it is through conversation that the world can be altered.[41] When an individual is confronted with a competing meaning system, that is, a different set of beliefs and values, the primary conditions for a possible shift from one universe to another are fulfilled. It goes without saying that only in a religiously pluralistic society is religious conversion possible. This process, when an individual moves from one symbolic universe to another, is called *alternation*,[42] and always involves the changing of plausibility structures. Since the individual is socialized into a subjective world, that is, a socially constructed symbolic universe, he or she must now be resocialized into the new one. This can be done only by means of *significant others* with whom the individual establishes strong affective identification.[43] There is thus always a social dimension in the changing of symbolic universe. An individual cannot remain within the boundaries of a certain universe without communicative interaction with others in the same universe and can never leave a certain universe without communicative interaction with people in another universe.[44]

Against this background, value-changing processes such as alterations in the religious system in connection with international migration become intelligible—migration can promote changes in the plausibility structure by exposing the individual to competing meaning systems with new plausibility structures. To be able to apply this theoretical concept to the Antiochean material we must proceed with a discussion of some relevant factors in the extremely complex group of problems connected with the relation between Judaism and Hellenism.

Without any doubt, Judaism in the Hellenistic era was deeply influenced by the surrounding Greco-Roman culture. The nature and degree of this influence has occupied scholars from different traditions ever since the beginning of the twentieth century.[45] Just to mention some examples: archaeological data suggest that the most important factors concerning synagogue architecture were local ones,[46] and the same might have been true for the synagogue communities,[47] which to some extent were organized with the *collegia* as a model.[48] Even though Diaspora Judaism and the Judaism of Palestine shared the same general ideology concerning purity, the practice of purification seems to have differed. While immersion was the normal means in Palestine, different kinds of ablutions or sprinklings were more frequent in the Diaspora, a usage probably influenced by the Gentile surroundings.[49]

Literature is another field in which the Hellenistic influence is evident. Evidence from Jewish inscriptions, papyri and other literature, including the LXX, indicates that to a large extent Greek was the language of the Jewish communities of the Diaspora,[50] even though, on account of constant immigration from Palestine,[51] Aramaic probably never died out, even in Egypt. Moreover, there are several examples of Jewish literature that bear witness to an oppositional attitude towards Hellenism, but at the same time show influences from Greek culture.[52] All this suggests not only influence but also familiarity with Hellenistic culture.

The Hellenistic impact on the Jewish communities in the Diaspora seems, however, to have varied from place to place and also over time. In general, Hellenistic influences appear to have increased over time.[53] In some Diaspora communities which had been established before Maccabean times, we find a more liberal attitude towards Hellenistic culture. As such, Alexandria seems to have held a key position.[54] There Jews were admitted to the Greek educational institutions and obtained through them what M. Hengel calls "a remarkably good education in rhetoric and philosophy."[55] But not even in Alexandria did this result in the complete assimilation of the Jewish community. Hengel states:

> [T]he Jewish Diaspora did not assimilate unconditionally to its Hellenistic environment. Jews went through the obligatory training of the gymnasium; they learnt Homer and classical poetry, and pursued further studies in rhetoric and philosophy; they went to the theatre and the games; they had social contacts with non-Jews and even entered upon a successful career in the Ptolemaic civil service. But they did not accept Greek polytheistic religion. They kept the Sabbath, avoided unclean food and attended worship in the synagogue, where more and more a polished didactic address in the style of the diatribe took its place alongside prayer and hymn and gave to the educated Jew the consciousness that he represented the true philosophy.[56]

This would probably be true for the majority of Alexandrian Jews. In general, there can be no doubt that the Jewish community resisted the temptation to assimilate.[57] However, some Jews, presumably from the upper classes, were at the same time striving for increased civil rights and a more general fusion of Hellenistic and Jewish culture.[58]

One curious expression of this is found in an interpretation of a papyrus, *CPJ* 519, in which A. Kerkeslager finds evidence for the appearance of a circumcised, nude Jew in an athletic context.[59] According to him the text refers to the situation in Alexandria sometime between 20 BCE and 41 CE. If his conclusions are correct, this text illustrates the highly complex relation between Judaism and Hellenistic culture in Alexandria. It seems that some Jews saw no contradiction in trying to combine Jewish identity with participation in Greek athletic activities.[60] Such a scenario would fit very well into Barclay's picture of some families who, without having any intention of breaking with Judaism, had attained citizen status.[61]

However, this would not have been a situation completely without problems. The text Kerkeslager is dealing with mentions both disgust and mockery among the reactions of the Gentile audience. The text presents, as Kerkeslager puts it, "the rather ironic image of a Jew whose very devotion to an expression of Greek identity makes his Jewish identity all the more inescapably obvious."[62]

There is other evidence of such efforts of combining elements from Judaism with elements from the surrounding society. Barclay has thoroughly analyzed several texts from Egypt that reveal such tendencies. Artapanus, writing sometime between 250 and 100 BCE, is loyal to his Jewish heritage but simultaneously fascinated by Egyptian religion.[63] Another expression of what Barclay labels "cultural convergence" is the presentation of the Exodus narrative in the form of Greek tragedy by Ezekiel, a contemporary of Artapanus.[64] The author of *The Letter of Aristeas* is supportive of Greek education ideals and moral and philosophical values and at the same time "unswerving in his loyalty to his fellow Jews."[65] This implies that there is no immediate connection between Hellenization and complete assimilation.[66] Alexandria provides a good example of this, but so does Jerusalem.

During the Roman era Jerusalem was in some respects the most Hellenized city in Palestine. Levine mentions, among other things, the size of the city, the residential quarters of the upper classes, their funerary monuments, the presence of a theater, a hippodrome, a gymnasium, the existence of a *polis*-like political organization and the use of Greek as reflecting Hellenistic influences.[67] On the other hand, Jerusalem was a Jewish city, as Levine puts it,

> in population, calendar, holidays, forms of religious worship, historical memories and more. Walking the streets in the first century, a visitor in all probability could not help but be struck by the absence of idols, statues, and figural art, an absence that distinguished Jerusalem from every other non-Jewish urban center in the Empire.[68]

Before the Maccabean revolt, the Hellenization of Palestine and above all, Jerusalem was extensive. The Hellenistic Jews, who had already deprived what we might call "reactionary" groups of political power, even started to make preparations for the transformation of Jerusalem into a Greek *polis*. One prerequisite for this was the annulment of Antiochus III's "letter of freedom," which granted the Jews the right to organize according to "ancestral laws."[69] This was accomplished through Antiochus IV Epiphanes' prohibition of the Jewish religion, which led to radical changes of the sacrificial cult and the suppression of institutions of particularly Jewish character, for instance, the Sabbath, festivals, circumcision, etc.[70]

While the Maccabean revolt by no means resulted in a complete "de-Hellenization"—in some respect rather the opposite[71]—it did have an important influence on the interpretation of Judaism. As Hengel puts it: "after the Maccabean revolt the tendency towards spiritual segregation from outsiders grew stronger, whereas on the other hand the Hasidic ideal of piety became dominant for the majority of Palestinian Jews."[72] Hengel, Judaism

The real issue at stake in the conflict between Hellenistic Jews and the Hasidim was the torah. One of the aims of the Hellenistic Jews was the complete abolition of the law of Moses, and a reaction against this "zeal against the law" would consequently involve a corresponding "zeal for the law."[73]

This implies that Jewish belief and practices in Palestine, and particularly Jerusalem, during the first century CE, up to the destruction of the temple and the sacrificial cult, was fairly homogeneous and dominated by one Hasidic branch—the Pharisees. Notwithstanding the diversified character of the Judaism of the period, there was much that most Jews had in common and to a large extent agreed upon. In comparison, Antioch was religiously a highly pluralistic milieu. Even though the "zeal for the law" also influenced the Jewish communities in the Diaspora, Judaism was but one of many religions practiced contemporaneously at Antioch.

The simple conclusion is that Antioch must have constituted a potential threat to the meaning system of any religious minority, independent of whether this minority had immigrated recently or had inhabited the city for generations. There is no doubt that the new group would be more vulnerable, but there is no guarantee that individuals within the established Jewish community would not develop strong affective identification with people outside the community. It is true that the Jewish community in Antioch, as elsewhere, must have developed strategies for dealing with deviant ideologies and for maintaining challenged realities. Since all religious worlds and, indeed, all kinds of socially constructed worlds are fragile, alternations are always a theoretical possibility. In a migration situation, when someone from a homogeneous society such as Jerusalem was confronted with the pluralism of, say, Antioch, the religious worlds would most certainly be exposed to stress, precisely by being confronted with an alternative. Berger and Luckmann state that "[t]he appearance of an alternative symbolic universe poses a threat because its very existence demonstrates empirically that one's own universe is less than inevitable."[74] If such strategies as Berger and Luckmann label "conceptual machineries of universe-maintenance"[75] fail to keep an individual within the same universe, the confrontation with an alternative universe could consequently result in the individual's shift between symbolic universes. The pluralism itself constitutes a potential threat, and, as we have seen, changes in an individual's plausibility structure, together with the failure of reality-maintenance processes, could result in "conversions." Since social reality is a social construction, it has to be transmitted to generations to come, and this process of socialization is in itself a complicated process and is never complete. Berger and Luckmann say "[t]he problem of legitimation inevitably arises when the objectivations of the (now historic) institutional order are to be transmitted to a new generation."[76] Once again we note the significance of the plausibility structure, which continuously legitimates the socially constructed reality of the individual. Berger and Luckmann state:

> [I]n situations where there is competition between different reality-defining agencies, all sorts of secondary-group relationships with the competitors may be tolerated, as long as there are firmly established primary-group relationships within which *one* reality is ongoingly reaffirmed against the competitors.[77]

We have already mentioned the term "assimilation" in this section, and this is of course a process which is closely connected to what has been discussed here. Assimilation has to do with social integration,[78] and could be described as an individual's change of symbolic universe in a social context. The close connection between "conversions" and plausibility structures implies that there is a social dimension of replacing one symbolic universe with another. A Muslim family in present-day Europe who converted to Christianity would almost certainly have done so as a result of changes in the plausibility structure. This must, of course, have had social consequences for the family as well.

To complete our analytical model, we now turn to a presentation of one way of depicting assimilation. With insights from this, together with what we have gained in understanding thus far, we will then look at the sources.

A theory of social integration

Variables of assimilation

As mentioned at the beginning of this chapter, Barclay has analyzed the Hellenization of the Egyptian Jews, which, as we have seen above, involved the process of assimilation. In his model he distinguishes between three *kinds* and *degrees* of Hellenization, namely, *assimilation* (social integration), *acculturation* (the non-material aspects of a cultural matrix, such as language and education) and *accommodation* (use of acculturation).[79] Barclay has thoroughly examined all available literary sources and found evidence of different kinds and degrees of assimilation. We recall that, due to the nature of the sources, Barclay considers it impossible to make the same kind of analysis of places outside Egypt. As stated above, I am in general more optimistic about the possibilities of making a similar analysis of the Syrian material. Such an analysis would, however, require a different method. Barclay's model is based on a situation where a reasonable amount of literary sources are available. For Antioch, we need a model with a higher degree of explanatory force, that is, where modern empirical material provides us with a pattern according to which it is possible to arrange the ancient sources. Barclay's analysis will, however, provide valuable comparative material.[80]

In a study of assimilation processes in the United States during the 1950s, M. M. Gordon presented a model that not only takes into account the degree of assimilation, but also focuses on the nature of assimilation, using different variables. Gordon takes as his point of departure a Weber-inspired "ideal type," namely the total and complete assimilation of a group into the culture and society of the host country. According to Gordon, such a complete process of assimilation would include seven sub-processes. When a sub-group has fused together with a host society, and thus for all intents and purposes ceased to exist as a separate group, this has 1) involved a change of the cultural pattern, including religious beliefs and observance. The minority group has furthermore 2) taken on large-scale primary relationships with the host society and has 3) fully intermarried and interbred. It has 4) taken over from the host society a sense of identity or ethnicity and 5) reached a point where its members encounter no discriminatory behavior or 6) prejudiced attitudes from the majority, and 7) no value or power conflicts exists with the civic host society.[81]

For our purpose six of these sub-processes could be useful. What Gordon refers to as "behavior receptional assimilation," that is, "absence of discrimination," is probably of no relevance to us, since this presupposes a society where discrimination is considered to be undesirable.[82] In the Roman Empire almost every human being was subject to what we would describe as discriminatory actions, especially since the common form of social relationship was built on the patron–client model.[83]

The first process, *acculturation* or cultural assimilation, Gordon defines as the "change of cultural pattern to those of host society."[84] In our scenario a more interesting aspect is the *process which precedes the change of the cultural pattern*, namely, the degree of familiarity with the cultural matrix of the host society. Familiarity with a society, as, for instance, being able to speak its language, is an obvious prerequisite for possible adaptation to its customs and values. Put in a different way, one must possess some basic knowledge of a society in order to fuse with it. As we will see, such familiarity, even a high degree of acculturation, can also be used in order to *avoid* assimilation. Thus, for the first step of the process of assimilation, I will emphasize the aspect of *familiarity* with the cultural host matrix rather than the *change* of cultural pattern to that of the host society. Figure 3.1 summarizes the assimilation model which will be used in the analysis of the Jews of Antioch.

Assimilation variables	
Designation	Description
Acculturation	Familiarity with the cultural matrix of the host society, including its language and education
Structural assimilation	Primary relationships with members of host society and entrance into cliques, clubs and institutions of host society on primary-group level
Marital assimilation	Marriage outside the group
Identificational assimilation	Development of sense of identity based exclusively on the host society
Attitude receptional assimilation	Absence of prejudice
Civic assimilation	Absence of power or value conflict

Figure 3.1 The assimilation process can be divided up into different sub-processes, which allow us, if sufficient data are available, to determine the *assimilation profile* for a specific group.

As Gordon points out, the assimilation process is not only a matter of degree; each of the sub-processes may take place to varying extents, which brings up questions of how these elements are interconnected. This is of special relevance for us, since it may well be that the sources can provide only an incomplete and fragmentary picture of the assimilation of a certain group. With some insight into the relationship between different aspects of assimilation we could reconstruct the assimilation of a specific group with greater precision. We will therefore proceed to examine the relationship between the sub-processes.

The process of assimilation

In our model *acculturation* is a necessary condition for the assimilation process. This means that assimilation can take place only if the minority group possesses some basic insight into the majority society.[85] If a minority group continues its path towards total assimilation, the natural and only way is through interaction with the host society at a primary group level. Such *structural assimilation* will lead to all the other types of assimilation. There is, for instance, an obvious connection between structural and marital assimilation. Once a minority group has begun to interact with the host society through different institutions, it will inevitably lead to a high frequency of intermarriage.

> If children of different ethnic backgrounds belong to the same play-group, later the same adolescent cliques, and at college the same fraternities and sororities; if the parents belong to the same country club and invite each other to their homes for dinner; it is completely unrealistic not to expect these children, now grown, to love and marry each other, blithely oblivious to previous ethnic extraction.[86]

The inevitable effect of structural assimilation, when fully realized, is the disappearance of the minority group. The minority has lost its ethnic identity, and *identificational assimilation* has taken place. Since individuals from the former minority group have become indistinguishable from the host society, they no longer experience prejudice or discrimination and there is no reason why there should be any value conflicts on civic matters. The assimilation process can now be said to include *attitude* as well as *civic assimilation*. Gordon summarizes the connections between the different aspects of assimilation as follows:

> *Once structural assimilation has occurred, either simultaneously with or subsequent to acculturation, all of the other types of assimilation will naturally follow.* It need hardly be pointed out that while acculturation, as we have emphasized above, does not necessarily lead to structural assimilation, structural assimilation inevitably produces acculturation. Structural assimilation, then, rather than acculturation, is seen to be the keystone of the arch of assimilation. The price of such assimilation, however, is the disappearance of the ethnic group as a separate entity and the evaporation of its distinctive values.[87]

My different use of the term "acculturation" would be of no relevance for the mechanism as such. There are of course many factors which can influence such a straightforward and ideal development.

One complicating factor in the process of assimilation is that cultural patterns can be said to exist in two different forms. An ethnic group's religious beliefs and practices, ethical values, literature and history constitute essential parts of that group's cultural heritage *and emanate exactly from that heritage*. Gordon refers to these cultural patterns as *intrinsic traits*. Other cultural patterns, such as dress, manner, examples of emotional expression and dialect, which are rather a result of a group's adaptation to a local situation *without being related to a specific ethnic heritage*, are referred to as *extrinsic traits*.[88] Gordon hypothesizes about which of these cultural traits is more relevant for the development of prejudice and states that, "at least in our era, differences in extrinsic culture are more crucial in the development of prejudice than those of an intrinsic nature."[89] With regard to the situation in antiquity and the relation between the Gentile and Jewish community, it was rather the intrinsic traits in the Jewish population that constituted the main source for prejudice against them.

Concomitantly, it was these very same intrinsic traits which prevented the Jews from becoming completely assimilated into the Gentile world. We noted above that, during the Hellenistic reform, the aim of the Hellenistic Jews was the complete abolition of the torah, the embodiment of *the codified intrinsic cultural traits* which effectively separated the Jews from other peoples and protected them from other cultural influences. Generally the Jews never assimilated fully. In the case of the Jews of antiquity there is no immediate connection between structural assimilation and all other types of assimilation. Very strong and religiously legitimated identity markers almost certainly slowed down or even prevented the assimilation process, since they functioned as efficient "conceptual machineries of universe-maintenance."[90]

With the inclusion of the distinction between intrinsic and extrinsic cultural patterns, we have completed the presentation of a model of assimilation by which we may describe not only the degree but also the nature of the assimilation of the Jewish population of Antioch, even though the model was not developed to analyze conditions during antiquity. We can test the model's ability as an interpretative instrument and at the same time deal with one particular intrinsic trait of great relevance for the assimilation process in our context, namely the Jewish practice of circumcision.

The assimilation profile—a test case

From a general point of view assimilation presupposes a situation where a minority group within a society risks being merged into a surrounding major society: as we have seen in dealing with the relation between Hellenism and Judaism, Hellenistic influences during certain periods could be regarded as a real problem for some groups even within Palestine—influences that can be understood only in terms of assimilation. In this case it is the cultural power from an imperialistic force that exercises influence within a conquered society. We recall, for instance, the narration in 1 Macc. 1:11–15:

> In those days certain renegades came out from Israel and misled many, saying "Let us go and make a covenant with the Gentiles around us, for since we separated from them many disasters have come upon us [πορευθῶμεν καὶ διαθώμεθα διαθήκην μετὰ τῶν ἐθνῶν τῶν κύκλῳ ἡμῶν ὅτι ἀφ᾽ ἧς ἐχωρίσθημεν ἀπ᾽ αὐτῶν εὗρεν ἡμᾶς κακὰ πολλά]." This proposal pleased them, and some of the people eagerly went to the king, who authorized them to observe the ordinances of the Gentiles. So they built a gymnasium in Jerusalem, according to Gentile custom, and removed the marks of circumcision [ἐποίησαν ἑαυτοῖς ἀκροβυστίας], and abandoned the holy covenant [ἀπέστησαν ἀπὸ διαθήκης ἁγίας]. They joined [ἐζευγίσθησαν] with the Gentiles and sold themselves to do evil.

It is not difficult to see our six sub-processes realized in this text. We can easily imagine that almost every Jew in Jerusalem possessed some knowledge about Hellenistic culture. To a certain degree they were all *acculturated*. The making of a covenant with the Gentiles, together with the authorization to follow the ordinances of the Gentiles and the building of the gymnasium, implies interaction with the Gentiles at a primary group level. This group of Jews has thus become *structurally assimilated*. According to Gordon we can now expect all the other aspects of assimilation to follow. As a first expression of this we can note the *marital assimilation*—the Jews, we are told, intermarried with Gentiles.[91] Furthermore, they are said to have "removed the marks of circumcision." This implies that the Jews were about to embrace also the *identificational aspects of assimilation*, since they evidently wanted both to act and to look like the Gentiles.

The decisive expression, which the author of 1 Maccabees conceives of as apostasy, is connected with the building of the gymnasium and consequently with the athletic activities held there.[92] It is well known that Greeks disapproved of circumcision, which they regarded as a mutilation of an otherwise perfect body; they even considered the retraction of the foreskin as ugly and crude, "reserved for satyrs, ugly old men, barbarians, and comic burlesque."[93] Even though aesthetic rather than moral aspects seem to be the underlying cause of the Greek, and later Roman, attitude, there can be no doubt about circumcision giving rise to negative reactions from the Gentile community.[94] It was, consequently, a barrier for Jews who wanted to join the Gentile community. Restoration of the foreskin, so-called epispasm, was therefore not unusual during antiquity. The earliest description of this surgical procedure is found in Celsus' *De Medicina*, from the first century CE: in 7.25.1 he specifically states that the operation is "not so very painful."[95]

There are several references in pre-rabbinic Jewish literature that confirm that Jews actually had this operation performed. Josephus mentions in *A.J.* 12.241 the same incidents narrated in 1 Macc. 1:11–15, but does not specifically mention epispasm. Instead he says that the Jews "concealed the circumcision of their private parts" (τὴν τῶν αἰδοίων περιτομὴν ἐπεκάλυψαν), but there is a high probability that what he actually refers to is epispasm.[96] The passage in *T. Mos.* 8:1–3 describes how those "who confess their circumcision" will be crucified during the events that will precede the final intervention by the god of Israel. Their sons will, furthermore, be subject to compulsive epispasm since they will be "cut by physicians to bring forward their foreskins." In 1 Corinthians 7:18, Paul admonishes the circumcised Jesus-believing Jews against having this operation performed (μὴ ἐπισπάσθω).

In several references in rabbinic literature there are hints of
epispasm which indicate that the custom was sufficiently extensive
to occasion mentions in halakhic discourses. In *m. 'Abot* 3:11 there is
a discussion about one who "make[s] void of the covenant of Abraham our father" (והמפר בריתו של אברהם אבינו). Almost the same wording
is used in *b. Sanh.* 99a (והמפר בריתו של אברהם). These expressions almost
certainly refer to epispasm, because, in *b. Sanh.* 38b, Adam is said to
have practiced epispasm (lit. "pulled his foreskin"; מושך בערלתו), and
this is connected to the breaking of the covenant. The same wording
is used in *b. Sanh.* 44a, with a reference to Achan, who is also said to
have transgressed the covenant. Similarly, in *b. Menaḥ.* 53b, Abraham
reproaches God for not having reminded the people of Israel about
"the covenant of circumcision" (ברית מילה); further, the transgressing
of the covenant is stated as one reason for the destruction of Jerusalem.[97] In the passage *b. Yebam.* 72a, we find a halakhic discourse on
whether a circumcised person who has drawn his prepuce forward to
cover up the corona, a so-called *mashuk* (משוך), has to be recircum-
cised in order to eat *terumah*.[98] *Leviticus Rabbah* 19.6 refers to one
rabbi who states that Jehoiakim pulled his foreskin (שמשך לו ערלה).
Finally, in *b. Yoma* 85b, the serious character of trying to hide one's
circumcision becomes clear, since R. Yehudah ha-Nasi is referred to
as having stated that the Day of Atonement covers almost all
transgressions except for one who "breaks the covenant" (ומיפר ברית)
and a very few other things. In these cases repentance is required
as well.[99]

We can conclude by saying that, since circumcision was thought of
as one of the foremost identity markers,[100] being directly linked to
covenantal theology and thus an intrinsic cultural trait,[101] any
attempt to undo circumcision would be regarded from an anti-
Hellenistic, Jewish standpoint as a complete break with Judaism.[102]
This means that, for the question of *civic* and *attitude receptional
assimilation*, we must conclude that the prospect of becoming
completely assimilated was entirely dependent on the possibility of
removing "the marks of circumcision." Even if we take into consideration the possibility that some Jews appeared in a Greek
gymnasium,[103] they would have been met with disgust and scorn,
which is also evident from the text Kerkeslager is analyzing.[104]

It is clear that these Jews had an extensive knowledge of
Hellenistic culture, and the same thing may be said of almost every
other Jew in Jerusalem. What is more important, however, is the way
they used this knowledge, an issue to which we will now turn.

The use of acculturation

One way of describing the development of the Hellenistic Jews during the reign of Antiochus IV Epiphanes is to say that they had used their familiarity with Greek culture in what Barclay calls an *integrative way*. By this he means that they had deliberately used their acculturation in order to be assimilated. Acculturation, we recall, is a necessary condition for the whole process of assimilation—it is the first step towards other sub-processes. According to Gordon, this could be *the only kind of assimilation* a group might experience. He states that *"cultural assimilation, or acculturation, of the minority group may take place even when none of the other types of assimilation occurs simultaneously or later, and this condition of 'acculturation only' may continue indefinitely."*[105]

This means that familiarity with a cultural environment, or even an adaptation to cultural patterns, does not have to result in assimilation. Intimate knowledge of a host society could in fact be used *in order to avoid being assimilated*. Barclay operates with separate scales for assimilation (social integration), acculturation (language/education) and accommodation (use of acculturation), and deals with the important question of how individuals use their acculturation. As he points out, "acculturation could be used to construct either bridges or fences between Jews and their surrounding cultures."[106] He points to the fact that a minority group could use its knowledge of a host society in two opposite ways—either "integrative," in order to submerge its own cultural uniqueness, or "oppositional," in ideological attacks on the host culture. Another way of using acculturation would be in different creative reinterpretations of the original meaning system.[107] This bears resemblance to the creative forms of expressing a Muslim identity that Rex found in Britain.[108] While I find Gordon's model generally better suited to identifying different groups within Antiochean society, this aspect of how acculturation is being used is of great value for our purposes and must be taken into consideration.

With this model for analyzing the *social integration* as well as the *religious differentiation* of the Jewish population, we will now begin an analysis of Antiochean Judaism. Firstly, however, based on the material above, what can we expect to find in Antioch? Are there some general assumptions that can be made about the Antiochean situation?

Generally speaking, on account of the pluralistic situation there is a high probability that we will find far more levels of Jewish religious commitment in Antioch than in Jerusalem.

1   We should be able to find groups strongly committed to traditional Jewish life. This could be either the result of a successful process of socialization or the consequence of a migration situation. In those cases where religiousness is a result of migration we could presumably speak of an *increasing religious commitment.* In their extreme variants such groups would probably have very few social contacts with the Gentile society and their assimilation would be minimal. Such groups would presumably have used their acculturation in an oppositional way. Borrowing Waardenburg's terminology, we could say that they had chosen the "religious option." We could perhaps alter Schiffauer's term "Islamization of one's self" and speak of a "Judaization of one's self."

2   On the other hand, there would be the opposite tendency—that is, groups with little or even no Jewish religious commitment at all. We would be able to find traces of immigrant groups or native Jewish Antiocheans with diminishing religious commitment: that is, groups who to different degrees had chosen the equivalent of Waardenburg's "secular option." In these cases we must assume that the socialization process towards Judaism had failed or that the world-maintaining legitimations had been insufficient. In the Antiochean context this would mean the abandonment of Judaism and adaptation to Greco-Roman religiousness. Such a process would be promoted by a high degree of social contact with Gentiles, leading to the formation of extensive networks of primary relationships. Such individuals or groups would naturally be highly assimilated, having used their acculturation in an integrative way.

3   Apart from such a polarization we would expect to find new creative forms of religious manifestations, which seek to adapt to new situations without leaving the overarching system of meaning.

Analysis—Antiochean Judaism revealed

Groups and factions

Crossing the boundaries—Antiochus the apostate

In *B.J.* 7.46–7, Josephus writes about Antiochus, the son of the chief magistrate of the Jews in Antioch:

> Now just at the time when war had been declared and Vespasian had recently landed in Syria, and when hatred of the Jews was everywhere at its height, a certain Antiochus, one of their own number and highly respected for the sake of his father, who was chief magistrate of the Jews in Antioch [ἄρχων τῶν ἐπ᾽ Ἀντιοχείας Ἰουδαίων], entered the theatre during an assembly of the people and denounced his own father and the other Jews, accusing them of a design to burn the whole city to the ground in one night; he also delivered up some foreign Jews as accomplices to the plot.

When describing this event, Binder labels the son of the ἄρχων in Antioch as belonging to a group of syncretistic Jews.[109] That is probably not entirely correct. Antiochus does not represent someone involved in a mixture between Judaism and other Hellenistic religions but someone who has left one fairly well-defined system (Judaism) for another fairly well-defined system (Hellenistic religion). Antiochus has evidently chosen the equivalent of the "secular option"[110] and left the religion of the minority for the religion of the majority. Josephus furthermore states, in *B.J.* 7.50, that Antiochus "further inflamed their fury; for, thinking to furnish proof of his conversion [μεταβολῆς] and of his detestation of Jewish customs by sacrificing after the manner of the Greeks [τὸ ἐπιθύειν ὥσπερ νόμος ἐστὶ τοῖς Ἕλλησιν]."

In this passage it seems clear that Antiochus, son of one of perhaps the most prominent Jewish leaders in the whole of Antioch,[111] had completely broken with his tradition and in all essentials become a Greek. One very strong argument in favor of this is the passage in which Antiochus is said to have sacrificed "after the manner of the Greeks." It is of course impossible to know for sure what motivated the actions of Antiochus, but it is possible that they were related to the question of citizenship, or more generally to "career necessities."[112] Josephus reports, in *B.J.* 7.52–3, that Antiochus gained authority over the Jews and hindered them from keeping the Sabbath. According to Barclay, this makes best sense if we assume that Antiochus was an officer in the Roman army.[113] If this was the case, it is possible that Antiochus tried to attain citizenship not in the *polis* of Antioch but in *Rome*, since one way of becoming a Roman citizen was through military service.[114] Judging from Josephus' statement, it seems clear that Antiochus' treachery to his family, people and whole culture was motivated by a wish to convince Gentile society, which may have doubted the seriousness of his "conversion." If that was the case, this might mean that such "conversions" were met with a certain resistance. All in all, in terms of assimilation Antiochus must have been one of the most assimilated Jews in Antioch.[115]

This is as far as a close reading of the source can get us: in Antioch, when "Vespasian had recently landed in Syria," there was a son of a prominent Jew who betrayed his family and traditions, ceased to be Jewish and became an assimilated Greek. Let us now turn to some crucial questions: apart from any issue of Josephus as a reliable source, can we from this reference to one individual and his relation to Greek culture and religion draw any general conclusions about, for instance, the existence of a group with similar behavior and opinions?

There are several factors which speak in favor of letting Antiochus represent one tendency within Antiochean Judaism, and which therefore allow us to assume the presence of a group who left Judaism for the Gentile alternative.[116] The studies of Waardenburg, Schiffauer and Hamberg show that such a development is exactly what we could expect in a place marked by religious pluralism. I have already mentioned that Antiochus seems to have chosen Waardenburg's "secular option." Even from a common-sense perspective, the existence of such a group seems more than plausible. In fact, the burden of proof belongs in my opinion to anyone who would raise doubts about the existence of such a group by suggesting that Antiochus was the only Jew, in a population of 20,000 to 40,000 Jews, who had left Judaism.[117] As for a historical analogy, we recall the narrative from 1 Macc. 1:11–15, cited and analyzed above, where the transformation to a Greek way of life seems to have been a group phenomenon. Barclay mentions Dositheos, son of Drimylos, who in *CPJ* 127d is described as a "priest of Alexander and the gods Adelphoi and the gods Euergetai" in 222 BCE, and in 3 Macc. 1:3 as one who had "changed his religion and apostatized from the ancestral traditions."[118] Kineas, son of Dositheos, is said to have been a priest for Ptolemy Philopator from 177/6 to 170/69 BCE, and his daughter Berenice was a priestess for Arsinoë Philopator in 169 BCE.[119] The most famous example of a transition from Judaism to a Gentile way of life in the first century CE is perhaps that of Philo's nephew Tiberius Julius Alexander, who was appointed Roman procurator of Judaea in 46 CE, and in 66 CE, as governor of Egypt, was responsible for the suppression of the Jewish uprising in Alexandria.[120] It is hard to avoid noting the striking resemblance between Antiochus and Tiberius Julius Alexander. Both had consciously left Judaism, culturally and religiously, both turned against their own people, and, on the condition that we accept Barclay's suggestion of Antiochus as a Roman officer, both made a military career.

With the exception of the situation in Egypt, the sources are few. Barclay has nevertheless found evidence of two cases of Jewish participation in a Gentile cult apart from that of Antiochus. In the temple of Amphiaraos in Oropus, Greece, an inscription, *CIJ* 711b, was made in the third century BCE which states that the Jew Moschos had received instructions from the gods Amphiaraos and Hygieia. In *CIJ* 749, from Iasus in Asia Minor, is Nicetas, son of Jason, contributing 100 drachmae to a Dionysiac festival.[121] Josephus (*A.J.* 18.141) mentions the grandchildren of Alexander, Herod's son, who "abandoned from birth the observance of the ways of the Jews and ranged themselves with the Greek tradition." Furthermore, L. H. Feldman refers to the inscription *CIJ* 742, which mentions a group of former Jews (οἱ ποτὲ Ἰουδαῖοι) in Smyrna who, early in the second century CE, had made benefactions to the city.[122] From Palestine we have, of course, R. Elisha ben Abuya, who was considered a heretic because of his interest in Greek philosophy.[123]

If we take into consideration these historical analogies as well as what we know from contemporary empirical material about the connection between religion and migration and permit this to be part of our hermeneutic pre-understanding, it seems reasonable to assume that Antiochus in Antioch was not one isolated case but was rather one of perhaps many Jews who consciously left Judaism and who had a corresponding clear interest in Hellenistic society and in Greek religion. It is possible that this group came from more prominent circles within Antiochean Judaism. The fact that Antiochus was the son of the ἄρχων could possibly be interpreted in such a direction.[124]

There can be no doubt that the Antiochus group was highly acculturated. From Alexandria we know that sons of prominent Jews were highly educated and attended the gymnasium.[125] Philo in fact praises parents who give their children the opportunity to attend the gymnasium and is himself a product of such an education.[126] The situation was probably the same in Antioch. It is reasonable to assume that Antiochus' whole family belonged to the most Hellenized in Antioch, and it is almost certain that Antiochus' father had provided his son with a Greek education. B. J. Brooten believes that the fact that Antiochus gives a public speech at the theater indicates he had received formal training in rhetoric.[127] This seems to be a very sensible interpretation.

Using Gordon's assimilation model, and taking into consideration the different assimilation variables mentioned above, we could now try to construct an *assimilation profile* for Antiochus and a hypothetical group of similar-minded Antiochean Jews. We noted in our dealing with the assimilation model above that acculturation does not have to lead to assimilation, and Barclay has, we recall, pointed to the fact that acculturation can be used in order to avoid assimilation. However, in the case of Antiochus and his assumed comrades, the process of assimilation had not stopped: instead, they had used their acculturation in an "integrative" way, resulting in the oppression of their own cultural uniqueness. This means that they had frequent contacts with persons representing Hellenistic culture. It is not a far-fetched conjecture that such contacts took place in the context of the *collegia*. In an analysis of Philo's attitude towards *collegia*, T. Seland finds that while Philo did not forbid participation in *collegia*, he was sceptical of joining and considered them dangerous groups that could lead to idolatry and apostasy (*Ebr.* 20–6; *Spec.* 1.176).[128] Philo's attitude shows that Hellenized Jews were concerned with preserving Judaism,[129] and that Jews even more Hellenized than Philo presumably participated in Greco-Roman *collegia*. In the case of Antiochus one could surmise that he was a member of one or several *collegia* as, for instance, Mithraism.[130]

This is evidently what Gordon described as structural assimilation. We recall that this is what he defined as the "keystone of the arch of assimilation."[131] Once structural assimilation has occurred, all the other sub-processes are likely to follow, and concerning Antiochus and his group it seems that this was the case. A well-founded conjecture would be that Antiochus and his assumed group married Gentile women, as did the Jews in 1 Macc. 1:15,[132] and that they developed a sense of identity based on the Hellenistic society. The attitude of receptional assimilation was an option only for those in the Antiochus group who had undergone epispasm. It would be almost impossible to become completely assimilated into the Gentile world if one was circumcised. If Antiochus was a Roman officer he had almost certainly removed the marks of circumcision and thereby clearly demonstrated the fundamental break with Judaism. Every Jew who wanted to be fully integrated into the Gentile world had to cease being Jewish. If this could be accomplished, there is no reason why value conflicts over civil matters should exist.

We may thus conclude this first analysis by depicting the assimilation profile of Antiochus. This is shown in Figure 3.2

In this case we have found a correspondence between the sources and the theoretical models, which makes it possible, on fairly good grounds, to assume the existence of a group of highly assimilated

Acculturation	Structural	Marital	Indentification	Attitude	Civic
Yes	Yes	Yes	Yes	Yes	Yes

Figure 3.2   Assimilation profile for the Antiochus group: the two last variables, attitude receptional and civic assimilation, are based on the condition that the individual male had undergone epispasm.

Jews. This could be summarized by saying that *there are several indications of a tendency towards separation from Judaism within some groups of the Jewish population.* This group, whose existence I have tried to make plausible, represents, of course, the culmination of such a process: the complete assimilation to the host society. It goes without saying that we must allow for other groups, ranging from a total or relatively high degree of observance to a more liberal attitude towards the torah. Let us start by looking for evidence of the other extreme of the ideological spectrum.

Observing torah—religious traditionalists

In *B.J.* 7.50, cited above, Josephus describes how Antiochus sacrificed "after the manner of the Greeks." Continuing the quote, we learn that Antiochus recommends that the Jews be forced to do the same, "as the conspirators would thus be exposed by their refusal." The story continues in 7.51: "[t]his test being applied by the Antiochenes, a few submitted and the recalcitrants were massacred."

It appears from this that some Jews faced death rather than give up their belief in the god of Israel. There is no reason to question the historicity of Josephus' statement. Martyrdom is generally a well-attested phenomenon from different religious traditions, and here is a clear indication of a group devoted to a life guided by the torah, no matter what the consequences. Even if only a minority of the Jewish population was prepared to pay such a price for obeying the torah, it is not far fetched to assume the existence of groups of very observant Jews. Sanders, for instance, states that most Jews maintained that the torah should be studied and followed but that the understanding of how this should be realized differed during various periods. He continues by stating that most Jews, in Palestine as well as in the Diaspora, worshiped daily and weekly, kept the Sabbath, circumcised their sons, observed certain purity regulations and supported the temple.[133] Despite mixed opinions on how this obedience would be realized, we can safely assume that the majority of the Antiochean Jews intended to live their lives obeying the torah.

There are admittedly not many indications of a group of very observant Jews existing in Antioch, for instance, living in isolation from the surrounding society. There may, however, be indications in favor of the existence there of a certain torah ideology, which specifically stated that torah obedience was worth dying for and to which Josephus' story could be related. Such ideology may have been especially vigorous, at least among some strata within Antiochean Judaism, since there is a possible connection between the tradition of the "Maccabean Martyrs" and Antioch. The story of the priest Eleazar, the seven brothers and their mother who, during the reign of Antiochus IV Epiphanes, were put to death on account of their faithfulness to the torah[134] is told in 2 Macc. 6–7 and retold in 4 Maccabees.[135] The overwhelming evidence points to Antioch as the place of the martyrdom as well as the place for the burial of the martyrs.[136]

From several sources we learn that the relics of the Maccabean martyrs were kept in a synagogue.[137] This statement seems rather startling given the laws of corpse impurity.[138] M. Schatkin, however, argues that these laws might generally have been less observed in the Diaspora and also in Palestine after 70 CE, since purity was related mainly to the temple,[139] and there are several examples of such burials from the early Christian era. In the Middle Ages a connection between a synagogue and a holy grave was considered normal, and contamination was prevented by the erection of cenotaphs.[140] As L. V. Rutgers has pointed out, this is quite irrelevant, since it says nothing about what was customary in antiquity, and it seems reasonable to conclude, with Rutgers, that there was probably never a synagogue in Antioch in which the earthly remains of the Maccabean martyrs were buried and that consequently there never was a Jewish cult of the Maccabean martyrs.[141] The reason for this is not only the improbability of a complete neutralization of the regulations connected to corpse impurity but, as Rutgers states, among all excavated synagogues in Israel and the Diaspora, there is not one example of a synagogue built directly over a grave.[142] Such a conclusion seems to be more in accordance with what we know of Diaspora Judaism during the first century. Referring to a passage in Philo, *Spec.* 3.205–6, Sanders has shown that the issue of corpse impurity in the Diaspora at least was considered worth reflecting upon.[143] It is true that the practice of ritual purification in the Diaspora could generally indicate a separation between purification and temple so that people started to look upon purification as an end in itself, but on the other hand, if we consider Binder's thesis of the synagogue as being linked to the central sanctuary in Jerusalem (see above pp. 38–9), ritual purification in a synagogue context becomes more intelligible.

If we have ruled out the possibility of a Jewish cult of the Maccabean martyrs, what about the literary composition of 4 Maccabees? It has been suggested that 4 Maccabees originated in Antioch, but there is indeed no consensus about that. J. H. Charlesworth mentions Egypt or Antioch as plausible locations,[144] while H. Anderson is more skeptical about an Antiochean provenance and suggests a more open attitude towards the question, at the same time giving the preference to a location in Asia Minor.[145] This is also J. W. van Henten's conclusion.[146] M. Gilbert, on the other hand, gives prominence to Antioch,[147] and Barclay too assumes an Antiochean origin.[148]

The dating of 4 Maccabees is also a complicated issue. Charlesworth states that most scholars consider a date between 40 BCE and 118 CE as reasonable;[149] having evaluated different scholarly opinions, Anderson proposes a period for composition between 19 and 54 CE.[150] Barclay, on the other hand, suggests a date at the end of the first century or early in the second century CE,[151] as do O. Eissfeldt and van Henten.[152]

We can thus conclude that, while there was probably no Jewish cult of the Maccabean martyrs in Antioch, 4 Maccabees may have originated there in the late first century CE, and we have in that case a slight indication of a torah ideology in Antioch that could be connected to a Jewish group who considered that obedience of the torah was worth dying for.

At first sight, a Jewish attitude towards Gentile olive oil, mentioned by Josephus, seems to point in a similar direction. In *A.J.* 12.120 we learn that Seleucus I Nicator

> gave orders that those Jews who were unwilling [τοὺς Ἰουδαίους μὴ βουλομένους] to use foreign oil should receive a fixed sum of money from the gymnasiarchs to pay for their own kind of oil; and, when the people of Antioch proposed to revoke this privilege, Mucianus, who was then governor of Syria, maintained it.

Whoever was responsible for the granting of this privilege— M. Goodman finds it more likely that it was Antiochus III[153]—it is clear from the latter part of the passage that the usage was established in the Roman period (Mucianus was governor of Syria from 67 to 69 CE).

This reference to Jews not willing to use Gentile oil could be interpreted as observation of the purity laws, and would thus be a sign of strict obedience of the torah.[154] This seems to be the view of Josephus, because in one account, *Vita* 74–6, he speaks of the Jewish inhabitants of Caesarea Philippi, who risked transgressing the laws (τὰ νόμιμα παραβαίνωσιν) as they had no pure (καθαρόν) oil to anoint themselves. This text, aimed primarily at a Jewish audience, would thus imply that using Greek oil would result in violating the torah; those Jews who refused to do so could consequently be defined as obeying the torah.

However, there are some problems connected with this view. In a perspicacious observation, Barclay draws attention to the fact that it is the gymnasiarchs who are said to be responsible for the oil distribution. He finds it unlikely that gymnasiarchs would be responsible for handling the complete oil supply for the whole city and states that the only institution where oil would be freely distributed was the gymnasium.[155] This implies that it was Jews training in the gymnasia as a step towards Antiochene citizenship who were granted money for alternative supplies. Two relevant questions emanate from this: first, if these Jews were so obedient to the torah, what were they doing in the gymnasia? Second, if they were not especially obedient to the torah, why bother about the origin of the oil?

The answer to these questions relates to another issue, namely, the number of Jews involved. How should the phrase in *A.J.* 12.120 (τοὺς Ἰουδαίους μὴ βουλομένους) be understood? It could be translated either as "the Jews, not wanting to use foreign oil" or "those Jews who did not want to use foreign oil." The grammatical construction makes both translations possible. In the first case *all* Jews are included. This is how Barclay understands the phrase, but he seems to believe that the alternative translation is more in accordance with the historical situation. Josephus, he states, "obscures the issue by generalizing it."[156] In the second case, as Goodman,[157] and R. Marcus in the translation in LCL understand the text, only some Jews are involved in the exchange of oil for money. On the other hand, in *Vita* 74–6, it is the Jewish inhabitants of Caesarea Philippi (Ἰουδαίους τοὺς τὴν Φιλίππου Καισάρειαν κατοικοῦντας) who lack pure oil. The same incident is also recorded in *B.J.* 2.591–2, where the narration is about "all the Jews of Syria" (πάντες οἱ κατὰ τὴν Συρίαν Ἰουδαῖοι). As Goodman points out, Josephus must have assumed that this would sound plausible to the Jewish readers.[158] It may well be, as Goodman further elaborates, that the custom of avoiding Greek oil was based not on biblical proof texts but rather on "pervasive religious instinct."[159] The ban on Gentile oil, obviously operative during the first century CE, was annulled during the third century by the rabbinic patriarch, something that is evident from an insertion in the Mishnah.[160] It appears from later rabbinic discussions[161] that the Amoraim were puzzled by the fact that no explanation, either for the original ban or for the annulment, is given in the Mishnah. Goodman's hypothesis is that the rabbinic patriarch R. Judah could not find any satisfactory arguments for keeping the prohibition and therefore declared it invalid.[162]

Thus Jews avoided Gentile oil, not because of a clear ban from an accepted authority, but because of a generally accepted custom based on social rather than strict religious reasons. If Goodman is right, the Jewish attitude to Gentile oil could not be used as evidence of religious observance or obedience to the torah, but merely as an indication of Jewish identity in a more general sense. The use of Gentile oil by a Jewish person would, on the other hand, be a clear indication of this person's repudiation of Judaism. Antiochus and Tiberius Julius Alexander were probably completely satisfied with Greek oil. Since the unwillingness to use foreign oil seems to have been widespread, Barclay's suggestion of the gymnasia as a general context seems more uncertain.[163]

In sum, there is nothing that unequivocally suggests that to refrain from Gentile oil should be taken as an indication of a "zeal for the law" rather than as a general Jewish identity marker. At the same time, while there is no doubt that observant Jews avoided Gentile oil, this could be true even for those with a more lax attitude towards the torah. We must therefore look for other indications of a traditionalistic interpretation of Judaism. One such indication could, in fact, be related to the temple in Jerusalem.

According to Josephus, *B.J.* 7.43, Syria in general and Antioch in particular were especially attractive for Jews partly on account of proximity to their homeland. This statement is somewhat misleading—for most of the time, due to historical reasons, the Jews' "homeland" was actually considered as being a part of Syria.[164] Migration within this area would consequently not be regarded as a migration from the Land of Israel to the Diaspora, but as moving from one part of the "homeland" to another.[165] A passage from the Mishnah could possibly reflect such an opinion. In the passage *m. Ḥal.* 4:11, it is stated in a discussion about the law of first-fruits (בכורים) that "[o]ne who buys in Syria is as he who purchases in the outskirts of Jerusalem" (הקונה בסוריא כקונה בפרוור שבירושלים). This is to be compared with what is said in the preceding passages, where various gifts are referred to as being refused due to their origin outside of Palestine.

Antioch was thus located in an area almost regarded as part of the Land of Israel, and there is evidence of a particularly strong connection between some Antiochean Jews at least and the temple in Jerusalem. As Sanders states, ancient authors attest that most Jews supported all aspects of temple worship[166]—indicated not least by the general payment of the temple tax.[167] Together with the synagogue and the home, the temple was one of three foci of the Judaism of the period.[168] As noted above, Binder has demonstrated a far-reaching connection in general between two of those: the temple and the synagogue. The synagogues, we recall, functioned as distant courts of the central sanctuary in Jerusalem.

This may be of special relevance for some Antiochean Jews, since Josephus informs us in *B.J.* 7.44 about how the Seleucid rulers, who succeeded Antiochus IV Epiphanes, "restored to the Jews of Antioch all such votive offerings as were made of brass, to be laid up in their synagogue." The fact that Josephus, *the priest*, seems to have thought highly of this synagogue, for instance by referring to it as τὸ ἱερόν,[169] indicates, at least according to Binder, that "there surely must have been a harmonious relationship between its congregation and the Temple hierarchy in Jerusalem."[170]

This could, of course, be interpreted in different ways, and need not necessarily be taken as an indication of torah obedience or of a certain degree of observance. The Essenes, for instance, while being critical towards the temple hierarchy in Jerusalem, certainly had a positive attitude in principle to the temple institution (in their own form),[171] and no one could accuse them of not taking religion seriously. On the other hand, the syncretistic temple cult during the Hellenistic reform attempt in Jerusalem could be described as anything but in accordance with a more traditional interpretation of the torah.[172] Furthermore, the extent to which the temple tax seems to have been collected indicates that most Jews supported it. Accordingly, it seems that the attitude to the temple, as was the case with the attitude to foreign oil, says nothing unequivocal about the religious commitment of an individual. A positive attitude to the temple does not necessarily indicate "zeal for the law," but someone who wanted to break with Judaism obviously did not support it. In the case of Antioch, however, taking into consideration Binder's evaluation of the relation between the synagogue and the temple, as well as the geographical/ideological aspects, I would be inclined to ascribe somewhat more importance to this "harmonious relationship." Due to the geographical/ideological circumstances, it is possible that the effect on Palestine of the Maccabean uprising in terms of what Hengel described as a "zeal for the law"[173] may have influenced a certain temple-oriented community in Antioch.

I would therefore conclude that we may cautiously assume the existence of a group more strongly committed to Jewish life than the main body of Antiochean Jews, taking the following aspects into consideration: 1) a general expectation of finding groups strongly committed to religion based on empirical studies of migration; 2) the reference from Josephus (*B.J.* 7.51), where it is stated that some Jews died rather than sacrificed in a Greek cultic context; 3) the possible existence of a group in Antioch which was ideologically connected to the tradition of the Maccabean martyrs as presented in 2 Maccabees, wherein we find a predominantly negative and hostile view of Gentiles, and that eventually resulted in the writing of 4 Maccabees around 100 CE; and 4) a possible strong connection between Jerusalem and a temple/torah ideology among some Antiochean Jews.

Such a group would be the result of either successful socialization or mechanisms in connection with migration. In the latter case, we could use Waardenburg's terminology and speak of individuals having chosen a "religious option," or we could imagine a process of "Judaization of one's self"[174] having been operative. This group must have been the definitive antithesis of the Antiochus group. In different ways it was presumably a closed group, having few contacts with the Gentile population. One could imagine that it had developed several ways of keeping its members within the ideological and social boundaries. The emphasis on torah obedience, of doing things the right way, would serve this purpose very well, but would at the same time make great demands upon the efficiency of legitimizing and reality maintenance processes. Isolation would, of course, serve such a purpose. I would think that the situation is comparable to that of the contemporary ultra-orthodox movement or of other similar groups, such as the Amish in the United States. The main strategy would thus involve 1) few contacts with the surrounding society, maintained by an organization which provided few opportunities to develop primary relationships with outsiders; and 2) great emphasis on socialization, together with different strategies for reality maintaining processes.[175]

Hence it follows that members of such a group would be assimilated to the surrounding society to a very small degree. It is likely that their assimilation profile would look something like that shown in Figure 3.3.

We could safely assume that they were acculturated, and that they must have had sufficient knowledge of Hellenistic society to know

Acculturation	Structural	Marital	Indentification	Attitude	Civic
Yes	No	No	No	No	No

Figure 3.3 Assimilation profile for the religious traditionalists, who possessed far-reaching knowledge about Hellenistic society, but used this knowledge in order to avoid being assimilated.

what to refrain from. The acculturation would hence have been used in an oppositional way, that is, their knowledge about Hellenistic society would be used to avoid influences or even to fight against its ideology. Fourth Maccabees is a good example of this, since the work displays strong influences from the same Greek culture it opposes.[176]

As for all the other variables, we must assume that Jews belonging to this group did not have frequent contacts with non-Jews. They certainly did not enter into gymnasia or into cliques, clubs and institutions of the host society: in short, they were *not* structurally assimilated. Moreover, we can be quite sure that they did not marry outsiders and did not develop a sense of identity with any other group. They most certainly experienced prejudice and power or value conflicts, as the incident related in *B.J.* 7.50–1 strongly indicates.

Evidence of Jewish residential districts in an urban environment is found in Egypt.[177] Josephus, for instance, mentions in *B.J.* 2.488 that the Jews of Alexandria were granted "a quarter of their own." As for the situation outside Egypt, Josephus (*A.J.* 14.260) mentions that the Jews of Sardis were given certain rights—among other things, a "place" (τόπος) "in which they may gather together . . . and offer their ancestral prayers and sacrifices." In Rome it seems that seven of the at least eleven known synagogues were located in the Transtiberene area,[178] but this area was the home of many other ethnic groups, not only Jews.[179]

How about the situation in Antioch? Is anything known about the existence of certain Jewish residential districts? According to G. Downey, the Jews during the reign of Antiochus IV Epiphanes lived in an area of their own, located near the south-western end of the city,[180] but this statement is almost impossible to verify. There is evidence of three synagogues from the first century BCE, one west of the city, near Daphne, one in the city and one east of the city,[181] and there were probably several others, but from this we can say nothing about the existence of certain Jewish residential areas. Kraeling may be right in stating that the existence of such settlements in Antioch is "entirely probable."[182] One thing is certain, however: if groups existed that were strongly committed to a traditional torah-obedient and extremely observant Jewish life, they probably lived by themselves in separate areas.

Constructing alternatives—messianism and Hellenism

The first century CE was an era of messianic movements. John the Baptist apparently led a quite important messianic movement, one of the more famous.[183] There were, however, others. *Antiquitates judaicae* 20.97–8 and Acts 5:36 inform us about Theudas, who had 400 adherents, and in *A.J.* 20.169–72 we hear about a somewhat later "Egyptian false prophet"[184] who sought to force his way to Jerusalem. According to *A.J.* 18.85, a Samaritan man led his followers to Mount Gerizim in search for the holy vessels of the temple, put there by Moses. In addition, in the revolts in 66–70, 115–117 and 132–135, "messianic hopes and figures played a prominent role."[185] There is evidence of messianic expectations in Alexandria.[186] Then, of course, we have the followers of Jesus from Nazareth.

In connection with the persecution of the *ekklēsia* in Jerusalem, Acts 8:1 describes how "all except the apostles were scattered throughout the countryside of Judea and Samaria." Later, in Acts 11:19, we are told that some of these reached Antioch and preached initially only for Jews, and in 11:20 that "some men of Cyprus and Cyrene who, on coming to Antioch, spoke to the Hellenists also, proclaiming the Lord Jesus." According to this account we are told that Hellenistic Jesus-believing Jews originally proclaimed the faith of this new Jewish faction among other Jews, but later also to Gentiles in Antioch.[187]

The question is how we are to evaluate the historical information given here. J. T. Sanders is very negative about the possibility of using Acts as a source for the situation in Antioch, since he finds the statement about the men of Cyprus and Cyrene nothing more than a narrative convenience.[188] W. A. Meeks and R. L. Wilken, J. P. Meier, F. W. Norris and, somewhat hesitatingly, C. C. Hill, on the other hand, find trustworthy the information that the mission to the Gentiles was initiated by Greek-speaking, Jesus-believing Jews.[189] In general, it seems wise to be skeptical of the historicity of a text where the ample amount of clearly legendary material is of such importance. The historicity of the statement concerning the introduction of the Jesus movement in Antioch is therefore dependent on its relation to the theological program of Luke.

There are, however, some aspects to indicate that we might have a reliable piece of information here concerning the introduction of this new kind of messianic Judaism in Antioch. The narrative structure of Acts 1–11 seems to lead to the legitimization of the mission to the Gentiles, but it is hard to attribute any narrative significance to the statement that the mission to the Gentiles in Antioch was initiated by Hellenistic, Jesus-believing Jews. This is, in fact, what we could expect, since it is reasonable to assume that those Jesus-believing Jews who directed their message to Gentiles, presumably in a synagogal context, had a positive and open attitude to Gentiles and to Hellenistic society in general. This is all the more probable since one of the Hellenists from Jerusalem, Nicolaus, was a former Gentile from Antioch[190] who had converted to Judaism and now joined with the Jesus-believing Jews. One may assume, as Meier does, that there was a connection between Nicolaus and the decision to go to Antioch.[191]

Even though this new messianic movement had originated not in Antioch but in Palestine, it seems as if one of its more distinctive features, namely, its relation to the Gentiles, became all the more accentuated in this new context. Irrespective of whether there was a Jewish mission or not, the accentuation of both a conscious mission to Jews and Gentiles and a messianic/apocalyptic message is a clear indication that we are confronted here with a new, innovative form of religious manifestation. This is exactly what we might expect to find in a religiously pluralistic milieu and in connection with migration. We noted above that there was an ongoing migration to the major cities in antiquity, and that there is every reason to assume extensive Jewish immigration to Antioch. Some Antiochean Jews were evidently attracted by this new messianic movement that had extended its mission even to the Gentiles, and we must assume that the majority of the Jewish adherents to the movement did not have any intention of leaving Judaism. Their engagement in the messianic movement was but one of many ways of being Jewish. This may, however, say something about their assimilation profile. As with most Jews in the urban centers in the Roman Empire, they were familiar with Hellenistic society, and were consequently acculturated. The openness towards Gentile society implies that they were structurally assimilated to some extent, since the mission to the Gentiles could be accomplished only by primary relationships with Gentiles.[192] During the period up to the Jewish War in 66 CE we may assume that there was no intermarriage between Jesus-believing Jews and Jesus-believing Gentiles, because the Jesus movement was a completely Jewish one with an unusual openness towards Gentiles. While Jews and Gentiles may occasionally have married, they could

Acculturation	Structural	Marital	Indentification	Attitude	Civic
Yes	Yes	No	No	No	No

Figure 3.4 Assimilation profile for Jesus-believing Jews and Hellenistic non-Jesus-believing Jews

not have done so while maintaining their original religious affiliations. We will deal more with the relations between Jesus-believing Jews and Jesus-believing Gentiles in the next chapter, but nothing indicates that the Jewish Jesus movement originally had any intention of leaving Judaism, and there was consequently nothing that motivated the adherents to strive for assimilation. Their assimilation profile ought therefore to have looked like that shown in Figure 3.4.

The same must have been true for another manifestation of innovative expressions of Judaism. Throughout this chapter we have noted the tendency among some Jewish groups to form a synthesis between Judaism and Hellenism. This was particularly common in Alexandria, but we noted above that there are indications that Antiochus may have had access to Greek education in Antioch, and that his family were probably highly acculturated. While Antiochus had clearly left Judaism, most Jews who were interested in Hellenism and wanted to create a Hellenistic Judaism were at the same time concerned with the preservation of a Jewish identity and had no intention of ceasing to be Jewish. It is unlikely that Jews and Gentiles married, but, as Gordon pointed out, structural assimilation may lead to all other kinds of assimilation, since contacts between different groups on a primary group level may lead to strong attachments between individuals. This is in accordance with Philo's warning that participation in Gentile *collegia* may lead to apostasy.[193] Philo himself, while certainly being both acculturated and structurally assimilated, did not approve of intermarriage,[194] but, according to S. J. D. Cohen, both he and Josephus were familiar with Jews who did.[195] The boundaries between Jews and Gentiles were generally rather strong, but it cannot be ruled out that intermarriage occasionally happened—as the case of Timothy suggests.[196]

In sum, we have found evidence of four different Jewish groups in Antioch. Firstly, a Jewish group on the very fringe of Judaism and clearly intending to leave Judaism; secondly, their complete antithesis, religious traditionalists with a strong commitment to torah obedience, possibly living in isolation both from other Jews and from Gentile society. We also found evidence of two innovative manifestations of Judaism, on the one hand, adherents of the messianic Jesus movement, and on the other very Hellenistic Jews who nevertheless looked upon themselves as Jews. We must, in addition, reckon with large groups of Antiochean Jews who would not have placed themselves in any of these distinct groups. Finally, we shall turn to the question of how this religious differentiation may have showed itself in relation to the synagogal institution.

The synagogue and religious differentiation

In the previous chapter, I reached the conclusion that there may have existed twenty to thirty synagogues in Antioch during the first century CE. How did the Jews of Antioch relate to these synagogues? There are basically two general alternatives. It may have been the case that all different manifestations of Jewishness could be found in every synagogue, or one could assume that one ideology dominated in each. The evidence as well as sociological considerations speak strongly in favor of the latter alternative.

We do not know of many sources of information about the designation of synagogues, but Rome and Jerusalem may give us hints about the situation in Antioch. From Rome we know of eleven, perhaps thirteen, different synagogues or congregations that bear individual names. At least four, maybe five, seem to have existed during the first century CE.[197] The "synagogue of the Hebrews" may refer to the first Jewish congregation in Antioch and was probably the oldest synagogue in the city.[198] The "synagogue of the Augustans" was evidently named in order to honor the Emperor Augustus, who had shown a far-reaching tolerance to Judaism and also made great contributions to the temple in Jerusalem.[199] The "synagogue of the Agrippans" was probably named after Marcus Vipsanius Agrippa, Augustus' chief lieutenant and heir, and the "synagogue of Volumnians" may have been named after the tribune in Syria.[200] According to P. Richardson, one inscription (*CIJ* 173), may refer to a "synagogue of the Herodians," named after Herod the Great.[201]

While these synagogues were named to honor persons of importance for the Jewish community, other synagogues in Rome show that names were given to indicate the origin of the founder or some characteristic of the members.[202] The "synagogue of the Vernaclesians," for instance, may have consisted of slaves born in the house of their owners, or of a group of Hellenistic Jews who in contrast to the Hebrews had adopted Roman customs, or of native Romans as opposed to immigrants.[203]

To turn to Jerusalem, in Acts 6:8–9, Luke informs us about the existence of perhaps five separate synagogues:[204]

> Stephen, full of grace and power, did great wonders and signs among the people. Then some of those who belonged to the synagogue of the Freedmen [Λιβερτίνων] (as it was called), Cyrenians, Alexandrians, and others of those from Cilicia and Asia, stood up and argued with Stephen.

The reference to the "synagogue of the Freedmen" is somewhat unclear—it may refer to descendants of Jews who were taken captive by Pompey in 63 BCE, or, as some manuscripts suggest, the word "Libyans" should be read instead of "Freedmen."[205] In any case, here we find that the name of a synagogue indicates a common origin of the individuals who belonged to it.

In sum, we find that names were given to synagogues according to several principles. Names could be given in honor of a patron or benefactor of the synagogue, to indicate the geographical origin of the founder, or to indicate the geographical or social origin of its members.

This shows that the synagogue was not a homogeneous institution, reflecting the diversity of Judaism:[206] the common denominator for the names of the synagogues is the assembling together of people who had something in common. While some names indicate that the members came from the same place or had a common social origin, we may also assume that they shared an ideology. To some extent these two aspects may have coincided. We know, for instance, that at least some Jews in Alexandria were Hellenized to a high degree. Is it possible that, for instance, the "Alexandrians" from Acts 6:9 not only originated from Alexandria but also shared a common concept of Judaism? At least according to one interpretation of the Vernaclesians in Rome we noted that they may have belonged to the more Hellenized Jews in Rome, perhaps in contrast to the members of the "synagogue of the Hebrews." It is obvious that Jews who revered the torah in a traditional way, using their knowledge about Hellenistic society to reject it, could not belong to the same synagogue in which members admired Hellenism and even welcomed Gentiles to their gatherings.

In the urban centers of the Roman Empire we must allow for a religious differentiation even in the organization of the Jewish communities. We may assume that some synagogues were more open to innovative ideas than others. That would be true both for the social experiment of combining Hellenism and Judaism and for a messianic, apocalyptic movement with a mission to the Gentiles. It is thus reasonable to assume that the Jesus-believing Jews in Acts 11:19–20, who first "spoke the word to no one except Jews," but later "to the Hellenists also," influenced synagogues with a positive attitude towards Gentiles.

In the previous chapter we noted that the Jewish communities were generally considered as *collegia* and that these usually existed on the condition that they did not violate public law. Given the regulations about the *collegia* in the empire, it is highly unlikely that the Jesus-believing Jews in Antioch were organized in any other way than as a synagogue. While the Jewish communities enjoyed protection as long as law and order were maintained, a new foreign cult did not. This is one consequence of the general, rather obvious assumption that the Jesus movement was originally part of Judaism and that Gentile adherents had to relate to the Jewish community. It is also in accordance with M. D. Nanos's interpretation of the situation in Rome. Nanos suggests that Paul, in Romans 13:1–7, argues that the Jesus-believing Gentiles should subordinate themselves not primarily to the authorities of Rome, but to the *synagogue authorities*.[207] This would make even more sense if we assume the existence of a synagogue consisting mainly of Jesus-believing Jews, considering themselves fully rooted within Judaism.

This is, in fact, the only reasonable way of depicting the organization of the early Jesus movement in Antioch. Some Hellenized Jesus-believing Jews, from Jerusalem, possibly including Nicolaus, the convert from Antioch, obtained a stronghold in at least one, but perhaps several, of the Hellenistic synagogues that consequently accepted Gentiles in their midst. I suggest that it is such institutions to which, for instance, Luke refers by the designation *ekklēsia*.[208]

Already in the Jewish biblical tradition the meaning of the Greek words ἐκκλησία and συναγωγή are intertwined—both can be used to translate the Hebrew word קהל.[209] While ἐκκλησία in the LXX is used to denote the Jewish community in a general, national way, there are texts that imply that it is rather the Jewish community in a more restricted sense that is meant—as a synagogal community. In Jdt 6:16–19, we find the account of an incident that implies a gathering at a place where the god of Israel is worshiped.

> They called together all the elders of the town, and all their young men and women ran to the assembly [εἰς τὴν ἐκκλησίαν]. They set Achior in the midst of all their people,

and Uzziah questioned him about what had happened. He answered and told them what had taken place at the council of Holofernes, and all that he had said in the presence of the Assyrian leaders, and all that Holofernes had boasted he would do against the house of Israel. Then the people fell down and worshiped God, and cried out: "O Lord God of heaven, see their arrogance, and have pity on our people in their humiliation, and look kindly today on the faces of those who are consecrated to you."

The terminology is of course dependent on definitions, but it seems we have here a synagogue in terms of a local council house in which communal discussions as well as worship took place.[210]

On the other hand, συναγωγή sometimes refers to a community of Jesus-believers, of meeting places, and even as a self-designation instead of ἐκκλησία. Of special interest is of course that Ignatius actually uses συναγωγή to denote cultic meetings, as in the passage *Pol.* 4:2, where the believers are admonished to have frequent meetings, πυκνότερον συναγωγαὶ γινέσθωσαν.[211] The best example, however, comes from the New Testament. A comparison between two verses in James makes it clear that the author of the letter thought of his community as a synagogue, and that both words, ἐκκλησία and συναγωγή, could be used as a designation of a community of Jesus-believers.

James 2:2: For if a person with gold rings and in fine clothes comes into your assembly [εἰσέλθῃ εἰς συναγωγὴν ὑμῶν], and if a poor person in dirty clothes also comes in . . .

James 5:14: Are any among you sick? They should call for the elders of the church [προσκαλεσάσθω τοὺς πρεσβυτέρους τῆς ἐκκλησίας] and have them pray over them, anointing them with oil in the name of the Lord.

We can thus conclude that the terminology does not speak against the view that the Jesus movement in Antioch was originally a synagogue consisting of Jesus-believing Jews, and that the Jesus-believing Gentiles related to this synagogue as any Gentiles related to any Jewish community.

In light of this, the remark in Acts 11:26, that the disciples were first called "Christians" (Χριστιανός) in Antioch, could make sense. We noted above that synagogues could be given names according to different principles. That a messianic Jewish community would be given a name by other Jews that manifested this is quite natural and does not imply any break with Judaism—rather the opposite.[212]

J. Taylor has suggested that the name was given by the Roman authorities, partly because of the political implications in the messianic claims. This is probably to overestimate the significance of the Jesus movement at this time. According to R. Stark, in the 40s CE there were about 1,000 believers *in the world*,[213] that is, both Jesus-believing Jews and Jesus-believing Gentiles, a figure accepted as a reasonable conjecture by J. T. Sanders.[214] That a riot in Antioch in 39–40 CE may have included messianic overtones is possible: this also applies to the Jewish War in 66–70, the revolt in 115–117 and the revolt of Bar Kokhba. But, as we will see in the next chapter, Malalas' account which Taylor uses is even less credible than is assumed by Taylor, and the followers of Jesus were certainly not the only messianic Jews in Antioch at this time.

According to M. Tellbe, the designation Χριστιανός shows that the difference between Jews or Christians (or alternatively of Christians as a distinctive Jewish faction) was publicly known, perhaps even in governing circles, because "Christ" and "Christians" "in non-Christian first century sources are consistently associated with public disorder and crimes."[215] Tellbe enters as evidence four texts, from which only three actually refer to first-century incidents: Pliny's letter to Emperor Trajan (*Ep.* 10.96) deals with an event in the beginning of the second century, and two texts, Tacitus *Ann.* 15.44, and Suetonius, *Nero* 16.2, refer to the incident during the reign of Nero (54–68). Suetonius reports only that the Christians (*Christiani*), who belonged to "a class of men given to a new and mischievous superstition," were punished.

Tacitus' remark is more interesting: he states that, in order to "scotch the rumour," Nero punished "with utmost refinements of cruelty, a class of men, loathed for their vices, whom the crowd styled Christians." We are furthermore told that the Christian movement had originated in Judaea and that the founder, Christus, was executed by sentence of Pontius Pilatus. Now Tacitus states that the reason why the Christians were convicted in Rome was "not so much on the count of arson as for hatred of the human race." The Christians are consequently referred to by an epithet generally used in connection with the Greco-Roman description of Jews! As will be shown in the next chapter, the literary motifs of *xenophobia/misanthropy/amixia* were common descriptions of the Jews as representing a life hostile to humankind and therefore a threat to ordinary society. Tacitus' claim

95

[handwritten margin note: they shared this w/ Jews but this does not make them Jews who weren't punished for their atheism]

that "this class of men" is "loathed for their vices" is an accusation that is completely in accordance with his own descriptions of *Jews*— for instance, in *Hist.* 5.4, where we are informed that "[t]he Jews regard as profane all that we hold sacred; on the other hand, they permit all that we abhor," and, in 5.5, the customs of the Jews are said to be "base and abominable, and owe their persistence to their depravity."

The Christians in Tacitus' account are thus geographically as well as ideologically connected to Judaism rather than to a separate cult. The story seems also to bear some resemblance to the event in Antioch when Antiochus accused the Jews of a desire to burn down the city (*B.J.* 7.46–7). According to Tacitus it seems as if it was the crowd rather than "governing circles" who were responsible for the accusations against the Christians, and that the emperor used rumors in order to find suitable scapegoats. It could be argued that when Tacitus relates the events during the reign of Nero, about fifty years after they first occurred, he incorporates anachronistic concepts from his own time, when Christianity certainly had begun to emerge as a non-Jewish, separate religion.[216] It may be worth mentioning that Tacitus, who himself had been the governor of a province of Asia, was also a close friend of Pliny the Younger, whom we know had close contacts with Christians.[217] It could, consequently, be argued that, while Tacitus may have thought that the "Christians" of the 60s in the city of Rome were the same "Christians" as those in the beginning of the second century with whom Tacitus himself may have been in contact, the former group was probably one faction within Judaism, comparable to the Pharisees. That Christianity eventually became a non-Jewish, separate religion does not mean that this separation must already have taken place by the first time we hear the term "Christian." The sources actually indicate the opposite.

Finally, the text from Josephus, *A.J.* 18.64, can hardly be said to indicate that the Jesus movement was "consistently associated with public disorder and crimes"[218] only because of its mention of the crucifixion. None of the texts referred to by Tellbe can, in fact, be used to indicate that the designation Χριστιανός in Acts was given by the civic authorities at the beginning of the 40s as a result of associations with public disorder. Tacitus' text indicates rather that "Christians" in Rome in the 60s were associated with Jews.[219] Regarding the origin of the designation, we must conclude that if the term really was in use in the middle of the first century, it is possible that we have here an intra-Jewish designation for a Jewish messianic synagogue in Antioch.

Summary and conclusion

The aim of this chapter has been to analyze the Jewish population in Antioch, with regard to its religious differentiation and, somewhat interconnected to this, its relation to Hellenistic society. One basic problem is that the available sources are few. In order to overcome this problem I suggested the use of a hermeneutic model based on the interaction between 1) a basic, general theoretical perspective of human society—the sociology of knowledge, 2) specific social-scientific theories used in empirical studies of modern societies, 3) comparative material from antiquity, and 4) primary sources.

It is a well known fact that Diaspora Judaism exhibits certain differences in comparison with Palestinian Judaism, and it has been assumed that the Diaspora status itself created certain differences in the religiousness of Diaspora Judaism. Studies of value changes among Hungarian immigrants to Sweden support the notion that international migration can promote changes in the individual's meaning system. The situation in antiquity was generally characterized by a high degree of mobility, and, as recalled from chapter 2, urban centers during antiquity were in constant need of new immigrants. Literary sources also support the idea that there was extensive Jewish immigration to Antioch. It thus seemed appropriate to use a theory of religious change derived from studies of international migration in Western Europe.

Studies of religious change among Muslim immigrants to several Western European countries have shown that religion among immigrants changes in three ways. One common denominator is that religion to some extent becomes optional, and the individual can within certain limits direct his or her own religious commitment. Some immigrants intensify their religious commitment and identity, while others become completely assimilated into the society of the majority. A third tendency that was observable in the studies was the formation of new, innovative religious manifestations. In short, and to generalize somewhat, some people tend to be more religious, some become less religious, and still others become religious in a new way.

The answer to why such alterations take place presumably lies in the change of plausibility structure. Migration promotes changes by confronting the individual with a competing reality with new plausibility structures. It is thus *pluralism* rather than the migration situation itself that is the decisive factor. It was argued that the Hellenistic world was characterized by a far-reaching pluralism, not least where religion was concerned, and its impact on the Jewish population was extensive but affected different groups in different ways and in varying degrees. It was demonstrated that Palestine, and especially Jerusalem, constituted a more religiously homogeneous society than the Diaspora. One vital aspect of the religiousness of Jews in the Diaspora is its relation to Hellenistic society. So in our analysis the theory of religious change had to be supplemented by a theory of social integration.

A model of assimilation, originally used in order to analyze assimilation processes in the United States in the 1950s, was adapted to suit the conditions during antiquity. Assimilation is a process involving several sub-processes that eventually result in a minority group fusing together with the majority society, and thus ceasing to exist. The sub-processes are: 1) *acculturation*—familiarity with the cultural matrix of the host society, such as language and education; 2) *structural assimilation*—primary relationships with members of the host society and entrance into cliques, clubs and institutions of the host society on a primary group level; 3) *marital assimilation*—intermarriage; 4) *identificational assimilation*—development of a sense of identity based exclusively on the host society; 5) *attitude receptional assimilation*—absence of prejudice; and 6) *civic assimilation*—absence of power or value conflict.

While it is possible for a group to be familiar with the culture of the host society without being assimilated, it was shown that the keystone in the process of assimilation was *structural assimilation*: it is likely that all other kinds of sub-processes will follow naturally once a group has experienced primary relationships with members of the host society. It was pointed out that one important aspect of acculturation is that familiarity with a culture can be used in two ways, either *integrative*, that is, assimilative, or in an *oppositional* way, that is, deliberately non-assimilative.

Since the effects noted in connection with international migration and the process of assimilation seem compatible with the overarching theoretical perspective, the sociology of knowledge, it was assumed that we could expect to find similar religious manifestations in the ancient material and that the assimilation model could be used in order to interpret the relation between different Jewish groups and Hellenistic society.

With the formulation of this theoretical concept, we turned to the sources and found a description of a former Jew, Antiochus, who had left Judaism, betrayed his family and people, and sacrificed to Greek deities (*B.J.* 7.46–7). Against the background of the studies of religious change, it was stated that there were probably other Jews with similar experiences, and therefore that it was legitimate to allude to a group of Jews that existed on the fringe of Judaism, clearly intending to leave Judaism. It was assumed that this group must have been almost completely assimilated into Greek society and that they had used their acculturation—their knowledge of Greek culture—in an integrative way, in order to achieve this.

We also found evidence of the completely opposite tendency, namely, Jews who were more committed to Jewish life and to torah obedience than the main body of Antiochean Jews. In *B.J.* 7.51, Josephus mentions some Jews who gave their lives rather than sacrifice to the Greek gods. While there probably never existed a cult of the Maccabean martyrs in Antioch, the assumed composition of 4 Maccabees in Antioch indicates a group of Jews who held torah obedience in high esteem. Such a group was probably only acculturated, that is, they possessed knowledge about Hellenistic society, but had used this knowledge in order to avoid being assimilated.

We found evidence of two innovative religious manifestations, namely, Hellenistic Jews, who without having any intention of leaving Judaism wanted to create a Hellenistic Judaism, and messianic, Jesus-believing Jews.

Finally, we discussed the relation between these Jewish interpretations of Judaism and the synagogue. Could it be assumed that all these Judaisms could be found in each and every synagogue, or is it more likely that one ideological tendency dominated each synagogue? It was argued that the latter alternative is the more likely. It was also suggested that the different names of synagogues in Rome and Jerusalem implied that people who shared the same ideology gathered together, and it was demonstrated that this is what could be expected from the perspective of sociology of knowledge. It was further argued that the Jesus movement originally influenced at least one of the synagogues in Antioch. This is the most natural state of affairs, since the Jesus movement originally consisted of Jews with no intention of leaving Judaism. The synagogue would consequently be the most natural institution for a completely Jewish interpretation of Judaism. Another strong argument in favor of this is shown by the regulations concerning the *collegia* in the Roman Empire. Since the synagogue was considered as a *collegium* and enjoyed protection, it is highly unlikely that the Jesus movement would organize in any other way than one that had the approval of the authorities of the city.

This study has thus revealed, with help from sociological theories, that several varieties of Judaism existed in Antioch, and that these differed from each other both concerning their relation to Hellenistic society and to their own religious tradition. In the next chapter we shall focus specifically on the interaction between Jews, including the Jesus-believing Jews, and Gentiles, including the Jesus-believing Gentiles.

Notes

1 See e.g., Davies, *Paul*; Herford, *Judaism*; Montefiore, *Judaism*; Moore, "Christian Writers"; Parkes, *Conflict*; Sanders, *Palestinian Judaism*.
2 Levine, *Ancient Synagogue*, 116.
3 Binder, *Temple Courts*, 228.
4 Barclay, *Mediterranean Diaspora*, 320.
5 Levine, *Ancient Synagogue*, 116. See also Barclay, *Mediterranean Diaspora*, 243–4.
6 See Downey, *Antioch in Syria*, 107, n. 101; Meeks and Wilken, *Jews and Christians*, 2–13; Levinskaya, *Diaspora Setting*, 128–35; Barclay, *Mediterranean Diaspora*, 245, n. 31; Binder, *Temple Courts*, 264–6; Levine, *Ancient Synagogue*, 116–18. These presentations are referring either directly to Krauss and/or Kraeling or to someone else who does. Binder, for instance, refers to Downey, Meeks and Wilken, Levinskaya, and Barclay.
7 Sanders, *Judaism*, 47.
8 Sanders, "Common Judaism," 5.
9 Ibid., 4.
10 Dunn, *Partings*, 18–36.
11 On the reasons for the appearance of the religious parties, see Sanders, *Judaism*, 13–29.
12 See, e.g., Porton, "Diversity," who mentions scribes, Hasidim, apocalyptic Jews, Samaritans, the Qumran community, Therapeutae, Sadducees, Pharisees and related groups, Zealots and Sicarii. Cohen, *Maccabees*, 25, also refers to "numerous teachers and holy men, each with his band of supporters," when characterizing first-century Judaism. Having taken into consideration new archeological and paleographical data, Kraabel, "Questionable Assumptions," 457–8, points to the social and economic diversity of Diaspora Judaism.
13 I do not intend to stress the cognitive or dogmatic aspects of a certain "belief," but rather what Aune, "Orthodoxy," 7, calls *"intentional-behavioral explications."*
14 Bauckham, "Parting," 137.
15 One might argue for a kind of Pharisaic influence in Antioch during the clash between Paul and Peter if we assume that those "believers who belonged to the sect of the Pharisees" in Acts 15:5 are connected to "certain people . . . from James" in Gal. 2:12.
16 Sanders, *Judaism*, 19–20.
17 Kraabel, "Unity," 30.
18 See, for instance, Brim and Kagan, *Constancy*; Inglehart, *Culture Shift*; Pettersson and Riis, *Scandinavian Values*.
19 Hamberg, "World-Views," 101.
20 Ibid., 102. See also Hamberg, *Livsåskådningar*, 177–86.

21 Meeks, *First Urban*, 17; Wallace and Williams, *Three Worlds*, 16–18.
22 See Barclay, *Mediterranean Diaspora*, 20–2, on Jewish immigration and settlement in Ptolemaic Egypt.
23 Kraeling, "Jewish Community," 134–5.
24 Ibid., 134.
25 Stern, "Jewish Diaspora," 138.
26 Waardenburg, "Institutionalization," 27–8. It is important to notice that Waardenburg not only refers to a "fundamentalist" attitude but emphasizes that the "religious option has many more varieties than the 'fundamentalist' one in any precise sense of the term."
27 Schiffauer, "Migration," 147–50.
28 Ibid., 151.
29 Ibid., 152.
30 Ibid., 156.
31 Ibid., 155.
32 Rex, "Religion," 19.
33 See for instance, Carlbom, "Sverige" (Muslim immigrants in Sweden), Finke and Stark, *Churching* (Catholic immigrants in the United States), Stark, "German-American Religiousness" (German immigrants in the United States), Hamberg, "World-Views" (Hungarian immigrants in Sweden).
34 Hamberg, "Migration," 83.
35 The reasons why an immigrant's religious commitment changes may, according to Hamberg, be related partly to his or her decision to emigrate. If a whole group migrates because they have suffered religious discrimination or persecution, religion will probably play a central role in the life of the group, and religious commitment could even increase in the new country. If migration is motivated by economic conditions or if religion has been enforced by social pressure, the role of religion may well be less significant, see Hamberg, "Migration," 72, and "International Migration," 27–8.
36 Cf. Hamberg, "World-Views," 102.
37 Berger and Luckmann, *Social Construction*, 113.
38 Ibid., 120.
39 Berger, *Sacred Canopy*, 45.
40 Berger and Luckmann, *Social Construction*, 174.
41 "Conversation" also embraces "the rich aura of non-verbal communication that surrounds speech"; see Berger and Luckmann, *Social Construction*, 172.
42 Ibid., 176.
43 Ibid., 176–7.
44 This first statement needs some clarification. Berger and Luckmann state that it is possible that the subjective reality remains relevant to a person who has been cut off from a community of people sharing his world. In such cases the face-to-face conversations have to be replaced by different reality-maintaining techniques, such as prayer and other kinds of religious procedures. In the case of a Catholic living for many years among people of other faiths, such means may "sustain his continued self-identification as a Catholic. They will, however, become subjectively empty of 'living' reality unless they are 'revitalized' by

social contact with other Catholics." See Berger and Luckmann, *Social Construction*, 175.

45 There is an immense amount of literature dealing with this topic, but for a brief and evaluative survey of modern history of research, see Levine, *Judaism*, 6–15.

46 Kraabel, "Social Systems," 266; Rutgers, "Diaspora," 94–5; Levine, *Ancient Synagogue*, 581. As for the synagogues of Palestine, Binder, *Temple Courts*, 226, regards them as having been built after the model of the temple of Jerusalem, which of course reflected Hellenistic influences; see Levine, *Judaism*, 68–72. Where the synagogues of the Diaspora are concerned, Binder states that the sources indicate "that these were consecrated edifices that bore an affinity to temples or cultic halls"; see *Temple Courts*, 337.

47 Kraabel, "Social Systems," 266.

48 "More successfully than any other of Rome's minorities, the Jewish population was able to adapt a Hellenistic Gentile social form, the private organization, to its particular social and religious purposes"; Kraabel, "Social Systems," 266. See also Sanders, "Common Judaism," 1–2. The same adaptation to local structures of organization is to be found when Muslim immigrant groups must find new legal solutions to the foundation of mosques in a non-Muslim society; see Waardenburg, "Institutionalization," 12, 15.

49 Runesson, "Water," 127; Sanders, *Judaism*, 218. Water had a prominent place in Greek religion and was used for many purposes. Ritual sprinkling was often required before entering a sanctuary. In sacrifices, the sprinkling of water was connected to preliminary rites; see Guettel-Cole, "Uses of Water," 162.

50 See Walser, *Greek*, who has argued in favour of a specific Greek used in the context of the synagogue.

51 Hengel, "Interpretation," 195. See also p. 195, n. 1, for examples of inscriptions from Ptolemaic Egypt.

52 One representative of such a literature, 4 Maccabees, with a possible origin in Antioch, is of special interest for us, and we will return to this work later. Charlesworth remarks that it displays Stoic influences and was composed by a Jew "who had mastered Greek thought and language"; see *Pseudepigrapha*, 151. Anderson describes the author's "extensive knowledge of Greek philosophy . . . his skill in Greek rhetoric"; see "4 Maccabees," 533. Gilbert labels the work as a "remarkable piece of Greek rhetoric" which shows "clear indications of Platonic and Stoic influences"; see "4 Maccabees," 317. Similarly, Barclay, *Mediterranean Diaspora*, 371, states that the author's "inventive vocabulary and his developed rhetorical skills confirm the picture of a Jew with an advanced Greek education who has gained a thorough training and a familiarity with the core disciplines of a Hellenistic schooling."

53 Levine, *Judaism*, 26. According to Hengel, Hellenization had already begun in the third century BCE and had been in progress since then. This is a pervading characteristic of Hengel's *Judaism and Hellenism*. A brief survey is to be found in Hengel, "Interpretation." This view has been heavily criticized by, for instance, Feldman: see, e.g., "How Much

Hellenism"; "Missionary Religion"; *Jew*, 3–44. A short summary of Hengel's work, as well as the criticism of it, may be found in Grabbe, *Judaism*, 148–53. See also Rajak, *Jewish Dialogue*, 3–10, for an evaluative discussion of both standpoints.

54 Cf. Hengel, "Interpretation," 211, who states that "[t]he role of Alexandria as the centre of operations for a Hellenistic Jewish education with a quite individual stamp has proved to be unique."

55 Ibid., 203.

56 Ibid., 204.

57 There is evidence of Jews from Egypt who became totally assimilated to the Greek environment: Dositheos, son of Drimylos was a Jew by birth but "changed his religion and apostatized from the ancestral traditions" (3 Macc. 1:3), and Philo's nephew Tiberius Julius Alexander made a successful career in the Roman administration (*A.J.* 20.100–3; *B.J.* 2.309; 5.45–6, 510; 6.237–42; Tacitus, *Ann.* 15.28); he may finally have become prefect of the praetorian guard in Rome; see Barclay, *Mediterranean Diaspora*, 106. Barclay is able to distinguish between three different levels of assimilation among the Jews of Egypt; see ibid., 103–24. Cf., however, Levine, *Judaism*, 28, who believes that there were very few Jews who integrated into Greco-Roman society, and Safrai, "Relations," 185, who states that we have no reason to believe that Jews who deliberately rejected Judaism "formed large circles or set up influential trends in Hellenistic Judaism."

58 See Barclay, *Mediterranean Diaspora*, 60–71, on the issue of legal status among the Alexandrian Jews.

59 Kerkeslager, "Jewish Identity." Cf., however Hengel, *Judaism: 2*, 51, n. 138, who suggests that the text refers to someone who has performed epispasm. On epispasm, see pp. 72–3.

60 Kerkeslager, "Jewish Identity," 32, concludes by stating that "the papyrus implies a period and a setting in which some Jews had reconciled the marks of Jewish identity with participation in the institutions of Greek identity." Cf. Hengel, *Judaism: 1*, 66, who ascribes great importance to the gymnasium in explaining the fusion of Hellenistic and Jewish culture in Alexandria.

61 See Barclay, *Mediterranean Diaspora*, 67.

62 Kerkeslager, "Jewish Identity," 33.

63 Barclay, *Mediterranean Diaspora*, 127–32.

64 Ibid., 132–8.

65 Ibid., 149.

66 Levine, *Judaism*, 27–8, states that "[a] conceptual mistake made frequently in the past equates Hellenization and assimilation. To assume a degree of Hellenization has often been construed as the Jews' loss of national or religious identity in favour of something else." Kraabel, "Questionable Assumptions," 458–9, finds no indications of assimilation from the excavated synagogues of Ostia, Stobi, Sardis or Dura. Even though pagan symbols are used "with boldness to express biblical themes," they are not used to "create some Judaeo-pagan hybrid religion."

67 Levine, *Judaism*, 46–61. See also Rajak, "Hasmoneans," 265–71.

68 Levine, *Judaism*, 93.

69 *A.J.* 12.138–44.
70 Hengel, *Judaism: 1*, 277–8, 292–302.
71 Hengel, "Interpretation," 220, states that "[i]t is clear . . . that the Hasmoneans did not stop the process of Hellenization in Palestinian Judaism, but as soon as they came to power rather carried it further."
72 Hengel, *Judaism: 1*, 179.
73 Ibid., 292. See also Sanders, *Judaism*, 22, who states that "[t]he fall of the Acra terminated any lingering hopes that the Hellenizers still had. Jewish distinctiveness would be maintained, circumcision would be kept, and the Mosaic law would be enforced." Levine, *Judaism*, 44, 93–4, points to the fact that no images appear on Hasmonean coins and suggests that the restricted use of figural art by Jews until the second century CE might have been a result of Hasmonean ideology. In addition, there are several other indications of observance, such as the presence of a large numbers of ritual baths. Dunn, "Issue," 299, states that, "in the piety crystallized and cherished among the Maccabees and their successors, zeal for the law, devotion to the covenant and loyalty to the nation had become inextricably interwoven."
74 Berger and Luckmann, *Social Construction*, 126.
75 Ibid., 122–34. By that term Berger and Luckmann refer to different mechanisms which legitimate symbolic universes, such as mythology, theology, philosophy and science. Closely connected to these are two applications of universe-maintaining conceptual machinery, namely, therapy and nihilation. Therapy aims at preventing the individual from leaving a given universe and functions by institutional arrangements such as exorcism, psychoanalysis, pastoral care, etc. Nihilation, on the other hand, functions by *denying* everything outside one's own universe. This can be done by giving the deviant reality a negative ontological status.
76 Ibid., 111.
77 Ibid., 172.
78 Cf. Barclay, *Mediterranean Diaspora*, 92, who understands the term as "social contacts, social interaction and social practices."
79 Ibid., 92–8.
80 See Rutgers, *Hidden Heritage*, 34–8, for a critique of Barclay's model. Apart from what seems to be a general skepticism concerning the use of models, one of Rutgers's main objections to Barclay's specific model is that it does not function as a tool for measuring diachronic change. While Rutgers may be right concerning this, his critique still seems somewhat unfair, since Barclay never claims his analysis has the ability to function as a diachronic instrument. For our purpose that aspect is beside the point: the diachronic dimension is not salient to the present study. Even Rutgers admits that Barclay's analysis takes into account "the dynamics of a particular situation." For a positive evaluation of Barclay's use of models, see Sanders, *Charisma*, 143–4, or "Early Christianity," 497–8.
81 Gordon, *Assimilation*, 69–70.
82 Ibid., 71.
83 Stambaugh and Balch, *Social World*, 63–4; Stegemann and Stegemann, *Jesus Movement*, 34–5.
84 Gordon, *Assimilation*, 71.

85 Cf. Barclay, *Mediterranean Diaspora*, 92, who believes that Jewish slaves in Greek households were highly assimilated even if they were acculturated to a very limited extent. It is hard for me to understand such a use of the term. How is it possible to think of an individual being assimilated into a society while having a very limited knowledge of, as Barclay puts it, "the linguistic, educational and ideological aspects of a given cultural matrix"?

86 Gordon, *Assimilation*, 80.

87 Ibid., 81.

88 Ibid., 79.

89 Ibid., 81.

90 Berger and Luckmann, *Social Construction*, 122–34. See also n. 75 above.

91 The general meaning of ζευγίζω is "to join" or "to fasten together," but in the passive tense more specifically "to be married."

92 On Greek education in general and the gymnasium in particular, see Hengel, *Judaism: 1*, 65–78.

93 Schäfer, *Judeophobia*, 105. See also Feldman, *Jew*, 153–8, on Greco-Roman views of circumcision.

94 See Whittaker, *Jews*, 80–5, for some examples of this.

95 See Rubin, "Decircumcision," for a detailed description of how Celsus' operation was performed and Goodwin, "Uncircumcision," for a description of the modern procedure. Tushnet, "Uncircumsicion," and Gilman, "Decircumcision," deal with uncircumcision in both ancient and modern times, and Hall, "Epispasm," covers epispasm in antiquity.

96 Hall has suggested that this refers to *infibulation* rather than to epispasm, Hall, "Epispasm," 73. This seems to be a rather odd suggestion, since infibulation, as described by Celsus, *presupposes the existence of a foreskin*: "the foreskin covering the glans is stretched forward" (*cutis, quae super glandem est, extenditur*), *Med.* 7.25.2. Cf., however, Hall, "Epispasm," 54, who also states that infibulation could be used by those who had been circumcised. That Jews who wished "to be Greeks even when unclothed," as Josephus puts it in *A.J.* 12.241, all practiced the more or less permanent covering of the glans used by Greek singers, for instance, is not very likely. On infibulation, see Schäfer, *Judeophobia*, 101.

97 The same connection between epispasm and the breaking of the covenant is also evident in 1 Macc. 1:15: ἐποίησαν ἑαυτοῖς ἀκροβυστίας καὶ ἀπέστησαν ἀπὸ διαθήκης ἁγίας.

98 The practice of setting aside *terumot* and *ma'aserot* ("heave offerings" and "tithes") continued even after the destruction of the temple when tithing became a kind of substitute for the sacrificial service, see Oppenheimer, "Terumot," 1027.

99 The discussion in the mishnah concerns under what conditions and for what transgressions the Day of Atonement procures atonement. In the gemara, where R. Yehudah ha-Nasi is referred to, it is clearly stated that the Day of Atonement really atones for epispasm, but only in combination with repentance. It is consequently somewhat misleading when Hall refers to this text as if it implied that the Day of Atonement under no circumstances could procure atonement for epispasm, see Hall, "Epispasm," 75.

100 In *Jub.* 15:25–6 it is even stated that salvation is impossible without circumcision on the eighth day.

101 See Dunn, "Issue," 303–5, for a short overview of the significance of circumcision within Jewish tradition.

102 The discussion in *b. Yebam.* 72a presupposes that the *mashuk*, the one who has drawn his prepuce forward, intends to remain within the boundaries of Judaism while at the same time to cover his circumcision, implying a certain openness to Hellenistic culture. Another possibility, as Hall, "Epispasm," 75, points out, is that the discussion concerns a person who wants to return to a more traditionalistic religious life. On the other hand, a person could actually have been prevented from being circumcised if his brothers had died as a result of circumcision. This could be the case if the child suffered from some hemorrhagic disease such as hemophilia (on the topic of hemophilia in rabbinic literature, see Rosner, "Hemophilia," 833–7). Under such conditions circumcision was forbidden according to *b. Yebam.* 64b. The mishnah on which the gemara is commenting, *b. Yebam.* 70a, originally deals with the question of what abnormalities (uncircumcision or mutilations) exclude a person from being entitled to eat *terumah.*

103 Harris, *Greek Athletics.*

104 Kerkeslager, "Jewish Identity," 20–3.

105 Gordon, *Assimilation*, 77.

106 Barclay, *Mediterranean Diaspora*, 98.

107 Ibid., 96–8.

108 Rex, "Religion," 19.

109 Binder, *Temple Courts*, 266. It is not easy to offer an exhaustive definition of such an ambiguous term as "syncretism," especially since Colpe, "Syncretism," 219, in his dealing with the meaning of the term, "cannot promise any certain results." McGuire, *Religion*, 34, simply defines the term as "the interweaving of new meanings into the traditional meaning system." On a very basic level, syncretism has to do with originally separate religious entities that relate to each other with the formation of new entities as a result. I find nothing that indicates such a development in the case of Antiochus.

110 Waardenburg, "Institutionalization," 28.

111 We recall that Binder considers the term ἄρχων as referring to functionaries at the top of the hierarchical structure, see Binder, *Temple Courts*, 371.

112 Cf. Segal, *Convert*, 89, who points to parallels in the modern secular Jewish community. With reference to the situation in antiquity, Safrai, "Relations," 185, states that there "were indeed individuals who felt drawn to the alien world outside, either because they deliberately rejected Judaism or because they wished to make their way in the surrounding world." As for the general situation, Barclay, *Mediterranean Diaspora*, 323, referring to Josephus, *A.J.* 18.141, and Tacitus, *Ann.* 2.85, among others, finds that "[o]ur sources describe a number of cases of Jews who abandoned the Jewish life-style, or at least crucial aspects of it, in order to ease some social dilemma or gain promotion in society."

113 Barclay, *Mediterranean Diaspora*, 322.

114 Kasher, *Jews*, 77–80. Cf. Smallwood, *Jews*, 361, who believes that Antiochus was a citizen in Antioch and held a magistracy.
115 Barclay, *Mediterranean Diaspora*, 322, states that "[t]his calculated renunciation of Judaism is the most extreme case of assimilation known to us."
116 Sanders, "Early Christianity," 140.
117 This, I believe, is a good example of the dangers involved in reading sources without an overarching theoretical superstructure. To assume that Antiochus represents an isolated case from which it is not possible to make generalizations is in my view a very unlikely proposal, but it is the obvious result of reading the source by itself—as it is written.
118 See Feldman, *Jew*, 82.
119 Barclay, *Mediterranean Diaspora*, 104.
120 Ibid., 105–6; Hengel, "Interpretation," 194.
121 Barclay, *Mediterranean Diaspora*, 321–2.
122 Feldman, *Jew*, 83.
123 Safrai, "Elisha," 668–9. Milton Steinberg's novel *As a Driven Leaf*, about Elisha ben Abuya's way from Judaism to Greek philosophy, is from the perspective of sociology of knowledge a very credible and fascinating presentation.
124 This is also the view of Binder, *Temple Courts*, 266.
125 Hengel, *Judaism: 1*, 66.
126 *Spec.* 2.229–30. Barclay, *Mediterranean Diaspora*, 160–1.
127 Brooten, "Jews," 32.
128 Seland, "Philo," 110.
129 See Niehoff, "Philo's Views," 136, who finds that Philo "generally tends to stress the religious boundaries between Jewish monotheism and pagan idolatry."
130 Mithraism was not exclusively a soldiers' society, but recruitment of new members often took place within such social groupings as the military organization, see Beck, "Mysteries," 177, 179.
131 Gordon, *Assimilation*, 81.
132 While there is no general biblical prohibition against intermarriage—Exod. 34:15 and Deut. 23:2–9 prohibit intermarriage with Canaanites only—during the period following the destruction of the temple in 586 BCE, marriage with Gentiles in general became a threat to Jewish identity; see also Ezra 9:12, 10:1–44; Neh. 9:2, 10:28–30. The prohibition against intermarriage with foreign women has its origin in this political situation and was further emphasized during the Hasmonean period, see Cohen, *Beginnings*, 260–1.
133 Sanders, *Judaism*, 236–7.
134 This is the only example of a martyrdom commemorated by both Jews and Christians. On the issue of the transformation of a Jewish martyrdom into a Christian, see Winslow, "Maccabean Martyrs."
135 On the relation between 2 and 4 Macc., see Anderson, "4 Maccabees," 540–1.
136 Schatkin, "Maccabean Martyrs," 98–102. Cf., however, Meeks and Wilken, *Jews and Christians*, 3, who find it more likely that the martyrdoms took place in Jerusalem.
137 Schatkin, "Maccabean Martyrs," 100–1, mentions Malalas, *Chron.*

206–7, which is supplemented in an Arabic version of a topographical description of Antioch, containing information "dating from no later than the sixth century AD (codex Vaticanus Arab. 286, s. XVI–XVII)." In addition to this there is a text, also mentioned by Schatkin, imbedded in a rabbinic version of the martyrdom on pp. 22a–25a of the MS of the "Arabic *Faraġ*-Book of Nissîm Ibn Shâhîn of Kairowân" (see Obermann, "Sepulchre," 253–60), without parallels in other rabbinic sources, in which it is said that this synagogue was the first to be erected after the second temple.

138 On corpse impurity, see Sanders, *Judaism*, 217–18.
139 Schatkin, "Maccabean Martyrs," 104.
140 Ibid., 104; Obermann, "Sepulchre," 265.
141 Rutgers, "Importance," 299–300, 302. See also van Henten, *Maccabean Martyrs*, 79, who also doubts the existence of a Jewish cult of the Maccabean martyrs.
142 Rutgers, "Importance," 299.
143 Sanders, *Judaism*, 218.
144 Charlesworth, *Pseudepigrapha*, 151.
145 Anderson, "4 Maccabees," 537.
146 van Henten, *Maccabean Martyrs*, 82.
147 Gilbert, "4 Maccabees," 318.
148 Barclay, *Mediterranean Diaspora*, 370, esp. n. 63.
149 Charlesworth, *Pseudepigrapha*, 151.
150 Anderson, "4 Maccabees," 534.
151 Barclay, *Mediterranean Diaspora*, 370, see also pp. 448–9 for an account of the scholarly discussion.
152 Eissfeldt, *Old Testament*, 615; van Henten, *Maccabean Martyrs*, 77–8.
153 Goodman, "Olive Oil," 229.
154 See, for instance, Binder, *Temple Courts*, 265.
155 Barclay, *Mediterranean Diaspora*, 256, n. 63.
156 Ibid.
157 Goodman, "Olive Oil," 228–9.
158 Ibid., 230
159 Ibid., 240
160 *m. ʿAbod. Zar.* 2:6.
161 *b. ʿAbod. Zar.* 35b–36a.
162 Goodman, "Olive Oil," 242.
163 Hoenig, "Oil," 66, believes that "the description of Josephus suggests that the repudiation of pagan oil was upheld even by non-observant Jews in the Seleucidean armies."
164 Bockmuehl, "James," 169–79; Barclay, *Mediterranean Diaspora*, 242.
165 Stern, "Jewish Diaspora," 137.
166 Only a few radical Jews inspired either by ideas found in biblical tradition or by Stoicism did not see the temple an indispensable part of religion, see Cohen, "Temple and Synagogue," 310, especially n. 45 for references.
167 Sanders, *Judaism*, 52, 237; Feldman, *Jew*, 48. The practice of temple tax seems to have been instituted by the Maccabees and maintained by the Herodians; see Cohen, "Temple and Synagogue," 311; Stegemann and Stegemann, *Jesus Movement*, 120.

168 Sanders, *Judaism*, 48.
169 On the general use of ἱερόν, see Binder, *Temple Courts*, 122–30.
170 Ibid., 266.
171 Betz, "Essenes," 461. On the history of the Essenes, see also Sanders, *Judaism*, 340–79, and Grabbe, *Judaism*, 491–9.
172 On the cult reform, see Hengel, *Judaism: 1*, 292–302.
173 Ibid., 292.
174 Constructed in analogy with Schiffauer's "Islamization of one's self"; see "Migration," 155.
175 See Shaffir, "Boundaries," 42–9, for an overview of relevant reality maintenance mechanisms in an American ultra-orthodox context.
176 See n. 52 above.
177 Cohen, *Beginnings*, 56.
178 Levine, *Ancient Synagogue*, 99; Binder, *Temple Courts*, 321; Barclay, *Mediterranean Diaspora*, 290.
179 Cohen, *Beginnings*, 57.
180 Downey, *Antioch in Syria*, 109.
181 Kraeling, "Jewish Community," 143. Cf. Meeks and Wilken, *Jews and Christians*, 9.
182 Kraeling, "Jewish Community," 141.
183 For an overview of messianic leaders during the first century, see Gager, "Messiahs," 39–40. For a short survey of the literary evidence of messianism from the Hebrew Bible to the early rabbinical period, see Schäfer, "Diversity," and, for a more comprehensive presentation, Horbury, *Jewish Messianism*. For an extensive discussion of the relation between John the Baptist and Jesus of Nazareth, see Meier, *Marginal Jew 2*, 19–233.
184 See also Acts 21:38.
185 Gager, "Messiahs," 40.
186 Pearson, "Christians," 208–9.
187 Witherington, *Acts*, 369, n. 12, comments that "Cyrene" probably refers to the area of Cyrenaica rather than to the city only, since Cyprus, which is not a city, is mentioned also. This seems quite probable. His suggestion that some of these men were of "African descent (and so Gentiles)" seems more improbable, since the narrative structure of Acts appears to be leading up to the introduction of the mission to the Gentiles.
188 Sanders, *Schismatics*, 153–4.
189 Meeks and Wilken, *Jews and Christians*, 15; Brown and Meier, *Antioch and Rome*, 33; Hill, *Hellenists*, 105–6; Norris, "Artifacts," 249.
190 Acts 6:5. Overman, "God-Fearers," 146–8, has argued that the designation προσήλυτος is not completely unambiguous and that Luke used the word in the same way as the LXX and Philo, namely, as also referring to Gentiles closely allied with the Jewish people but distinct from Jews—that is, strikingly similar to the concept of god-fearer. He argues that it would be nonsense if Luke had meant "convert to Judaism" in Acts 2:10 and 13:43, since proselytes, who are strictly speaking Jews, are here mentioned together with the Jews. While it is probably quite correct that the term carried different meanings, it should, however, be noted that proselyte in the sense of "convert to

Judaism" could be mentioned along with Jews, since proselytes were considered a separate class of Jews, see Feldman, *Jew*, 339–41. See also Goodman, *Mission*, 72–3, who has similarly argued that the term was *becoming* a technical term among Jews for converted Gentiles. Cf., however, Kuhn, "προσήλυτος," who concludes that "contemporary Jewish usage differentiated sharply between προσήλυτοι who had become Jews by circumcision and the σεβόμενοι τὸν θεόν who in spite of their personal piety were still Gentiles according to Jewish estimation."

191 Brown and Meier, *Antioch and Rome*, 33.

192 See Barclay, *Mediterranean Diaspora*, 326, who states that there are indications "that it was not uncommon for such [Christian] Jews to associate with Gentile believers on terms which indicate quite a high level of assimilation."

193 Seland, "Philo," 110.

194 *Spec.* 3.29.

195 Cohen, *Beginnings*, 245.

196 Acts 16:1: "Timothy, the son of a Jewish woman who was a believer; but his father was a Greek." Cf. Eberts, "Plurality," 315, who assumes that "[s]ome Hellenists permitted, even encouraged, intermarriage between Greek-speaking pagans and Greek-speaking Jews."

197 Levine, *Ancient Synagogue*, 97; Richardson, "Augustan-Era," 23.

198 Levine, *Ancient Synagogue*, 97; Richardson, "Augustan-Era," 20. As noted by Levine, *Ancient Synagogue*, 97–8, n. 132, references to synagogues of the Hebrews have been found in Philadelphia (*CIJ* 754) as well as Corinth (*CIJ* 718).

199 Barclay, *Mediterranean Diaspora*, 293; Richardson, "Augustan-Era," 20–1.

200 Ibid., 22.

201 Ibid., 23–8.

202 Hedner-Zetterholm, "Jewish Communities," 137.

203 Ibid., 137, n. 92.

204 Cf. Conzelmann, *Acts*, 47, who suggests that Luke refers to one synagogue "which had a varied makeup." Munck, *Acts*, 58, makes the same interpretation and so does Bruce, *Acts*, 156, while admitting that it is also possible to understand Luke as referring to five, four or two synagogues. Haenchen, *Acts*, 271, notes that, from a syntactical point of view, the groups mentioned fall into two categories. Marshall, *Acts*, 129, argues along the same line and assumes the existence of two synagogues.

205 Levine, *Ancient Synagogue*, 53–4.

206 The diversity of the synagogues of Rome has been demonstrated by Williams, "Structure."

207 Nanos, *Mystery*, 289–336.

208 Acts 5:11; 8:1, 3; 9:31; 11:22, 26; 12:1, 5; 13:1; 14:23, 27; 15:3, 4, 22, 41; 16:5; 18:22; 20:17, 28. Cf. Meeks, *First Urban*, 75–84, who has investigated four models from the environment: 1) the household, 2) the voluntary association, 3) the synagogue, and 4) the philosophic or rhetorical school. While he found several similarities between "early churches" and the assumed models, he finally refuted them all. Instead, he tried to show how the Pauline Christians developed a unique

culture. Kloppenborg, "Edwin Hatch," 237–8, on the other hand, is more inclined to accept the statement that Pauline churches can be fitted into the spectrum of the Greek and Roman voluntary associations. While Ascough, "Thessalonian," has argued that the Thessalonian Christian community was similar to a professional voluntary association, Tellbe, *Synagogue and State*, 93, has recently suggested that the Thessalonian church was organized as a *collegium domesticum*. For an overview of the field, see Ascough, *Formation*.

209 Schmidt, "ἐκκλησία," 528; Schrage, "συναγωγή," 802.
210 This type of synagogue has been labelled *public synagogue* to be distinguished from the *national assembly* and the *semi-public synagogue*, see Runesson, *Origins*, 213–32, 329. For the use of συναγωγή and ἐκκλησία to denote local Jewish assemblies, see, e.g., *Pss. Sol.* 10:6–7. Cf. Horsley, *Galilee*, 339, n. 7.
211 See Schrage, "συναγωγή," 840–1, for further references.
212 See Taylor, "Disciples," 76–82, for an overview of different scholarly interpretations of why the disciples were called "Christians."
213 Stark, *Rise of Christianity*, 7.
214 Sanders, *Charisma*, 136.
215 Tellbe, *Synagogue and State*, 66.
216 Taylor, "Social Nature," 128.
217 Meier, *Marginal Jew 1*, 91.
218 Tellbe, *Synagogue and State*, 66. See Meier, *Marginal Jew 1*, 59–69, on the *Testimonium Flavianum*.
219 See Williams, "Domitian," 202, who states that, "[a]s for the Christian sect at Rome, it is surely too much to assume that the authorities were sufficiently interested in its ethnicity to make a precise distinction between its Jewish and non-Jewish adherents."

4

EVIDENCE OF
INTERACTION

Was sollen wir Christen denn
nun mit diesem verworfenen,
verdammten Volk der Juden tun?
Martin Luther, *Von den Juden und ihren Lügen*

Introduction

In this chapter we are going to address the question of how the Jews
and Gentiles interacted in Antioch. In the previous chapter we
reached the conclusion that there were several different ideas of how
to live a Jewish life guided by the torah; we will now focus on how the
Jews of Antioch related to their Gentile neighbors.

We will begin by looking at the relations between Jews and
Gentiles as regards the prevalent attitudes towards Jews in the
Roman Empire. We will then proceed by studying some texts that
deal specifically with the situation in Antioch and try to get a feeling
of how the events connected to the Jewish War may have affected
these relations negatively. Thereafter we will examine the opposite
aspect: although it is well known that relations between Jews and
Gentiles in antiquity were strained there are indications of a certain
widespread admiration of Judaism and of Gentiles associating themselves with the Jewish communities. We will study the different
ways this could be done within the political/religious system of a
Greek *polis* under the dominance of Rome. Finally, we will look at a
specific and extremely important aspect of Jewish–Gentile relations:
namely, how members of the Jesus movement struggled with the
question of whether and how the present messianic age would affect
their relations with the Gentiles.

Riots and reactions

In a study on anti-Semitism in the Greco-Roman world, *Judeophobia: Attitudes toward the Jews in the Ancient World* (1997), P. Schäfer deals with several Greek and Roman authors from the third century BCE and onwards and focuses on how the origin of the Jews and specific Jewish cultural traits are presented in these texts.[1] Schäfer shows, for instance, how somewhat legendary anti-Jewish traditions about how the Jews were driven out of Egypt were transmitted in literary texts for several centuries. In combination with motifs such as the "impiety," "misanthropy" and "xenophobia" of the Jews, these Exodus traditions were transformed into a powerful anti-Jewish literary tradition with implications even into modern times.[2]

It is true that there was a general distinction between Greeks and barbarians within Hellenistic culture. Among other things, barbarians were considered uneducated, unfriendly to strangers, cruel and by nature slaves, while the Greeks were masters and manifested their superiority through a particular life style.[3] This distinction was transmitted throughout the Greek expansion to newly established *poleis*, and the Hellenistic concept of *paideia* was efficiently disseminated by the educational institutions such as the gymnasium.[4] To a certain extent the negative Greek attitude towards Jews was part of a general negative attitude towards any people not belonging to the pan-Hellenic community and must be understood in the context of one culture trying to avoid being assimilated by another.[5] However, according to Schäfer one must also allow for specific anti-Semitism: that is, "hostility directed at the Jews which distinguishes the Jews from other ethnic groups."[6]

In trying to distinguish between anti-Judaism and anti-Semitism, between justifiable and unjustifiable action taken against Jews, between the legitimate and the illegitimate, Schäfer argues that the motifs mentioned above became part of a process where Jews and Judaism were seen as a constant threat to the civilized, that is, Greek world. He concludes:

> The Jews as the "evil incarnate," denying and perverting in their xenophobic and misanthropic hatred all cherished values of humankind, conspiring against the civilized world—this, I would like to argue, is the allegation which crosses the line from the "justifiable" to the "unjustifiable," from "anti-Judaism" to "anti-Semitism." It is directed against "the" Jews, that is, not only some but all Jews, and it has no regard

for what Jews do and do not in reality—"the" Jews are identified as the outcasts of human civilization. To be sure, it has a "kernel of truth," in that the Jews do separate from others in certain circumstances, but it is precisely this conscious perversion of the "truth," the phobic mystification of the outgroup, which distinguishes the "anti-Semitic" from the "anti-Jewish" attitude. Since it is the peculiar result of the amalgamation of Egyptian and Greek prejudices, one might argue that only the idea of a world-wide Greco-Hellenistic civilization made it possible for the phenomenon we call anti-Semitism to emerge.[7]

A. F. Segal has argued that anti-Semitism was known but not very prevalent during the Hellenistic period and that the anti-Jewish writings are to be seen in the context of a general dislike of foreigners.[8] It is true that one must be aware of the dangers of anachronism when using a designation with such specific meaning attached to it, but what we find here is a phenomenon that is not to be considered within the context of a general xenophobia. The evidence suggests that the Jews were hated and feared to an extent that is not comparable with the attitude felt towards other ethnic and/or religious groups, and it is certainly justified to speak of anti-Semitism in antiquity in the way Schäfer does. We will see further evidence of this in the next chapter.

The texts that Schäfer has used in his study reflect mainly the standpoint of the intellectuals, and, while this certainly provides us with important information about attitudes towards Jews, it is in the streets of the cities of the Diaspora that these attitudes would or would not become operative. In his treatment of intellectual prejudice against the Jews, L. H. Feldman concludes that "[t]he influence of the intelligentsia on rulers or assemblies was, to say the least, minimal."[9] It is probably true, as Feldman states, that the attitudes of Cicero, Seneca or Tacitus were not transformed into anti-Jewish political measures against the Jews, but it is naive to believe that there is no connection between the attitudes of the elite and the manifestations on the streets. The following analysis will surely serve the purpose of showing this.

The incident at the circus

In the sixth-century *Chronicle* of John Malalas we read about an incident at the circus in Antioch that, according to the narrative (*Chron.*

244–5), had devastating consequences for the city and presumably also for the continuing relations between Jews and Gentiles:

> From the first year of Gaius Caesar the Green faction assumed from him licence to do as they chose and rioted in Rome and every city for three years until the end of his reign, for he favoured them. In the third year of his reign, in Antioch in Syria, the supporters of the Blue faction in that city chanted in the theatre against the Greens there. "Time raises up and casts down: the Greens are lechers," while the consular governor, Petronius, was watching the races. There followed a great faction riot and disaster fell on the city. For the Hellenes of Antioch fought with the Jews there in a faction brawl, killed many Jews and burnt their synagogues. When the priest of the Jews in Palestine, named Phineas, heard of this, he collected a large number of Jews and Galileans who were citizens. With about 30,000 of these he came suddenly to the city of Antiochos from the city of Tiberias and killed many there, for he made a single unexpected attack with armed men.

There are several problems involved in the interpretation of this text. Despite the fact that the chronicle has a special Antiochene focus since Malalas was especially familiar with the situation in the city,[10] it seems that this narrative contains several errors.

Malalas describes a pogrom that is triggered by a conflict between supporters of the two factions racing at the arena. The part where Phineas intervenes with 30,000 men is certainly an exaggeration, and, as C. H. Kraeling has noted, the impossibility of such an event "jeopardizes the value of the story as a whole."[11] Unfortunately, there are additional problems with Malalas' account, since it seems as if the references to the faction riot are also erroneous. It is true that there was an area for horse- and chariot racing in Daphne at least from the late third century BCE, and that a hippodrome modeled on the Circus Maximus existed from the middle of the first century BCE.[12] It is likewise true that the history of Antioch records several riots,[13] but there is not one single piece of evidence in favor of the existence of factions of the Roman kind before the fourth century in any of the eastern cities of the empire.[14]

It is hard to determine the historicity of one aspect in a narrative where the author seems to have got almost every other verifiable detail wrong. There are some circumstances, however, that allow a certain plausibility regarding a riot in Antioch at this time. In Alexandria there had certainly been riots. Since the summer of 38 CE, the situation in Alexandria had been catastrophic for the Jewish population. The visit of the newly appointed Jewish king, Agrippa, resulted in street violence which soon got out of control, and an atrocious period followed. It was only when Gaius was assassinated early in 41 CE that peace could be re-established. In connection to this, two delegations from Alexandria were sent to Rome in order to try to restore the political status of the Jewish community. This resulted in an edict from Gaius' successor, Claudius, which on the one hand confirmed the right of the Jewish population to exercise their religion and requested that the Alexandrians behave in a friendly manner towards the Jews.[15] On the other hand, the edict finally put an end to the ambition of some strata within the Jewish community to integrate into the social and political life of the city—the Jews are not "to aim at more than they have previously had" (*CPJ* 153.88–90). The experiment of combining Judaism and Hellenism was over.[16]

These events probably had some bearing on the political climate in Antioch.[17] According to Josephus, Claudius' edict was also sent to Syria, and if this is true it could imply similar conditions there.[18] In the papyri version of the edict it is stated that the Jews in Alexandria were now forbidden to "bring in or invite Jews coming from Syria or Egypt" (*CPJ* 153.96–7), which is an indication that there had been contacts. There are reports from Syria of several other incidents in the period from 39 to 44 CE, and it is thus not unlikely, as J. M. G. Barclay suggests, that they may have been triggered by the Alexandrian pogrom.[19] The period was also troublesome as a result of Gaius' plan to invade Judea and erect a statue of himself in the Jerusalem temple.[20] The project failed thanks to the hesitation of Petronius, legate of Syria, to carry out Gaius' orders, but when the legions were assembled and were waiting in Antioch it is reasonable to assume that Jewish protests may have stirred up the feelings of the Gentile community.

In the edict Claudius also orders the Jews not "to intrude themselves into the games presided over by the *gymnasiarchoi* and the *kosmetai*" (*CPJ* 153.92–3). This has been understood as a parallel to Malalas's account of the incident at the arena in Antioch,[21] but a more probable interpretation is that the text refers to the fact that the games were originally intended for the citizens of Alexandria and were thus connected to the issue of the striving for citizen rights in that city.[22] If there was a riot in Antioch in 40 CE, it may have been connected to a similar situation rather than to circus factions, which is also suggested by Josephus' report of Claudius' having sent the edict to Syria.

We can thus conclude that the essence of Malalas's narrative reflects a plausible scenario in an Antiochean context. It is clear that this is an expression of anti-Jewish feelings. Irrespective of the fact that the Jews made up a considerable part of the population and were usually tolerated, and to some extent even assimilated, tolerance could easily be transformed into hatred. We can also notice two official attitudes towards Jews that may have contributed to the behavior of the masses. On the one hand, during the reign of Gaius, the official attitude in a way legitimated violence against Jews; on the other hand, Claudius also rebuked the Gentile faction in the Alexandrian conflict. It is easy to imagine what consequences this may have had on the relations between Jews and Gentiles on an everyday basis.

Apart from the incident in 40 CE, the period up to the outbreak of the Jewish War in 66 CE seems to have been characterized by comparative tranquillity for the Jews in Antioch. Josephus even reports that, when enmity between Jews and Gentiles increased in Syria as a result of the rebellion in Palestine, the inhabitants of Antioch, Sidon and Apamea spared the Jews. In *B.J.* 2.479 Josephus attributes rather noble feelings to the inhabitants of Antioch—he believes that "their pity for men who showed no revolutionary intentions" prevented them from killing or imprisoning a single Jew. In reality it is possible that the presence of the Roman legions and King Agrippa had a restraining influence on both sides.[23] Peace would not last for long, however.

Antiochus, Titus and the Jews in Antioch

In connection with the Jewish War of 66–70 CE Josephus, in *B.J.* 7.46–53, reports a series of incidents starting with what seems to have been an ancient equivalent of Crystal Night:

> Now just at the time when war had been declared and Vespasian had recently landed in Syria, and when hatred of the Jews was everywhere at its height, a certain Antiochus, one of their own number and highly respected for the sake of his father, who was chief magistrate of the Jews in Antioch, entered the theatre during an assembly of the people and denounced his own father and the other Jews, accusing them of a design to burn the whole city to the ground in one night;

he also delivered up some foreign Jews as accomplices to the plot. On hearing this, the people, in uncontrollable fury, ordered the men who had been delivered up to be instantly consigned to the flames, and all were forthwith burnt to death in the theatre. They then rushed for the Jewish masses, believing the salvation of their native place to be dependent on their prompt chastisement. Antiochus further inflamed their fury; for, thinking to furnish proof of his conversion and of his detestation of Jewish customs by sacrificing after the manner of the Greeks, he recommended that the rest should be compelled to do the same, as the conspirators would thus be exposed by their refusal. This test being applied by the Antiochenes, a few submitted and the recalcitrants were massacred. Antiochus, having next procured the aid of troops from the Roman general, domineered with severity over his Jewish fellow-citizens, not permitting them to repose on the seventh day, but compelling them to do everything exactly as on other days, and so strictly did he enforce obedience that not only at Antioch was the weekly day of rest abolished, but the example having been started there spread for a short time to the other cities as well.

We have already dealt with parts of this text in the previous chapter when we looked for evidence of a group of Jews wanting to leave Judaism, but, in our present dealing with the text, it is its significance for our understanding of the relations between Jews and Gentiles that we are highlighting.

When trying to explain the sudden violence against the Jewish population, it is not sufficient to refer only to the revolt in Palestine. Josephus connects the outbreak of violence with Vespasian's arrival in Syria in 67 CE, which probably meant Antioch, since the Roman army was located there. Antiochus may even have been an officer in that army. It is also evident that the "Antiochus case" carries socio-psychological overtones. As he was a "convert" from Judaism to Greco-Roman society, the political pressure on Antiochus to prove loyal to Rome must have been extremely heavy. Antiochus' ambition to force the Jews to submit to such a devastating test of loyalty is probably also to be seen in the context of the political situation. It is only natural that the Gentile community of Antioch feared the vast Jewish population: when the Jews rioted in other places, the issue of loyalty became urgent.[24] It is also possible that some Antiocheans had actually been involved in the war in Palestine, since the Romans sometimes supplemented their legions with auxiliary forces that were in large part recruited from Syria.[25]

But the consequences of Antiochus' accusations and the readiness of the Antiochean population to take part in the massacre is intelligible only when seen against a profound fear and hatred of "Jews." Here we find the practical consequences of the literary motifs of *xenophobia/misanthropy/amixia*: the concept of Jews representing a life hostile to humankind and therefore threatening "ordinary" society. It is in this context that the ban against the Sabbath is to be understood. It is the intolerable strangeness of the Jews combined with accusations of *xenophobia/misanthropy/amixia* that this cultural matrix turned into a "monstrous conspiracy against humankind and the values shared by all civilized human beings."[26]

For the Jews in Antioch things got even worse when a fire really did break out. This would have led to an atrocity of enormous dimensions had it not been for the intervention of the Roman authorities, who, according to Josephus, instituted inquiries and found the Jews innocent of all accusations.[27]

This illustrates that, while the masses of Antioch needed few excuses to start massacres, Roman authorities usually acted in favor of preserving the special status of the Jewish community.[28] Riots and massacres did not serve Rome's purpose well. This can be seen in several texts. In *A.J.* 12.120, a text we also dealt with in the previous chapter, Josephus reports about Jewish privileges in Syria.

> [Seleucus Nicator] gave orders that those Jews who were unwilling to use foreign oil should receive a fixed sum of money from the gymnasiarchs to pay for their own kind of oil; and, when the people of Antioch proposed to revoke this privilege, Mucianus, who was then governor of Syria, maintained it.

Mucianus was governor of Syria in 67–69 CE, and Barclay suggests that this incident took place during the troubles just mentioned.[29] This seems very plausible, but the general context of Josephus' account is of minor importance for the moment. What is striking is that the people of Antioch wanted this Jewish privilege revoked, *while Roman authorities instead confirmed its validity.*

In *B.J.* 7.96 Josephus reports another similar incident in connection with the end of the Jewish War. After having conquered Jerusalem, Titus "exhibited costly spectacles in all the cities of Syria through which he passed, making his Jewish captives serve to display their own destruction." Such spectacles most certainly took place also in Antioch, even though Josephus does not state that explicitly.[30] When the people of Antioch heard that Titus was approaching, they hastened to meet him, not only men, Josephus reports, but also women and children. He continues in *B.J.* 7.102–4:

> And when they beheld him approaching, they lined the road on either side and greeted him with extended arms, and invoking all manner of blessings upon him returned in his train; but all their acclamations were accompanied by a running petition to expel the Jews from the town. Titus, unmoved by this petition, listened in silence to what was said; but the Jews, uncertain as to his opinion and intentions, were kept in deep and distressing alarm.

Then Titus left, but on his arrival shortly afterwards he was invited to the theater where the population had now gathered (*B.J.* 7.108–11):

> Once more they persistently pressed and continuously entreated him to expel the Jews from the city, to which he pertinently replied: "But their own country to which, as Jews, they ought in that case to be banished, has been destroyed, and no other place would now receive them." So relinquishing their first request the Antiochenes turned to a second, petitioning him to remove the brazen tablets on which were inscribed the privileges of the Jews. But this, too, Titus refused, and leaving the status of the Jews of Antioch exactly as it was before, he set out for Egypt.

Apart from the clear tendency in Josephus' narrative to present Titus in a favorable light, the essence of the story makes a credible impression,[31] and we notice again how Rome protected the Jews of Antioch and confirmed the validity of their time-honored privileges.

We must ask ourselves what consequences this may have had in everyday situations. Antioch was originally a Greek city, and above we noticed a certain anti-Semitic tradition among Greek authors. We have also seen examples of how this could express itself. Demands for having the Jews expelled, or at least for revoking their privileges, were raised, and riots and massacres were initiated. Rome intervened and established peace, rebuked the Gentile population, and confirmed time and again the validity of the Jewish privileges. The effect on the relations between Jews and Gentiles must have been considerable—*Rome, conqueror also of Antioch*, protected the misanthropic Jews regarded as the outcast of the Hellenistic world.

This does not mean that Rome could not take a hard line against the Jews. In the Jewish War, the power of Rome made itself clear, echoing Claudius' warning to the Alexandrian Jews three decades earlier: "[i]f they disobey, I shall proceed against them in every way as fomenting a common plague for the whole world" (*CPJ* 153.98–100). As we noted above, Titus "exhibited costly spectacles in all the cities of Syria" (*B.J.* 7.96), using Jewish captives, and Malalas reports that, on the road to Daphne, Titus set up winged bronze figures called cherubims which were supposed to have come from the temple, but most certainly were imitations. The symbolic effect was probably not dependent on their authenticity. On the gate was placed a bronze figure of the Moon with four bulls facing Jerusalem. In Daphne, possibly on the site of a synagogue destroyed to make room for it, a theater was constructed with the inscription *ex praeda ivdaea*, "from the Jewish spoils."[32] These actions are to be seen in the context of a conqueror celebrating his victory, however, and seem not to have been an expression of any specific hatred against the Jews.

In trying to sum up how attitudes against Jews became operative in everyday situations, it would be an oversimplification to describe the relations between Jews and Gentiles in the Syrian cities as wholly antagonistic. Jews had lived in Antioch for hundreds of years, and we noted above that some Jews were structurally assimilated, which implies not only familiarity with the cultural matrix but also primary relationships with members of the host society. There must consequently have existed strong interpersonal relations, at least between some Jews and some Gentiles. On the other hand, the evidence presented above can hardly be interpreted in any other way than that many Jews in Antioch lived under the constant threat of one day being burnt at the stake by a former neighbor.

The paradox of attraction

Converts, admirers and god-fearers

In spite of this disheartening picture of the relations between Jews and Gentiles in Antioch there is, rather surprisingly, evidence of Gentiles who felt drawn to Judaism. Whereas the Greek attitude, with roots in Egyptian traditions, seems to have been explicit, Roman authors present a more complex picture, revealing a certain ambivalence between "dislike and fear, criticism and respect, attraction and repulsion."[33] There are two texts that specifically mention Gentile interest in Judaism in Antioch. We noted in the previous chapter that one of the Hellenistic Jews in Jerusalem, who presumably belonged to the group that began preaching to the Gentiles in Antioch, was "Nicolaus, a proselyte of Antioch" (Acts 6:5). Everything indicates that he was a former Gentile who had become Jewish and now had joined the Jesus-believing Jews in Jerusalem.

The other passage comes from Josephus. In *B.J.* 7.45, he states that the Jews of Antioch "were constantly attracting to their religious ceremonies multitudes of Greeks, and these they had in some measure incorporated with themselves." It is not entirely clear what is meant by this phrase. M. Goodman and Feldman believe that Josephus here refers to god-fearers,[34] while S. J. D. Cohen finds the context better served if the reference is to conversion.[35] I do not intend to deal with the question of whether Judaism during the first century was a missionary religion or not: for the present analysis, this is of little relevance.[36] No one can seriously doubt that Gentiles did convert to Judaism during the first century CE. There may be different views regarding the extent to which this occurred and the reason why it took place, but there is no doubt that it happened.[37]

More relevant for the present discussion is whether there was a group of Gentiles with a clear interest in Judaism who may even have adopted several Jewish customs and who participated in the activities in the synagogue without having converted to Judaism. In two influential articles A. T. Kraabel and R. S. MacLennan have questioned the whole concept of god-fearers. Their main arguments are that no inscriptions indicate the existence of god-fearers, and that the concept has a specific theological role in the narrative of Luke, who more or less invented it in order to show how Christianity legitimately became a Gentile religion.[38] Finally, according to Kraabel and MacLennan, references in Classical Greco-Roman literature are few and are interpreted against the background of Acts.

It is, of course, worth drawing attention to the fact that the terminology was by no means univocal and that one has to be aware of the dangers of letting such a tendentious writing as Acts determine the meaning of a term *that in truth does not even occur in the writings of Luke.* It is also beneficial to be reminded that different theological biases may produce the same kind of exaggerations. Kraabel and MacLennan mention D. Flusser's and M. Hengel's completely opposing interpretations of the supposed high number and great influence of the god-fearers. While Flusser saw in this the overwhelming success of Judaism, Hengel found that the presence of a multitude of god-fearers showed the complete failure of Judaism, which could be corrected only in Christianity.[39]

The main thesis in Kraabel's and MacLennan's articles, namely, that a group of Gentiles traditionally referred to as "god-fearers" did not exist, is, however, not convincing. For instance, the assumption that a group of interested Gentiles, if it existed, must of necessity have left traces in epigraphic remains, and thus the absence of epigraphical evidence must mean the non-existence of such Gentiles, is in itself questionable. As pointed out by J. A. Overman, this argument is mainly *ex silencio*,[40] and besides, if one does not focus so narrowly on the term θεοσεβής, there is epigraphical and papyrological evidence of the phenomenon, as pointed out by Feldman.[41] The Aphrodisias inscriptions from the third century CE, which specifically mention fifty-four god-fearers who appear to be other than born Jews but are still distinguished from three proselytes, is perhaps the best evidence of the existence of a group of Gentiles closely attached to the synagogue and also denoted as θεοσεβεῖς.[42] There remains other evidence. While it may be possible to question some of Feldman's references to Gentile god-fearers, his collection of evidence in favor of the existence of interested Gentiles associated with the synagogue is still impressive.[43] Overman's statement that "there is every reason to assume that the presence of a class of Gentiles associated with the synagogue is an authentic reflection of the diverse composition of diaspora Judaism in the late first century" seems to be a reasonable conclusion.[44]

Cohen has dealt with the complexity of Gentile attitudes towards Judaism in a very credible way.[45] He distinguishes between several ways for a Gentile to show respect or affection for Judaism. Gentiles could, for instance, admire some particular aspect of Judaism. This is sometimes seen in the writings of Greek or Roman authors, who, for instance, express admiration of Moses.[46] Gentiles could also acknowledge the power of the god of Israel by incorporating him in the pantheon. This would be a normal way for anyone within the Greco-Roman religious system to relate to a foreign god. Some Gentiles financially aided the Jews or were conspicuously friendly to them. We know of several Gentile benefactors who were honored by the Jewish communities by being given honorary titles.[47] It is correct, as Cohen states, that the fact that Gentiles supported Jewish communities does not necessarily imply that they had any special affection for Judaism; however, from a social perspective they are to be considered closer to the Jewish community than Gentiles who only acknowledged the power of the god of Israel because they had a friendly relationship with the Jewish community.[48]

Some Jewish practices or rituals seem to have attracted Gentile attention. During the first century CE, at least in the city of Rome, the habit of adopting different Jewish customs seems to have been fairly widespread: Seneca, for instance, reacted against this Jewish influence upon Roman life. In a famous statement, cited by Augustine in *Civ.* 6.11, Seneca states, "the customs of this accursed race have gained such influence that they are now received throughout the world. The vanquished have given laws to their victors."[49] It is possible, as will be argued in the next chapter, that Domitian's measures taken against Jews during the late first century CE were motivated partly by a fear of Jewish influence on Roman culture. This way of relating to the Jewish community is of special relevance for us, since it emphasizes that Jewish behavior need not be an indication of Jewishness.[50] A Gentile who observed Jewish practices could be mistaken for a Jew, and Gentiles could refer to themselves as Jews and be called such by others. From an outside perspective it was not always possible to distinguish between someone *called* a Jew and someone who really *was* a Jew.[51]

Finally, Gentiles could convert to Judaism, which according to Cohen would include three elements: practice of the Jewish laws, exclusive devotion to the god of Israel, and integration into the Jewish community. Such a person would not only be called a Jew but would in a sense also become one.[52] There are, however, indications that may lead us to assume that the status of a convert was somewhat ambiguous. As Feldman states, "[i]t is a mistake, however, to think that the attitude toward proselytes was uniformly favorable."[53]

Ethics, survival rates and the attraction of the Jews

But why did Judaism exercise an influence on Gentile society at all? Feldman has indicated three aspects that attracted Gentiles: namely, the antiquity of Judaism, the cardinal virtues, and Moses as the ideal leader.[54] As we noted at the beginning of this section, this shows that a certain ambivalence existed especially among Roman authors. Jews were hated *and* admired, feared *and* respected, and, as we stated when we dealt with the negative attitudes towards Jews, such attitudes (the negative more than the positive) may have affected even popular strains of the population. While these mainly intellectual opinions about Jews and Judaism may have had an impact on the general population, it seems reasonable to look for a social-scientific explanation as well.

In his attempt to explain the rise of Christianity, R. Stark has among other things pointed to two vital aspects that made Christianity successful in becoming the dominant religious force in the Western world: namely, low mortality and high fertility among the Christians. Stark argues, for instance, that their moral code led to higher Christian survival rates during several severe epidemics during the first centuries CE. Because of a religiously motivated desire to care for the sick, more Christians survived than other Gentiles, who lacked a religious motivation to express mercy. According to Stark, Christianity was better equipped to handle natural or social disasters, since the theological system could provide explanations for human suffering. This, together with a divinely ordained love towards all mankind, led to a more efficient mobilization of human resources. Christians even extended their charity to include Gentiles, and the strong attachments that evolved between such Gentiles and the Christians eventually led to Gentile conversions to Christianity.[55] Regarding fertility, Stark points out that, while birth control, abortion and even infanticide were accepted and even encouraged in Greco-Roman society, Christianity condemned all three. According to Stark this led to higher fertility rates among Christians because more female children survived, which led to a surplus of women in Christian subcultures. Many Gentile women had also been rendered infertile as a result of damage connected to abortions and contraceptive devices and medicines. Abortion often resulted in the death of both the fetus and the mother.[56]

This "Christian moral code" is, of course, nothing but basic Jewish ethics.[57] From this it follows that what may have been effective in the relations between Christianity and Gentile society must likewise have been operative mechanisms in the interaction between Jewish communities and Gentile society. Let us first recapitulate some of the basic social conditions in Antioch. We recall from chapter 2 that Antioch, like every ancient city, was densely overpopulated: this together with sanitation problems and shortage of water created ideal conditions for the spread of infectious diseases. Mortality rates were very high, which can be explained partly by the fact that in populations over 250,000 persons there are always recurrent outbreaks of epidemics. Therefore, any ancient city had to rely on a constant influx of people just in order to maintain its population. The consequence of this is that the big ancient cities were populated to a great degree by recent newcomers, who were uprooted from their original social networks and were consequently strangers to each other. The *collegia* provided the required social networks to some extent, as we noted in chapter 2: fictive kinship for those uprooted from their original families and even fictive polities for those who otherwise were denied the possibility of political activities within the *polis*.

Migration, however, always implied social isolation to some extent. This is partly due to the organization of the *collegia*, which were local associations. Membership in one *collegium* could thus not be transferred to another *collegium* in another *polis*, since there was no inter-*polis* organization. Such trans-city organizations would have been perceived as a threat to the imperial government and would almost certainly be suppressed.[58] Recent newcomers confronted with the harshness of life in the metropolis no doubt existed in a social and religious vacuum.[59] However, in this environment, characterized to such a degree by human isolation and social chaos, the synagogue represented an institution which transcended city borders. The synagogue's role as community center where a wide range of charitable activities took place[60] emphasized exactly the aspects of life that these migrants lacked.

It is reasonable to assume that the social character of the synagogue exerted considerable influence on Gentiles who had recently arrived at the *polis*. We may, for instance, assume lower mortality rates within the Jewish communities compared to those in the general population on account of an organized system of caring for the sick and poor. During epidemics Stark reckons with the possibility that care, even without any medications would have cut mortality rates by at least two-thirds.[61] These effects would have been much more significant when epidemics spread all over the empire, causing society to collapse. However, if one part of the population of Antioch could rely on a social network that had not only the family and home as basis, but also the synagogue and the Jewish community, this would probably show itself also in higher survival rates in the recurring epidemics. In addition, the restrictions against contraceptive methods, abortions and infanticide resulted in higher nativity rates, with the effect that more children reached adulthood, even given the same child mortality rate as in the Gentile population.

We can only imagine what impact this may have had on recent immigrants, lacking every aspect of social fellowship, but also on ordinary inhabitants in the *polis*. Ancient cities were to a high degree characterized by sickness and sudden and violent death. In the midst of all this there was a considerable group of people centered around a common institution and the worship of one single deity who seemed to cause the adherents of the cult to prosper.[62] It is possible that the blessings of the covenant from Deuteronomy 28 were perceived to some extent as a living social reality in Antioch. Apart from a profound and sincere interest in Judaism, we must not overlook the purely social and pragmatic motivation for people to associate with the Jewish community. From the perspective of a Gentile lacking initial social contacts, it would seem to be a very rational decision to associate with the Jewish community, since it could provide a social network of decisive importance. Despite Tacitus' comment in *Hist.* 5.5 that "the Jews are extremely loyal toward one another, and always ready to show compassion, but toward every other people they feel only hate and enmity," it is reasonable to assume that some Gentiles were also embraced by the charitable activities in the synagogue.

Jews, god-fearers and civic authorities

But why was there a class of Gentiles who were apparently interested in both the religious aspects of Judaism and the social intercourse in the Jewish community, but who did not convert to Judaism? If Judaism offered such advantages socially and religiously, why not go the whole way and become part of the covenant of the god of Israel? There are several reasons why conversion to Judaism was not the most natural alternative. For instance, the idea of exclusive worship of one god was foreign to Greco-Roman religious reflection. From the perspective of the Jewish community there is an increasing understanding of the possibility of religious conversion to Judaism from the Hasmonean period onwards,[63] but for most Gentiles embracing the ordinary Greco-Roman religious system the idea of abandoning all other deities for the god of Israel seemed preposterous and unnecessary. Many, as noted above, just incorporated the god of Israel in their pantheon and continued to worship the other gods, but may also have adopted Jewish practices. We must not underestimate the problems involved for a Gentile to convert to Judaism. To become part of the covenant people, a Gentile had to become solely affiliated with Judaism, not only theologically but also socially.[64] This could seriously affect one's social and political career, since much of civic life included participation in cultic activities from which Jews should refrain. Besides, to become a proselyte meant being not really accepted as a Jew by the Jewish community but twice as hated by the Gentile community: both for being a renegade politically and religiously and for being Jewish.

For some Gentiles, however, having the position of god-fearer would be a very attractive alternative, since this could mean having the best of both worlds: that is, maintaining a Gentile social and religious identity but at the same time reckoning on being embraced by the salvation of the god of Israel. As we will see below, many Jews believed that at least some Gentiles would have a share in the world to come.

It is likely that the "god-fearer," to some extent, was a product of the religious/political system in Greco-Roman cities. We may recall from chapter 2 that inhabitants, if not Jewish, were expected to express loyalty towards the *polis*, including the emperor, by participating in official cultic activities and by fulfilling their religious duties on a family level. Negligence to do so could lead to reprisals from the *polis* or from Rome. Anyone in a Greek *polis* who existed in a religious no man's land was in danger of being accused of impiety.[65] During the Classical period, foreigners who lived in a Greek *polis* and wanted to establish a new cult had to seek the permission of the assembly.[66] The same was true even during Roman times. As we recall, a conquered Greek *polis* was principally autonomous, but the assembly acted as the extension of the power of Rome. Accordingly, a Gentile could not neglect his or her obligation to the *polis* and to the emperor. From the reign of Augustus, as M. Tellbe states, "all inhabitants of the Roman empire, including adherents to foreign cults, were expected to make a token gesture of acknowledging Roman gods so as not to jeopardize the *pax deorum* by a failure to perform the established rituals."[67] In addition, Gentiles had to participate in the cult of the *polis* and perform their duties as family members. Only formal conversion to Judaism, if that was possible, would exempt a Gentile-born person from his or her religious obligations.[68]

The Jewish community was well informed about this state of affairs. The only reasonable way of understanding the relation between god-fearers and those communities that welcomed such Gentile admirers in their midst is that the Jews in fact accepted the double loyalties of the Gentiles, since they were not considered formally as Jews. As Goodman has pointed out, the prevalent attitude to Gentile worship of their ancestral deities was tolerance. As long as Gentile worship was kept outside the Land of Israel, Jews in general would have few objections.[69] *Hence, it is most likely that the Jewish communities urged the Gentile god-fearers not to neglect their commitment to the official cult, since accusations of having led Gentiles astray could easily affect Jewish privileges.*[70] *Collegia*, we recall, existed on the condition that they did not violate public law.

There is actually some evidence that could be used to support this. In 1976 the so-called Aphrodisias inscription was discovered by chance in connection with preparations made for the construction of the Aphrodisias museum. The marble block, which dates from the third century CE, contains two lists of names of Jews, proselytes and god-fearers who had all contributed to a memorial.[71] We noted above that this inscription is an important piece of evidence in determining the relationship between god-fearers and the Jewish community. In one listing appear nine names of people who are called god-fearers but at the same time are identified *as members of the city council.*[72] It is thus clear that these Gentile god-fearers managed to combine their engagement in the Jewish community with an official position in the city council *that certainly involved Gentile cultic activities, such as public sacrifices at the openings of all council meetings.*[73] This makes perfect sense only if one assumes that the Jewish community did not oppose Gentile involvement in the official cult as long as they remained Gentiles.

It is possible, but less obvious, that the inscription *CIJ* 766, where Julia Severa is said to have built a synagogue, indicates the same conditions. Local coinage shows that this donor was politically active in the mid-first century CE, and is known to have been a high priestess in the local cult.[74] Nothing indicates that she was a god-fearer in a more narrow sense: she is probably better seen as representing the patron–client system in the Roman world.[75] However, as Cohen has pointed out, one who actually supports the Jews is from a social perspective closer to the Jewish community than one who admires Judaism from a theological perspective.[76] What is important to note, however, is that the Jewish community apparently had nothing against her involvement in the local cult,[77] since they obviously accepted her donations and honored her by publicly acknowledging their gratitude.

We may conclude that there was a rather wide spectrum of relations between Jews and Gentiles in Antioch during the first century CE. While it was possible to cross the boundaries between Judaism and Greco-Roman religion—a Jew could really become a Gentile and *vice versa*—it is evident that this process was not uncomplicated. Due to a certain reluctance from both the Jewish and the Gentile community to accept cultural and religious transmigration, Hellenized synagogues became important places for cultural interaction.[78] In the life of the synagogue, Jews interested in Greco-Roman religions and culture could meet with Gentiles interested in Judaism. Under some specific circumstances this could, however, give rise to serious intra-Jewish debates. We are now going to direct our attention to one such incident.

The incident at Antioch

From Galatians 2:11–14(21) we know of an event that seems to have occurred in Antioch sometime in the early 50s.[79] Paul reports in

Galatians 2:12 that Peter, one of the Jewish adherents to the early Jesus movement, used to eat with the Gentiles, but at the arrival of certain people from James (τινας ἀπὸ Ἰακώβου) "he drew back and kept himself separate for fear of the circumcision faction" (ὑπέστελλεν καὶ ἀφώριζεν ἑαυτόν φοβούμενος τοὺς ἐκ περιτομῆς). This behavior of Peter attracted Paul's wrath, and he rebuked Peter sharply, accusing him of hypocrisy.

This text is of course of great importance for anyone interested in the interaction between Jews and Gentiles, or rather between Jesus-believing Jews and Jesus-believing Gentiles. The complex of problems connected to the interpretation of this text and its relation to other texts, as for example, Acts 15 (which is apparently ignorant of this conflict), is, however, immense. Even though the problem of the incident at Antioch has long occupied scholars, there is virtually no consensus about neither what actually gave rise to the quarrel nor what the result of it was.[80] This can be easily illustrated by studying some important contributions during the last decades.

The scholarly debate

Purity and tithing

J. D. G. Dunn's article "The Incident at Antioch (Gal. 2:11–18)" appeared in 1983. It was motivated by his notion that "there has been remarkably little detailed work done on the incident itself."[81] Dunn argued that table-fellowship between Jews and Gentiles was generally a complicated matter during antiquity and that the main obstacles to unrestricted table-fellowship were the laws concerning *unclean foods*, *ritual purity* and *tithing*. Dunn stated that, because of these laws, there was a tendency within Judaism to avoid social intercourse as much as possible,[82] but concluded that there must have been a broad spectrum of social relations between Jews and Gentiles regardless, and that the degree of social intercourse was dependent to some extent on the degree of the individual's religious observance.

Having evaluated different exegetical alternatives, Dunn suggested that table-fellowship in Antioch involved observance of at least the basic dietary laws, since the Jesus-believing Gentiles were originally god-fearers. The men from James, shocked at what they regarded as too casual an attitude, demanded a higher degree of observance, especially with regard to ritual purity and tithing. According to Dunn, they referred to the earlier agreement made in Jerusalem (Gal. 2: 1–10), where Paul's mission to the Gentiles was agreed upon but where the specific issue of table-fellowship was never considered. Dunn argued that this agreement in no way changed the obligation to torah obedience for the Jesus-believing Jews.[83]

According to Dunn, the reason why Peter suddenly withdrew from the table-fellowship was that "[h]e could not deny the logic of Jerusalem's demand, that a Jew live like a Jew."[84] Continued table-fellowship could therefore lead to a severe loss of authority in relation to Jewish–Christian communities in Palestine. In Dunn's view, Paul's reaction is related to his increasing understanding of the relevance of the principle of justification through faith. It is in fact the incident at Antioch that allows Paul to see that the basic contradiction between traditional Judaism and the principle of justification through faith "rules out not just justification by works of the law, but life lived by law (covenantal nomism) also."[85] It was not possible to live at the same time "in Christ" and "in accordance with the law."

To sum up Dunn's view: the issue at stake, from James's point of view, was the *degree of observance*, especially with regard to ritual purity and tithing. What James's representatives insisted on was that the Jesus-believing Jews in Antioch were to return to a proper torah-obedient behavior. Peter accepts this and withdraws from table-fellowship while waiting for the Jesus-believing Gentiles to adapt to this code of conduct. From Paul's viewpoint this meant a complete contradiction, since the principle of justification through faith had ruled out justification through the torah as well as a life lived by the torah.

In *The Partings of the Ways* (1991) as well as in *A Commentary on the Epistle to the Galatians* (1993), Dunn returned to the incident at Antioch, but seems, in all essentials, to maintain the view of the article outlined here.

Circumcision and table-fellowship

In 1987 P. F. Esler presented a rather different picture in *Community and Gospel in Luke–Acts*. Esler's understanding of the incident at Antioch differs from Dunn's on several decisive points. Esler rejected the idea that a diversity of attitudes concerning eating with Gentiles was prevalent among the Jews of the period. While not claiming that there were no exceptions, Esler, having surveyed various literary and historical evidence, nevertheless presupposed the existence of a Jewish ban against eating with Gentiles. Consequently, the problem at stake cannot have been related to *degrees* of table-fellowship, only "the stark choice between no fellowship and fellowship following circumcision and acceptance of the Jewish law."[86] In Esler's view James demanded that table-fellowship could be maintained only on condition that the Jesus-believing Gentiles were circumcised and thus became Jews, since Jews could eat only with other Jews. The heart of the conflict is thus related to the *status* of the Jesus-believing Gentiles. The reason why James (and Peter) withdrew from table-fellowship was not only theological considerations but also that "such a practice threatened to destroy the boundaries which preserved the separate identity of the Jewish people: their [James's and Peter's] motivations were social and ethnic, as much as theological."[87]

Critique and revision

In 1990 E. P. Sanders made several important contributions to the discussion in the article "Jewish Associations with Gentiles and Galatians 2:11–14." Sanders first pointed out that Dunn's idea that the problem of the incident was related to the Gentiles' ritual impurity, and that the food had not been tithed, rests on incorrect presumptions. It might well be the case that Jews during the first century considered all Gentiles impure, Sanders argued, but this impurity did not affect social intercourse between Jews and Gentiles, since "all Jews, including Pharisees, were impure more or less all the time."[88] Sanders drew attention to the fact that ritual impurity was removed only when one entered the temple, to eat the Passover and the second tithe, and that impurity otherwise was the rule, something which did not affect social intercourse even between Jews. "All the impurity meant," Sanders stated, referring to the Gentiles, "was that they could not enter further into the temple."[89]

Secondly, Sanders commented on Esler's critique of Dunn's idea of a broad spectrum of social relations between Jews and Gentiles, some even involving table-fellowship. Sanders emphasized that Esler's literary evidence, which certainly indicates restrained relations between Jews and Gentiles, does not represent the general Jewish view and is also misinterpreted. He found that the texts Esler put forth indicate rather that it was not the act of eating together which was the problem *but the food itself*. While not denying that there is evidence of significant Jewish separatism, Sanders nevertheless found that Dunn's view, of a broad range of social intercourse which was dependent on the degree of religious observance of the individual, must be maintained. When reaching a conclusion on what might have been the problem in Antioch, Sanders suggested that generally it involved the degree of association as well as the particular food itself. James worried on the one hand that too many contacts could lead to unwanted consequences, while on the other hand, due to a general dislike on his part for eating Gentile food, he might have considered Peter to have been not cautious enough.

Circumcision and oath-taking

In 1994 Esler addressed once more the question of the incident at Antioch in a chapter of *The First Christians in their Social Worlds*. Here Esler adds several important pieces to the picture presented in 1987. Presupposing that Galatians is to be defined as analogous to a *deliberative speech*, Esler argued that we might expect its *narratio* (in which we find the account of "the incident of Antioch") to be of relevance for the whole letter. Since the problem in Galatians is related to circumcision of Gentiles, we can assume that the situation in Antioch in one way or another was similarly related to circumcision. Esler thus maintained the view from 1987.

In 1995 Esler dealt with one further aspect of the conflict at Antioch in the article "Making and Breaking an Agreement Mediterranean Style," where he addressed the decisive question of whether James's action in Antioch was a result of his breaking the earlier agreement or not. According to Galatians 2:9, James, Peter and John, "who were acknowledged pillars," gave to Paul and Barnabas "the right hand of fellowship, agreeing that we should go to the Gentiles and they to the circumcised." If Paul and James reached an agreement on the issue of the mission to the Gentiles, but James later insisted on the circumcision of Jesus-believing Gentiles in Antioch as a condition for continued table-fellowship, James would be seen as having broken that agreement. In an attempt to show how such behavior could be intelligible, Esler presupposed that "the values and meanings shared by contemporary Mediterranean villages are closer to those of the ancient Mediterranean than are those of modern North Americans or Northern Europeans."[90] Accordingly, he employs a model of social interaction from the field of Mediterranean anthropology and suggested that, within a framework of honor and shame, James could break the agreement without losing honor since he had not confirmed the agreement with an oath, merely by the shaking of hands.[91] According to Esler, this reluctance for oath-taking could have been motivated by a general antipathy possibly originating from the teaching of Jesus (Jas 5:12; Matt. 5:33–7). In *Galatians* (1998), Esler continued to argue for this view of table-fellowship and the incident at Antioch.

Christian identity

Quite an opposite view on James is advocated by B. Holmberg, who in the article "Jewish *Versus* Christian Identity in the Early Church" (1998) aimed at interpreting the incident at Antioch as a question of different "self-definitions." Holmberg criticized Esler for operating with what Holmberg labeled "an individualistic and psychologizing model, instead of a more social-scientific one."[92] Furthermore, Holmberg found Esler's proposition that James explicitly demanded circumcision of the Jesus-believing Gentiles, as well as having reneged on the agreement for whatever reason, to be historically improbable. He was consequently not persuaded by Esler's effort to place the incident within a Mediterranean context.[93]

Instead, Holmberg suggested that James demanded a higher degree of observance not on the part of the *Jesus-believing Gentiles* but on that of the *Jesus-believing Jews*, and furthermore a virtual separation of the Christian community into two commensality groups. In Holmberg's view James looked upon Jesus-believing Gentiles as being part of the covenant, but in their own way, while they perceived the proscription to mean that they had been excluded from the covenant people, thus experiencing a strong pressure to become full, circumcised converts to Judaism. To James and Peter, the Jerusalem agreement made no difference in how the Jesus-believing Jews related to the torah, while Paul requested that the demands of a Jewish identity should cede to those necessary for maintaining a common Christian identity.

The need for a different approach

As we can see, suggestions on how to solve the problem with the incident in Antioch are *legion*. The reason for this is, of course, that the text contains several gaps that must be filled in through an act of interpretation. The fact that scholars put forward different and sometimes even contradicting suggestions to solve a given historical problem often emanates from the character of the text: what we want to know is simply not in the text but must be supplemented from outside the text world.

This is evident in the different suggestions of what the incident in Antioch really was about. Was it the degree of observance (Dunn), or the food (Sanders), or the social intercourse (Esler), or identities (Holmberg)? And what did James actually demand and from whom? Was it the Jesus-believing Jews who were the target for James's critique (Holmberg), or the Jesus-believing Gentiles (Esler), or both (Dunn)? Did James explicitly demand that the Jesus-believing Gentiles should be circumcised (Esler), or did he simply suggest a separation of the community into two commensality groups which resulted in an implicit demand for circumcision (Holmberg)?

The different interpretations given by scholars are to some extent a result of assumptions or perspectives on a meta-level, which have arisen from the interpretation of other ancient sources or are the result of modern approaches or models. This emphasizes the fact that the answer to the question "what gave rise to the incident?" is to be found not in the semantic or syntactic aspects of the text but in extra-linguistic circumstances in the *universe of discourse* to which the text refers.[94] Consequently, I intend to offer not a new text commentary on Galatians *but a different interpretative frame* through which the text about the incident at Antioch may be read.

Other circumstances in the text are more explicit, and there are rather uncontroversial aspects of Galatians that may help us direct our search for a plausible context to the incident at Antioch. One specific reference in the letter leads us to assume that it is Jesus-believing Gentiles that are Paul's primary focus. In Galatians 4:8 Paul refers to a time when the addressees "were enslaved to beings that by nature are not gods."[95] This almost certainly refers to the period before the Gentiles became adherents of the Jesus movement, possibly to their former status as god-fearers maintaining the religious obligations to the official religion.

One of Paul's main concerns in the letter is to discourage the Gentile believers from submitting to circumcision. This is specific-ally stated in the passage 5:2–5, where Paul creates a dichotomy between circumcision and Christ. It is evident that the Jesus-believing Gentiles in Galatia have been under some pressure to convert to Judaism. Already in 1:7 we are informed that some advo-cates of what Paul refers to as "another gospel" are confusing the Galatians and, as Paul puts it, "want to pervert the gospel of Christ." In 6:12–13 it is evident that their primary demand has been to force the Galatians to submit to circumcision.[96] The problem Paul is facing in Galatia is thus related to the issue of the status of the Jesus-believing Gentiles within the Jesus movement: are Gentile adherents to be circumcised or not?[97]

Now, circumcision also plays an important part in the Antioch incident, since Paul states that Peter refrained from table-fellowship with the Jesus-believing Gentiles because of fear of the "circumcision faction" (Gal. 2:12). Esler's reading of the rhetorical structure of

Galatians has led him to assume a connection between what is stated in the *narratio* (in which the Antioch incident appears) and issues dealt with in the main part of letter, and he reaches the conclusion that the problem in Antioch was the same as the one Paul encountered in Galatia.[98] His suggestion that it is reasonable to assume a thematic correspondence between the *narratio* and the main part of the letter seems justifiable,[99] and we may thus assume that, since the problem in Galatians is connected to the status of the Gentiles within the Jesus movement as well as the justification of the Gentiles apart from the torah,[100] this was also the problem in Antioch.

It is important to note the eschatological aspect involved in this. As will be evident in the following, the urgency with which the status and salvation of the Gentiles were dealt with indicates that there existed a consciousness of living in the end time. This is also hinted at in Galatians 1:4, where Paul states that Christ has sacrificed himself "to set us free from the present evil age."[101] The eschatological context is also possibly indicated in Acts 15:1 where it is reported that "certain individuals" questioned whether Gentiles could be saved unless they were circumcised, and in 15:5 it is explicitly stated that "some believers who belonged to the sect of the Pharisees" made the same remark. We may thus conclude that the incident at Antioch occurred in a context where the eschatological status of the Gentile adherents to the Jesus movement was at stake.[102]

One way of addressing the issue of what the conflict was actually about would thus be to relate what is stated in the text on a semantic/syntactic level to concepts of the eschatological status of Gentiles within the Judaism of the period. Hence, I will begin by asking how Jews in general understood the relation to the Gentile world in an eschatological perspective and relate the assumed positions of the agents in the conflict to such a common Jewish understanding. By approaching the problem from this point of departure, that is, from a basic Jewish understanding of the Gentiles' destiny in an eschatological context, we may avoid the anachronistic pitfall.

Covenant and conflict

The eschatological status of Gentiles

Generally speaking, a wide range of ideas about the eschatological destiny of the Gentiles seems to have existed at the time of Galatians. The author of *Jubilees* belongs to the more pessimistic faction, predicting the complete destruction of the Gentile nations. In the passage *Jub.* 22:20–2, which deals with intermarriage, the destiny of the Gentiles becomes clear. Jacob is warned against taking a wife from any of the seed of the daughters of Canaan:

> [B]ecause all of his seed is [destined] for uprooting from the
> earth;
> because through the sin of Ham, Canaan sinned,
> and all of his seed will be blotted out from the earth,
> and all his remnant,
> and there is none of his who will be saved.
> And for all of those who worship idols and for the hated ones,
> there is no hope in the land of the living;
> because they will go down into Sheol.

Similar views are evident already within the Bible. Micah 5:9–15, for instance, describes how the god of Israel in the messianic age will purge Israel from foreign elements and how he influences and vindicates the people's rights by punishing the Gentile nations which have violated Israel:[103]

> Your hand shall be lifted up over your adversaries, and all
> your enemies shall be cut off. In that day, says the Lord, I will
> cut off your horses from among you and will destroy your
> chariots; and I will cut off the cities of your land and throw
> down all your strongholds; and I will cut off sorceries from
> your hand, and you shall have no more soothsayers; and I will
> cut off your images and your pillars from among you, and
> you shall bow down no more to the work of your hands; and I
> will uproot your sacred poles from among you and destroy
> your towns. And in anger and wrath I will execute vengeance
> on the nations that did not obey.

In Zephaniah 2:4–15 we read about the divine judgment regarding the Gentile nations, how they are to be destroyed and how the faithful shall plunder their cities and inhabit them. The reason for this is stated in vv. 10–11:

> This shall be their lot in return for their pride, because they
> scoffed and boasted against the people of the Lord of hosts.
> The Lord will be terrible against them; he will shrivel all the
> gods of the earth, and to him shall bow down, each in its
> place, all the coasts and islands of the nations.

We see in these texts a common theme which finds expression not least in the prophetic tradition and describes the judgment regarding the nations for their pride and violence against Israel.[104] Also in other Jewish literature, as we noted above, such views are evident.[105] We may thus conclude that the view that the Gentile nations were ultimately to be destroyed or subordinated to Israel is to be found in different Jewish texts,[106] from the Bible to the sectarian literature of the Essenes in Qumran.[107]

On the other hand, such texts are supplemented by others in which the future salvation of the Gentiles is envisaged. We can thus read in Isaiah 19, after seven chapters of detailed descriptions of the coming judgment, how there will be "an altar to the Lord in the center of the land of Egypt" (19:19); how the god of Israel will send them "a savior, and will defend and deliver them" (19:20); how the Egyptians together with the Assyrians will worship the god of Israel, who will bless them, saying, "[b]lessed be Egypt my people, and Assyria the work of my hands, and Israel my heritage" (19:25). In *1 En.* 10:21, Michael is told that "all the children of the people will become righteous, and all nations shall worship and bless me; and they will all prostrate themselves to me." A common theme is that the Gentile nations in the end will stream to Zion in what has been labeled *the eschatological pilgrimage.*[108] In these texts the Gentiles are often presented as full participants in an eschatological salvation. Isaiah 2:2–3 presents us with the following scenario:[109]

> In days to come the mountain of the Lord's house shall be established as the highest of the mountains, and shall be raised above the hills; all the nations shall stream to it. Many peoples shall come and say, "Come, let us go up to the mountain of the Lord, to the house of the God of Jacob; that he may teach us his ways and that we may walk in his paths."

Post-biblical literature displays the same theme. In Tob. 13:11, for instance, we find a similar expectation:[110]

> A bright light will shine to all the ends of the earth; many nations will come to you from far away, the inhabitants of the remotest parts of the earth to your holy name, bearing gifts in their hands for the King of heaven. Generation after generation will give joyful praise in you, the name of the chosen city will endure forever.

138

These few examples indicate that the Judaism of the first century CE probably did not have *one* view of the eschatological destiny of the Gentiles and certainly not a predominantly negative one. In biblical, pre-rabbinic, and even Tannaitic literature,[111] where a positive attitude predominates,[112] we find different solutions regarding what will happen to the Gentiles. Discussing "eschatological situations," P. Fredriksen finds that the material can be clustered around two opposite poles, ranging from destruction to salvation,[113] and, having noted that *Jub.* 15:26–32 pictures the Gentile nations as being destined for destruction, T. L. Donaldson notes that "[m]ore hopeful and optimistic attitudes towards those outside the covenant are also present within the literature of the period."[114] Sanders has found six discernible predictions about Gentiles in biblical and post-biblical literature.[115] It is worth noting that several of these are to be found within the same literary work.[116] It seems absolutely clear that the earlier prevailing view, in which it was claimed that biblical religion in the age of the prophets had turned corrupt during post-exilic Judaism and was overwhelmingly negative towards the Gentiles (and in this respect was corrected by Jesus), is impossible to sustain, something which has been emphatically pointed out by Sanders.[117]

The fact that there were *both* positive and negative traditions about Gentiles has an important bearing on the Antioch incident. The early Jesus movement certainly seems to have been influenced by traditions with a positive attitude towards Gentiles. This becomes evident in the fact that the movement was a missionary one. "[T]he overwhelming impression is," Sanders states, "that Jesus started a movement which *came to see the Gentile mission as a logical extension of itself.*"[118] In other words, something in the words and/or actions and/ or attitudes of Jesus seem to have convinced his disciples that following Jesus was *not* incompatible with a positive view of the salvation of the Gentiles. Exactly what Jesus thought about Gentiles and their eschatological relation to Israel or of eschatology in general is, of course, way beyond the scope of this study,[119] but there can be no doubt that the first adherents of the Jesus movement found missionary activities directed towards Gentiles as being a vital part of the ideology of the movement.[120]

As we have seen, a positive attitude was generally not foreign to Judaism—many Jews probably thought that at least some Gentiles were to be embraced in some way by the eschatological salvation of Israel.[121] Jesus and the early Jesus movement would have been no exception. On the other hand, again in Sanders's words, "[w]e understand the debates in early Christianity best if we attribute to Jesus no explicit viewpoint at all."[122] Nothing indicates that Jesus formulated a specific theological program for the inclusion of the Gentiles. If, however, we assume that he confirmed that Gentiles were to be embraced by the final salvation, it is not strange that within the early Jesus movement *different* concepts developed of how to relate to Gentiles and of how the actions of the god of Israel, through Christ, would also relate to the nations of the world. As a result of an increasing identification of Jesus as the Messiah, the issue of the salvation of the Gentiles became more and more intense. The awareness of living in a period in history when the final intervention was about to take place triggered specific strata within the common religious tradition, not least discourses dealing with the future destiny of the Gentile nations. Ideology had to be transformed to social reality, and, since this process was dependent on existing concepts of salvation and of Gentiles, we must regard some aspects of the concept of salvation within the Judaism of the first century CE.

A covenant for Gentiles?

The foundation of the relation between Israel and its god was the covenant. In his monumental work on Palestinian Judaism, E. P. Sanders reached the conclusion that the common pattern in all surveyed literature can be described in terms of *covenantal nomism*. In this system, the god of Israel rewards obedience and punishes transgressions. However, since the torah provides means of atonement, the covenantal relationship can thus be maintained or, when needed, re-established, but, even more important, *everyone living within the boundaries of the covenant and remaining in the covenant through obedience and atonement will be saved!* [123] This statement seems to have been true for the Tannaitic rabbis, the Qumran community and probably every other kind of Judaism of the period.[124]

This soteriological system was, of course, for Jews only. Exactly how the Gentiles would be saved is less clear. Were they perhaps expected ultimately to convert to Judaism? Having analyzed several texts dealing with the eschatological pilgrimage, Donaldson points to the fact that there is no indication that Gentile men were to undergo circumcision, while some texts imply torah obedience.[125] At the same time it is nowhere explicitly stated that Gentiles are to be exempt from the torah,[126] something that reveals a certain ambiguity in connection to the issue of Gentile salvation. This ambiguity could imply, Donaldson suggests, that the conversion of the Gentiles is taken for granted.[127] In connection with this Fredriksen has, rightly I think, pointed out that a Gentile who has converted to Judaism *is no longer to be considered Gentile*. One must, according to Fredriksen, distinguish between *moral* and *halakhic* conversions. Gentiles who turn to the god of Israel and, from a Jewish standpoint, cease worshiping idols are still Gentiles. The saved Gentiles in texts dealing with the eschatological pilgrimage of the Gentiles are consequently saved *as Gentiles*.[128] This is the conclusion Donaldson finally reaches, stating that "this strand of Jewish eschatological tradition tended to anticipate the inclusion of the Gentiles *as Gentiles*."[129]

Included in what? Could it be argued that these Gentiles were included in the *covenantal* community of Israel? There are several factors that speak against this as being the general Jewish view. We recall that Donaldson found no indication that male Gentiles who came to Zion were to undergo circumcision. It is highly unlikely that Jews in general could imagine that any man could be included in the covenant without circumcision.[130] It is true that N. J. McEleney has argued that it was possible to convert to pre-rabbinic Judaism without being circumcised,[131] and that Sanders, who believes that circumcision was generally regarded as an essential part of Jewish practice, reckons with the possibility that not every Jewish community required circumcision of converts.[132] However, McEleney's standpoint has been adequately refuted by J. Nolland, who concludes that "none of the texts brought forward stand scrutiny as firm evidence for a first-century Jewish openness to the possibility of accepting . . . a convert to Judaism who felt unable to undergo circumcision."[133] We must conclude that, if there were Jewish communities who accepted uncircumcised converts, they have left no traces.

In general the view must be maintained that the majority of Jews during the first century CE found a strong connection between male circumcision and covenantal nomism. We may recall the discourse about epispasm from the previous chapter, where I concluded that, if a man wanted to leave Judaism to become completely assimilated to the Gentile society, the best way would be to have his prepuce re-created. *There was an immediate connection between circumcision and covenantal theology*. Several texts from different periods—pre-rabbinic, Tannaitic and Amoraic—all establish a strong connection between epispasm and the breaking of the covenant of Abraham.[134] No uncircumcised male, not even a Jew who had been prevented from being circumcised due to a hemorrhagic disease,[135] was allowed to take part in the Passover meal,[136] which is permeated with covenantal theology, as stated in Exodus 12:48:

> If an alien who resides with you wants to celebrate the Passover to the Lord, all his males shall be circumcised; then he may draw near to celebrate it; he shall be regarded as a native of the land. But no uncircumcised person shall eat of it.

Jubilees 15:26 even attributes relevance to the point of time for the circumcision, a standpoint that must have made conversions impossible:

> And anyone who is born whose own flesh is not circumcised on the eighth day is not from the sons of the covenant which the Lord made for Abraham since [he is] from the children of destruction.

This certainly reflects a rather extreme standpoint, but nevertheless reveals something of how seriously this biblical commandment was taken. In *Jub.* 15:33–4 the author predicts how the "sons of Israel" will deny the ordinance of circumcision in the future and thereby abandon the covenant. For this sin there will be no forgiveness. This, together with the texts dealing with epispasm, indicates that some Jewish groups existed on the fringe of Judaism and that some Jews had left Judaism and ceased to circumcise their sons, something which is in accordance with the results of the analysis in the previous chapter. Other Jews, like the author of *Jubilees*, evidently considered this as a threat. The reaction is not incomprehensible.

It is evident that, while there certainly were traditions which were positive to the eschatological salvation of the Gentiles, the question of *how* this would come about had not been reflected upon. Quite naturally, Jewish theologians had been occupied with creating a concrete soteriological system for the present. By the first century CE, "covenantal nomism" was the common pattern of religion. By living in a covenantal relationship with the god of Israel, that is, by obeying the torah and by using the means of atonement provided by it and relying on the mercy of the god of Israel, Jews thought that they would ultimately be saved. On the one hand, the covenant provided salvation for those within; on the other hand, the covenant was for Jews only.

This is the ideological context in which the incident at Antioch took place. Thus, when the early Jesus movement was constructing a pragmatic solution to the issue of how to relate to the Gentiles, it had to base its work on the building blocks from this symbolic world. Let us now turn to the prolegomena of the conflict—*the apostolic council in Jerusalem.*

The agreement at Jerusalem and the apostolic decree

Most scholars believe that Galatians 2:1–10 basically relates the same incident as the one in Acts 15,[137] and this is also my assumption in the following discussion. According to Acts 15:1, "certain individuals" came from Judea "teaching the brothers, 'Unless you are circumcised according to the custom of Moses you cannot be saved'" (ἐὰν μὴ περιτμηθῆτε τῷ ἔθει τῷ Μωϋσέως, οὐ δύνασθε σωθῆναι). This resulted in discussions and debates, and it was decided that a delegation from Antioch should go up to Jerusalem "to discuss this question with the apostles and the elders" (15:2). *It is thus the soteriological status of the Gentiles that is on the agenda.* According to 15:5, those in Jerusalem who most vigorously argue for Paul's case, against "some believers who belonged to the sect of the Pharisees," are Peter and James—the latter, however, introducing some regulations, the so-called *apostolic decree*, to be kept by the Jesus-believing Gentiles.

This narration stands in sharp contrast to Paul's account. According to Galatians 2:2, Paul went to Jerusalem together with Barnabas and Titus. In Jerusalem some "false believers" (2:4) wanted Titus circumcised, while Paul "did not submit to them even for a moment" (2:5). In a statement, hard not to understand as ironic and bitter,[138] Paul makes clear that "those who were supposed to be acknowledged leaders" (τῶν δοκούντων εἶναί τι) did not impose anything on him (2:6). Instead the representatives reached an agreement of divided areas of responsibility. Having recognized "the grace that had been given to me," Paul states, "they gave to Barnabas and me the right hand of fellowship, agreeing that we should go to the Gentiles and they to the circumcised" (2:9).

It is certainly not easy to evaluate the information in these texts. Both texts are far from being objective accounts of a historical incident. Luke is occupied with defending the mission to the Gentiles and presents us with a rather harmonious situation where James becomes the most anxious spokesman for the circumcision-free mission.[139] On the other hand, Paul's version of the story has a specific function within the overarching rhetoric of the whole letter.[140]

There may, however, be some general reasons to give more credence to Paul's version.[141] The text is earlier than Luke's, which in itself is no guarantee for historical accuracy, but Paul was actually involved in the course of events and had thus immediate access to what really happened.[142] At the same time, "what really happened" is, of course, from Paul's perspective. He naturally relates those parts relevant to him in a way that serves his purposes. But the insight that we are dealing with a rhetorical discourse does not have to lead to a complete repudiation of Galatians as a historical source, as suggested by R. G. Hall.[143] Esler has, for instance, pointed out, in his critique of Hall, that much of what Paul says in Galatians 1:13–2:14 could be checked, since it was part of the public domain.[144] Paul was not alone in having direct access to what had happened. Esler also claims that one must take into consideration the nature of Paul's audience. They are addressed in a way ("brothers," "members of God's family," etc.) which shows that they were not "some amorphous body of citizens unrelated to him [Paul]," which leads Esler to the conclusion that "by Mediterranean standards it would have been disgraceful to dissemble to persons such as these."[145]

We are thus in possession of two sources to the apostolic council; as we are well aware of the rhetorical component in Galatians as well as the harmonizing tendency in Acts, we can extract some information about the historical situation. As for the use of Galatians as a historical source, we can state that, irrespective of the function of the text about the apostolic council and the subsequent incident in the rhetorical structure of the letter it certainly reflects a historical nucleus.[146] *Both accounts of the apostolic council contain a common denominator; the new situation needs halakhic clarification.*

In relation to the prevalent views of Gentiles and the soteriological function of the covenant, this is hardly surprising. The Jesus movement was convinced that the end of the present age was at hand. Consequently, the question of the Gentiles had to be solved, but exactly what was agreed upon is in fact very hard to decide. Both Luke and Paul seem to agree that circumcision and a general obedience to the torah were not to be imposed on the Jesus-believing Gentiles and that the areas of responsibility should be divided up. Acts 15:20, 28–9, adds the four prohibitions,[147] known as the apostolic decree, while Paul in Galatians 2:6 specifically states that the Jerusalem leaders contributed nothing to him (ἐμοὶ γὰρ οἱ δοκοῦντες οὐδὲν προσανέθεντο). What he actually refers to here is not entirely clear. What is clear, however, is that both parts agreed that the coming of the eschatological kingdom also involved an active mission directed towards Gentiles.

The predominant view is that it is hardly likely that this fourfold prohibition was originally part of the Jerusalem agreement but instead in some way reflects the reality of the Lukan community.[148] Contrary to this consensus, M. D. Nanos has suggested *that Paul both knew of and taught the apostolic decree.*[149] This would place Paul firmly within the Judaism of the first century. If it can be demonstrated that Paul and James were in agreement about the apostolic decree, this would rule out several suggestions regarding what caused the incident in Antioch.

Nanos suggests that a halakhah that governed the relation between Jews and god-fearers was operative during the first century, and that the apostolic decree represents one stage in the development of what was later known as the Noahide laws or commandments, first codified in the Tosefta (*t. ʿAbod. Zar.* 8:4).[150] It is of course doubtful whether one should refer to the apostolic decree as Noahide theology, taking into consideration the differences both in content and context. D. Novak, for instance, has objected to "[t]he lumping together of the phenomenon of the *sebomenoi* with the concept of Noahide law."[151] Novak is certainly right in pointing out that the Noahide commandments are "a body of moral principles to govern a humanity which transcends the religious community itself,"[152] while the apostolic decree applied only to Gentile adherents to the Jesus movement. One could add that there are seven Noahide commandments but only four in the decree, and that the ethical dimension seems to be stressed more in the Noahide commandments than in the apostolic decree, etc. Novak concludes that there is no evidence for a Noahide catalogue in New Testament times. This is, of course, true if we accept Novak's definition of Noahide commandments/theology.

If, however, we understand the Noahide commandments as one expression of different Jewish ways of reflecting upon the relation between Jews and Gentiles, it is hard to state that the apostolic decree constitutes something essentially different from Noahide theology.[153] In fact, if we leave out the laws imposed on the stranger living in Israel,[154] there is still evidence of another kind of pre-rabbinic commandment to be applied on Gentiles, admittedly with a rather different outlook.[155] In *Jub.* 7:20 we read:

> And in the twenty-eighth jubilee Noah began to command his grandsons with ordinances and commandments and all of the judgements which he knew. And he bore witness to his sons so that they might do justice and cover the shame of their flesh and bless the one who created them and honor father and mother, and each one love his neighbor and preserve themselves from fornication and pollution and from all injustice.

In *Jubilees* these regulations are used primarily as criteria of the judgment against the giants, whose sins bring about the flood. Considering the pessimistic view on the future salvation of the Gentiles, which according to *Jub.* 15:26 are "to be destroyed and annihilated from the earth," the theology of *Jubilees* serves a secondary function, that of legitimizing the condemnation of the Gentile nations.

We have already noticed that the eschatological future of the Gentile nations was an issue of interest in biblical and post-biblical literature. In Tannaitic literature we find that the Noahide theology is fully developed, which implies that there was also an interest in how to relate to Gentiles at that time. There is every reason to assume that such an interest (irrespective of whether we call this Noahide theology or not) existed during the first century as well, since we know that Judaism exercised a considerable influence on Gentile society. If Gentiles interacted with Jews and participated in activities in the synagogue, there was certainly a need for halakhot regulating relations between Jews and Gentiles. The political/religious system in the Greek *polis* is another reason for the need for halakhic reflection upon the status of god-fearers and other Gentile admirers and benefactors. It is a reasonable assumption that the apostolic decree reflects such a halakhic tradition and that the delegates participating in the Jerusalem conference agreed upon its continued validity.[156] If the apostolic decree has its *Sitz im Leben* in the context of Gentile god-fearers participating in the activities of the synagogue, why would Paul not agree on its continuing validity?[157]

However, one problem is that Paul's way of dealing with the situation in Corinth seems to contradict what is stated in the apostolic decree (Acts 15:20, 29), namely, that the Jesus-believing Gentiles are to abstain from things "polluted by idols" (ἀπέχεσθαι τῶν ἀλισγημάτων τῶν εἰδώλων) or "what has been sacrificed to idols" (ἀπέχεσθαι εἰδωλοθύτων). Is it possible that Paul could have agreed to the decree *which specifically states that one should avoid meat offered to idols*, while in 1 Corinthians 10:25 he states that one may eat "whatever is sold in the meat market without raising any question on the ground of conscience." Since the probability is high that much of the meat sold at the market had or would be involved in some cultic activity, Paul's recommendation seems strange especially if one considers his prohibition against idolatry in 10:1–22 and also in 5:10–11. Similarly, in 10:27 he states that one may eat whatever is served when being invited to an unbeliever. On the other hand, in 8:4–12 it seems as if Paul argues that in fact no idols exist at all and that the reason to avoid eating meat offered to idols is only out of consideration for those who would take offence. The complexity of the section dealing with idol foods has led scholars to doubt the unity of the letter, and several attempts to divide 1 Corinthians into two or more letters have been made.[158] However, what is perceived as inconsistency and contradiction could, in fact, constitute the rhetorical strategy of Paul, and it is entirely possible to consider the section 8:1–11:1 as one literary unit.[159]

P. J. Tomson has argued that this section, which is most likely part of a response to a previous letter from the Corinthians,[160] represents a halakhic discourse aimed at prohibiting all forms of idolatry, including meat offered to idols. Tomson has shown that there was within the Tannaitic tradition two ideas: on the one hand, there was a realistic, rational view of idolatry—idols were not considered real in an ontological sense. On the other hand, idolatry was connected to belief in a spiritual world dominated by demons as opposed to angels.[161] Paul seems to connect to both: in 1 Corinthians 8:4–6 he clearly alludes to a realistic view of idolatry, while in 10:19–21 he both refers to the imaginary status of idols and equates Gentile sacrifices with sacrifices to demons. Tomson argues that Paul in 1 Corinthians 8 addresses those in the Corinthian community who have raised doubt about a previously stated prohibition against food offered to idols.[162] It is interesting to note that this corresponds well to the suggestion above that the Jewish community did not oppose Gentile involvement in the official cult of the *polis* and the empire. If we assume that the Jesus-believing Gentiles were recruited among former god-fearers who had previously related to a Jewish community and simultaneously upheld their obligations towards the official cult, their reluctance to refrain from this usage is understandable.

While having reached the conclusion in 10:1–22 that idol food may under no circumstances be eaten, Paul in 10:23–11:1 now turns to the issue of how to define what is idol food in doubtful cases. By drawing parallels to rabbinic discussions about idolatry, Tomson reaches the conclusion that, according to some halakhic traditions, *it is the specified intention towards idolatry that makes an object forbidden.* Paul's way of arguing bears some resemblance to the terminology used in relation to sales to Gentiles.

> Goods of specified intention פירושן, i.e. which by quality or condition are evidently meant for idolatry, are forbidden. But if unspecified סתמן, i.e. not in this sort of quality or condition, they are permitted and one may sell 'without anxiety'; and there is no need to inquire. Even if there are idolatrous intentions, they were not openly uttered and did not represent the power of idolatry. 'But if [the pagan] specified, even water and salt are forbidden' (*t. A. Z.* 1:21).[163]

Tomson has shown that this aspect may very well be covered by the word συνείδησις, which is used by Paul in the discussion in 10:25–9.[164] According to Tomson, συνείδησις is best understood as "consciousness" and thus refers to *the act of signifying one's intention towards an object.* This implies that what Paul really states is that meat sold at the market is not to be considered principally as idol food. However, if a Gentile specifically states how he regards the meat, that is, *considering it to be idol food,* the meat would be forbidden, as in the example in 10:28. That is why it is the "consciousness" of the other that makes the difference in 10:29. By signifying his intention towards the meal, the Gentile host has turned the otherwise allowed meat into forbidden idol food. Tomson's reconstruction makes sense: by combining analogies from admittedly later rabbinic sources with insights into Paul's rhetorical strategy, it becomes all the more likely that Paul actually embraced the ideology of the apostolic decree and that it was part of his program of the mission to the Gentiles. The section 1 Corinthians 8–10 does not contradict this hypothesis. Quite the opposite: if we accept Tomson's interpretation, it rather confirms it.

It is clear that under no circumstances would Paul accept that the torah be imposed on the Jesus-believing Gentiles. From the paraenetic parts of Paul's letters, it could be asserted, however, that Paul nevertheless made great demands upon Gentiles who wanted to associate with the god of Israel.[165] They were certainly to remain Gentiles but, following Nanos, *they were not to remain pagans.*[166] If Paul accepted that the apostolic decree was applicable to Jesus-believing Gentiles, this would not mean that he imposed the torah on them, since, strictly speaking, the halakhah for righteous Gentiles or god-fearers was *not the torah but something to be observed by Gentiles not having been blessed with the gift of torah.* Thus, there is nothing contradictory in stating that the Gentiles should not obey the torah while at the same time demanding that they should observe the apostolic decree. As Gentiles they were completely free, but as believers they must subordinate their freedom to worship the god of the whole world and thus accept the halakhah for "righteous Gentiles" operative during the first century CE. As Nanos very eloquently puts it:

> Paul's view of liberty must be understood in the context of his commitment to the inherent compromise of monotheism present in any insistence on "righteous gentiles" becoming Jews. Christian gentiles are not Jews and thus are theoretically free of purity laws. Nevertheless, their assertion of freedom must be examined in the relative context of Jewish and

gentile relationship and the function of Torah for each. There is a law higher than the freedom to seek one's own rights, for purity behavior applies in the context of the unification of both Jew and gentile in the eschatological restoration of God's rule on earth.[167]

This view of the apostolic decree and Paul's relation to it has the clear advantage of using components prevalent in the symbolic world of first-century Judaism. Such a basic assumption is as justifiable as the traditional view that Paul broke with and left Judaism. The "burden of the torah" is, of course, a Christian invention. Religious Jews generally did, and do, regard the torah as a blessing and something to rejoice at. In Paul's mind, it had not ceased to be relevant for Jews and had never been relevant for Gentiles.

If Paul and James, Peter and John all agreed on the apostolic decree, that is, an already existing halakhah regulating the commensality between god-fearers and Jews in the synagogue, and furthermore agreed that circumcision and a general obedience to the torah were not to be imposed on the Jesus-believing Gentiles and that the areas of responsibility should be divided up, *what was the fuss really about?* To be able to answer that question, we must first turn to a vital aspect of social interaction between Jews and Gentiles.

Who ate with whom—the issue of table-fellowship

As we noted above, Esler holds the view that Jews in principle could eat only with other Jews and that there was a general ban against eating with Gentiles. His interest in this matter relates to what he considers to have been the problem in Antioch. Esler assumes that the meal in Antioch was the eucharistic meal[168] and, because of a likewise assumed general ban observed by all Jews within the religious community against table-fellowship, that commensality constituted the real problem.[169] It must be emphasized that Esler here uses "table-fellowship" in an extremely limited sense. He defines table-fellowship "in the full sense" as sitting around a table sharing the same food, wine and vessels.[170] This definition is only relevant for Esler's specific interest in table-fellowship in the context of the eucharistic meal. While the identification of the meal in Antioch with the eucharist cannot be completely ruled out, we must note that the text indicates neither eucharistic nor common meals.[171] One strong argument against the view that the meal in Antioch was the eucharist is that Paul elsewhere uses a technical term for designating it, namely κυριακὸς δεῖπνον in 1 Corinthians 11:20. It is hard to understand why Paul leaves out any allusion to the eucharist if this was what the conflict was really about.

Esler may be right in stating that "as a general rule Jews did refrain from eating with Gentiles."[172] Greek and Roman sources certainly reveal a Jewish refusal to associate or eat with Gentiles.[173] We have already noted a general unwillingness to use Gentile oil. Some Jewish texts either forbid or at the least problematize eating with Gentiles or eating Gentile food.[174] We noted in the previous chapter that, regarding assimilation, most Jews in the Diaspora were *structurally assimilated* but they seldom went so far as *marital assimilation*. There is certainly evidence of a Jewish separatism.

The question is, however, whether this suggests that *all Jews* observed a general ban and, irrespective of the kind or degree of religiousness, refrained from eating with Gentiles. That presumes a rather stereotyped picture of Judaism and Jews. As we noticed in the previous chapter, Judaism was diversified not only with regard to different factions: the Jews of the first century CE also had different ideas of how to carry out the commandments in the torah. We found evidence of people on the fringe of Judaism, some clearly intending to leave Judaism. On fairly good grounds we assumed the existence of a rather traditionalistic group with a strong commitment to obey the torah. We found evidence of Jews who wanted to combine Hellenism with Judaism. We also concluded that, since the majority of people did not live in complete isolation from the surrounding society, which might have been the case with some traditionalistic groups, social intercourse of varying degrees was part of everyday life. *We cannot assume that these different groups of Jews held the same view of table-fellowship with Gentiles.*

This does not prove, of course, that Jews habitually ate "in the full sense" together with Gentiles, but it draws our attention to the fact that Judaism, as every other religious system, was, and is, so full of nuances that to speak of *one* Jewish attitude to table-fellowship (or any other aspect of human life) represents an oversimplification of little analytical use. From this follows that *the degree of association* with Gentiles does not necessarily say anything about *the degree of religiousness*, but rather of *the kind of religiousness*.[175] It is only when we set a later, ideologically more uniform rabbinic Judaism, or even the modern ultra-orthodox community, as a standard for what Judaism must have been that all evidence of other religious expressions appears to be anomalous. Would not some Jews who still wanted to be loyal to their religious heritage and at the same time believed that Judaism and Hellenism could be combined—who admired parts of Greek culture, were inspired by Greek authors, attended theaters, the circus, the gymnasium—have found it appropriate to eat together with Gentiles or even to accept dinner invitations from Gentiles?[176]

This is related to what Sanders pointed out in his criticism of Esler, namely that the interpretation of the texts to which Esler refers is not unambiguous. Sanders rightly draws attention to the fact that the ideology of not mixing with Gentiles in, for instance, *Joseph and Asenath*, "is not sociological evidence that Jews did not eat with Gentiles or marry them; on the contrary, the author was trying to check a practice he considered threatening."[177] Do these no doubt censorious sources reflect the common Jewish view of this kind of social intercourse with Gentiles, *or do they rather imply that table-fellowship "in the full sense" between Jews and Gentiles actually existed, since the authors of these texts found it necessary to comment adversely on such behavior?* Esler answers this criticism by analogously stating that the existence of the torah has not been questioned, notwithstanding that "[t]here were always Israelites who disobeyed the Torah and others who called them back to its observance."[178] This would imply, according to Esler, that one "cannot reasonably doubt its [the ban's] existence merely because it is propounded by a particular author."[179] But the issue at stake is not whether there was an ideology that did not approve of table-fellowship with Gentiles, but whether such an ideology was embraced *by all Jews within the religious community*. The evidence presented by Esler does not prove the latter, only that *some* Jewish groups took it amiss to eat with Gentiles. Surely other Jews may have disapproved—the texts to which Esler refers show that. Most Pharisees disapproved, and the Qumran community disapproved of anything but their own halakhah—they would not have eaten even with a Pharisee—but such views do not determine or even reflect what Jews in general thought about table-fellowship with Gentiles.[180] I would say that Sanders still has a point here.

If we leave out Esler's narrow definition of table-fellowship and concentrate on the phenomenon in a broader sense, there are several indications that it was possible. In his dealing with the incident in Antioch, Tomson asks "what degrees of Jewish–Gentile fellowship were possible according to the halakha, both in Palestine and the diaspora?"[181] He continues:

> [T]here are convincing indications that in spite of the restrictions in the halakhic areas of idolatry, food and purity, marriage and sexual relations, Jews did not refrain from

table-fellowship with gentiles either in gentile homes or their town, and were even proud of their hospitality.[182]

One such indication is found in the passage *m. ʿAbod. Zar.* 5:5, which seems to describe a situation from real life.

> If [a Jew] was eating with him [—an idolater—] at a table, and he put a flask [of wine] on the table [and] a flask [of wine] on the side-table, and he left the other [there] and went out, what [wine] is on the table is prohibited, and what [wine] is on the side-table is permitted, and if [the Jew] had said to him, 'Mix [thy wine] and drink', [the wine] which is on the side-table is also forbidden.

The problem in this situation is related to the Gentile custom of offering some wine in a libation to Gentile gods, thus making all wine unserviceable for Jewish guests.[183] The point, however, is that here we have halakhic instructions regulating table-fellowship between Jews and Gentiles. Tomson also refers to traditions about Rabbi Meir, who lived during the mid-second century, that deal with several halakhot concerning the situation of Jews eating in Gentile homes.[184] As can be expected, this tolerant view was not universally prevalent. As we noted in our discussion of Jewish concepts of the eschatological destiny of Gentiles, there were diametrically opposed concepts. The situation seems to have been the same when it comes to the issue of table-fellowship. Tomson quotes the passage *t. ʿAbod. Zar.* 4:6, attributed to R. Shimon ben Elazar, a student of R. Meir referred to above. Here all partaking in Gentile meals is considered idolatrous. Tomson concludes, "R. Meir and R. Shimon ben Elazar seem to represent two divergent views on relations with gentiles within the same pious tradition."[185]

Furthermore, some texts to which Esler refers as evidence for a ban against table-fellowship in his restricted sense seem, in fact, to indicate the opposite: namely, that precisely such table-fellowship between Jews and Gentiles existed. This is, for instance, the case with Judith, who certainly eats at Holofernes' banquet, but eats food and wine prepared by her maid (Jdt 12:17–19).

> So Holofernes said to her, "Have a drink and be merry with us!" Judith said, "I will gladly drink, my lord, because today is the greatest day in my whole life." Then she took what her maid had prepared and ate and drank before him.

Esler states that this is not proper table-fellowship but "a meal in parallel," according to his definition, which, as we will see, does not fit into the cultural matrix of antiquity. Even if we accept Esler's statement for the sake of argument, it is nevertheless clear that it is the food that constitutes the main obstacle in this case. Provided with the proper food, table-fellowship seems to be possible. Or is this only a lifeless image of real intimate, ancient table-fellowship? There are circumstances that should make us inclined to think otherwise. Let us turn to the text in *Let. Aris.* 181, where the translators of the LXX are invited to a royal banquet. The king invites his Jewish guests and assures them that everything "will be served in compliance with your habits; it will be served to me as well as to you."

What follows is a description of how everything is arranged in order to please the Jewish guests. The priest Eleazar is even invited to offer the introductory prayer instead of "the sacred heralds, the sacrificial ministers, and the rest, whose habitual role was to offer the prayers" (*Let. Aris.* 184). One certainly gets the impression that the whole banquet has been arranged in order to establish exactly such a table-fellowship whose existence Esler denies. There is no problem with the food or with the wine, since we must assume that no libations had taken place: a Jewish priest offered the prayers. Esler even believes that the servants were Jews and states that the wine had "expressly not been subject to any rites akin to libation to pagan gods."[186] Despite this, it does not constitute table-fellowship, according to Esler, but a meal "conducted in parallel, not in common."[187]

He specifies two main reasons for this. First, he states that, since the king does not use the usual Greek word for "to eat together," συνεσθίειν, but instead the phrase δειπνῆσαι σήμερον μεθ᾽ ὑμῶν, this would "create an impression of a rather less intimate form of table-fellowship."[188] This is simply not correct: the normal designation for an official banquet in Hellenistic times was either δεῖπνον or συμπόσιον, so all the text is saying is that the guests are invited to an official banquet.[189] Besides, Esler's argument implies that Revelation 3:20 suggests a less intimate form of table-fellowship between Jesus and the one who looks for his company, since we find here exactly the same use of the verb δειπνέω plus the preposition μετά.

Listen! I am standing at the door, knocking; if you hear my voice and open the door, I will come in to you and eat with you, and you with me (εἰσελεύσομαι πρὸς αὐτὸν καὶ δειπνήσω μετ᾽ αὐτοῦ καὶ αὐτὸς μετ᾽ ἐμοῦ).

This is not a very likely reading, and we must conclude that Esler's philological argument simply does not work.

Secondly, Esler states that the Jews are "spatially separated from their gentile host (so there is no sign of any food or drink being passed from him or to them or vice versa)."[190] It is obvious that Esler has narrowed his definition of table-fellowship to such an extent that it is doubtful whether any ancient meal could meet his demands. A normal Roman *cena* would probably not live up to Esler's standards. K. Bradley states that the diners often had their own tables from which they ate their food individually. He continues:

> So, with diners constantly moving their recumbent bodies towards and then away from private tables, it might be questioned whether Roman habits could encourage anything quite comparable to the commensality of the modern situation, despite the intimacies that might follow from proximity on the couches. This is not to say that the Roman table was devoid of all symbolic significance. Some thought that the very word *"mensa"* conveyed an idea of centrality, though how widely this antiquarian speculation circulated is unknown. Others regarded the loaded table as a symbol of nature's beneficence, with the table itself—round, stable and nurturing—representing the earth. To others it was simply a token of civilised living. In none of this, however, is there anything remotely close to the idea of "commensality" as defined above, a word, incidentally, for which there is no analogue in classical Latin.[191]

This is most illuminating, since it becomes all the more apparent that it is not improbable that Esler's definition of table-fellowship "in the full sense" *never existed in antiquity but is based on modern concepts of commensality.*[192]

Furthermore, it is hard to imagine anyone not being spatially separated from the other guests at a large banquet. Since the rule was one diner per couch, the conditions at the royal banquet described in *The Letter of Aristeas* seem perfectly normal.[193] One could hardly imagine the king functioning as a waiter. Normally food and, after the meal, wine were served by waiters at a side-table.[194] The text does not suggest any special spatial separation between the host and the Jewish guests, rather the opposite. We can also read about how the banquet continued for seven days and every evening after an interval there was time for conversation and the drinking of wine. This certainly implies a *symposion*.

A Greek banquet was composed of two parts,[195] the meal itself and a following part where wine was drunk, the *symposion*, during which conversation and entertainment took place.[196] In the account of the banquet we find descriptions of the conversations that took place between the king and the guests and how the king, pleased at his Jewish guests' ability to eclipse even his own philosophers in wisdom, drank to their health.[197] We are also told that the king was "mingling among the guests with geniality and great delight" (*Let. Aris*. 274). This is a most interesting piece of information, since this could indicate that wine was actually passed from one person to another. In Cicero's *Verr*. 2.1.26.66, there is a reference to a proposal to drink "in the Greek fashion." This is usually considered to mean either drinking a fixed amount of wine *supplied by the host of the feast*, or drinking a toast *and passing the cup to the person toasted*.[198] It is thus likely that Esler's definition of table-fellowship "in the full sense," that is, sharing the same food, wine and vessels,[199] could actually be applied to the table-fellowship at a banquet. This, together with the statement that the king ate the same food as the Jewish guests, shows that this is table-fellowship even by Esler's standards.[200]

We must conclude that there unquestionably existed a certain reluctance among Jews to associate with Gentiles. As Sanders states, "Jews were in general less willing to mix than were the other peoples of the empire."[201] In spite of this, social intercourse existed in almost every area of life with one general exception—marriage. As for table-fellowship between Jews and Gentiles, we have seen that it did exist and was perfectly possible, given the right circumstances, which must have depended on the specific individual's degree of halakhic observance. This may have varied for different groups and probably even geographically. We have noted that some groups may have considered all table-fellowship with Gentiles abominable while other groups had a more open attitude. In the previous chapter I described the existence of different groups in Antioch with different ideological outlooks. It is important to note that the texts above imply that table-fellowship was possible even in the home of a Gentile, although the reluctance to eat with a Gentile would generally have been much less *if the meal were to be taken in the home of the Jew*, where the Jew was in control of what was served and knew where the ingredients came from. We must now proceed by asking the following: if table-fellowship *per se* did not constitute a problem, what did?

Covenantal theology in the making

Let us for a moment recapitulate the findings and positions taken in this section so far. First, in dealing with the different concepts of the eschatological future of the Gentiles, we noticed that there were both negative and positive traditions within first-century Judaism. Some traditions certainly envisaged the future salvation of Gentiles, but *how* this salvation would be accomplished was not specified. The identification of Jesus as the Messiah within the Jesus movement triggered specific strata within these traditions and resulted in missionary activities directed towards Gentiles.

Secondly, we learnt from Sanders that *covenantal nomism* was the general type of Judaism during this period and noted that soteriological significance was ascribed to the covenant itself. Entering into the covenant required conversion to Judaism, and we found a very strong connection between male circumcision and covenantal nomism. Male individuals inside the covenant means circumcised males. To undo circumcision was synonymous with leaving the covenant.

Thirdly, regarding the apostolic council, I sided with Nanos that Paul agreed with the apostolic decree, which was probably a prevalent halakhah regulating the commensality between Jews and god-fearers. It is obvious that an agreement was reached, but less clear what was really agreed upon besides the facts that the apostolic decree should be observed, that male circumcision and a general obedience to torah were not to be imposed on the Jesus-believing Gentiles, and that there would be a division of the areas of responsibility.

Fourthly, while Jews generally refrained from eating with Gentiles, certain Jews could have table-fellowship with certain Gentiles.

With this background we can now begin to reconstruct the social interaction in Antioch. We must note first that the early Jesus movement seems to have been trapped in a dilemma. On the one hand, the Gentiles were to be embraced by the salvation of the god of Israel, but the only institution that could provide this was reserved for Jews only. I suggest that it is this tension that underlies the incident at Antioch and that the heart of the conflict consists of *different concepts of covenantal theology*.[202] In order to find a way out of the dilemma, I suggest that Paul emphasized the soteriological aspects of covenantal nomism by stating that, in order to be saved, Gentiles had to be *included in the covenant.*

This implies that Paul also embraced the pattern of covenantal nomism. Sanders, who has convincingly shown that covenantal nomism was the prevalent religious system of Palestinian Judaism before the destruction of the temple, believes, however, that Paul's soteriology is of another kind. Sanders finds that Paul denies two important pillars of Judaism, namely, "the election of Israel and faithfulness to the Mosaic law."[203] He states, furthermore, that Paul *"explicitly denies that the Jewish covenant can be effective for salvation, thus consciously denying the basis of Judaism."*[204]

I find it hard to follow Sanders here.[205] He assumes that Paul's soteriological system must be applicable to both Jesus-believing Jews and Jesus-believing Gentiles—in short, to "Christians." As a result, what Paul states about the torah is also valid for Jews. However, as pointed out by several scholars, Paul's main concern was the Gentiles, and in his mind the torah had not lost its validity for Jesus-believing Jews.[206] The problem arises from the failure of not making the important distinction between Jesus-believing Jews and Jesus-believing Gentiles. Paul does not deal with the problem of how the Jesus-believing Jews are to be saved because the covenant provides the means for salvation for Jews. Through Christ the covenant was certainly to be perceived in a new way, *but it was the same covenant.* As W. D. Davies has argued in connection with the interpretation of the term "Israel" in 2 Corinthians, "just as the new covenant conceived by Jeremiah, Jubilees and the sectarians at Qumran did not unambiguously envisage a radical break with the Sinaitic covenant but a reinterpretation, so Paul's new covenant."[207] Paul's intention was rather to find a way to include the Gentiles in the salvation of the god of Israel, and, as L. Gaston has shown, the inclusion of the Gentiles, without excluding the Jews, is a major theme in Romans.[208]

Above we reached the conclusion that the idea that Gentiles could be included in the covenantal community of Israel was foreign to Jewish theological reflection. If Gentiles were considered as embraced by eschatological salvation, this was not thought of in covenantal terms. *However, this seems to be exactly the case with Paul.* The inclusion of the Gentiles meant for Paul the inclusion in *the covenant*, since it was the covenant that provided the ultimate means of salvation. By connecting the inclusion of the Gentiles with the promise given to Abraham in Galatians 3:7–29, Paul interprets the salvation of the Gentiles in *covenantal terms*, since the promise given to Abraham is a *covenantal promise* as stated in Genesis 15:18: "[o]n that day the Lord made a covenant with Abram."[209]

However, Paul was stressing that Gentiles had a place in this renewed covenant *exactly as Gentiles*—they were *not* to convert to Judaism, and were consequently *not* to undergo circumcision.[210] If, however, they underwent physical circumcision, the works of Christ would have been of no benefit to them,[211] and the god of Israel would be the god of the Jews only and not of the Gentiles. In Romans 3:28–31 Paul's view is quite clearly spelled out.

> For we hold that a person is justified by faith apart from works prescribed by the law. Or is God the God of Jews only? Is he not the God of Gentiles also? Yes, of Gentiles also, since God is one; and he will justify the circumcised on the ground of faith and the uncircumcised through that same faith. Do we then overthrow the law by this faith? By no means! On the contrary, we uphold the law.

The reason why Paul so emphatically prevents Gentiles from becoming Jews may be connected to his belief in the one god. In commenting on these verses Nanos has argued that Paul considered "the universalistic oneness of God" to be lost if Gentiles were to become Jews:

> His oneness has been compromised if he is *only* the God of Israel, *only* the God of the circumcised, *only* the God of Torah, and not *also* the God of the nations, not *also* the God of the uncircumcised, and not *also* the God of those outside the Torah. The Torah would not be established, and all Israel would not be saved, because the One God who called Israel and gave them the gift of Torah would not be the one God of all who believe in him, whether the Jew first or also the Greek.[212]

Paul thus simultaneously obliterates and accentuates the differences between Jews and Gentiles. They are certainly "one in Christ," but it is precisely as "Jews" and "Gentiles" that they constitute this unity. In building up this theological construction, Paul makes use of traditions deeply embedded in his own religious tradition. Monotheism, the eschatological pilgrimage of the Gentiles, and covenantal nomism are combined with a firm conviction of living in the messianic age, resulting in a soteriological model for the inclusion of the Gentiles into the covenant that provides salvation for both Jews and Gentiles.

Paul was not involved in a process of creating a new religion where the torah was no longer valid for Jews. His mission was rather to emphasize that the torah was not for Jesus-believing Gentiles.[213] To state, as Dunn does, that Paul thought it not possible to live at the same time "in Christ" and "in accordance with the law" is to invert the set of problems.[214] For 2000 years, one of the problems for the Christian church has been to define the position of the Jews in a Christian world. It is a long way from the accusation of Melito of Sardis that the Jews killed god (*Peri Pascha* 96) to *Nostra Aetate* of the Second Vatican Council, where it is stated that Jesus' passion "cannot be blamed upon all the Jews then living, without distinction, nor upon the Jews of today," and that "the Jews should not be presented as repudiated or cursed by God."[215] However, both standpoints reflect the fact that ever since the Jesus movement became a predominantly Gentile, non-Jewish religion, the question of how to relate to Jews and Judaism has been at the heart of Christian theological reflection. The rather anachronistic picture which emanates from this state of affairs assumes that, since Paul had become a Christian, that is, non-Jewish, he had to deal with rejecting the torah for both Jews and Gentiles. Paul becomes the establisher of the law-free gospel—the first true Christian hero, the liberator of Christianity from its Jewish burden. *But, within the early Jesus movement, the problem was not the Jews, but the Gentiles; the problem for Paul was not that the Jews must abandon the torah but to explain why the Gentiles should not adopt it.*[216]

To return to the problem in Antioch: we noticed that table-fellowship between Jews and Gentiles was possible under the right circumstances. The situation where a Gentile was invited to dinner in a Jewish home and the Jewish host consequently had full control of the food and wine would no doubt be the least complicated, especially if the guest was a god-fearing Gentile who had adopted certain Jewish customs perhaps equivalent to the apostolic decree. Dunn thinks that not even James would have had anything against eating with an uncircumcised person. He finds it unlikely to assume "that Titus ate his meals in splendid isolation when he visited Jerusalem" and believes that the reason for this was that Titus "observed a high standard of ritual purity."[217] As we have seen, this was probably not the case. The conflict at Antioch had nothing to do with ritual purity of this kind. If Dunn is right in assuming that the Jews in Jerusalem had table-fellowship with the uncircumcised Titus, *this was exactly because the meal was taken within a Jewish context, and almost any Jew could (or can) eat with a Gentile during such circumstances.*

It appears from Galatians 2:11–13 that some Hellenized Jews in Antioch thought it possible to eat together with Gentiles. This custom may have had nothing to do with the specific theology of Paul and the Jesus-believing Jews but may have been part of a local

Antiochean halakhah prevalent among Hellenized Jews in general. If the Jesus-believing Jews in Antioch are considered to be part of the general Jewish community, one must assume that the apostles kept the torah according to the local halakhah and that they found nothing contradictory in living as observant Jews and eating with Gentiles.[218]

However, there are two circumstances that imply that the relations between Jesus-believing Jews and Jesus-believing Gentiles were more intimate than those usual between Jews and Gentiles. Firstly, in the previous chapter we reached the conclusion that it is likely that Gentiles within the Jesus movement were closely attached to the synagogue because of the legal system. It is likely that this led initially to an increased group solidarity within the Jesus movement in Antioch.

Secondly, this social reality was ideologically motivated and encouraged. The fact that Paul considered the Jesus-believing Gentiles to be covenantal partners implied that Jews and Gentiles within the Jesus movement were equal to one another. If "there is no longer Jew or Greek" or "slave or free," not even "male and female," if all "are one in Christ Jesus" (Gal. 3:28), if neither "circumcision nor uncircumcision counts for anything" (Gal. 5:6),[219] and since "real circumcision is a matter of the heart—it is spiritual and not literal" (Rom. 2:29),[220] if the Gentiles had "been cut from what is by nature a wild olive tree and grafted, contrary to nature, into a cultivated olive tree" (Rom. 11:24), and if "there is no distinction between Jew and Greek; the same Lord is Lord of all and is generous to all who call on him" (Rom. 10:12), would this not affect commensality? The question is: in what ways?

I find it likely that, as a result of a prevalent halakhah in Antioch, possibly reflected in the apostolic decree that made social contacts between Jews and Gentiles possible, in combination with the political system reinforced by the ideology of Paul, the Jews in the Jesus movement in Antioch felt free to accept dinner invitations from Gentiles and to use food prepared and brought by Gentiles for common meals.[221] It is, however, unlikely that the torah, as interpreted in Antioch, was ever violated.[222] That Jews and Gentiles should have eaten together without any regard to the food laws, as suggested by C. K. Barrett, among others, is highly improbable.[223] Such a proposition does not take seriously the conditions under which the Jesus movement developed. Its underlying assumption is that Jews during antiquity only waited for an opportunity to disregard the food laws of the torah. In reality it seems to have been the other way round: Gentile god-fearers adapted to the Jewish food standard. Jewish adherents to the Jesus movement did not question whether the torah was still valid for Jews since this was self-evident. If the majority of Jesus-believing Gentiles were recruited among former god-fearers, they had certainly already adapted to a Jewish life style, since their motive for associating with Jews in the first place was a profound interest in Judaism. God-fearers did not want to separate from Judaism. Quite the contrary, *one of Paul's major problems was to prevent Gentiles from becoming Jews.*

When James heard how the Antiochean community carried out the agreement of the Jerusalem council it is not surprising that he reacted by sending a delegation to Antioch.[224] In the same way as the messianic status of Jesus gave rise to certain associations and expectations, so did the idea of the inclusion of the Gentiles in the covenant. In Jerusalem, where torah-obedient ideology had prevailed since the Maccabean uprising, too close an association with Gentiles may in general have been regarded as a threat to Judaism itself. One can only imagine how Jews in Jerusalem would have reacted *if Gentiles were said to be part of the covenant of circumcision without circumcision.* Non-circumcision in a covenantal context, we remember, signaled a clear break with the covenant and consequently with Judaism. We also recall the narration in 1 Macc. 1, where it is said that the Hellenistic Jews made a *covenant* with the Gentiles *and* removed the marks of *circumcision.*

It is likely that James, in accordance with prevalent ideas of how Jews and Gentiles should associate, considered the Jesus-believing Gentiles to be connected to the Jewish community as *god-fearers.* It seems as if he did not consider the coming of the Messiah as a point in history when Gentiles, as Gentiles, should be fully incorporated in the covenant, while he still regarded them to be enclosed by the final salvation. *But, from James's point of view, there was no need for a new way of relating to Gentiles, since there was already an established and halakhic-defined way of social intercourse: Gentiles could become god-fearers and as such be embraced by the final salvation.*

What James consequently demanded was that such unrestricted table-fellowship had to cease and that the Jesus-believing Gentiles should form a separate commensality group.[225] As noticed above, Esler suggested that Peter, with James's backing, demanded instead that the Gentiles should be circumcised. This entails that the agreement from Jerusalem had been revoked: Esler takes pains to show that this would have been possible within a context of Mediterranean intrinsic cultural traits such as honor and shame.[226] While this cannot in general be ruled out, Esler's application of every detail of the model makes his reconstruction improbable. It is doubtful if it is possible to work with a social-scientific model at such a low degree of abstraction in a historical perspective.

Furthermore, if James really demanded that the Gentiles should be circumcised, it is hard to understand why this demand would primarily affect commensality. Judging from the effect his demand seems to have had, the simplest conclusion is that he in fact demanded what Peter actually brought about—a separation into two commensality groups.[227] What οἱ ἐκ περιτομῆς made perfectly clear was that, if Jesus-believing Gentiles claimed part in the *covenant* with the god of Israel, they had to be circumcised and were to keep the whole of the torah. If circumcision was their only alternative, this would certainly have implied that the agreement from Jerusalem had been revoked. But on this issue the sources (Acts 15:23–9; Gal. 2:1–10) are in fact in agreement—at the Jerusalem council everyone seems to have accepted that Gentiles, as Gentiles, were enclosed by the final salvation through the works of the god of Israel in Jesus Christ.

In practice, the explicit demand for a separation of the community would soon, of course, function as an *implicit* demand on the Jesus-believing Gentiles formally to become Jews. This would, however, result in a new dilemma, since, according to Pauline teaching, the Jesus-believing Gentiles would risk cutting themselves off from Christ if they submitted to circumcision.[228] The Jesus-believing Gentiles must have perceived this social separation as excluding them from the people of God and, as Holmberg has noted: "Paul's characterization of Cephas' behavior as τὰ ἔθνη ἀναγκάζεις ἰουδαΐζειν is not without foundation."[229]

It is possible that both parties in the conflict thought that the other part had broken the agreement reached at the Jerusalem council, but in reality it could very well be that the question of how to relate to Gentile adherents to the Jesus movement had never been dealt with in detail.[230] Both sides argued from preconceived presuppositions of covenantal theology, of commensality in general and halakhah concerning table-fellowship in particular. The probability of communication problems and complete misunderstandings is immense. The reason why James succeeded in convincing Peter, Barnabas and the other Jews about his model was that, from a Jewish point of view, his solution of relating to Gentiles must have been considered the most natural. *Thus, the weight of tradition and the authority of the brother of Jesus make it perfectly clear why Paul suffered an ideological defeat.*[231]

Before summarizing this complicated and lengthy discussion we must deal with one additional aspect which further points to a covenantal context. As mentioned above, some scholars assume that the meal in question was in fact the eucharistic meal. While this cannot be completely ruled out, we must note that the text indicates neither eucharistic nor common meals. One strong argument against the view that the meal in Antioch was the eucharist is that Paul, as mentioned earlier, elsewhere uses a technical term for designating it. It is hard to understand why Paul should omit any allusion to the eucharist if this was what the conflict was really about. On the other hand B. Chilton interprets the incident in Antioch as a conflict about *eucharistic* different covenantal models. Chilton finds six types of eucharist within the New Testament material.

According to Chilton, the community in Antioch would have interpreted the eucharist partly with the help of Petrine tradition presenting Jesus' meal with his disciples as a covenantal sacrifice, a kind of sacrifice of sharings, presupposing the continuing validity of the temple worship and as conveying the Mosaic stature of Jesus.[232] This tradition was to be elaborated by Paul, however, who emphasized the connection between Jesus' death and the eucharist, presenting the eucharist as a sacrifice for sin, but at the same time insisting that the last meal occurred on the night Jesus was betrayed, not on Passover.[233] As Paul used the Petrine tradition for shaping his own understanding of the eucharist, so did James by accomplishing a revision of the Petrine tradition. The reason for this "Jacobean program" was, according to Chilton, "to integrate Jesus' movement fully within the liturgical institutions of Judaism, to insist upon the Judaic identity of the movement and upon Jerusalem as its governing center."[234] James's interpretation of the eucharist was modeled instead after the Passover, which had far-reaching consequences. If Jesus' last supper was seen strictly as paschal it would have conveyed three limitations: 1) temporally, the meal would only take place at Passover; 2) geographically, Jerusalem would be the only place for celebration; and 3) socially, *the participants would have to be Jews*,[235] and *nota bene*, not only Jews but *circumcised Jews*! We can thus draw the important conclusion that, if the discussion of suitable table-fellowship in Antioch also carried eucharistic overtones, the covenantal motif is still central, and it is evident that the problem from James's point of view would have been solved once the Gentiles either withdrew from table-fellowship or submitted to circumcision.

I have argued that the conflict at Antioch ultimately concerned different ideas of how the Gentile nations would be embraced by the eschatological salvation of the god of Israel. It was thus the status of

Gentile adherents to the Jesus movement that constituted the real problem at stake. Paul's model of including the Gentiles in the covenant as Gentiles stood in sharp contrast to James's model, in which the Gentiles had to become Jews to be considered covenantal partners. James certainly regarded the Jesus-believing Gentiles as being associated with the Jewish community in some way—certainly not as equals, and certainly not as being included in the covenant with the god of Israel. Paul, however, stressed that, "in Christ," all distinctions between men become, on one level, superfluous. But here comes the paradox: this unity "in Christ" is arrived at *only when the social distinction between Jew and Gentile is maintained*. It is as "Jew" and "Gentile" that mankind becomes "one in Christ," since the god of Israel is the god not only of the Jews, but of all humanity.

The importance of this interpretation cannot be overstated: in the Antiochean conflict we find the earliest evidence of how ideological and social mechanisms working together brought about a social division between Jesus-believing Jews and Jesus-believing Gentiles. In Antioch the Jesus-believing Jews supporting James's model won the day. In the long run, however, they would suffer a devastating defeat.

Summary and conclusion

In the Hellenistic world there was a far-reaching contempt for Jews and Judaism. This can be explained partly by the fact that the Greeks considered all other peoples to be barbarians. There are, however, reasons for assuming that the Jews were feared and hated to such a degree that it is justifiable to speak of an ancient anti-Semitism. Especially within a Greek intellectual tradition, "xenophobia," "misanthropy" and "impiety" were common motifs in the denigration of the Jewish people.

In Antioch there were certainly strained relations both before and after the Jewish War, explainable partly by this general anti-Semitic trend in Hellenistic society but also because the Jews actually provoked several serious revolts and strove for increased political influence. Occasionally, Gentile reactions resulted in riots and pogroms. During the aftermath of the fall of Jerusalem, one serious incident took place. Antiochus, whom we dealt with in the previous chapter, accused his own people of planning to burn down the city and brought about a massacre of the Jews who did not sacrifice to the Greek gods. In connection with Titus' arrival at the city, the population of Antioch appealed twice to the general that the Jews should be thrown out or at least be deprived of their special privileges. Titus refused and confirmed instead the rights of the Jews. It is clear that the prejudice among the elite could have rather far-reaching consequences on a popular level, something that may have been aggravated due to Rome's policy of protecting the Jews.

Within Roman literary tradition there is, however, evidence of an ambiguous attitude towards Jews. This showed itself partly in the somewhat unexpected phenomenon among Gentiles of adopting different Jewish practices such as the Sabbath. Other Gentiles went even further in their admiration of Judaism. While some probably converted to Judaism, there existed several ways of relating to the Jewish communities. Some Gentiles, usually referred to as god-fearers, associated themselves rather closely with the synagogue without becoming converts and maintained their religious and social relations to the Gentile community. This was possible because of the juridical system of the cities and the tolerant attitude of some Jews towards other peoples' native cults.

The social importance of the attraction that the Jewish communities exercised on part of the Gentile population should not be under-estimated. For people lacking family and social networks and subject to the harsh conditions of the urban environment, the Jewish communities' emphasis on charity and fellowship must have made a strong impression. It cannot be ruled out that the Jewish prohibition against contraceptive methods, abortion and infanticide contributed to attracting Gentiles, who in reality could see the blessings of the god of Israel.

Within the Jesus-believing Jewish community, the interaction between Jews and Gentiles gave rise to specific problems. In Galatians 2:11–14(21), we are told about an incident with far-reaching consequences. Peter, one of the Jewish adherents to the early Jesus movement, who used to eat with the Gentiles, suddenly, on the arrival of representatives of the early Jesus movement from the Jerusalem community, drew back and separated himself from the Jesus-believing Gentiles: he was sharply rebuked by Paul because of this.

This incident has been the subject of a great number of studies, but one cannot say that there is any consensus either about the reason for the schism or about its consequences. It is suggested here that this event is to be seen against the background of Jewish eschatological concepts of the destiny of the Gentiles. It is argued that the conflict was basically about two different ways of relating to the Gentiles and concerned mainly the status of the Gentile adherents within the Jesus movement. In order to emphasize the soteriological aspects, Paul believed that the Gentiles had to be incorporated in the covenant, which, according to prevalent conceptions, provided salvation for those within. This, however, ultimately created a conflict, since Paul also advocated the view that Gentiles should remain Gentiles as Jews should remain Jews—otherwise the god of Israel would be the god only of the Jews and not of the whole world. According to Paul, through the death of Jesus there was a new possibility for a new fellowship—Jews and Gentiles with maintained boundaries would constitute one unity in Christ.

James, on the other hand, while having agreed on the principle that Jesus had died also for the Gentiles, found no reason for any soteriological innovation, since there was already an established way of relating to Gentiles. They could be god-fearers and associate with the Jesus-believing Jewish community and through Christ also be saved, since the common Jewish view on the destiny of the Gentile nation assumed the salvation of at least some righteous Gentiles. This model would be more in accordance with common Jewish concepts of the relation between Jews and Gentiles, and James would have had no difficulty in convincing Peter and the other Jews in the Jesus-believing Jewish synagogue about the fairness of his model. From a common Jewish perspective, Paul's soteriological solution threatened basic Jewish identity markers and may have triggered fears of a development as in 1 Macc. 1:11–15, where epispasm and making covenant with Gentiles clearly implied apostasy.

Using his authority as the brother of Jesus, James demanded a separation of the community into two commensality groups, one for Jews, the other for Gentiles, since too close social intercourse would have confused the boundaries between Jews and Gentiles. He further suggested a covenantal fellowship that, according to him, and presumably most Jews, would require that the Gentiles converted to Judaism. In this incident we find the embryo of what later became a virtual separation between Jews and Gentiles, between Judaism and Christianity.

Notes

1 For an extensive collection of Greek and Latin texts, translations and commentaries on Jews and Judaism, see Stern, *Greek and Latin*. Another, less extensive, collection of texts is found in Whittaker, *Jews*. See also Gabba, "Growth," for a concise overview of Greek attitudes towards Jews, and Hidal, "Jews," on Roman attitudes in particular.
2 Schäfer, *Judeophobia*, 15–33.
3 "This xenophobia was, historically speaking, somewhat ironical, since the Greeks and Romans alike owed an enormous part of their civilisation to foreigners"; see Grant, *Social History*, 123.

4 Hengel, "Interpretation," 170–1, and also Hengel, *Judaism: 1*, 65–78, on the role of education within Hellenism.

5 "School and gymnasium together gave the Greek minority support against the threat of assimilation to the 'barbarian' environment"; Hengel, *Judaism: 1*, 66.

6 Schäfer, *Judeophobia*, 197.

7 Ibid., 206.

8 Segal, *Rebecca's Children*, 26.

9 Feldman, *Jew*, 175–6.

10 Malalas probably wrote, or at least composed the first edition of his work in Antioch; see Croke, "Malalas," 4.

11 Kraeling, "Jewish Community," 148.

12 Humphrey, *Roman Circuses*, 457. This hippodrome was badly damaged during the earthquake in 115 CE and thoroughly reconstructed by Trajan or Hadrian.

13 Haddad, *Aspects*, 145–52.

14 Cameron, *Circus Factions*, 198–200.

15 On the riots in Alexandria and the embassies to Gaius in general, see Smallwood, *Philonis Alexandrini*, 14–27, and Barclay, *Mediterranean Diaspora*, 48–60. Claudius' edict exists in two versions: *A.J.* 19.280–5 and *CPJ* 153. The latter version is to be preferred since there is some doubt about the authenticity of some passages in Josephus' version connected to the issue of the legal status of the Alexandrian Jews, see Barclay, *Mediterranean Diaspora*, 58, and Schäfer, *Judeophobia*, 149.

16 On the Alexandrian pogrom, see Barclay, *Mediterranean Diaspora*, 48–60, and Schäfer, *Judeophobia*, 136–60.

17 Barclay believes that Malalas's account contains "an element of truth in referring to violent attacks on the Jewish community"; see Barclay, *Mediterranean Diaspora*, 251, and n. 51. Downey, *Antioch in Syria*, 193, describes Malalas' account as "inadequate and distorted," but continues: "it seems possible to recover from it some suggestions of the significance of the events."

18 Barclay, *Mediterranean Diaspora*, 251, n. 52.

19 Ibid., 251–3.

20 *A.J.* 18.261; *B.J.* 2.184–6.

21 Downey, *Antioch in Syria*, 194.

22 Tcherikover and Fuks, *CPJ: 2*, 53.

23 In *B.J.* 2.481 Josephus mentions that Agrippa had taken to Antioch. See also Kraeling, "Jewish Community," 150.

24 Josephus states the opposite. In *B.J.* 2.479 he reports that the reason why the Antiocheans did not kill or imprison any Jews was that, "with their own vast populations, these cities disdained the possibility of Jewish risings."

25 Farmer, "Post-Sectarian," 241–2.

26 Schäfer, *Judeophobia*, 210.

27 *B.J.* 7.60. Kraeling has argued that Josephus recorded two accounts of the same event; see "Jewish Community," 150–2. But cf. Downey, *Antioch in Syria*, 586–7.

28 There were, of course, exceptions. We have already noted how the Roman official attitude, during Gaius' reign, caused rather than

prevented disturbances in Alexandria. Gaius' predecessor, Tiberius, had many Jews expelled from Rome, and during the reign of Claudius there are reports of actions taken against the Jews of Rome; see Barclay, *Mediterranean Diaspora*, 298–306.
29 Ibid., 256–7. Cf. Downey, *Antioch in Syria*, 587.
30 Millar, *Near East*, 79.
31 Barclay, *Mediterranean Diaspora*, 257.
32 Malalas, *Chron.* 261. See also Downey, *Antioch in Syria*, 206.
33 Schäfer, *Judeophobia*, 210.
34 Goodman, *Mission*, 87; Feldman, *Jew*, 350.
35 Cohen, "Respect," 417.
36 See Svartvik, *Mark*, 333–41, and Paget, "Proselytism," for overviews of the discussions. In general I tend to side with Paget's conclusion that there is no evidence that Gentile converts were actively sought out, but that there probably existed a missionary consciousness among some Jews.
37 See Feldman, *Jew*, 288, n. 1, for an extensive bibliography on proselytism.
38 Kraabel, "Disappearance," 124, 126, 127; Kraabel and MacLennan, "God-Fearers," 136, 140.
39 Ibid., 132.
40 Overman, "God-Fearers," 145.
41 Feldman, *Jew*, 358–62. Several sources mentioned by Feldman do actually use the word θεοσεβής, but other designations that presumably refer to the same phenomenon also occur.
42 Reynolds and Tannenbaum, *Jews and Godfearers*, 56–7. See also Feldman, *Jew*, 362–9.
43 See Feldman, *Jew*, 244–358, and "Omnipresence."
44 Overman, "God-Fearers," 152. Cohen, *Beginnings*, 62, states, with a reference to the term "god-fearer," that "the debate about the precise meaning and application of this term ought not to obscure the fact that such gentiles existed." See also Levinskaya, *Diaspora Setting*, 51–103, for an extensive discussion of the problems connected with the assumed existence of god-fearers, and Gager, "Jews," for a profound critique of Kraabel's position.
45 Cohen, *Beginnings*, 140–74.
46 This has been developed by Gager, *Moses*, and Feldman, *Jew*, 233–87.
47 Rajak and Noy, "*Archisynagogoi*," 87–9; Rajak, "Synagogue," 161–4.
48 Cohen, *Beginnings*, 147.
49 See also Seneca, *Ep.* 95.47.
50 Cohen, *Beginnings*, 149–50.
51 Ibid., 66–8.
52 Ibid., 160.
53 Feldman, *Jew*, 339. See also pp. 338–41, and McKnight, *Light*, 30–48, for overviews of attitudes towards converts, including references to primary sources.
54 Feldman, *Jew*, chs 6–8.
55 Stark, *Rise of Christianity*, 73–94.
56 Ibid., 115–28.
57 Cf. Tacitus' report in *Hist.* 5.5, about the Jewish disgust at infanticide.

58 Walker-Ramisch, "Greco-Roman," 135–6.
59 Cf. Oberschall, *Social Movements*, 52: "[Recent urban migrants] are members of solidary groups in villages and small towns, but remain unorganized for a time in the city milieu."
60 Levine, *Ancient Synagogue*, 132.
61 Stark, *Rise of Christianity*, 89.
62 Tacitus noted that the Jews, admittedly in their homeland, were "healthy and hardy"; see *Hist.* 5.6.
63 Cohen, *Beginnings*, 136–7.
64 Ibid., 168–9.
65 The most famous example during the Classical period is, of course, Socrates, who in 399 BCE was found guilty of refusing to acknowledge the gods recognized by the state, of introducing new divinities, and finally of corrupting the youth; see Price, *Ancient Greeks*, 85–8.
66 As in Athens; see ibid., 76.
67 Tellbe, *Synagogue and State*, 34.
68 See Baron, *Social History*, 179, who points out that god-fearers were often kept from conversion to Judaism only by legal difficulties. "A grave obstacle," Baron states, "was the conflict between the duty of every citizen of a pagan municipality and a member of a pagan family to worship a local deity, and the extreme condemnation of all idolatry by Jewish law."
69 Goodman, *Mission*, 49–59.
70 Mitternacht, "Foolish Galatians," 431–2; Nanos, *Irony*, 257–71.
71 Reynolds and Tannenbaum, *Jews and Godfearers*, 22–3.
72 Καὶ ὅσοι θεοσεβῖς. Ζήνων Βουλ(ευτής) Τέρτυλλος Βουλ(ευτής); see Face *b* ll. 34–5 in ibid., 6–7. City councillors as patrons are known also from Sardis, see Levine, *Ancient Synagogue*, 350.
73 Reynolds and Tannenbaum, *Jews and Godfearers*, 58.
74 *MAMA* 6.263. See also Rajak, "Jewish Community," 162–3, 166–7; Levine, *Ancient Synagogue*, 111–12.
75 Feldman, *Jew*, 310 states that she "sympathized with Judaism"; Rajak, "Synagogue," 168, finds that "she is fairly unlikely to have been in the process of any sort of conversion"; and Levine, *Ancient Synagogue*, 350, states that she "remained fully pagan." The fact is that we do not know—Julia Severa could have been anything from a completely uninterested donor to a god-fearer in a more narrow sense. It is, however, less probable that she was Jewish, as suggested by Applebaum, "Legal Status," 443.
76 Cohen, *Beginnings*, 147.
77 Goodman, *Mission*, 55.
78 This may, as Cohen, *Beginnings*, 173, has pointed out, have varied from place to place. While the Jewish community in Aphrodisias may have seen themselves as part of general society and accepted Gentiles as god-fearers in their communities, the relations between Jews and Gentiles in Alexandria were more strained, so we may even doubt that there were any sympathizers at all.
79 The question of whether the account of the Antioch incident ends with 2:14 or includes also 2:15–21 as a summary of the speech Paul held in Antioch has been subject to an extensive debate. Commentators who

focus on the rhetorical structure usually find that the *narratio* ends with v. 14 and that the *propositio* begins with v. 15: see, e.g., Betz, *Galatians*, 113–14; Longenecker, *Galatians*, 80–1; Witherington, *Grace*, 148, 169; Esler, *Galatians*, 59–61. See also Gaston, *Paul*, 68. Other scholars take a middle position and state that Paul addresses both Peter and the Galatians: see, e.g., Dunn, *Galatians*, 130; Fung, *Galatians*, 105; Martyn, *Galatians*, 229–30; Lührmann, *Galatians*, 43–4. Kieffer, *Foi*, 13–17, and Holmstrand, *Markers*, 157–65, on the other hand, argue that the account of the incident continues throughout v. 21. In my opinion it is not possible to reach a clear-cut decision concerning how the sections relate to each other. For the present study it may be sufficient to say that it is reasonable to assume the existence of some connection between the sections. The argument against Peter thus continues irrespective of whether it constitutes part of Paul's speech to Peter. At the same time it seems clear that the whole situation and the argumentation are relevant for the situation in Galatia; see Holmberg, "Sociologiska perspektiv," 74, n. 2.

80 See Wechsler, *Geschichtsbild*, or Kieffer, *Foi*, 80–132, for overviews of the general scholarly discussion.
81 Dunn, "Incident," 4.
82 Ibid., 17–18.
83 Ibid., 31, 35–6.
84 Ibid., 34.
85 Ibid., 37.
86 Esler, *Community*, 77.
87 Ibid., 87.
88 Sanders, "Jewish Associations," 175, 176.
89 Ibid., 176.
90 Esler, "Making and Breaking," 289.
91 Ibid., 292.
92 Holmberg, "Christian Identity," 410.
93 Ibid., 408.
94 Cotterell and Turner, *Linguistics*, 87.
95 Dunn, *Galatians*, 223; Esler, *Galatians*, 17; Nanos, *Irony*, 77–8.
96 For a short overview on the opponents of Paul in Galatia, see, e.g., Dunn, *Galatians*, 9–11; Esler, *Galatians*, 69–72; Witherington, *Grace*, 21–5. For more extensive and critical evaluations, see Longenecker, *Galatians*, lxxxviii–xcviii; Mitternacht, *Forum*, 26–38; Nanos, *Irony*, 110–99.
97 Esler, *Galatians*, 36–7.
98 Esler, *First Christians*, 61–2.
99 Cf. Martyn, *Galatians*, 229–30, who states that "Paul's failure formally to close the quotation in v 14 is no accident. It reflects his determination to connect his account of the Antioch incident to the situation in Galatia."
100 See, e.g., Gal. 3:1–18; 5:1–12.
101 As pointed out by, e.g., Longenecker, *Galatians*, 8, the focus in the verse is soteriological. The deliverance mentioned is not a removal from the world, but a rescue from the evil that dominates the present age. Cf. Betz, *Galatians*, 42, who points to the fact that Paul speaks of a

liberation out of the present evil age and not a change of eons. See also Martyn, *Galatians*, 90–1, who holds the view that this verse actually "serves as one of the topic sentences for the whole of the letter," and indicates "a distinctly apocalyptic frame of reference."

102 See also Stendahl, *Among Jews*, 27, who finds that the doctrine of justification "originates in Paul's theological mind from his grappling with the problem of how to defend the place of the Gentiles in the Kingdom."

103 Hillers, *Micah*, 73–4.

104 See, e.g., Amos 1:3–2:3; Isa. 13:1–19:15; Jer. 46:1–50; Ezek. 25:1–30:26.

105 *Jub.* 23:30; *1 En.* 91:9; Bar. 4:25, 31–5; *Sib. Or.* 3:669–701, *T. Mos* 10:7; 1QM 1:6, 11:11–17, 12:10–12, 14:5–7. For the identification of the eschatological enemies as Gentiles in the writings of the Qumran community, see Sanders, *Palestinian Judaism*, 247.

106 Several more examples can be found in Sanders, *Jesus and Judaism*, 214, Sanders, *Judaism*, 291–2, and Donaldson, "Proselytes," 7–8.

107 The Qumran sect perhaps represents the only discernible group with a unequivocally negative view of Gentiles; see Sanders, *Palestinian Judaism*, 243–57, on how the sect pictured its enemies.

108 Jeremias, *Promise*, 57.

109 See also Mic. 4:1–2; Zech. 8:20–3; and Jeremias, *Promise*, 57–60, who mentions several more references.

110 See also *1 En.* 10:21, 90:30–3, 91:14; *Sib. Or.* 3:564–70; and Donaldson, "Proselytes," 8, for more references.

111 "There is no one view of the situation of Gentiles which prevailed throughout the Tannaitic period. The general impression is that the Rabbis were not ungenerous except when special circumstances moved them to view Gentiles with bitterness"; Sanders, *Jesus and Judaism*, 210. See also *t. Sanh.* 13:2, where R. Eliezer denies the Gentile a place in the world to come while R. Joshua states that righteous Gentiles will have a share in the world to come, a statement that Jeremias remarkably enough leaves out.

112 Fredriksen, *From Jesus*, 149; Sanders, *Jesus and Judaism*, 215.

113 Fredriksen, "Judaism," 220–1.

114 Donaldson, "Proselytes," 3.

115 1) The wealth of the Gentiles will flow into Jerusalem, 2) Gentile nations will serve Israel, 3) Israel will be a light to the nations, 4) the Gentiles will be destroyed or 5) defeated, and 6) Gentiles will survive but will not dwell with Israel; see Sanders, *Jesus and Judaism*, 214.

116 Four of those occur within Isaiah, and *Sib. Or.* 3:489–808 also presents what Sanders, *Jesus and Judaism*, 214, calls "multivalenced attitudes."

117 See Sanders's critique of Jeremias's picture of Judaism by the time of Jesus as being overwhelmingly negative towards Gentiles; Sanders, *Jesus and Judaism*, 212–16.

118 Ibid., 220.

119 For an overview of Jesus and eschatology, see Allison, "Eschatology." See also Sanders, *Jesus and Judaism*, 218–21, on Jesus's relation to the Gentiles.

120 As Theissen, *Religion*, 86, has noted, the ambiguity regarding the

eschatological destiny of the Gentiles manifested itself also in different messianic expectations. On the one hand, the Messiah will conquer the Gentiles and drive them out (see *Pss. Sol.* 17:21–5); on the other hand he will have them streaming to Zion in the pilgrimage of the nations (see *Pss. Sol.* 17:31).

121 Sanders, *Jesus and Judaism*, 218.
122 Ibid., 221.
123 Sanders, *Palestinian Judaism*, 422.
124 "Covenantal nomism must have been the general type of religion prevalent in Palestine before the destruction of the Temple"; Sanders, *Palestinian Judaism*, 428. "When we turn to Hellenistic Jewish literature . . . we see that membership in Israel is no less important for determining salvation"; see Sanders, "Covenant," 22. The only exception seems to be *4 Ezra*; see *Palestinian Judaism*, 409, and "Covenant," 15. See also Dunn, "Issue," 298–303.
125 *1 En.* 91:14; *T. Levi* 18:3, 9.
126 Donaldson, "Proselytes," 26–7.
127 Ibid., 26.
128 Fredriksen, "Judaism," 221–5, and *From Jesus*, 149–50.
129 Donaldson, "Proselytes," 27.
130 With the exception of a man whose brothers had died as a result of circumcision; see chapter 3, n. 102.
131 McEleney, "Conversion," 328–33.
132 Sanders, *Judaism*, 214.
133 Nolland, "Uncircumcised," 194. Goodman, *Mission*, 81, agrees.
134 See also Schäfer, *Judeophobia*, 93: "[c]ircumcision was thus the external sign of the covenant between God and Abraham/Israel, the non-observance of which was considered as the ultimate break with this covenant, dissociation from the community of Israel."
135 *b. Yebam.* 64b.
136 At least within rabbinic Judaism there is a strong connection between circumcision and the Passover seder, since both involve blood symbolizing salvation. "Blood now became the dominant symbol of covenant, both sacrificially (as the lamb) and through circumcision. One form of blood recalls the other; the blood of the paschal lamb and the blood of circumcision become merged because both are items given by God specifically to effect salvation"; Hoffman, *Covenant*, 109.
137 Dunn, *Galatians*, 88; but cf. Bruce, *Epistle*, 43–56, Longenecker, *Galatians*, lxxvii–lxxxiii, and Witherington, *Grace*, 13–20, who equate Acts 11 with Gal. 2. For a short listing of the most common arguments *pro* and *contra* a connection between Gal. 2:1–10 and Acts 15, see Witherington, *Grace*, 14–15, and for a more extensive discussion, Fung, *Galatians*, 9–28.
138 Lambrecht, "University," 185.
139 Brown and Meier, *Antioch and Rome*, 36.
140 On the general discussion of the rhetoric of Galatians, see Esler, *Galatians*, 59–61, Witherington, *Grace*, 25–36, and, more exhaustive, Mitternacht, *Forum*, 153–233.
141 Brown and Meier, *Antioch and Rome*, 36; Segal, *Convert*, 189.
142 See Farmer, "James," 149–51, for a dicussion of why Paul's account should take precedence over the account in Acts.

143 Hall, "Historical Inference."

144 See Esler, *Galatians*, 61–8, on the problem of rhetoric and history, and pp. 62–4 for his discussion of Hall.

145 Ibid., 63.

146 The function is to some extent dependent on the genre. While from the beginning of the rhetorical treatment of Galatians there seems to have been a consensus that the incident at Antioch is part of a *narratio*, the genre discussion has been more complicated. From Betz's suggestion in his commentary that Galatians is forensic, the pendulum shifted towards defining the letter as deliberative, while Longenecker found both forensic and deliberative aspects in the rhetorical structure; see Porter, "Paul," 541–7, for an overview of how Galatians has been treated. See also Nanos's discussion of the problems with the rhetorical classification of Galatians, *Irony*, 323–31.

147 Following the Alexandrian text, see Conzelmann, *Acts*, 118, for discussion and references.

148 "Most exegetes agree that the 'kosher' observances from Lev. 17–18, imposed on Gentile converts in Acts 15:20, 29, do not belong historically to the Jerusalem agreement"; see Brown and Meier, *Antioch and Rome*, 38. "Gal. 2:6 excludes the possibility that the decree was decided upon at the Apostolic council"; see Conzelmann, *Acts*, 119. Esler believes that the apostolic decree "represents the core of a compromise agreement reached between Jewish Christians and Gentile Christians, with the Gentiles undertaking to adhere to the four prohibitions, and the Jews in return re-establishing table-fellowship"; Esler, *Community*, 106. Dunn finds that the Jerusalem council settled only the circumcision issue and that the apostolic decree reflects a later agreement; see Dunn, "Incident," 38. See also Catchpole, "Apostolic Decree," 430–1, Bruce, "Apostolic Decree," 117, and Barrett, "Apostolic Decree," 53.

149 Cf. Hurd, *Origin*, 259–62. He suggested that the debate in Corinth was occasioned by a previous letter from Paul, who attempted to enforce the apostolic decree in Corinth. See also Bockmuehl, "James," 190.

150 Nanos, *Mystery*, 52.

151 Novak, *Image*, 25.

152 Ibid., 26.

153 Cf. Segal, "Jewish Voice," 17, who finds that the rules in the apostolic decree "are quite similar to the formulation of the Noahide Commandments." Taylor, "Jerusalem Decree," 374–7, argues that the apostolic decree is a kind of proto-Noahide theology, and Bockmuehl, "Noachide Commandments," 100, concludes that the underlying ideas of the Noahide commandments are prevalent in texts from the period of the second temple.

154 Lev. 17:7–16, 18:6–26; Exod. 12:18–20, 20:10.

155 Cf. Goodman, *Mission*, 53, who argues that the existence of pre-rabbinic passages cited as parallels to Noachide laws "constitute evidence of the *lack* of a Jewish theology about gentiles before 100 CE." On the other hand, Segal, "Jewish Voice," 12, finds that the Noahide laws are traceable to *Jubilees*.

156 Cf. Callan, "Background," 295–7, who argues that the apostolic decree specified the minimal standards for conversion to Judaism.

157 Cf. Barrett, "Paul," 50–1, 56–7.
158 See Hurd, *Origin*, 43–7.
159 Eriksson, *Traditions*, 137, 172–3.
160 Fee, *Corinthians*, 6–10.
161 Tomson, *Jewish Law*, 157.
162 Ibid., 193.
163 Ibid., 218.
164 Ibid., 208–16.
165 "[Paul] clearly applied purity concepts and language to matters of table-fellowship, sexual conduct, discipline, and as the foundation of proper behavior within the community. And he continually described the actions of Christ Jesus in sacrificial and priestly terms (3:25 [ἱλαστήριον as the sacrifice of Yom kippur]; 5:2; 8:3, 34; 15:8)"; Nanos, *Mystery*, 194–5.
166 Ibid., 197.
167 Ibid., 197.
168 Esler, *First Christians*, 52–3. See also Chilton, *Feast*, 8, 98, and *passim*; Fung, *Galatians*, 106; Holmberg, "Christian Identity," 405.
169 Esler, *Galatians*, 93.
170 Esler, *Community*, 84.
171 Catchpole, "Apostolic Decree," 440.
172 Esler, *Community*, 77, or *Galatians*, 95.
173 Esler, ibid., mentions Hecataeus of Abdera, Apollonius of Molon, Diodorus of Siculus, Pompeius Trogus, Tacitus and Philostratus.
174 In Esler, ibid., we find references to Dan. 1:3–17, Jdt 10–12, Add. Esth. 14:17, Tob. 1, *Let. Aris.*, *Jub.*, *Jos. Asen.*, Mishnah and Talmud.
175 While wrongly, I believe, considering the ritual laws of purity (cf. Sanders versus Dunn above) as the cause for a Pharisaic restricted attitude towards Gentiles, Segal, *Convert*, 202, nevertheless reaches a similar conclusion apropos social intercourse when stating that "one can allow a fairly high amount of laxness without assuming that the lax Jews were automatically apostates. It depended on the perspective of the actors in the first century." See also Barclay's clarifying discussions regarding deviance in "Who Was Considered," and "Deviance," 114–19.
176 See Bockmuehl, "James," 168: "so many of the same people must have eaten with Gentiles, without ceasing to be Jews."
177 Sanders, "Jewish Associations," 177.
178 Esler, *Galatians*, 110.
179 Ibid., 110.
180 Dunn also reckons with "a broad range of social intercourse between faithful Jew and God-fearing Gentile" but defines those willing to associate with Gentiles as "less scrupulous" and the others as "strict"; see Dunn, "Incident," 23. Dunn's conclusion is confirmed by Sanders, "Jewish Associations," 180. Holmberg, "Christian Identity," 402, suggests that one must distinguish between different levels of social interactions, i.e., between the *intimate* and the *common sphere*, but he is thus also open to a certain range of association.
181 Tomson, *Jewish Law*, 230.
182 Ibid., 231.

183 See Esler, *Galatians*, 102–4, on Greek and Roman table-fellowship, and pp. 104–5 on the problem with Gentile wine.
184 Tomson, *Jewish Law*, 232.
185 Ibid., 234. Esler, *Galatians*, 106–7, also refers to Tomson's treatment but finds that they do not refer to his table-fellowship of "the relevant type."
186 Esler, *Galatians*, 114.
187 Ibid., 115.
188 Ibid., 113.
189 Nielsen, "Royal Banquets," 103.
190 Esler, *Galatians*, 114.
191 Bradley, "Roman Family," 49.
192 See also Noy, "Sixth Hour," 141, who states that "[t]here is no evidence that the Jews in general had any developed belief in the importance of table-fellowship . . . the only time at which the meal in itself acquired much ideological value was at Passover."
193 Dalby, *Siren Feasts*, 13, but cf. Esler, *Galatians*, 102.
194 Boardman, "Symposion *Furniture*," 126; Bradley, "Roman Family," 48.
195 We cannot assume that every meal in a Greek context developed into a drinking party or had the character of a banquet. "[D]inner parties and drinking parties were surely (in Athens as in most societies) less ubiquitous than their frequent occurrence in memoirs and fiction would suggest"; Dalby, *Siren Feasts*, 12–13.
196 Burkert, "Oriental," 7; Dalby, *Siren Feasts*, 16–20. See also d'Arms, "Heavy Drinking," 304–8, on Roman attitudes to drinking and drunkenness.
197 See especially *Let. Aris.* 235, 261, 274.
198 Dunbain, "Ut Greco," 81.
199 Esler, *Community*, 84.
200 See Bockmuehl, "James," 167: "Philip Esler's forceful and somewhat contrived denial of widespread commensality seems unreasonable."
201 Sanders, "Jewish Associations," 180.
202 Cf. Taylor, "Jerusalem Decree," 379–80, who finds that the crisis emanated from different interpretations of the apostolic decree. Taylor argues that the decree can be understood in terms of proto-Noahide commandments giving the Gentiles a separate status but at the same time keeping them at a distance from the covenant. On the other hand, the decree could be understood as precepts binding on foreign residents. This way of looking at Gentiles would rather result in their being brought closer to the people of Israel. According to Taylor, James advocated the former interpretation and Paul the latter, which gave rise to the conflict. While certainly being an intriguing theory with some points in common with the suggestion in the present work, it fails to take into consideration the eschatological context of the conflict. For that reason, the suggestion that the conflict was about the soteriological status within the Jesus movement seems more likely to me.
203 Sanders, *Paul, the Law*, 208.
204 Sanders, *Palestinian Judaism*, 551.
205 See Gager, *Reinventing Paul*, 46–9, for a critique of Sanders's view of Paul. He concludes, rather pertinently, that "[w]hat is so intriguing

with Sanders's work is that it comes so close to a radical break with the traditional view, yet misses it by a mile."

206 See e.g., Meyer, "Romans," 66; Tomson, *Jewish Law*, 237; Lapide and Stuhlmacher, *Paul*, 42; Gaston, *Paul*, 77; Nanos, *Mystery*, 21–40.

207 Davies, "Jewish," 11. Davies argues that the adjective חדשה in Jer. 31:31, which is translated καινή in LXX (Jer. 38:31) and by Paul in 2 Cor. 3:6, could be applied to the new moon, "which is simply the old moon in a new light."

208 Gaston, *Paul*, 116–34.

209 It is generally accepted that Paul's arguing implies an inclusion in a covenantal fellowship with the god of Israel, while the implications of this usually follow the traditional view of Paul as dealing with the salvation of both Jews and Gentiles; see, e.g., Martyn, *Galatians*, 341; Boers, *Justification*, 63–4; Dunn, *Galatians*, 173; Wright, *Climax*, 137–56.

210 1 Cor. 7:18–20.

211 Gal. 5:2.

212 Nanos, *Mystery*, 184.

213 Ibid., 178–9.

214 Dunn, "Incident," 37.

215 "Declaration on the Relationship of the Church to Non-Christian Religions"; see Abbott, *Vatican II*, 666.

216 As Segal, *Convert*, 192, observes in connection with Luke's depiction of the Jerusalem conference: "[n]o one says that Jews should not be circumcised."

217 Dunn, "Incident," 33.

218 Tomson, *Jewish Law*, 228.

219 Gal. 6:15 and 1 Cor. 7:19 state the same.

220 Cf. Col. 2:11.

221 So also Hill, *Hellenists*, 140.

222 Sanders, "Jewish Associations," 186.

223 Barrett, "Paul," 54.

224 I assume that James was behind the delegation from Jerusalem and that this delegation is identical with "the circumcision faction," and that Peter's reaction was caused by their arrival in Antioch (Gal. 2:12). This is certainly not the only way to understand the text; see, e.g., Nanos, "Peter's Eating," 286–92. However, to understand the reference to "the people from James" as merely a temporal determinator (see ibid., 286, 291–2) does not do justice to the construction of the phrase. The contrast between the very accentuated πρὸ τοῦ γὰρ ἐλθεῖν at the beginning of the phrase and ὅτε δὲ ἦλθον in the second clause strongly suggests that Paul meant to imply a causal relationship between the arrival of the people from James and Peter's reaction. Thus, if such causality is made probable, it is likely that James was the real source of Peter's fear. As Painter has noted, given the position of Peter within the Jesus movement, "some great authority must have been behind the circumcision party and been the source of his fear. This can only be James"; *Just James*, 69. Cf. the discussion and further references in Betz, *Galatians*, 107–8. See also Taylor, *Paul*, 128; Fung, *Galatians*, 107; Bockmuehl, "James," 180; Hallbäck, "Jerusalem," 309; Witherington, *Grace*, 152–6; Dunn, *Galatians*, 117–24.

225 Holmberg, "Christian Identity," 410.
226 For Esler's arguments, see "Making and Breaking."
227 Holmberg, "Christian Identity," 410; Lührmann, *Galatians*, 44.
228 Gal. 5:2–6.
229 Holmberg, "Christian Identity," 411.
230 Cf. Esler, who finds it "extremely unrealistic to assume that the question of table-fellowship could somehow not have come up during the Jerusalem meeting"; Esler, *Galatians*, 136. But this presupposes that table-fellowship generally was considered so problematic that it deserved special attention, something I have taken pains to show was not the case.
231 Cf. Holmberg, "Sociologiska perspektiv," 87–8. On the authority of James, see Farmer, "James," 140–2, and Painter, *Just James*, 84, 96, 269–76.
232 Chilton, *Feast*, 75–92, 148.
233 Ibid., 109–30, 149.
234 Ibid., 149.
235 Ibid., 99–100, 148–9.

5

POLITICS AND
PERSECUTION

Crede mihi, bene qui latuit, bene vixit . . .

Ovidius, Tristia

Introduction

This chapter will present a suggestion as to how the theologically motivated social division between Jesus-believing Jews and Jesus-believing Gentiles, combined with socio-political circumstances, brought about a separation between the communities. It will be argued that this process, which eventually resulted in the emanation of a new religion, was the result of a conscious strategy that can be compared to other expressions of collective action, such as tax rebellions, political uprisings, revolutions or, in short, *social movements*.[1]

By interpreting the separation between Judaism and Christianity in terms of a social movement, we will be able to look at the complex process from a new perspective that may lead us to discover aspects other than those usually focused on. The methodological consideration is also motivated by the number of sources available. The reconstruction of the process of separation between Judaism and Christianity is to a high degree dependent on how the few sources are viewed. In this chapter the theoretical assumptions will therefore be crucial for the interpretation. I would like to remind the reader of the hermeneutical model used in this study: analytical results are dependent on the interaction between 1) a basic, general, theoretical perspective regarding society, 2) specific social-scientific theories derived from empirical studies of human societies, 3) comparative material from antiquity, and 4) primary sources.

One result of using social movement theories is that the socio-political situation will be given due attention. It will be argued that Roman legislation concerning foreign cults as well as the socio-religious system of the Greek cities, combined with a confusion within the Jesus-believing Jewish movement about how to relate to Gentile adherents, gave rise to a situation that could be solved only by a separation between Jews and Gentiles in the Jesus movement. It will be shown how the harsh anti-Semitic statements and the overtaking of the Jewish religious tradition by the Gentile church become intelligible seen from this perspective. The relation between the community of Matthew, formative Judaism and the community of Ignatius will also be given a new interpretation. We will, however, begin with a short survey of some vital aspects of social movement theories.

Constructing analytical tools

A theory of social movements

Social movements and collective action

The history of humanity displays many examples of how people have joined together in order to obtain a common goal. Individual efforts are occasionally mobilized into what we may call *collective action*, which, to use C. Tilly's rather general definition, consists of "people's acting together in pursuit of common interest."[2] Strikes, tax rebellions, different forms of demonstrations, rioting mobs as well as revolutions are examples of how people have acted together collectively, and as a result inherited institutions and established groups have been challenged and their legitimacy has been called into question. One form of collective action is the *social movement*, which may be understood as "nonroutine concerted actions in and through which people try to change their lives and to create situations within which they may—ideally and/or materially—live in comfort."[3] A. Oberschall defines social movements as "large-scale, collective efforts to bring about or resist changes that bear on the lives of many."[4] Tilly refers to the concept of social movement within a Weberian tradition as when "a group of people somehow orient themselves to the same belief system and act together to promote change on the basis of the common orientation."[5]

What is important for the present analysis is that the underlying empirical concept of social movements is based on a set of hypotheses "used for explaining everyday routine behavior, whether it be that of isolated individuals, small groups, large, permanently organized social units, or ephemeral crowds."[6] The concept of social movements is thus connected to the underlying assumption from the sociology of knowledge that *homo sapiens* is also *homo socius*,[7] and this is the reason why it can be assumed that the mechanisms, with cultural variations, involved in a social movement are operative in all human societies, with the possible exception of very homogeneous and closed ones. It is thus a reasonable assumption that these theories might be used to interpret the situation in Antioch during the first century CE.

The rationality of social behavior

One theoretical aspect that is assumed in most recent renderings of social movements is that, when humans are faced with choices, they try to select the most rational or reasonable option. While still considered controversial by some social scientists,[8] this assumption, known as *rational choice theory* (RCT), is in some way or other shared by the leading approaches to social theory.[9] It is important when dealing with the rationality of collective action to note that the term pertains to rationality *within the referential system of the individual*. This means that different people, and cultures, form various concepts of what is rational. Even martyrdom, which for most modern people appears to be a non-rational act, can be interpreted within the theoretical concept of RCT.[10] It is, furthermore, important to note that choices are taken by error-prone humans, who occasionally have faulty, incomplete and irrelevant information available and whose actions influenced by other humans in a complex social context. It is also important to note that RCT is used not as an independent analytical tool, but rather as an underlying perspective. All these aspects are taken into consideration in the following formulation of the principle of human rationality by R. Stark and R. Finke: "*Within the limits of their information and understanding, restricted by available options, guided by their preferences and tastes, humans attempt to make rational choices.*"[11]

Another way of picturing the rational aspect of human behavior is Oberschall's reference to collective behavior as *adaptive* and *normative*.[12] Behavior is adaptive, Oberschall states, when people "choose the alternative for which net benefit, that is, benefit minus cost, is the greatest." While this formulation is somewhat narrower than the one above, it is clear from Oberschall's comments on RCT that his use of the concepts corresponds to that of Stark and Finke.[13] It is, however, his reference to collective behavior as *normative* that is of some importance for the present analysis. Oberschall states that behavior is normative "when people limit the goals they seek and the means of obtaining them to conform to law, convention, rules of conduct and other people's notions and expectations about what is right and appropriate."[14]

One important consequence of collective action being both adaptive and normative is that both goals and means are results of deliberate choices that in turn 1) *are based on experience of what has worked in the past,* and 2) *usually conform to the expectations and norms of the society as a whole.*[15] The repertoire of means used by a social movement is thus restricted by the specific cultural matrix, as is the formulation of goals. But why is it that people gather together at all and formulate such culturally determined goals: in short, what causes social movements to arise?

The origin of social movements

There are several ways of explaining the emergence of social movements. Some theorists consider them to be a result of high levels of dissatisfaction, while others find them to be dependent on the breakdown of institutions providing stability.[16]

Those who emphasize *social breakdown theory* are usually in agreement about three propositions. Firstly, social movements will flourish in periods of rapid social change; secondly, there is a correlation between the degree of hardship and the number of movements, sects, and their adherents; and thirdly, the most dissatisfied people are the most likely adherents of movements and sects. However, as Oberschall notes, negative conditions may exist for a long time and may even worsen without the emergence of a social movement,[17] and, while the propositions appear plausible and may account for some movements, the empirical evidence for applying social breakdown theories on a global level for the emergence of social movements is lacking.[18]

Instead of accentuating societal conditions, an alternative *solidarity theory* emphasizes two other dimensions, namely, 1) changes in the capacity to act collectively and 2) changes in opportunities for success. According to this theory, social movements originate *when social bonds, shared identity, a potential leadership and organization exist in a group and contribute to the capacity of the group to act collectively.* In this perspective organizational aspects are highlighted, since both the capacity to act collectively and changes in opportunities for success are dependent to some extent on the ability of the social movement to mobilize resources from its adherents. Thus, the *mobilization of resources* as well as the *organization* of a social movement deserve some attention.

181

The mobilization of resources

Oberschall refers to the mobilization as "the process through which individual group members' resources are surrendered, assembled, and committed for obtaining common goals and for defending group interest."[19] Tilly, on the other hand, puts more stress on the degree of activity of the participants: "'mobilization' conveniently identifies the process by which a group goes from being a passive collection of individuals to an active participant in public life."[20] For Tilly, the resources are thought of in rather concrete terms, such as "land, labour, capital, perhaps technical expertise as well."[21]

Ideology, however, is a vital part of a social movement, and according to L. d'Anjou it performs two functions: 1) ideology is used as an instrument in resource mobilization, and 2) it includes inherently a challenge to the authorities. We will return to the second function below, but for the moment dwell upon the question of whether ideas and symbols, that is, *ideological components*, besides functioning as instruments in the process of resource mobilization, can also function as resources. F. Kniss relates a discussion of the role of cultural or ideological factors in connection with resource mobilization theories. According to Kniss there has been a certain reluctance to consider ideological components as resources, but recently scholars have begun to reconsider the role of ideal or cultural factors. Kniss makes a statement of great importance for the present analysis, namely that "[i]deas and symbols play a central role in most religious conflicts and religious actors are skilled in the mobilization and manipulation of such resources."[22]

The prospect of reconstructing the division of labor or monetary resources in the early Jesus movement is small, but our sources reveal enough of the ideology of the movement for us to be able to understand the mobilization of ideological resources, especially in situations of conflict. Kniss distinguishes between two kinds of cultural resources, namely, *abstract cultural resources*, that is, ideas and beliefs, and *concrete cultural resources*, for instance, architecture or liturgical forms. Since abstract resources may cover a broad range of meanings, they are more manipulable and more easily mobilized in conflicts over other kinds of resources. Concrete resources are less divisible than abstract resources, which may imply that they are also the object of intense, uncompromising conflicts—it is, as Kniss rightly notes, "difficult to think of someone only partially wearing a black hat."[23]

Resource mobilization quite naturally has consequences for the organization of a social movement. It is vital for the leadership of a movement to create a feeling of solidarity among the members. Tilly has summarized some important aspects of the relationship between group structure and organization in stating that *solidarity* in an organization is a product of shared identity and the existence of the specific kind of interpersonal bonds that link people together.[24] The more extensive its common identity and internal networks, the more organized the group. One way of creating a group characterized by solidarity is to mete out negative sanctions to non-contributors and selective incentives to contributing members.[25] These effects are sometimes observable when different groups join together. Social movements usually start from existing groups that already have an organization, leaders, social bonds, meeting places, etc. Occasionally, such pre-existing groups with common goals may unite and form a social movement together. Such *federations* or *coalitions* may affect the group's solidarity level positively, since loyalty to the group and commitment to the common goal will be decisive for participation. In these situations positive incentives and negative social sanctions operate in pre-existing networks and emphasize participation.[26]

Finally, we will turn to perhaps the most important characteristic of a social movement, namely, *the challenge of one or several aspects of the social system.*

Social movements and social conflict

We noted at the beginning of this survey that social movements involve a process wherein people collectively are trying to bring about or resist changes in order to live in harmony, ideally and/or materially. "Social movement actions," d'Anjou states, "are in part motivated by the fact that existing institutional arrangements fail (or are perceived to fail) to cater to the needs and interests of the excluded groups and categories in society."[27] The effort to change these conditions *always* involves conflict with the dominant authorities in society. This challenge or struggle is carried on at different levels: at the systemic level and, more importantly, always on a cultural level.[28] This implies that conflicts in which a social movement is involved lead to *a process of meaning construction or reconstruction*, since cultural or ideological components are being used as vital resources in order to motivate participants of a movement to commit themselves to the goal of the movement. "A social movement," d'Anjou states, "is a meaning construction process because in every movement its initiators and leaders have to provide a rationale for action that tells people what is wrong and what they have to do to redress this wrong."[29]

The struggles or social conflicts that are the result of the emergence of a social movement's challenge of the dominant order are often very complex, involving several actors interacting in a variety of ways. Tilly's *polity model*, whose basic terminology we will use in the following analysis, takes several important aspects into consideration.

According to Tilly, in any *population* there exists a *government* that controls the main, concentrated means of coercion within the population. In this model we also find two kinds of *contenders* who use resources in order to influence the government, namely, *members* of the polity, who have low-cost access to the resources controlled by the government, and *challengers*, who lack this access to the resources of the government. The *polity* consists of the collective action of the members and the government.

In its most primitive and static version, which should be sufficient for our needs and suited to our sources, all contenders attempt to realize their goals. Federations between different contenders may occur, and even between contenders and the government. All contenders struggle for power but the challengers struggle in particular to enter the polity, while the members of the polity strive to remain in the polity (Figure 5.1).[30]

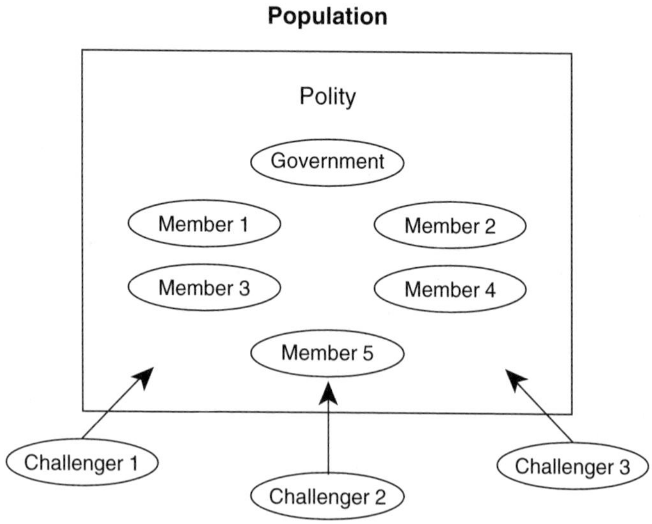

Population

Figure 5.1 Tilly's elementary *polity model*: the *members* of the *polity* strive to remain in the polity, while *challengers* above all strive to enter, in order to get access to routine, low-cost resources controlled by the *government*.

184

Let us now turn to the situation in ancient Antioch and begin with the general socio-political situation that gave rise to a social movement clearly aimed at separating itself from Judaism. Using the assumptions from the theories about social movements, we will turn to the sources and interpret the separation process as a result of collective behavior.

Analysis—the struggle for independence

The call for collective action

The socio-political situation after the Jewish War

The war against Rome ended in catastrophe and with the fall of the temple in 70 CE it was essentially over. For the population of Judea the situation was devastating: entire communities had been completely destroyed, and there are reports of severe casualties among the population.[31]

In the previous chapter we dealt with some aspects of the consequences of the Jewish War. We recall that the Gentile population instituted a more or less systematic persecution of the Jews of Antioch that seems to have been aimed at the complete abolition of Jewish privileges, including religious practices.[32] We noted that Rome's celebration of the victory over the Jews certainly affected Antioch in several ways, but that the Jews at the same time enjoyed protection by their conquerors—Titus even restored their former rights. This, we concluded, probably did not help to improve the strained relations between the Gentile and the Jewish communities of Antioch.

The end of the war had, of course, drastic and immediate political consequences. The most important for the present analysis was the institution of the poll tax *fiscus Judaicus*, which was founded shortly after the end of the war by Vespasian. Its original name was probably *denarii duo Judaeorum*—"the two *denarii* of the Jews." All Jews, male and female alike, and including slaves from the age of three to sixty or sixty-two, were liable to pay annually 2 *denarii*, initially to finance the rebuilding of the temple of Jupiter Capitolinus which had been burnt down in 69 CE.[33]

Apart from the financial burden of the tax, which may have been substantial,[34] the political and social consequences were significant. Due to the tax, Jews were constantly associated with the rebellion in Judea, and, for Hellenized Jews, the striving for increasing integration into Hellenistic society was finally put to an end.[35] Traditionalistic torah-obedient Jews had to cope with the fact that the price they had to pay in order to continue worshiping the god of Israel was a subscription to Jupiter.

From the beginning, only Jews who belonged to the Jewish community had to pay the tax. This means that only Jews who considered themselves Jewish, who worshiped the god of Israel and who observed the torah were intended to pay the tax. There are two texts that support this view. Dio Cassius reports in 65.7.2 that Vespasian "ordered that the Jews who continued to observe their ancestral customs [τοὺς τὰ πάτρια αὐτῶν ἔθη περιστέλλοντας] should pay an annual tribute of two denarii to Jupiter Capitolinus." In B.J. 7.218, Josephus states that "[o]n all Jews, wheresoever resident (τοῖς ὁπουδηποτοῦν οὖσιν Ἰουδαίοις), he imposed a poll-tax of two drachms, to be paid annually into the Capitol as formerly contributed by them to the temple at Jerusalem." E. M. Smallwood has commented that there is a discrepancy between the two texts insofar that one could take Josephus' statement to mean that all Jews irrespective of whether they were observant or not would be liable to the tax, but as she herself remarks, the discrepancy is apparent rather than real.[36] The texts seem to indicate that Jews who had formerly paid the temple tax were now liable to pay the *fiscus Judaicus*: that is, Jews practicing Judaism, both in Palestine and in the Diaspora.[37]

This seems to have been the way that the tax was imposed up till the reign of Domitian (81–96), who, however, made an important alteration in how it was exacted.[38] Suetonius has described the reform in *Dom.* 12.2.

> Besides other taxes, that on the Jews was levied with the utmost rigour [*acerbissime actus est*], and those were prosecuted who without publicly acknowledging that faith yet lived as Jews [*inprofessi Iudaicam viverent vitam*], as well as those who concealed their origin and did not pay the tribute levied upon their people [*dissimulata origine imposita genti tributa non pependissent*].

Suetonius clearly mentions two categories of people. The second is the less controversial. It almost certainly refers to highly assimilated Jews who had left Judaism.[39] Among those who would be affected by the extension of the tax, we would, accordingly, find Julius Tiberius Alexander,[40] and, if the tax enforcement was pursued also outside Rome, Antiochus from Antioch.

The first category is a somewhat more complicated issue. It is usually taken to refer to Gentiles who had adopted Jewish cultural traits or even converted to Judaism without publicly acknowledging this.[41] As we noted in the previous chapter, Gentile admirers of Judaism may have included not only converts and god-fearers who were loosely affiliated with the synagogue: there was a variety of ways in which Gentiles could express admiration for Judaism. During the first century there were, at least in Rome, many Gentiles who, for instance, celebrated the equivalent to the Jewish Sabbath by lighting candles and, strangely enough, by fasting. The crucial question is whether Domitian intended to impose the tax on these categories of Gentile admirers of Judaism, as well as on converts.[42]

L. A. Thompson has asserted that it is unlikely that Domitian meant to impose the tax on god-fearers and converts. If those categories were intended, he argues, the result would be a contradiction, since converts to Judaism would be liable to the tax, while god-fearers and sympathizers would be accused of atheism and run the risk of being executed. According to Thompson, this would imply "a virtual legalization of conversion to Judaism, and that by an emperor who, as is well known, took very severe measures against conversion and Judaizing on the part of Roman citizens."[43] Given the negative attitudes towards Judaism during the period, such legislation would be highly improbable, but Thompson's solution to this problem is, nevertheless, not convincing. He suggests that *both* categories refer to "apostates" and non-Jewish, but circumcised, *peregrini*.[44]

P. Schäfer may have a point in criticizing Thompson for missing the historical reality in his zeal to find a logical solution, namely, that an accusation of atheism was not an official instrument of Roman legislation but a political continuance for eliminating dangerous rivals.[45] This is indeed correct, but the problem remains—how can on the one hand, god-fearers and converts to Judaism be liable to pay tax and, on the other, be accused of atheism?

There is certainly evidence of people being accused of atheism and even executed. Dio Cassius (67.14.1–2) describes how two of Domitian's relatives, among others, suffered this fate.

> Domitian slew, along with many others, Flavius Clemens the consul, although he was a cousin and had to wife Flavia Domitilla, who was also a relative of the emperor's. The charge brought against them both was that of atheism, a charge on which many others who drifted into Jewish ways [τὰ τῶν Ἰουδαίων ἤθη] were condemned. Some of these were

put to death, and the rest were at least deprived of their property. Domitilla was merely banished to Pandatereia.

The interpretation of the phrase "drifted into Jewish ways" has caused some dispute. Are we to consider Flavius Clemens and his wife as Gentile god-fearers, or as converts to Judaism or to Christianity?[46] The most reasonable solution to this problem is that Flavius Clemens and his wife were god-fearers who consequently had adopted different Jewish cultural traits.[47] To some extent they had "drifted into Jewish ways," but Flavius Clemens could hardly have formally converted to Judaism, since this would have required him to break with all cultic duties that were connected to his political office;[48] however, as a god-fearer he could have maintained his link to the official cult. For the same reason it is improbable that he had joined the Jesus movement, and, as pointed out by Smallwood and P. Keresztes, this would almost certainly have left traces in Christian tradition.[49]

The most reasonable way of understanding the action taken by Domitian is that, in addition to extending the tax-base (resulting in increasing income), the emperor wanted to take action against prominent Roman citizens who had adopted Jewish customs.[50] One reason for the severity in exacting the tax may have been a need for money,[51] but it is hard to avoid the suspicion that the underlying anti-Semitism in Hellenistic culture was the most important factor.[52] I suggest both the imposition of the tax on assimilated ex-Jews—that is, people who in all the essentials had ceased being Jewish—and the persecution of Romans with a partiality for Judaism were two expressions of the same phenomenon, namely, fear that Jewish influence on Roman culture would taint the Roman spirit.[53] Thus, the simplest way to understand Suetonius' text is to assume that Domitian never intended to extend the tax to include either god-fearers or recent Gentile converts to Judaism, but only to Jews who had assimilated to Hellenistic society. Recent converts, god-fearers and other sympathizers were instead in danger of being accused of atheism. In such an atmosphere of terror, accusations of atheism or Judaism could easily be used in political struggles for power, as in the case of Flavius Clemens and his wife Flavia Domitilla.[54]

One example of the brutality of this anti-Semitic program is found in the continuation of Suetonius' *Dom.* 12.2 cited above: "I recall being present in my youth when the person of a man ninety years old was examined before the procurator and a very crowded court, to see whether he was circumcised."

This text is often assumed to demonstrate how the Romans, eager to find more Jews on whom to impose the tax, checked whether people were circumcised (= Jewish) or not.[55] Because this man was ninety years old, it is assumed that the original regulations of the tax had been abandoned, since those liable for the *fiscus Judaicus* were men and women between *three and sixty or sixty-two*.[56] While such a change is by no means impossible,[57] another understanding seems more plausible. If we imagine that the aim of this investigation was to decide not whether the man was Jewish *but whether he was Gentile*, and as such possibly guilty of atheism, that is, having "drifted into Jewish ways," the account makes perfect sense.

The consequence of Domitian's enforcement of the *fiscus Judaicus* was in sum that Jewishness and Jewish identity were brought into focus. The humiliating component in the original realization of the tax was even more accentuated, since Jewishness was now apparently considered an ineffaceable quality—once a Jew, always a Jew! The fact that Domitian focused to such a degree on those who had left Judaism and who apparently wanted to be fully integrated into Hellenistic society adds some perspective to the analysis in chapter 3, where I reached the conclusion that there was a group of Jews who clearly intended to leave Judaism. If it was considered by Rome worthwhile to track down such former Jews in order to impose the tax on them, this may give us a hint of the proportions of the phenomenon. The Jewish community was also affected by the increased anti-Semitic atmosphere, but their special privileges seem to have been untouched,[58] since the idea of the tax was to trade religious freedom for money. It may be the case that great parts of the society, at least in the city of Rome, were negatively affected by Domitian's policy.

When Domitian was assassinated in 96 CE, his successor, Nerva, made radical alterations in the way the tax was exacted. One indication of how profound the terror was during the reign of Domitian is that Nerva minted coins with the legend *fisci Juidaici calumnia sublata* (the cessation of malicious accusations relating to the Jewish tax), proclaiming the end of the period. Dio Cassius (68.1.2), reports:

> Nerva also released all who were on trial for *maiestas* [κρινομένους ἐπ᾽ ἀσεβείᾳ] and restored the exiles . . . and no persons were permitted to accuse anybody of *maiestas* (ἀσεβείας) or of adopting the Jewish mode of life ['Ιουδαϊκοῦ βίου].

189

It seems clear that the new emperor's policy was a relief for many groups in society. For the Jews in general, the situation did not change in a fundamental way—negative attitudes towards Jews certainly prevailed. But since the pressure lessened on Gentiles who had adopted Jewish customs, as well as on god-fearers and converts, the focus may have shifted away from Jews and Judaism, and the Jewish community probably experienced some relief during the reign of Nerva. Gentile admirers of Judaism and god-fearers could evidently continue associating with Jews without risk of being accused of atheism. Assimilated, former Jews were probably exempted from paying the *fiscus Judaicus*.

So far we have dealt only with the consequences of the Jewish War, primarily in the context of the city of Rome, and focused on how different Gentile admirers of Judaism as well as Jews were affected by the *fiscus Judaicus* and its anti-Semitic enforcement during the reign of Domitian. In the following we will discuss what bearing this had on the Jewish community in Antioch with its Gentile admirers, focusing particularly on the relation between the Jesus-believing Jews and the Jesus-believing Gentiles and the *polis* of Antioch. We will, however, begin by summing up some aspects of the relationship between Jews and Gentiles in order to get an idea of how the normal relations between Jews, Gentiles and the civic authorities may have been like.

Jews, Gentiles and the fiscus Judaicus *in Antioch*

There is no specific evidence about how the imposition or the reinforcement of the tax made by Domitian affected the Jewish community in Antioch. J. M. G. Barclay has commented that we do not possess any evidence indicating that the issue of tax evasion or atheism was pursued outside Rome.[59] While this is true, it is not the same thing as stating that Domitian's enforcement of the *fiscus Judaicus* did not reach outside the city of Rome. This we simply do not know.

Regarding the tax itself, it is clear that it concerned the whole empire. The ostraka from Appolinopolis Magna shows that from 71/72 the tax was levied in Egypt,[60] and that was probably true for Syria as well. The administrative organization of the tax was already available, since it was probably ordinary tax-collectors who were used to collect this tax also.[61] It is likely that Domitian's reinforcement of the tax had the most severe consequences in the city of Rome, and that its character of witch-hunt was most perceptible in that milieu where it is likely that the political dimension was most salient.

However, if the motivating factor behind Domitian's measures against the Jewish influence was anti-Semitism, as I suggested above, would it not be desirable to have the alterations of the tax imposed empire-wide? Despite the lack of evidence, one cannot take for granted that Domitian's enforcement of the *fiscus Judaicus* and the anti-Semitic program affected only the city of Rome. The Roman presence was very tangible in Antioch, since the provincial administration had its headquarters there.[62]

When it comes to the issue of atheism and potential charges of impiety, we must also bear in mind that the situation in Rome differed from that in Antioch in one respect. The religious/political system in Rome was more homogeneous than that in Antioch, which was basically a Greek city, conquered by the Romans and incorporated in the religious/political system of the empire. As we noted in chapter 2, Greek cities that came under Roman dominance established cults of Roman emperors modeled on existing cults of the gods, and there is every reason to assume that the cult of Roman emperors spread rapidly through the empire.[63] The cult of Domitian was, accordingly, most certainly established also in Antioch. However, since Antioch was originally a Greek city and administered by members of the local elite, participation in the cultic activities of the city was also considered a religious/political duty. In this way one could say that there existed two levels of religious/political control that partly coincided. On the one hand, Rome was in charge of the overarching political structure and their cultic activities. On the other hand, participation in the religious obligations that had to do with being an inhabitant in the Greek *polis* concerned primarily the local authorities of Antioch. The Greek *polis* was principally autonomous—but under the dominance of Rome.[64]

The normal inhabitant of Antioch—Greek, Roman, Syrian, Egyptian, Cretan or Jewish—would have had nothing to fear from the authorities. Foreign cults were organized as *collegia* and existed on the condition that they did not violate public law and that they expressed loyalty to the *polis* as well as to the empire. The Jewish community, while considered one of many *collegia*, had privileges that exempted Jews from participation in the cult of the emperor as well as the official cult of the *polis*. Such privileges were bestowed on the Jewish community during the Seleucid Kingdoms and were only reconfirmed by Rome.

It is clear that, besides participating in the official religion, Gentiles in Antioch also showed interest in Judaism. This constituted no problem in principle—the eclectic character of Greco-Roman religion was simply part of religious expression.[65] In general, most Gentiles remained Gentiles in spite of a profound interest in Judaism, and in most, if not all, cases the interest or admiration did not affect their own Gentile identity. For instance, Gentiles who admired some aspects of Judaism could do so from within a Gentile symbolic universe. Gentiles who acknowledged the power of the god of Israel simply incorporated the new divinity in their pantheon. Benefactors could be fully rooted within the Gentile religious system, and even Gentiles who practiced one or many Jewish rituals did so without leaving their original religious system.

This was possible only because of the tolerant attitude of at least some Jewish communities towards Gentile cults. It was even in the interest of the Jewish communities that Gentile god-fearers did not neglect their cultic obligations towards the *polis* and the empire. God-fearers did not constitute any threat to society. Both god-fearers and the Jewish community thus existed within the polity and within the juridical system and had, accordingly, everything to gain from maintaining the boundaries and everything to lose by not doing so. The relation between god-fearers, the Jewish community and the government is depicted in Figure 5.2.

M. Goodman, however, has argued that, in the period before the *fiscus Judaicus* was imposed, there existed a certain confusion about who was Jewish and who was Gentile, and that the *fiscus Judaicus* promoted the development of a more stringent Jewish identity.[66] To some extent Goodman is right. We have seen evidence in antiquity of a far-reaching confusion regarding who was a Jew and who may have been called a Jew, and that it was impossible to discern between Jews and Gentiles from an outside perspective: however, there is every reason to assume that *the Jewish community knew exactly who was Jewish and who was not.* To some extent, the need to maintain the boundaries

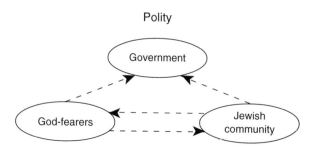

Figure 5.2 The relations between god-fearers, Jews and the government were positive, since all actors existed within the legal system.

192

between Jew and Gentile was part of the concept of being separated from the nations of the world. It was important for the Jewish community to know the status of the people in the synagogues for halakhic reasons. Social interactions of various kinds, such as table-fellowship and marriage, required that the status of specific individuals be made clear.[67] The religious/political dimension also necessitated a clear distinction between those who were exempted from the official cult and those who were not. It may be true that the authorities had difficulties in deciding the religious identity of an individual, but that is not the same as assuming that the Jews were uninterested in or ignorant of the status of people with whom they socialized.

The *fiscus Judaicus* consequently sharpened the boundary between Jew and Gentile in Antioch, especially from the Roman point of view, but there is no reason to assume that such a consciousness did not exist before the introduction of the tax. In fact, the temple tax on which the *fiscus Judaicus* was originally modeled may have functioned in a similar way. The annual contribution to the temple of a half shekel was probably instituted during the Hasmoneans, and in spite of being voluntary it was probably paid by most Jews, who thereby acknowledged their Jewishness and their loyalty to the temple in Jerusalem.[68] While Gentiles occasionally contributed to the local Jewish communities and to the temple in Jerusalem, it is probable that the temple tax was reserved only for Jews.[69] One passage in *m. Šeqal.* 1:5 states that the half shekel would not be accepted from the hand of a Gentile or a "Cuthean" (הנכרי והכותי). The Pharisees referred to the Samaritans as "Cutheans," who were consequently considered as non-Jews.[70] Since the temple tax paid for the communal sacrifice, that is, the sacrifice of *the community of Israel*,[71] there may have existed a certain reluctance to accept contributions from Gentiles and Samaritans, with a reference to texts such as Ezra 4:1–3.[72] We see that there were several reasons for the Jewish community in Antioch to maintain the boundaries between Jew and Gentile, and this is relevant when we discuss how the Jesus-believing communities dealt with the problems of tax, identity and authorities.

The rationality of separation

If we recapitulate the situation in Antioch before the Jewish War, we recall from chapters 3 and 4 that in the late 40s CE there existed several synagogues with different ideologies and different ways of relating to Gentile society. Some of these synagogues were more positive to Gentiles than others, and the messianic Jesus movement

had apparently influenced such synagogues. Given the juridical conditions, the *ekklēsia* in Antioch is best understood as an ordinary
synagogue influenced by the Jesus movement. The only real difference between this synagogue and others was that here the Jews were
Jesus-believing Jews and the Gentiles were *Jesus-believing* Gentiles.

We must assume that the Gentiles who joined the Jesus-believing
Jews were mainly people who had previously related to the synagogue
as god-fearers. Before the introduction of the messianic element they
had thus already adopted Jewish customs, since their motivation for
having associated themselves with the Jewish community in the first
place was a profound interest in Judaism, theologically and/or socially.
As the elite in Rome had done, they had picked up different Jewish
religious practices. They may even have *called* themselves "Jews" and
may have been called so by others,[73] but they *were* Gentiles, and they
fulfilled their religious obligations towards the *polis*, as discussed in
the previous chapter.

With the introduction of the messianic element, some things
would change. As a result of the theology of Paul, *the Gentiles connected
to the Jesus movement understood themselves as part of the covenant that was
originally made between Israel and the god of Israel, and their status had
thus shifted from god-fearer to something more.* However, it is clear that
being incorporated in the covenant made the Gentile relation to the
official cult impossible. In the previous chapter we noted that Paul
both knew and taught the apostolic decree, *which specifically states that
the Gentiles should refrain from things polluted by or sacrificed to idols.*[74] In
this respect the Jesus movement differed from other Jewish ways of
relating to Gentiles, and we must conclude that the halakhah that was
imposed on the Jesus-believing Gentiles was probably more strict than
the halakhah regarding Gentiles practiced by other Jewish groups.[75]

For the Jesus-believing Gentiles, the benefits of this arrangement
far exceeded the costs. As a member of the Pauline Jewish community
in Antioch, a Gentile was part of the soteriological system of Judaism
to a degree never experienced before. Through Christ, Gentiles were
incorporated into the covenantal system that provided salvation
without prior conversion to Judaism. *Non-conversion to Judaism was a
necessary condition.* In addition to this we must not underestimate the
social component: in the previous chapter we reached the conclusion
that social intercourse in this community was less restricted than in
other Hellenistic synagogues. Since Jews and Gentiles now constituted one unity "in Christ," Jesus-believing Jews probably even
accepted dinner invitations from Jesus-believing Gentiles and also
food brought by Jesus-believing Gentiles to communal meals.

According to Antiochean halakhah, the torah, however, was never violated.

The potential cost of belonging to the messianic community was the risk of being exposed as someone not fulfilling the religious obligations of the *polis*. Many Jesus-believing Gentiles were recruited from the group of recent newcomers who lacked social networks, however, and since it was not possible to tell the difference between Jews and Gentiles from an outside perspective, the risk of getting caught must have been insignificant—anyone acting Jewish could easily pass as a Jew. From the perspective of the authorities and other Jewish communities, there was little or nothing that distinguished this Jewish community from others—a kernel of Jews, associating themselves with interested Gentiles, who if necessary could claim to be Jews.

As already mentioned, M. D. Nanos has argued that Romans 13:1–7 refers to the subordination of the Jesus-believing Gentiles to the synagogue authorities and not, as is usually assumed, to the civic authorities of the Roman Empire.[76] If he is correct, this was certainly motivated by theological considerations, but at the same time Paul shows here awareness of the religious/political implications of a theology that prevents Gentiles from participation in the official cult. By subordinating themselves to the synagogue authorities and not striving for separation from the Jewish community, the Jesus-believing Gentiles would have a chance of existing in a religious/political no-man's-land. As Gentiles without the protection from the Jewish community, they would certainly "incur judgment."[77]

The conflict at Antioch did not affect the external appearance of the community as much as the internal. The conflict concerned primarily the covenantal status of the Gentiles and only secondarily different halakhic views on the proper degree of social intercourse. But it did bring about a theologically motivated social division between Jesus-believing Jews and Jesus-believing Gentiles. According to James, and probably every other Jewish faction, no one could enter into the covenant with the god of Israel without prior conversion to Judaism, including male circumcision. The Jesus-believing Gentiles were certainly considered to be embraced by the final salvation, through Christ, as Gentiles, but outside the covenant. This led not only to a theological distinction, but also to a social separation between Jesus-believing Jews and Jesus-believing Gentiles. The Jesus-believing Gentiles became reduced to the status of Jesus-believing god-fearers. The difference between this community and other Jewish communities after the incident at Antioch was accordingly even smaller.

For the Jesus-believing Gentiles the situation became more complicated. According to Pauline ideology the Gentiles should remain Gentiles: *they were not to convert to Judaism*. On the other hand they could not solve the formal problem regarding their relation to the authorities by relating to the Jesus-believing Jewish community as ordinary god-fearers, that is, by also having a relation to the official cult. After Paul left, the Jesus-believing Gentiles were reduced to the status of god-fearers without access to the covenant of the god of Israel *and without any separate religious identity*. They were certainly not Jews—they were even forbidden to convert to Judaism—and they were not proper Gentiles, since they were also forbidden to express the religious/political identity into which they had been socialized.[78] Since they were socially and theologically separated from Jews and Gentiles, the only unifying trait was their belief in Christ, as the one who had suffered and died for them too. In this situation we find the embryo of what would become a separate religious identity and we may already note the most salient characteristic of what would later become "Christianity," namely, *non-Jewishness*.

The Jesus-believing Jews would have no identity problem, since the messianic element had not affected their Jewish identity to any great extent. This messianic/apocalyptic element of the Jesus movement was, of course, genuinely Jewish, and nothing indicates that Jesus-believing Jews ever saw themselves as anything but Jews. Did these Jews pay the temple tax? This is a tricky question, since there is certainly evidence of a critical attitude towards the temple in the New Testament.[79] It is likely that the gospels' report of Jesus predicting or threatening the destruction of the temple is historical.[80] Luke's formulation of Stephen's speech in Jerusalem certainly shows that the Jesus movement had picked up this element from the traditions about Jesus.[81] While Luke reports that Paul refers to the same attitude to the temple in the speech before the Athenians,[82] he also pictures Paul as confirming his commitment to the tradition by sacrificing in the temple.[83] On the other hand, Matthew 17:24–7 specifically states that Jesus paid the temple tax. W. Horbury takes this as evidence of a halakhic conflict between Jesus and the Pharisees in which Jesus takes a position more profound than that expressed by the priests and by the Qumran community. Jesus paid, but only in order not to cause offence.[84]

One can find strains of severe criticism of the temple in Jewish tradition. One of the most profound appears in the passage *Sib. Or.* 4:27–30, which envisages a time when mankind "will reject all temples . . . altars too, useless foundations of dumb stones . . . defiled with blood," and only "look to the great glory of the one God." The majority of critical attitudes towards the temple, however, are directed not against the temple institution or the sacrificial cult *per se*, but, as in the case of the Qumran community, against the current administration and in the context of an eschatological restoration theology.[85] Jesus' attitude towards the temple is also best seen in such a theological context, and in this respect he continued traditions prevalent within the Judaism of the period.[86] In general, people seem to have been positive to the temple and to the sacrificial cult that was thought to atone for the sins of Israel.

Given this diversity within first-century Judaism, it is unlikely that there was *one* single view within the early Jesus movement of how to relate to the temple tax. It is more likely that individual Jews who joined the Jesus movement continued the praxis they had followed before they joined the movement. There may have been Jews who did not pay the tax, but, since it seems as if most Jews did, *there is every reason to assume that most Jesus-believing Jews paid it, thereby expressing their identity as Jews and their loyalty to the temple of Jerusalem.*[87]

But what about the Jesus-believing Gentiles: did they also pay the temple tax? I believe that we must distinguish between Paul's attitude and that of the rest of the Jewish Jesus movement in this matter. According to Nanos, in Romans 13:7 Paul urges the Jesus-believing Gentiles connected to the Jesus-believing Jewish community in Rome to pay "taxes to whom taxes are due" (τῷ τὸν φόρον τὸν φόρον). Nanos takes this to refer to the temple tax and he argues that the payment of this tax was part of the halakhah that "righteous gentiles" were obliged to keep (we have already dealt with this in connection with the apostolic decree). While I am somewhat reluctant to accept the suggestion that god-fearers in general paid the temple tax, Nanos is probably right in assuming that Paul considered it proper for the Jesus-believing Gentiles to support the temple in Jerusalem. This would be completely in accordance with Paul's theology of including the Jesus-believing Gentiles in the covenant, as argued in the previous chapter. Thus, they were obliged to share the responsibility for the community sacrifice, not as Gentiles, *but as covenantal partners.*

I am inclined to imagine, however, that James thought differently. He, and the majority of the Jesus movement after the Antioch incident, considered that the Jesus-believing Gentiles were not to be included in the covenant, but that they would be saved according to the theology of god-fearing Gentiles. This was almost certainly the position of the majority of the Jews. The Jesus-believing Gentiles may have called themselves Jews, been called Jews by others, and have been seen as Jews from the perspective of the authorities, but within the Jesus-believing community everybody agreed that Jesus-believing Gentiles were not Jews, and non-Jews, as we recall, probably did not pay the temple tax. We may conclude that, after the incident at Antioch, the status of the Jesus-believing Gentiles within the polity of Antioch was somewhat unclear.

While the Jesus-believing Jewish community still had a relation with the authorities of Antioch, the Jesus-believing Gentiles had lost theirs by not fulfilling their religious duties as Gentile inhabitants in a Greek *polis*. They were completely dependent on their relation to the Jesus-believing Jewish community, since it gave them the possibility of passing as Jews. In this way the Jesus-believing Gentiles' religious/political status was disguised by their relation to the Jesus-believing Jewish community.[88] With the fall of the temple and the replacement of the temple tax with the *fiscus Judaicus*, things would, however, change dramatically (Figure 5.3).

While the temple tax in principle had been voluntary, the *fiscus Judaicus* was not: while the decision to contribute to the temple had rested upon the individual, it was now the authorities who decided who had to pay Vespasian's tax.[89] Not paying the temple tax did not necessarily affect Jewish identity: some Jews, the priests for instance, probably did not pay and considered this to be in accordance with being Jewish. The *fiscus Judaicus*, however, had serious consequences for identity: if someone claimed to be not liable to pay the tax, he or she could not at the same time insist on being Jewish and demand to be exempted from participation in the official cult. Inversely, if someone was considered as liable for the *fiscus Judaicus*, this was the

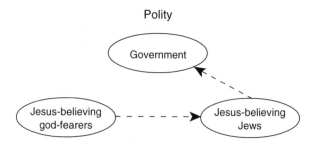

Figure 5.3 The status of the Jesus-believing Gentiles after the incident in Antioch was reduced to that of god-fearers. They had lost their intimate relationship with the Jewish community, and also their religious/political relationship to the *polis*, since this was dependent on the participation in the official cult.

same as being defined as Jewish. Consequently, a direct connection between the tax and Jewish identity grew up and the tax was the price the Jewish community had to pay in order to maintain its religious and political privileges.

Let us now consider the situation of the Jesus-believing Jews as well as the Jesus-believing Gentiles after the Jewish War, and after Vespasian's introduction of the *fiscus Judaicus*. The Jesus-believing Jews almost certainly considered themselves as nothing but Jews, and were probably organized as a usual Jewish institution—a synagogue, properly defined as one of many *collegia*. As such they were recognized by the civic authorities in the *polis* of Antioch, admittedly with some help from Titus. We recall that the inhabitants of Antioch wanted to have the Jews thrown out, or alternatively have them stripped of their rights, and that Titus instead confirmed the Jewish privileges (*B.J.* 7.102–11). There can be no doubt that Jesus-believing Jews must have been considered liable to pay the *fiscus Judaicus*, regardless of whether they had previously paid the temple tax or not. The only way for them to avoid paying now would be to renounce their Jewishness and claim that they were Gentiles, but that would, of course, require them to participate in the official cult. Given the increased hostility directed against Jews in the aftermath of the Jewish War, it is not likely that Gentile society would accept Jewish defectors. It was never easy to leave Judaism, and the war had not made it easier. It is possible that Antiochus' violent behavior against his own family and people is to be seen against the background of conflicts of loyalty within the Antiochean society. By betraying and falsely accusing the Jews of having intended to burn down the city, and by severely punishing them, he assured the empire and the *polis* of his loyalty. The consequence of this for the Jesus-believing Jewish community was *a reinforcement of their Jewish identity*, since those who were considered liable for the tax were defined as Jews.

The situation of the Jesus-believing Gentiles, which had certainly been complicated even before the war, was now even more convoluted. From the perspective of the civic authorities they were defined as Jews, since this was the only way to cloak their vulnerable relation to the *polis*.[90] Now, however, there was a price to pay for being Jewish. By paying the *fiscus Judaicus*, the Jesus-believing Gentiles would resolve the tension in relation to the civic authorities: they would, however, be defined even more clearly as "Jews" and thereby pay the price for their religious freedom. *This must, in fact, have been their only alternative.* To deny being "Jewish" would almost certainly have led to severe reprisals from the authorities and from the general population

199

as well, since their collaboration with the former enemy, the Jews, would have been looked upon with utmost scepticism. To return to an ordinary Gentile life would certainly have required them to renounce their relationship with the Jews in the most profound way—and they would thus lose their relation to the god of Israel who, through Christ, provided salvation for everyone who believes. Without the Jesus-believing Jewish community they would certainly be lost, in every aspect of the word.

Being associated with Jews and Judaism during the period immediately after the war was far more fraught with social problems than before it. Already from the period *before* the outbreak of the war the population of the Syrian cities, thus including Antioch, was conscious of the potential double loyalties of people who associated themselves with the Jews. Josephus writes in *B.J.* 2.462–3:

> The whole of Syria was a scene of frightful disorder; every city was divided into two camps, and the safety of one party lay in their anticipating the other. They passed their days in blood, their nights, yet more dreadful, in terror. For, though believing that they had rid themselves of the Jews, still each city had its Judaizers (τοὺς ἰουδαΐζοντας), who aroused suspicion.

According to S. J. D. Cohen, ἰουδαΐζω could refer here either to Gentiles who had sided with the Jews in their political struggles or to Gentiles who had adopted Jewish customs. He continues, "on either account they were suspected, presumably of collaboration with the Jews, but were not killed."[91] We have seen how the anti-Jewish attitudes increased after the war, and there is every reason to assume that the Gentile population kept the Gentile admirers of Judaism under suspicion to an even higher degree than before.

Theologically, the Jesus-believing Gentiles realized that they were not to be considered Jews. Both Paul and James had been in agreement about this: the clash in Antioch concerned how *the Gentiles* should be understood to relate to the Jewish community and the degree of social intercourse between Gentiles and Jews, not whether Gentiles should become Jews or not. Moreover, their association with the Jesus-believing Jews resulted in their having to endure the persecutions that had fallen upon the Jews of Antioch. Being lumped together with the Jews meant that they could continue to exist without a separate religious and social identity, but it could also mean being beaten up or killed as a Jew or as a Gentile collaborating with the Jews. During Domitian's enforcement of the *fiscus Judaicus*, we can assume that things got even worse.

Now, if we assume that human behavior is basically rational, how would the Jesus-believing Gentiles react to this social-ideological dilemma? What action would be the most rational if one embraced an ideology that made Gentile identity a necessary condition for salvation, *but at the same time required a Jewish definition in order for it to be maintained?* Moreover, if the connection to the Jesus-believing Jewish community *that had established a social and theological division between the communities led to persecution for being Jewish, would this not give rise to a desire to create a situation within which one may—ideally and/ or materially—live in comfort?* Furthermore, during the turn of the first century, the second generation of Jesus-believing Gentiles was becoming integrated into the social world of the Jesus movement. We must also allow for new Gentile adherents to the movement as a result of missionary activities. For these categories the present conditions were not obvious but had to be made part of the individuals' symbolic world through the process of socialization (in the case of the second generation) and resocialization (in the case of new adherents to the movement) (Figure 5.4).

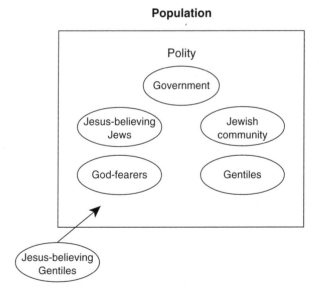

Population

Figure 5.4 To be able to obtain a position within the polity, the Jesus-believing Gentiles must place themselves outside the polity, thus taking the position of challengers.

I suggest that this socio-political situation gave rise within parts of the Jesus-believing Gentile community to a mobilization of ideological resources which established a social movement resulting in an effort to separate the Jesus-believing Gentile community from the Jesus-believing Jews. Given the juridical and political conditions, such a process would of necessity include the establishment of a separate organization that could be recognized by the authorities: a *collegium* for Jesus-believing Gentiles fully separated from Judaism.

To be able to succeed with this perilous task, the Jesus-believing Gentiles would have to disassociate themselves from Jesus-believing Jewish community in order to acknowledge their true Gentile identity, and in this situation they would be extremely vulnerable.[92] In order to get *into the polity of Antioch*, they must cut themselves off from the Jesus-believing Jewish community that provided them with cover, *and place themselves outside the polity*, as in Figure 5.4.

Such collective behavior would conform exactly to Oberschall's reference to the rational aspect of human behavior, since it implies that the social movement of separation would base its action on what worked in the past, that is, the institution of the *collegia*, and it would furthermore have conformed to the expectations and norms of society as a whole: that is, by accepting the prevalent juridical conditions. From this it follows that the parting of the ways in Antioch was primarily a separation—not between "Judaism" and "Christianity" —but between Jewish and Gentile adherents to the Jesus movement.

Using theories about collective action, I will show in the following how the scanty sources make the scenario that I have suggested plausible. I will demonstrate how this perspective, together with the results we have hitherto reached and our overarching theoretical assumptions, will present us with a coherent picture of the parting of the ways, primarily in Antioch but with possible wider implications.

I will begin at a point in history when we are able to find clear evidence of a Gentile Christian movement in Antioch for the first time: namely, in the writings of Ignatius. Here we find the ideological goal of the movement revealed in the harsh conflict between the synagogues of the Jesus movement and those Jesus-believing Gentiles who chose to remain in the Jewish community as Gentile god-fearers. At the same time we find evidence of the vigorous reaction of Rome, both in the writings of Pliny the Younger and in the way Ignatius' life ended.

Christianity as a social movement

Judaism, Christianity and Ignatius of Antioch

Ignatius of Antioch is one of the first authors *within the Jesus movement* who writes from a perspective *clearly outside Judaism.*[93] In Ignatius' world, the separation between Judaism and Christianity had to some extent already taken place. This is not to say that the separation process was completed, but, in the symbolic world of the bishop in Antioch, Christianity was, or at least should be, a non-Jewish movement. If this separation was a result of a social movement possessing a sufficiently clear ideology to effect such a change as a result of the socio-political situation as outlined above, it would not be surprising if we were to find traces of the goal and ideology of that movement in the writings from a period when the movement was fully active. I will argue that this is exactly the case: in the writings of Ignatius we will find not only the goal of the movement, but also signs of social conflict, an organizational adaptation to the current situation, and insights in what may have functioned as the main ideology of the movement. Let us begin with the most evident: the goal of the movement.

The most evident indication of the goal of the assumed movement is, of course, the presence of texts that clearly state the difference between Judaism and Christianity. In the first chapter, we looked at some of those texts and reached the conclusion that Ignatius assumed that Judaism and Christianity were two incompatible religious systems. This is, of course, nothing but the ideological goal of the social movement that emanated from the need to create a religious movement in order to separate from Judaism. Eighty, ninety years after the death of Jesus, we find a Gentile movement whose present leader, Ignatius, embraces the ideology that adherents to the movement must refrain from Jewish influences. We remember from the first chapter that Ignatius in *Magn.* 10:3 states that, "[i]t is monstrous [ἄτοπόν ἐστιν] to talk of Jesus Christ and to practise Judaism [ἰουδαΐζειν]."

The verb ἰουδαΐζω is used here in the sense "to live according to Judaism," and, while the phrase has been taken to refer to Jewish life in general,[94] Cohen has pointed out that the context suggests that the specific issue at stake was connected with the problem of when to celebrate the Lord's Day.[95] What we find here is the echo of the goal of the movement Ignatius represents: withdraw from Judaism!

This raises, of course, the question of what Ignatius meant by the term "Judaism." The text above, and especially the use of ἰουδαΐζω, which is often employed in the context of non-Jews adopting Jewish customs, suggests that Ignatius had Gentile "Judaizers" in mind.[96] During this period, Jews cannot "Judaize," only non-Jews can.[97] What Ignatius meant is that for a Gentile adherent of the Jesus movement it is out of the question to adopt Jewish customs—in this actual case, the celebration of the Sabbath instead of the Lord's Day. While this text refers to the local situation in Magnesia, Ignatius' concept of the relation between Christians and Jews is no *ad hoc* solution, but emanated from the local situation in Antioch.[98] Thus, in Ignatius' handling of the local problems in Magnesia and Philadelphia, his view of what constitutes Jewishness becomes evident.[99]

In what context can we expect to find a Gentile adopting Jewish customs? In general, god-fearers who associated themselves with the Jewish community would fit such a description, but in this case it becomes strikingly clear that Ignatius refers to a special faction of Judaism and god-fearers: namely the very same kind of Jesus-believing Jewish community from which Ignatius and his community had separated. Let us take a fresh look at another text from Ignatius, namely, *Phld.* 6:1:

> But if anyone interpret Judaism to you [ἐὰν δέ τις ἰουδαϊσμὸν ἑρμηνεύῃ ὑμῖν] do not listen to him; for it is better to hear Christianity from the circumcised than Judaism from the uncircumcised [ἄμεινον γάρ ἐστιν παρὰ ἀνδρὸς περιτομὴν ἔχοντος χριστιανισμὸν ἀκούειν, ἢ παρὰ ἀκροβύστου ἰουδαϊσμόν].

We will return to the potential identity of the first category later and for the moment focus on those uncircumcised who interpret Judaism. The most reasonable suggestion regarding the identity of such a group is that they represent some kind of Gentile adherents to some form of Jesus movement. By reading together different texts about Judaism and assumed docetic opponents, L. Gaston reaches the conclusion that the group in Philadelphia represents "a group of Gentile Christians with a docetic christology."[100] I believe him to be right about the "Gentile Christian" part, but, as pointed out by J. L. Sumney, the question of whether Ignatius faced one, two or several different opponents is dependent on whether the letters are to be read together or, as he suggests, individually.[101] Taken by itself, this letter shows no traces of docetism.[102] W. R. Schoedel also believes that the latter group in the text above are Gentile Christians. He states that Ignatius has in mind "(a) a group of circumcised Jewish Christians and (b) a group of uncircumcised Gentile Christians and regards the latter as followers of the former."[103] He continues by stating that the uncircumcised condition of the Gentile adherents can be explained since circumcision was not always required of proselytes.[104] As we noted in the previous chapter, J. Nolland found no indication of any Jewish group who admitted uncircumcised proselytes, at least not during the first century CE.[105] Due to the very strong connection between the covenant and circumcision, it is highly unlikely that any Jewish faction would have admitted uncircumcised converts. Not even Paul did this, since he did not consider the Gentile adherents to the Jesus movement to be Jews. We have also noted that it was perfectly normal that Gentiles associated with the Jewish community.

Schoedel is close to the truth anyway: I suggest that Ignatius in Philadelphia encountered an ordinary community of Jesus-believing Jews with some Gentile Jesus-believers cloaked as Jews. We will return to the specific ideology below and for the moment confine ourselves to saying that the community seems to have based its case on the interpretation of the LXX as indicated by the passage *Phld.* 8:2.[106] If we take seriously the statement that the early Jesus movement was a Jewish faction with different ways of relating to Gentiles, but one which basically used models already prevalent within first-century Judaism, there is nothing strange in finding one expression of this in Philadelphia.

This solution has the clear advantage of sparing us from inferring the completely unconfirmed and unlikely *ad hoc* hypothesis that this Jewish community was "unorthodox" in perhaps not demanding circumcision from converts. From Ignatius' point of view, the uncircumcised Gentile adherent to the Jesus-believing Jewish community interpreted "Judaism," since there did not exist a specific term for "Jewish Christianity." As a result of the introduction of the *fiscus Judaicus* the Jesus-believing Jewish communities' Jewish identity had become even more accentuated. In order to avoid participation in the official cult, Gentile adherents to the movement had to disguise their existence by pretending to be Jews. Even though Ignatius and those following him, in Antioch as well as in other places, intended to separate from Judaism, *not every Gentile adherent to the Jesus movement found this to be the only solution.* It is likely that many Gentiles chose to remain in close connection to a Jesus-believing Jewish community, as their motivation for having associated themselves with the Jews in the first place was a profound interest in Judaism. Consequently, they had no intention of leaving messianic Judaism for a Gentile religion stripped of almost every Jewish influence except the idea of the

Messiah and the Holy Scriptures of the Jews. From Ignatius' point of view, such an understanding represented a Jewish rather than a Christian standpoint. We recall that in his view it is not *impossible*, but *monstrous*, to talk of Jesus Christ and at the same time live according to Judaism.[107]

There is another source that can be interpreted in a way that would confirm the existence of Gentiles living disguised as Jews. A couple of decades before Ignatius wrote to the Philadelphians, the author of Revelation specifically mentioned the community in Philadelphia (Rev. 3:19):

> I will make those of the synagogue of Satan who say that they are Jews and are not, but are lying [τῶν λεγόντων ἑαυτοὺς Ἰουδαίους εἶναι, καὶ οὐκ εἰσὶν ἀλλὰ ψεύδονται]—I will make them come and bow down before your feet, and they will learn that I have loved you.[108]

The identity of those who call themselves Jews but according to the author are not really Jews has caused some debate.[109] According to the majority of scholars, the text refers to the local Jewish community.[110] While this is by no means an unlikely reading, the perspective I have suggested opens the way for an alternative understanding. It may be the case that what Ignatius and the author of Revelation refer to is one kind of manifestation of the Jesus movement that evidently includes Gentiles who hid their existence by pretending to be Jews.[111] The author of Revelation, representing a Jesus-believing Jewish standpoint, may have reacted against an increasing Gentile influence on the Jesus-believing community, while Ignatius, a couple of decades later, would have reacted against those Gentiles who still wanted to associate themselves with the Jesus-believing Jewish community. From his perspective, their existence rested on an incorrect interpretation of the scriptures,[112] and was still a kind of Judaism, *namely the same kind of Judaism that Ignatius' social movement was about to leave.*

It is evident that we have here a social conflict which is exactly what we might expect if we are dealing with a social movement consisting of people acting together in pursuit of a common interest. We remember the proposition that social movements are partly motivated by the fact "that existing institutional arrangements fail (or are perceived to fail) to cater to the needs and interests of the excluded groups and categories in society."[113] The attempt to manage such a situation always leads to conflicts with dominant authorities in society. In the case of Ignatius and the Gentile separation movement, we expect to find two sources of conflict: 1) one in connection with the separation from the Jesus-believing Jewish community and 2) the other connected to the role of being a challenger and the efforts to get back into the polity, but on equal terms with other members in the polity. We will start by dealing with the first conflict.

Apparently Ignatius' conflict with Judaism, that is, *primarily Jesus-believing Judaism*, is intense. Now, if it is true that Ignatius' "Christianity" had emanated from a former relationship with a Jesus-believing Jewish community and that the Gentile adherents had previously disguised their existence by pretending to be Jews, we should be able to find some indications of this. The nature of the conflict could actually be taken as evidence of the relation between Ignatius and his opponents: that is, indicating that the conflict, as I suggest, was primarily between Ignatius, representing the Jesus-believing Gentiles, and the Jesus-believing Jews.

In his classic reformulation of some of G. Simmel's propositions concerning social conflict, L. A. Coser distinguished between two basic kinds of conflicts:

> Conflicts which arise from frustration of specific demands within the relationship and from estimates of gains of the participants, and which are directed at the presumed frust-rating object, can be called *realistic conflicts*, insofar as they are means toward a specific result. *Nonrealistic conflicts*, on the other hand, although still involving interaction between two or more persons, are not occasioned by the rival ends of the antagonist, but by the need for tension release of at least one of them. In this case the choice of antagonists depends on determinants not directly related to a contentious issue and is not oriented toward the attainment of specific results.[114]

According to this definition it is evident that the conflict between the Jewish and Gentile faction in the Jesus movement was a *realistic conflict*. It was the Gentile adherents' frustration at being reduced to Gentile god-fearers and being trapped in the religious/political system without any possibility of expressing their true religious identity, that is, as covenantal partners, that triggered the social movement of separation. The conflict was thus directed at the frustrating object, that is, the Jesus-believing Jewish leadership, that according to the Gentile movement misinterpreted the scriptures in not allowing Gentile adherents full covenantal status as Paul had done. Instead, they had been forced to pretend to be Jews, which they were not, neither according to their own ideology nor according to that of the Jesus-believing Jews. That Paul played a vital part in the ideology of Ignatius is certain. In two of his letters he refers directly to Paul,[115] and it is assumed that Ignatius knew several of Paul's letters and honored him as a source of instruction.[116]

The conflict that emanated from the formation of the new Gentile movement was certainly a means towards a specific result: namely, the separation from every kind of Jewish influence. At the same time it meant maintaining some specific Jewish religious traits as the Holy Scriptures and the concepts of covenant and the Messiah, while certainly "de-Judaizing" them and transforming them into a new Gentile religion—Christianity.

According to the writings of Ignatius and other texts that reveal the conflict between the Gentile and Jewish factions of the Jesus movement, the conflict seems to have been fierce. In addition to the text we have studied here, we may note that the "demonization" of Judaism had already begun: in *Phld.* 6:1–2, Judaism is identified with "tombstones and sepulchres of the dead" and with "wicked arts and snares of the prince of this world." According to Coser, close ties and great involvement may result in deeper conflicts, and one may even assume a greater intensity in conflicts where the participants had had to suppress hostile feelings.[117] Thus, the strength of the conflict between Ignatius and Judaism *may indicate that there had originally been a close relationship between the participants.* This fits very well into the scenario I have suggested, as does Coser's statement about suppressed feelings. Before the rise of the social movement, there were few possibilities for the Jesus-believing Gentiles to express their dissatisfaction at having been reduced to the status of god-fearers, since they were completely dependent on the Jewish community. This relationship may have been even more complicated if Paul, as suggested by Nanos, had insisted that the Jesus-believing Gentiles should subordinate themselves to the synagogue authorities and that this ideology was operative among the Jesus-believing Gentiles.[118]

This suggested former intimate relationship also indicates that the two groups were basically in agreement about the fundamental values and goals of the movement. To use Coser's terminology, the Gentile group that broke away from the Jesus-believing Jewish community constituted a *heretical* group who upheld the central interests of the Jesus movement, "only proposing different means to this end or variant interpretations of the official creed."[119] According to Coser, conflicts within a close group are more passionate and more radical: "[t]he coexistence of union and opposition in such relations makes for the peculiar sharpness of the conflict."[120] This corresponds well to the suggested picture of the relation between Jesus-believing Jews and Jesus-believing Gentiles: as it seems, the only major aspect of disagreement was the status of Gentile adherents to the Jesus movement. This was at the heart of the conflict in Antioch between James and Paul and which led to the social/theological division between Jesus-believing Jews and Jesus-believing Gentiles. It is probably this issue that was at stake in the conflict between Ignatius and his opponents in Philadelphia, too. In *Phld.* 8:2 Ignatius states:

> For I heard some men saying, "if I find it not in the charters in the Gospel I do not believe," and when I said to them that it is in the Scripture, they answered me, "that is exactly the question."

It is clear that it is the Jewish Bible, probably in the form of LXX, that is meant by the word "charter" (τὰ ἀρχεῖα).[121] Nothing, however, indicates what Ignatius and his opponents disagreed about. What is it that Ignatius finds in the scriptures, but his opponents do not? If we assume that the major conflict between Jesus-believing Jews and Jesus-believing Gentiles was the status of Gentiles within the Jesus movement and that this conflict in combination with socio-political circumstances gave rise to the social movement, as I have suggested, it is likely that Gentile status was in fact the cause for the dispute also in Philadelphia. What the Jesus-believing Jews could not find in the Jewish Bible was that Gentiles should be included in the covenant without prior conversion to Judaism, and therefore they refuted any gospel that presumed such a Gentile status. They were probably right: it takes a rather advanced hermeneutical re-reading of the biblical texts in order to reach such an understanding, and, while the exegesis of the rabbis from later periods indicates that they could very well have reached such a strained understanding of the text (Paul did), the challenging of the covenantal theology was certainly a restraining factor. This is probably why Ignatius refrains from continued exegesis: he refers rather to a higher authority: the cross, death and resurrection of Christ.

There is still one aspect of Coser's conflict theory that is of interest to us. Coser states that one example of a *non-realistic conflict* is anti-Semitism, "except where it is caused by conflicts of interests or values between the Jewish and the other group or individuals."[122] The example is apt and gives our hypothesis further support, since Coser furthermore states that "[i]f total personalities are involved, there is also a greater likelihood that nonrealistic elements will enter into realistic conflict situations."[123] We noted above that Ignatius in *Phld.* 6:2 connected Judaism with the activities of "the prince of this world," and that he in *Magn.* 8:1 probably used popular prejudice against Jews in describing Judaism as being based on myths and fables.[124] In the previous chapter we noted that intellectual attitudes that are best understood as anti-Semitism certainly existed. It is well known that, in the decades after the death of Ignatius, Christian literature abounds in developing anti-Semitic themes. We can thus conclude that the nature of the conflict, as it appears in the writings of Ignatius, indicates a *realistic conflict within a close group that eventually acquired non-realistic elements*. This, in turn, could be taken as evidence for the proposed hypothesis that the parting of the ways was primarily between Jewish and Gentile manifestations of the Jesus movement, that is, a conflict originating within a close group.

Finally, if the Gentile separation from the Jesus-believing Jewish community can be interpreted in terms of a social movement, we should be able to find an adequate leadership organization, and this is, in fact, exactly the case. If we compare the leadership structure in the 50s with the one in the letters of Ignatius,[125] we certainly find that the authority of the ministry has been strengthened.[126] The ministry as reflected in the letters of Ignatius clearly centers around the bishop. In *Smyrn.* 8:1 we read how the *bishop* is associated with Christ and the *presbytery* with the apostles, and how the deacons shall be reverenced "as the command of God."[127]

This is exactly what we might expect. We recall that a social movement may originate *when social bonds, a shared identity, a potential leadership and an organization exist in a group and contribute to the capacity of the group to act collectively*. Hitherto, we have found evidence of the social bonds and the shared identity in the social situation of the Jesus-believing Gentiles, who in order to avoid reprisals from the authorities pretended to be Jews, thus suppressing their own ideology and identity as covenantal partners. As a result of the Antioch incident their former status as covenantal partners had been reduced to that of god-fearers, *thus without the possibility of intimate fellowship either with the Jewish part of the community or with the Gentile community*. We have noted the goal of the movement: to separate from Judaism. We have seen that Ignatius was involved in a serious social conflict with the Jesus-believing Jewish communities. We have now found the presence of a strong, rather well-developed hierarchic leadership in the community of Ignatius, as well as in those he writes to or visits.

We will now direct our attention to how the leaders in Ignatius' community in Antioch used their authority in order to mobilize ideological resources for the separation from the Jesus-believing Jewish community. For this purpose we will turn to a document that seems to have functioned as a source and an expression of the main ideology of the movement—the Gospel of Matthew.

Resource mobilization and the Gospel of Matthew

It is clear that Ignatius knew the Gospel of Matthew in one form or another. Schoedel, for instance, finds evidence of the use of Matthew in one or two passages of Ignatius and "gospel material of a Matthean type not derived from the Gospel" in one or two passages.[128] J. P. Meier, on the other hand, finds about a dozen possible allusions to the Gospel and four texts that clearly show dependence on Matthew.[129] He considers the simplest explanation to be that Ignatius in fact knew and used Matthew rather than pre-Matthean traditions,[130] and this is also what he refers to by the term εὐαγγέλιον.[131] While it is not certain that the Gospel originated in Antioch,[132] it is a historical fact that Ignatius not only knew but also used the Gospel of Matthew in some form in the situation in which he lived.[133]

The nature of Matthew, its clearly Jewish orientation and its obvious tendency to shape creatively the traditions it used have resulted in an interest in the relation between the Matthean community and Judaism and occupied scholars throughout the twentieth century. The discussion will presumably continue even during this century, since the question of the social and historical location of the Matthean community has by no means been resolved. In a recent study, *The Controversy Stories in the Gospel of Matthew* (2000), B. Repschinski concludes a very extensive *Forschungsbericht* by stating, "[t]he harsh distinction between Jews and Gentiles of early redaction criticism has given way to a more fluid perception of Matthew's gospel reflecting the transition from Judaism to a Gentile church."[134] D. Senior makes a similar remark in his comprehensive introduction entitled *What Are They Saying About Matthew?* (1996), and points out that all hypotheses about the setting of the Matthean community point to a church in transition "from a predominantly Jewish Christian church to an increasingly Gentile church."[135] There is consequently a fairly well-established consensus about the existence of a process of transition from a Jewish context to a Gentile one, but there remain different views on how and when this transition took place.[136] The perspective on the separation process between Judaism and Christianity that I have suggested may also have some implications for our under-standing of the relations between the Matthean community, Judaism and the community of Ignatius. We will therefore turn to the question of the role of Matthew in an Ignatian setting.

It would not be too bold a hypothesis to assume that the presence of the Jewish Gospel of Matthew in the hands of the Gentile non-Jewish and even anti-Jewish community of Ignatius in some way represents a culmination of the process of transition from a Jewish to a Gentile setting. The insights that Ignatius' community both *knew and used* the Gospel of Matthew, irrespective of its origin, and that Ignatius at the same time understood "Christianity" to be something profoundly different from "Judaism" raise, however, questions about the role of Matthew in the separation process between Ignatius and the Jesus-believing Jewish community of Antioch. If we accept the suggestion that Ignatius led a social movement that intended to separate from Judaism, primarily understood as a Jesus-believing Jewish community, the leadership of which we have found evidence must have been involved in mobilizing resources from the members of the community. Ideology, we recall, performs a twofold purpose: it is used as an instrument in resource mobilization and embodies the challenge of the authorities. Ideological components in the form of *abstract cultural resources* are easily mobilized in conflicts, and we recall that religious actors are usually skilled in the manipulation of such resources. In a resource mobilization perspective, what role would Matthew have had in the conflict with the Jesus-believing Jews? Assuming that Ignatius' community functioned as a social movement, what impact would Matthew have had in this specific socio-historical situation, irrespective of its original *Sitz im Leben?* If Matthew could be shown to have fulfilled the function of ideological resource in the conflict with the Jesus-believing Jewish community, this could be taken as further evidence for the hypothesis that Ignatius represented a social movement aimed at separation from Judaism. We will thus turn to the question of how the text of Matthew could have func-tioned as a cultural resource in the social conflict between the community of Ignatius and the Jesus-believing Jews.

In a social movement, the leadership will try to create a feeling of solidarity among its members and establish a group with strong interpersonal bonds and a shared identity. Several aspects of the Gospel of Matthew could well serve such a purpose. For instance, Matthew presents us with a clear in-group/out-group perspective. This is evident already in the presentation of the disciples. It is a well-known fact that Matthew knew nothing of the disciples' lack of understanding that is so prominent in the Gospel of Mark.[137] In Matthew, the disciples are the primary recipients of the teaching of Jesus, and the major speeches are directed mainly to Jesus' own disciples. By a combination of having been given the gift of under-standing and having been properly instructed by Jesus, the disciples understand his teachings fully.[138] S. Byrskog has summarized the relationship between Jesus as the only teacher and the pupils by stating *"Jesus is as teacher the essential identity marker for a group of pupils."*[139] Byrskog furthermore finds that the disciples in the narrative are not merely figures of the past, but that they also exhibit traits that make it likely that the readers/hearers of the Gospel *could identify with the disciples.*[140] It is evident that this theme from the presentation of the disciples in Matthew may have been used in the community of Ignatius as a means of creating a shared identity in the community. The true disciples are those who understand the teaching of Jesus.

In the Gospel of Matthew we also find how negative sanctions are meted out to non-contributors while incentives are allotted to those within. Several texts are structured in a similar way: to those loyal to the teaching of Jesus, rewards will be meted out, while those outside will face punishments of different kinds. This is rather well exemplified in Matthew 13:47–52:

> Again, the kingdom of heaven is like a net that was thrown into the sea and caught fish of every kind; when it was full, they drew it ashore, sat down, and put the good into baskets but threw out the bad. So it will be at the end of the age. The angels will come out and separate the evil from the righteous and throw them into the furnace of fire, where there will be weeping and gnashing of teeth. "Have you understood all this?" They answered, "Yes." And he said to them, "There-fore every scribe who has been trained for the kingdom of heaven is like the master of a household who brings out of his treasure what is new and what is old."

In this text it is evident that it is the attitude towards Jesus' teaching that determines whether a person belongs to the in-group or to the out-group.[141] Those outside do not understand the teachings of Jesus. This is the most pertinent characteristic of the false disciples of Matthew, and the whole section of 13:1–53 is dedicated to developing this theme. Matthew seems in general to have a clear idea of who belongs to the community and who does not.

As Overman has pointed out, Matthew deleted the story of the so-called strange exorcist found in Mark 9:38–40 and Luke 9:49–50. The saying about allegiance in Mark 9:40 and Luke 9:50 ("[w]hoever is not against us/you is for us/you") is instead found in an inverted Q version in Matthew 12:30: "[w]hoever is not with me is against me, and whoever does not gather with me scatters." In Matthew's world it is unthinkable that there would be a genuine exorcist who was not a member of the Matthean community, and membership in that community is a result of a conscious decision.[142] A skilled leader would have no problem in using these *cultural resources* in order to create a feeling of shared identity and a group characterized by solidarity.

In Ignatius' version of group identity, membership in the community also depends on the attitude towards the bishop. In *Phld.* 3:2, Ignatius states "[f]or as many as belong to God and Jesus Christ,—these are with the bishop," which could reflect a distant echo from the Gospel of Matthew concerning allegiance. Furthermore, we have seen how Ignatius was engaged in disputes over the interpretation of the scriptures, and in *Phld.* 7:2 he refers explicitly to the *spirit of god* who legitimizes the authority of the bishop. It is rather evident that Ignatius is of the opinion that he has been entrusted with the gift of understanding the teaching of Jesus, and in the dispute in *Phld.* 8:2 he identifies the "charters" with "Jesus Christ." *It is evident that the Gospel of Matthew could serve the purpose of both creating group solidarity and legitimizing the interpretative authority of the bishop.*

This leads us to the question of how the Gospel of Matthew may have been used in mobilizing resources for the social conflict. Repschinski has analyzed the controversy stories in Matthew in order to determine the relation of the Matthean community to Judaism. His redaction-critical analysis shows, hardly surprisingly, that Matthew not only took over the traditions handed down to him, but reworked them to suit his purpose. This is evidenced, for instance, in the appearance of the opponents, *who are clearly defined as the Pharisees*. Together with this concentration on the Pharisees as the main antagonists in the controversies, Matthew's redaction reflects that the conflict is *not only between Jesus and the opponents but also involves his disciples*.[143] Moreover, Repschinski's analysis of the narrative context shows that "the controversy stories are part of the Matthean agenda to delegitimize the Jewish leaders."[144]

Both these aspects would fit well into a situation where the Ignatian community was involved in a conflict with a Jesus-believing Jewish community. We remember that Byrskog found that the disciples in Matthew exhibit traits *that make it likely that the readers/ hearers of the Gospel could relate to the disciples*. Thus, by taking over the

214

roles of the disciples in the narrative world of Matthew, the community of Ignatius could use Matthew as an ideological resource in the conflict with the Jewish leadership in the Jesus-believing community. Ignatius' divinely legitimated leadership, bestowed with the gift of interpreting the scriptures as the true disciples of Jesus, could engage in a conflict similar to that of Jesus. As Jesus, presented in Matthew as "the superior interpreter of scripture and Law,"[145] was involved in a conflict over the interpretation of the torah, so was Ignatius' community. Even though the opponents of Ignatius in Antioch also believed that Jesus of Nazareth was the Messiah, their inability to understand the scriptures in the way Ignatius did excluded them from being "Christians":

> Not everyone who says to me, 'Lord, Lord,' will enter the kingdom of heaven, but only the one who does the will of my Father in heaven. On that day many will say to me, 'Lord, Lord, did we not prophesy in your name, and cast out demons in your name, and do many deeds of power in your name?' Then I will declare to them, 'I never knew you; go away from me, you evildoers.'

This text from Matthew 7:21–3 may very well have been used in order to assure Ignatius' community that even if the Jesus-believing Jews claimed to act in the name of Jesus this was, in fact, not true. Only Ignatius' community could claim to do the will of their Father in heaven.

It is obvious that the Gospel of Matthew, despite its Jewish orientation, could be used as an instrument in the process of mobilizing resources both inwards (creating a group with a shared identity and characterized by solidarity) and outwards (in the conflict with the Jesus-believing Jewish community). This leads us to the question of why the Jewish Gospel of Matthew became the property of the Gentile community of Ignatius at all.

We noted in the beginning of this section that there is consensus about Matthew representing a transition from Judaism to a Gentile church. However, the scenario that I have suggested allows not for a gradual transformation *but for a radical break*. This presents a rather interesting avenue of exploration when it comes to explaining how Ignatius' community came to be in possession of the Gospel of Matthew. The simplest explanation is that the Jesus-believing Gentiles *used the same text after the separation from the Jesus-believing Jews as they had used before the separation*. This leads to the rather astounding

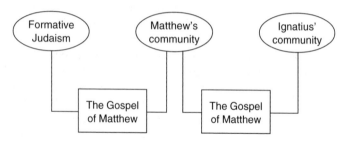

Figure 5.5 The community of Matthew was simultaneously involved in a
conflict with the Jesus-believing Gentiles and with formative
Judaism. The Gospel of Matthew was used as an ideological
resource for both Matthew's community and the Jesus-believing
Gentiles' community.

conclusion that, if the community that created the Gospel of
Matthew was located in Antioch, which is possible, *it may be the case
that the community of Ignatius, in fact, broke off from Matthew's community.*
Since the community of Matthew was involved also in a conflict with
formative Judaism,[146] we reach the conclusion that the Gospel of
Matthew was used *both, and even simultaneously, in the conflict between the
community of Matthew and the Pharisees and their successors after the fall of
the temple and in the conflict between Ignatius' community and the Matthean
community.* We would thus have the scenario that is illustrated in
Figure 5.5.

What we find here is the first step in the adaptation of the Jewish
Holy Scriptures by the Jesus-believing Gentiles that would eventually result in the takeover and transformation of a complete religious
tradition. For some Jews, the combination of a repudiation of Jews but
assent to their religious tradition may have appeared as an attractive
alternative.

Federations and the mission to the Jews

Contrary to the prevalent consensus, R. Stark has suggested that Jews
on a large scale converted to Christianity, not only initially but up to
the fourth century. He takes his point of departure from a few
sociological propositions derived from empirical studies of religious
conversions in the present-day United States. For instance, Stark
claims that converts to new religious movements are recruited mainly
from the religiously inactive and discontented and those affiliated with
the most accommodated religious communities. There is, furthermore,

a tendency for people to be more willing to adopt a new religion if it retains cultural continuity with the religion they are already familiar with. Finally, social movements grow much faster if they spread through pre-existing networks.[147] Stark goes on to say that, since the Hellenized Jews of the Diaspora had adjusted to a life in the Diaspora, they had become marginal in relation to the Judaism practiced in Palestine. On the other hand, because of their commitment to the torah, they were prevented from participating in the civic life of the Hellenistic cities. "In short," Stark concludes, "large numbers were no longer Jews in the ethnic sense and remained only partly so in the religious sense."[148] However, these marginalized Hellenistic Jews could resolve the tension inherent in their situation by becoming Christians; they would then no longer have to keep the torah, and the hindrance from becoming part of Hellenistic society would thereby be removed.

While Stark has certainly indicated interesting mechanisms, there are some obvious problems with his analysis that are connected to his understanding of Judaism and Christianity. This, I believe, makes his suggestion less applicable to the general situation. With some minor modifications it will, however, be possible to use his analysis to show that some Jews certainly joined the Jesus movement. The question is: *did they join the Jesus-believing Jews or the Jesus-believing Gentiles—and for what reason?*

Firstly, Stark's view of Diaspora Judaism is in need of some refinement.[149] The suggestion that the Jews of the Diaspora were marginalized is probably not entirely correct. Some Jews certainly were: the analysis in chapter 3 showed that there were Jews who lived on the fringe of Judaism and wanted to be completely assimilated to Hellenistic society but who nevertheless encountered severe difficulties on account of the prevalent attitudes towards Jews. Domitian's attitude towards those Jews who concealed their origin may indicate that this phenomenon was of considerable proportions. To assume that *all* Jews of the Diaspora believed that adaptation to Hellenistic society contradicted torah obedience is, however, a mistake and is based on a stereotyped view of Jews and Judaism. On the contrary, Judaism of the Diaspora had managed to adapt to the conditions and had found means to make halakhic adjustments that enabled a fully Jewish life. It may have been a different kind of Judaism than the one in Jerusalem—the analysis of the Antioch incident showed that there were different views on how to relate to Gentile society—but in general it was possible to maintain a Jewish identity in the Diaspora. That the Jews of the Diaspora were only waiting for someone to invent a torah-free version of Judaism is part of the Christian confessional discourse and should be rejected as such. In reality, the Judaism of the Diaspora was far more complex than to fit the description "marginalized Hellenized Jews."

However, Stark's attempt at explaining aspects of the rise of Christianity is hard to reject entirely. It is not unthinkable that Jews would be attracted to the Jesus movement: the question is which Jews and what kind of Jesus movement? There is one group who would certainly fit nicely into Stark's description of people who are mainly drawn to new religious movements: namely, those Jews who felt alienated and clearly intended to leave Judaism. We recall Stark's assumption that converts to new religious movements are *recruited mainly from the religiously inactive and discontented and those affiliated with the most accommodated religious communities.*

Despite their clear desire to become assimilated into Hellenistic society, very Hellenized Jews may have encountered severe difficulties in achieving this. We noted in our previous treatment of Antiochus from Antioch that the action he took against his family and people may have been motivated by a wish to show clearly where his loyalty lay. It is likely that the period before and after the Jewish War was not well suited for Jews who wanted to leave Judaism and become part of Hellenistic society. Domitian's alteration of the *fiscus Judaicus* to include also assimilated ex-Jews is one indication of the attitudes towards Jews at the turn of the first century CE. In fact, the entire first century had been a disappointment for those who wanted to combine Judaism and Hellenism: already in the 40s Claudius had put an end to the Hellenistic program of the Alexandrian Jews, and a copy of his edict was also sent to Antioch. The Jewish War resulted in an increased distrust of and suspiciousness against Jews, and anti-Semitic strains within Hellenistic culture, prevalent before these and subsequent revolts, crystallized further.

Thus, those who wanted to cross the path between Judaism and Hellenistic religion and culture found that the road was closed. At the same time, the desire to leave Judaism during this period must have been even more marked, since they were being persecuted. Ironically, these Jews had to endure this persecution from the very group they wanted to join because they belonged to another group they wanted to leave. The situation of these Jews resembled that of the Jesus-believing Gentiles, who wanted to separate from Judaism. In fact, the goal of both these groups seems to have been congruent. Could not Gentile Christianity have been an alternative for these Jews?

One could, of course, argue that there would be little to gain for these Jews if they joined the Jesus-believing Gentiles, since during this period the latter were persecuted by the authorities, as indicated by the famous letter of Pliny the Younger to Trajan.[150] Could it be considered rational to exchange one persecution for another? This, I suppose, depends on whether the prevalent difficulties were considered transient or not. The hypothesis that the Jesus-believing Gentile movement intended to split off from Judaism leads to the assumption that they also attempted to gain recognition as an independent *collegium*. This would be in accordance with the presumption that collective action is *adaptive* and *normative*: people usually attempt to 1) make rational choices, 2) base their action on what has worked in the past, and 3) conform to the law, convention and people's notions and expectation about what is right and appropriate.

There are indications that Ignatius' movement was involved in the process of getting back into the polity of Antioch. We recall from chapters 2 and 4 that the Romans had a weakness for ancient traditions. Julius Caesar, we recall, prohibited all *collegia* empire-wide, *with the exception of the ancient ones*—for instance, Judaism. Suetonius in *Aug.* 93 reports that Augustus had a restrained attitude towards new cults but "treated with respect such foreign rites as were ancient and well established."[151] L. H. Feldman has devoted one whole chapter in his *Jew and Gentile in the Ancient World* (1993) to the topic of the attraction of the Jews due to the antiquity of their religion. He points, for instance, to the seemingly general principle during the Hellenistic and Roman periods that "the older and more eastern things were, the more divine and the more credible they were."[152] He notes furthermore that, of Tacitus' six accounts of Jewish origins, four contain "pro-Jewish intimations, all of which impute great antiquity (so much admired by the ancients, especially by the Romans, who lacked it) to the Jews."[153]

We may conclude that if a new religious association during the reign of Trajan were to have a chance of becoming a legally recognized *collegium, its chances of success would certainly have increased if it could prove to be as ancient as Judaism.* On the other hand, Judaism proper would probably not serve as the best model for a new *collegium*, since Jews were associated with rebellion—the Jewish War 66 to 70 CE was followed by local revolts in Egypt and Cyrenaica, and possibly even in Palestine, 115–117 CE.[154] The *fiscus Judaicus* was still levied on all who were defined as Jews—a constant reminder of the rebellious spirit of the Jews. From Pliny's letters we know that Trajan was extremely restrictive in allowing new *collegia*, since he feared that they could become political associations.[155] But *what if a new religious association claimed antiquity on a par with Judaism by emphasizing that its members were the true Gentile heirs to the religious heritage of the rebellious Jews and stressed that this correct understanding of the Jewish religion could only be realized in a non-Jewish context?*[156]

One theme that is specially developed in much Christian *Adversus Iudaeos* literature is that the *Jews had misunderstood their own Holy Scriptures and as a result had lost the right to them*. This right had instead passed over to the Christian church, which now represents the true people of the god of Israel. Such tendencies are evident already in texts from the end of the first century CE, for instance, in Hebrews and *Barnabas*, but more developed in texts from the second century, as in Justin's *Dialogue with Trypho*, *Apology* and Melito of Sardis' *Peri Pascha*. We have already seen that Ignatius was involved in disputes regarding the interpretation of the scriptures, and he is actually taking over parts of the Jewish religious tradition: the prophets were in fact not Jews but a variety of Christians. This is the logical consequence of their not living according to Judaism but according to Jesus Christ, as Ignatius states in *Magn.* 8:1–2:

> Be not led astray by strange doctrines or by old fables which are profitless. For if we are living until now according to Judaism [εἰ γὰρ μέχρι νῦν κατὰ Ἰουδαϊσμὸν ζῶμεν], we confess that we have not received grace. For the divine prophets lived according to Jesus Christ. Therefore they were also persecuted, being inspired by his grace, to convince the disobedient that there is one God, who manifested himself through Jesus Christ his son, who is his Word proceeding from silence, who in all respects was well-pleasing to him that sent him.

First, Ignatius' exhortation not to be led astray by doctrines and fables is best understood as a warning *against Jewish interpretations of the scriptures*. It is likely, as Schoedel states, that the identification of Christ as the word from silence refers to the supposed inability of the Jews to understand their own religious tradition: the appearance of Christ from silence brings the divine hidden purpose to light.[157] The radical "Christianization" of the prophets is one indication of how profound this inability is, and how extensive the hostility is between Judaism and Christianity. The ideological message is clear: the Jews do not understand what their sacred texts are really about. Even within the seemingly Jewish tradition, there have always been true followers of Christ, the prophets, who did not feel obliged to observe the torah, as indicated by their reluctance to observe the Sabbath (*Magn.* 9:1). As indicated by the example of the prophets, true followers of Christ have always been persecuted by true followers of Judaism. According to this ideology, Christianity is the true manifestation of the divine revelation at Sinai, and Judaism, including the Jewish faction of the Jesus movement, represents a misconception. What we find in the conflict with the Jews and in the "Christianization" of Jewish traditions *is the mobilization of ideological resources to be used in the struggle for a position in the polity.* The Jesus-believing Gentile movement had been forced voluntarily to place itself outside the polity—this was a result of the separation from the Jesus-believing Jewish community: now was the time for the struggle for a position within the polity—but on their own terms.

There is some evidence that confirms that the Gentile Jesus movement tried to influence the civic authorities. In his *Ecclesiastical History*, Eusebius preserved an apology attributed to a certain Quadratus, who probably presented his defense for Christianity to Hadrian during his stay in Asia Minor in 123–124 or in 129.[158] Eusebius writes in *Hist. eccl.* 4.3.1:

> When Trajan had reigned for nineteen and a half years Aelius Hadrian succeeded to the sovereignty. To him Quadratus addressed a treatise, composing a defence for our religion because some wicked men were trying to trouble the Christians. It is still extant among many of the brethren and we have a copy ourselves. From it can be seen the clear proof of his intellect and apostolic orthodoxy.

This could be interpreted as evidence for how the Jesus movement tried to influence the civic authorities in order to be legally recognized as a *collegium*, fully separated from Judaism. The same is true for the epistle to Diognetus, presumably from the beginning of the third century.[159] The letter, written to a high-ranking Gentile, is full of anti-Jewish statements and stresses the peaceable character of the Christians as well as their moral qualities.[160] These texts show that Christians tried to influence the authorities, and it is reasonable to assume that the goal of the lobbying was to convince the civic authorities of the rationality in admitting this non-revolt-prone, non-Jewish, ancient cult into the polity.

Thus, the Hellenized Jews who wished to leave Judaism in order to become more assimilated to Hellenistic society found in the Jesus-believing Gentile movement *Gentiles* who wanted to *separate* from

Judaism and *create a place in the polity of Antioch* as a *non-Jewish Gentile collegium*. Now, we recall that pre-existing groups with common goals may sometimes *unite and form a social movement together*. This is exactly what we find here. By joining the Jesus-believing Gentile movement, some very Hellenized Jews found a way, perhaps the only way, to put their plans for assimilation into action and to do this without abandoning the fundamental aspects of their original culture. People, we recall, are more willing to adopt a new religion if it retains cultural continuity with the religion they are already familiar with. In the Gentile Jesus movement, Jews found a way to retain Judaism but to cease being Jewish and instead become Gentiles. We may now return to the text from *Phld.* 6:1: "it is better to hear Christianity from the circumcised than Judaism from the uncircumcised [ἄμεινον γάρ ἐστιν παρὰ ἀνδρὸς περιτομὴν ἔχοντος χριστιανισμὸν ἀκούειν, ἢ παρὰ ἀκροβύστου ἰουδαϊσμόν]."

Now we understand that the circumcised from whom Christianity can be heard may very well refer to those Jews who had joined the Gentile Jesus movement and, by doing so, for all intents and purposes ceased to be Jewish.

Summary and conclusion

During certain conditions people join together in order to obtain a common goal. One form of such collective action is the social movement that can be defined as a group of people orienting themselves to the same belief system and acting together to promote change on the basis of this common orientation. It has been argued that the emergence of a Gentile Jesus movement can basically be understood as a social movement and that theories about social movements can be used to understand the separation between Judaism and Christianity.

One salient feature of social movement theory is that human behavior is rational. This rational aspect implies that social movements limit their goals to conform to law, convention and other people's notions of what is right and appropriate, and that the aim of the movement is often based on experience of what has worked in the past.

It is argued that the emergence of the goal within parts of the Jesus movement was a result of such a rational, conscious choice based on several circumstances. The ideology of the Jesus-believing Jewish community differed in one aspect from other Jewish communities in that they did not allow the Jesus-believing Gentiles to perform their cultic obligations to the *polis* and at the same time relate to the Jesus-believing Jewish community. As a result, Gentiles had to cloak their existence by subordinating themselves to the synagogue authorities and by pretending to be Jews. During the period before the Jewish War this was possible, but there is evidence from Antioch that shows that the Gentile population was aware of the ambivalent position of god-fearers.

In the period following the Jewish War, the possibility of existing in a religious no-man's-land was reduced due to the imposition of the *fiscus Judaicus*. During the reign of Domitian there is, furthermore, evidence that the tax was levied even more efficiently and was combined with a program of reducing the cultural influence of Judaism on the Roman population.

The result of this was that religious adherence rather than being automatic became a matter of a conscious decision. Someone who wanted to adhere to Judaism had to pay the *fiscus Judaicus* and was thereby identified as Jewish and could claim exemption from participation in the official cult of the *polis*. The possibility of retaining a Gentile identity and at the same time refraining from cultic duties could lead to accusations of atheism and result in the death penalty. The reasonable assumption is that the majority of the Jesus-believing Gentiles solved this potential conflict with the civic authorities by paying the Jewish tax and remaining subordinate to the synagogue authorities. This, however, resulted in a dilemma. On the one hand, the Jewish identity of the Jesus-believing Jews was further reinforced by the Jewish tax, on the other hand, both Jews and Gentiles within the Jesus movement agreed that the Gentile adherents were still Gentiles and should not become Jews. It was exactly this situation that had led James's faction to exhort the Jesus-believing Jews to refrain from intimate social intercourse with the Jesus-believing Gentiles. The outcome of the incident in Antioch had resulted in a separation of the community into two commensality groups and the status of the Jesus-believing Gentiles had been reduced to that of god-fearers. However, because of the reluctance of the Jesus movement to allow the Gentile adherents to participate in the official cult, the Jesus-believing Gentiles became deprived of all social and religious identity.

Probably during the reign of Domitian, there emerged in the Jesus-believing Gentile community a leadership that formulated a separate theological program, presumably based on a one-sided understanding of Pauline ideology about Jews, the covenant, the torah and the eschatological destiny of the Jewish people.

This ideology is to some extent observable in the writings of

Ignatius. We find in his letters a clear understanding of Christianity as something profoundly different from Judaism. It is no longer possible to combine Jewishness with Christianity. It is "monstrous to talk of Jesus Christ and to practice Judaism," Ignatius writes to the community in Magnesia. The writings of Ignatius also exhibit a tendency to take over the religious heritage of Judaism. In matters of interpretation Ignatius claims to have been granted the gift of understanding the Jewish scriptures in a more correct way than the Jews.

This perspective implies that the separation between Judaism and Christianity was, in fact, a separation between Jesus-believing Jews and Jesus-believing Gentiles. This could also explain the fact that the community of Ignatius was in possession of the Gospel of Matthew. Presuming that the community that created the Gospel of Matthew was located in Antioch, the simplest explanation as to why the Jewish-oriented text of Matthew ended up in a non-Jewish Gentile religion is that the parting of the ways in Antioch occurred between Matthew's community and that of Ignatius. This implies that the text of Matthew was involved in two conflicts, since Matthew's community also seems to have been involved in a coincident conflict with formative Judaism. We consequently reach the intriguing conclusion that both Matthew's and Ignatius' communities used the same text as an ideological resource in their respective conflicts. Ignatius used Matthew in the struggle for independence and in an effort to create a legally recognized *collegium*, separated from Judaism, while the Matthean community used the text to create a new kind of Judaism.

Notes

1 To see Christianity as a social movement is nothing new: see, e.g., Blasi, *Early Christianity*, who applies this concept to the entire early Jesus movement. His conclusions tend, however, to be rather general. This could be explained by the fact that the scope of the work is very broad and does not really take into account the social and political conditions in the Roman Empire or the dynamics of the interaction between different Jewish and Gentile groups.
2 Tilly, *Mobilization*, 7.
3 d'Anjou, *Social Movements*, 40.
4 Oberschall, *Social Movements*, 2.
5 Tilly, *Mobilization*, 40.
6 Oberschall, *Social Movements*, 11.
7 Berger and Luckmann, *Social Construction*, 69.
8 For an extensive critique of rational choice approaches to religion, see Bruce, *Choice*, and, for a brief survey, Bruce, "Critique." See Beckford,

"Start Together," 491–2, for a short account of positive as well as negative criticism of RCT.

9 See McAdam, McCarthy and Zald, "Social Movements," 707, for a short survey of rational choice theory in connection with social movement theory.

10 Stark, *Rise of Christianity*, 163–89.

11 Stark and Finke, *Acts of Faith*, 38.

12 The terminology is not univocal. While crowd insurgencies in the early and middle twentieth century were usually labelled *collective behavior*, there has been a tendency during the last decades to prefer the term *collective action*; see Lofland, *Social Movement*, 11. On Tilly's use of the term, see Hunt, "Collective Action."

13 See Oberschall, *Social Movements*, 34–5.

14 Ibid., 11.

15 One exception is the riot where everyday norms are being suspended; see ibid., 16.

16 Ibid., 16–19.

17 Ibid., 17, 47.

18 Ibid., 17–19, 47.

19 Ibid., 56.

20 Tilly, *Mobilization*, 69.

21 Ibid., 69.

22 Kniss, "Ideas," 8. See Hart, "Cultural Dimension," for a critical evaluation of movement culture in recent research, especially pp. 93–6, where Hart deals with the culture in relation to resource mobilization tradition.

23 Kniss, "Ideas," 9.

24 Tilly, *Mobilization*, 62–4.

25 Oberschall, *Social Movements*, 57. Similar effects have been analyzed by Iannaccone, who has shown that strictness, or even sacrifice, screens out members who lack commitment and stimulates participation among the remaining members; see "Sacrifice" and "Strict Churches."

26 Oberschall, *Social Movements*, 24.

27 d'Anjou, *Social Movements*, 40.

28 Ibid., 41.

29 Ibid.

30 Tilly, *Mobilization*, 52–4.

31 Schäfer, *History*, 131.

32 Goodman, "Diaspora Reactions," 30.

33 On the *fiscus Judaicus* in general, see Tcherikover and Fuks, *CPJ: 1*, 80–2, and *CPJ: 2*, 110–16, and *CPJ* 160–229. See also Carlebach, "Rabbinic References," for a treatment of one explicit mention of the *fiscus Judaicus* in rabbinic literature.

34 The liability to pay the tax rested upon the master of a Jewish family, who had to pay for his wife, his unmarried daughters and minor sons and his slaves, probably even for any non-Jewish slaves in the household; see Tcherikover and Fuks, *CPJ: 2*, 114. Barclay, *Mediterranean Diaspora*, 77, remarks that a family with two children would face an annual bill increasing by 60 percent.

35 Smallwood, *Jews*, 374.

36 Smallwood, "Domitian's Attitude," 2.
37 Cf. Barclay, *Mediterranean Diaspora*, 311, n. 68, who is less certain of whom Vespasian thought liable to pay the tax.
38 Cf. Barclay, ibid., who makes the remark that whether one chooses to describe Domitian's action as an extension of the tax-base or merely as a "clamp-down" on tax evasion is a matter of perspective.
39 Barclay, *Mediterranean Diaspora*, 311; Keresztes, "Jews," 5. Smallwood, "Domitian's Attitude," 3, has suggested that "Jews who had become Christians" may have been intended, and Schäfer, *Judeophobia*, 114, agrees. See also Sanders, *Schismatics*, 167, who is open to the possibility that "Christians" may have been present in *both* groups.
40 Goodman, "Nerva," 41; "Diaspora Reactions," 32.
41 Cohen, *Beginnings*, 42; Barclay, *Mediterranean Diaspora*, 311; Smallwood, "Domitian's Attitude," 3.
42 Smallwood, ibid., 4, suggests that "Domitian extended the incidence of the tax, so that it fell not only (as before) on practising Jews (i.e., Jews by religion as well as by race), but also on non-practising Jews and on gentile converts."
43 Thompson, "Domitian," 335.
44 Ibid., 339–40.
45 Schäfer, *Judeophobia*, 114. Barclay, *Mediterranean Diaspora*, 312, Smallwood, "Domitian's Attitude," 7, and Rutgers, "Roman Policy," 106–7, also point to the political dimension.
46 For instance, Lane, "Social Perspectives," 225 (Christians), Smallwood, "Domitian's Attitude," 9 (god-fearers), Keresztes, "Jews," 27 (converts to Judaism).
47 Barclay, *Mediterranean Diaspora*, 312, n. 72; Schäfer, *Judeophobia*, 116; Feldman, *Jew*, 347.
48 Ibid.
49 Smallwood, "Domitian's Attitude," 7; Keresztes, "Jews," 14–15.
50 Barclay, *Mediterranean Diaspora*, 311–12.
51 Keresztes, "Jews," 3; Barclay, *Mediterranean Diaspora*, 310–11.
52 Williams, "Domitian," 204–5.
53 That Roman society accommodated such attitudes has been sufficiently demonstrated by, e.g., Schäfer, who summarizes them by stating that "the peculiarity of the Roman attitude toward the Jews seems better expressed by the term 'Judeophobia' in its ambivalent combination of fear and hatred"; see *Judeophobia*, 210. See also Barclay, *Mediterranean Diaspora*, 313, who concludes that the evidence "does suggest an atmosphere in which Judaism was presented as un-Roman and even anti-Roman."
54 Rutgers, *Hidden Heritage*, 183.
55 Barclay, *Mediterranean Diaspora*, 323; Goodman, *Mission*, 123.
56 Stern, *Authors 2*, 131.
57 Cf. Goodman, *Mission*, 122–3, who, in connection with Domitian's exaction of the tax, states that "[n]o sources suggest any change in the formal definition of the tax."
58 Smallwood, "Domitian's Attitude," 6.
59 Barclay, *Mediterranean Diaspora*, 312, n. 73.
60 *CPJ* 160–229. Nos. 182–92 refer to the reign of Domitian.

61 Keresztes, "Jews," 2. In Egypt, however, special tax collectors were appointed with the sole responsibility of collecting the Jewish tax, see Smallwood, *Jews*, 375.

62 Downey, *Antioch in Syria*, 169.

63 Winter, "Imperial Cult," 93–7.

64 Tcherikover, *Hellenistic*, 36.

65 Martin, *Hellenistic Religions*, 10.

66 Goodman, "Nerva"; *Mission*, 46–7, 120–8.

67 Goodman, ibid., 46–7, is in fact conscious of this, but makes a distinction between theory and practice. He states that a census, as in Roman society, that recorded citizenship and social rank, did not exist, but this is, in my opinion, to tone down the significance of informal networks and social control functions.

68 Sanders, *Judaism*, 156, and *Jesus and Judaism*, 64. On the history of the temple tax see Horbury, "Temple Tax," 277–82. It is possible that the Essenes did not pay or paid only once in a lifetime, and the priests seem to have claimed exemption; see Horbury, "Temple Tax," 282. See also Mandell, "Who Paid," for the rather odd suggestion that the temple tax was paid only by the Pharisees and that Vespasian's tax was also levied only on the Pharisees and those who associated themselves with them, and finally Cohen, *Beginnings*, 62, n. 150, where, *inter alia*, he comments on Mandell.

69 Ibid.

70 Purvis, "Samaritans," 592. See, e.g., Josephus *A.J.* 9.288.

71 Sanders, *Judaism*, 104–5.

72 Nanos, *Mystery*, 309, states that there are several historical references that indicate that "righteous gentiles" paid the temple tax. The texts he refers to, Josephus, *A.J.* 14.110, and Tacitus, *Hist.* 5.5, however, do not explicitly state that Gentiles paid the *temple tax*, but that Gentiles *contributed to the temple* in Jerusalem. The difference may be vital. On the other hand, it cannot be ruled out that god-fearers were occasionally allowed to pay the tax as well. I am, however, not convinced.

73 Cohen, *Beginnings*, 58–62.

74 Acts 15:20, 29.

75 It is interesting to note that the "proto-Noahide" theology of *Jub.* 7:20 completely fails to mention idolatry.

76 Nanos, *Mystery*, 289–336.

77 Rom. 13:2.

78 See Barclay, *Obeying*, 58, who emphasizes these aspects regarding the situation in Galatia.

79 See Dunn, *Partings*, 57–74.

80 See Sanders, *Jesus and Judaism*, 61–76, for an overview of scholarly discussions about Jesus and the temple as well as Sanders's own hypothesis that Jesus is likely to have predicted the destruction of the temple and carried out a symbolic act of its destruction.

81 Acts 7:48.

82 Acts 17:24; cf. 7:48.

83 Acts 21:26.

84 Horbury, "Temple Tax," 285.

85 Sanders, *Judaism*, 362–3, 376–7.

86 See Sanders, *Jesus and Judaism*, 77–119, for a thorough discussion of restoration theology within Judaism.

87 Cf. Mandell, "Who Paid," 228, who states that "[t]here is no indication that such sects as the Samaritans or the Jewish Christians were required to pay it [the temple tax]." That is certainly true, but we have found evidence that possibly indicates that the Samaritans *were not even allowed to pay the temple tax*. That the Jesus-believing Jews paid the temple tax is very likely, since nothing indicates that they ever saw themselves as anything but Jews.

88 Cotter, "Collegia," 88.

89 Cohen, *Beginnings*, 62, n. 150; Goodman, "Nerva," 42.

90 Cf. Collins, "Insiders," 196–7, who finds it likely that Christians who were indistinguishable from Jews and who shared in the legal status of the local Jews existed in western Anatolia at the end of the first century.

91 Cohen, *Beginnings*, 185.

92 Regarding the situation in western Anatolia, Collins, "Insiders," 199, states that "Christian groups which separated definitively from civic institutions and from Jewish associations (*politeumata* or *synodoi*) would have become outsiders socially or legally. If they caused noticeable unrest or disturbances, they would have come to the attention of the Roman governor. They could also have been accused before the governor by Romans, Greeks, Greco-Asiatics or Jews. Motivations for such accusations would have varied but would have included atheism, that is, the impious rejection of the traditional gods, on part of the Gentiles, and infringement of Jewish tradition and laws, on part of the Jews. If brought to trial, they could have been punished by beating with rods, whipping, simple expulsion from the city, relegation or deportation, which may have involved confiscation of property, or execution."

93 Cf. Hengel and Barrett, *Conflicts*, 37, who state that Ignatius "in his polemics shows himself to be the first author of a purely Gentile Christianity."

94 Schoedel, *Ignatius*, 126.

95 Cohen, *Beginnings*, 187.

96 Lieu, *Image*, 31; Stanton, "Early," 180.

97 The reference of the word to someone who has become Jewish or someone who is Jewish is first attested in the writings of Clement of Alexandria and Origen; see Cohen, *Beginnings*, 188–9.

98 So Meeks and Wilken, *Jews and Christians*, 20, who state with reference to all statements about Judaism in Ignatius' letters that the polemical passages almost certainly reflect "also Ignatius' experience of Judaeo-Christians in Antioch." See also Trevett, *Study*, 39.

99 Sumney, "Opponents," 365.

100 Gaston, "Judaism," 39.

101 Sumney, "Opponents," 347–9. See Barrett, "Jews and Judaizers," 221–30, for an overview of the discussion of Ignatius' opponents, and Goulder, "Docetists," who suggests that Ignatius' opponents are Ebionites; concerning this cf., however, Schoedel, "Theological Norms," 35.

102 Sumney, "Opponents," 359. See also Barrett, "Jews and Judaizers," 224, and Schoedel, *Ignatius*, 209.

103 Ibid., 202.

104 Schoedel, *Ignatius*, 202, and "Theological Norms," 34. So also Barrett, "Jews and Judaizers," 234.

105 Nolland, "Uncircumcised," 194.

106 See Barrett, "Jews and Judaizers," 232–5, and Schoedel, *Ignatius*, 202–3, 207–8, for discussions of the ideology of the opponents in Philadelphia.

107 *Magn.* 10:3. See Trevett, *Study*, 86, who states that "[t]he language of the anti-judaizing passage *Magn.* 6–10 suggests that Ignatius was opposed to Christians (not Jews proper) who retained elements of Jewish orthopraxis."

108 A similar phrase appears in the letter to the community in Smyrna; see Rev. 2:9.

109 See Collins, "Insiders," 205–6, or "Vilification," 310–14, for an overview of different suggestions.

110 See, e.g., Collins, "Insiders," 206; Aune, *Revelation*, 175–6, 162–5; Lohse, "Synagogue"; Cohen, *Beginnings*, 26.

111 See Gager, *Origins*, 132.

112 Schoedel, *Ignatius*, 202.

113 d'Anjou, *Social Movements*, 40.

114 Coser, *Functions*, 49.

115 *Eph.* 12:2; *Rom.* 4:3.

116 Trevett, *Study*, 20. See also Koester, *Introduction 2*, 281–7.

117 Coser, *Functions*, 68.

118 Nanos, *Mystery*, 289–336.

119 Coser, *Functions*, 70.

120 Ibid., 71.

121 Sumney, "Opponents," 355; Schoedel, *Ignatius*, 207–8; Lieu, *Image*, 37.

122 Coser, *Functions*, 49.

123 Ibid., 69.

124 Lieu, *Image*, 28.

125 See Holmberg, *Paul and Power*, 196–204, for a concluding summary of authority in the "primitive church."

126 Schoedel, *Ignatius*, 22.

127 See also *Magn.* 2–3.

128 Schoedel, "Reception," 175.

129 Meier, "Matthew," 182, 180. See also Sanders, *Schismatics*, 154–5.

130 Meier, "Matthew," 186.

131 Brown and Meier, *Antioch and Rome*, 25; Meier, "Matthew," 186. See also Trevett, *Study*, 22–3.

132 See, e.g., France, *Matthew*, 91–5; Meier, *Law and History*, 7–9; Senior, *About Matthew*, 16–19; or Painter, *Just James*, 72.

133 Meier, "Matthew," 179. See also Legarth, *Guds tempel*, 117–18.

134 Repschinski, *Controversy*, 61.

135 Senior, *About Matthew*, 19.

136 See, e.g., Brown and Meier, *Antioch and Rome*, 45–72, and Sanders, *Schismatics*, 154–9, for suggestions of the development of the Matthean community.

137 Overman, *Matthew's Gospel*, 133. On the presentation of the disciples in Mark and the relation to Matt. and Luke see Fowler, *Let the Reader*, 256–60, and on the narrative function of the disciples in Mark, Tannehill, "Disciples."

138 Byrskog, *Jesus*, 228, 234; Overman, *Matthew's Gospel*, 133.
139 Byrskog, *Jesus*, 235.
140 Ibid., 235–6.
141 See also Matt. 13:47–50; 22:1–14; 24:45–51; 25:14–30.
142 Overman, *Matthew's Gospel*, 109–11.
143 Repschinski, *Controversy*, 344.
144 Ibid., 345.
145 Ibid., 344.
146 Overman, *Matthew's Gospel*, 147–9; Repschinski, *Controversy*, 344.
147 Stark, *Rise of Christianity*, 55.
148 Ibid., 58.
149 See Sanders, *Charisma*, or Sanders, "Early Christianity," for a somewhat more expanded version.
150 *Ep.* 10.96.
151 See also Cotter, "Collegia," 78–9.
152 Feldman, *Jew*, 177.
153 Ibid., 194.
154 Smallwood, *Jews*, 393, regarding Palestine; cf., however, Grabbe, *Judaism*, 597.
155 See Cotter, "Collegia," 82–4, referring to *Ep.* 10.92, 93.
156 See Hedner-Zetterholm, *Portrait*, 181–9, on how the image of Laban in rabbinic literature developed into that of an enemy as a hermeneutical side-effect. This study draws attention to the general mechanism of vilifying the other in order to make oneself appear in a more favorable light.
157 Schoedel, *Ignatius*, 122.
158 Quasten, *Patrology 1*, 191.
159 Ibid., 248.
160 See *Diogn.* 5.

EPILOGUE

Summary and implications

The main results of the study

This study has suggested that the separation between Judaism and Christianity in Antioch was principally a separation between Jesus-believing Jews and Jesus-believing Gentiles. This development, it is argued, was a result of both ideological factors and socio-political circumstances. The Jewish Jesus movement that meant itself to be living in the eschatological end time found reasons within its own religious tradition to believe that the Gentile nations were to be included in the final salvation. When it came down to transforming this theology into practice, however, different solutions seems to have emerged.

Paul's standpoint of including the Gentiles in the covenant was perceived as an attractive solution for the Gentile adherents to the movement, since they thereby became more intimately connected to the Jewish adherents. This, however, was considered as a serious threat to many other Jewish factions. By manipulating aspects of Jewish covenantal theology, Paul was unintentionally playing with fire. This is evident from the reactions his ideology caused with other Jews, not least James.

James's way of dealing with the Gentile problem was probably more in line with a general understanding of the relations between Jews and Gentiles. I have suggested that James found no reason for creating a new way of relating to Gentiles, since there was already a well-tried institution for Gentiles interested in Judaism: Gentiles could become god-fearers and relate to the Jewish community as such. From a Jewish point of view this model would have been preferable, since it did not threaten Jewish identity. However, the fact that the Jesus movement did not allow the Gentile adherents to maintain their cultic obligation towards the *polis* created a complex social and identity problem for the Jesus-believing Gentiles.

According to the religious-political system in the Greek *polis* even during the Roman period, inhabitants in a *polis* were expected to participate in the official cult. The Jewish communities that welcomed Gentile god-fearers were certainly aware of this problem. Thus, it is reasonable to assume that the Jewish communities accepted that god-fearers participated in Gentile cultic activities and simultaneously associated with Jews in the milieu of the synagogue. Accordingly, it would be no problem for any Gentile admirer of Judaism to pursue this interest.

However, Gentiles within the Jesus movement would face a serious problem. It was obviously not entirely possible to use god-fearers as a model. To retain a relationship with the Jesus-believing Jews implied a break with Gentile religion. This, in turn, exposed the individual to possible interest from the authorities. It is not necessary to assume the existence of a secret police force who spied on the inhabitants to check whether they upheld their cultic obligations or not to understand that Jesus-believing Gentiles existed in an embarrassing legal greyzone which gave rise to a situation *that could be used against them*. It is likely that Jesus-believing Gentiles solved this dilemma by pretending to be Jews and by subordinating themselves to the synagogue of the Jesus-believing Jews, since the Jews were exempted from participation in the official cult.

According to the analysis in the present study, the so-called incident in Antioch was a conflict that actualized the problems of transforming ideology to social reality. This conflict was basically related to *the status* of the Jesus-believing Gentiles in relation to Jewish identity. According to Paul, Gentiles were to be included in the covenant, while James advocated that they should remain god-fearers, though without any cultic relation to the *polis*. Since this model from a Jewish point of view, however, may have been perceived more natural and in no way threatening to Jewish identity, the Jesus-believing Jewish community, compelled by the authority of James, the brother of Jesus, broke off the more intimate social intercourse with the Gentile adherents to the movement. The result was a division of the community into two commensality groups. In reality the division was even more profound: the Jesus-believing Gentiles may have experienced this as being excluded from the people of god.

Thus this theologically motivated situation affected the social reality of the community: the utopian Pauline vision of the eschatological community consisting of torah-obedient Jews and righteous Gentiles united in Christ had being replaced by a problematic compromise. Shortly after the end of the Jewish War, Vespasian introduced a tax to

232

EPILOGUE: SUMMARY AND IMPLICATIONS

be paid by every Jew between the ages of three and sixty or sixty-two. It is clear that Jewish identity from now on came to be connected with the payment of this tax. It is reasonable to assume that Jesus-believing Jews felt obliged to pay it. *This reinforced their Jewish identity even more.* Given the socio-political conditions in the empire, we must draw the conclusion that the Jesus-believing Gentiles also paid the tax in order to maintain their disguise as Jews. Thus, even their "Jewish" identity became more salient.

This led to a serious conflict, however. According to the ideology of the Jesus movement Gentiles should remain Gentiles and were not to become Jews—Paul had even stated that Gentiles who converted to Judaism risked cutting themselves off from Christ. However, according to Paul, the fact that Gentiles were considered as covenantal partners within the Jesus movement resulted in close social relations between Jews and Gentiles. After the incident at Antioch, the division between Jew and Gentile within the Jesus movement there had been reinforced. Thus, the Jesus-believing Gentiles were forced to act as Jews in relation to the authorities but could not take full part in the social activities in the synagogue, since every Jew within the Jesus movement considered them to be Gentiles. In addition, as a result of the Jewish War, anti-Jewish attitudes had become more accentuated, which implies that the Jesus-believing Gentiles may have had to endure persecution for being Jews.

It is suggested that it was this combination of theological and socio-political elements that eventually gave rise to a movement within the Gentile part of the Jesus movement to become a legally recognized *collegium*, completely separated from Judaism. Thus, the parting of the ways in Antioch was primarily between Jesus-believing Jews and Jesus-believing Gentiles.

Implications

In this conflict it is clear that the Jesus-believing Gentiles made use of an anti-Jewish ideology that was already prevalent in society. The political situation further added fuel to such feelings. It is important to note that the anti-Judaism of early Christianity was part of a realistic conflict and used as a resource in an attempt to convince the authorities of the splendid qualities of this new Gentile movement. An important part of this program was the vilification of the Jesus-believing Jewish movement. It is possible that one reason why the church carried on with this, and denigrated the Jews and Judaism even further might be that the program to become a legal non-Jewish religion failed. Thus, the vilification of the Jews became part and parcel of the ongoing project of being accepted by the authorities. By the time that this had been achieved, in the fourth century, anti-Judaism had become part of the theological outlook of the church.

Is it possible to draw any general conclusions about the separation between Judaism and Christianity from this study? There are some elements in the Antiochean situation that may have been operative wherever Christianity emerged as a non-Jewish religion. It seems reasonable that the problem of the status of the Gentile within the Jesus movement was also experienced in other locations. To some extent this has to do with the nature of Judaism in combination with the socio-political conditions in the Roman Empire. The situation in Galatia and the correspondence between Ignatius and the different communities in Asia Minor suggest that those communities experienced comparable situations. These contacts between different church leaders indicate that the implied social movement in Antioch *was part of a much larger movement in Asia Minor.* Similar conflicts are also evoked by the Gospel of John and Revelation. In addition, we find strains of anti-Jewish literature from different locations from the period after the death of Ignatius.

It may thus be the case that some mechanisms identified in this study were operative even at other locations and in other periods. One important factor would have been the various strategies involved in dealing with Gentile adherents to the Jesus movement, given the socio-political conditions in the empire and the constitution of Judaism. Another would have been the anti-Jewish discourse originating from the desire on part of the Jesus-believing Gentiles to become a legally recognized *collegium*, and the failure of that vision. If this scenario is correct, it implies that the suggestion that the separation was mainly between Jesus-believing Jews and Jesus-believing Gentiles may also have a bearing on the general understanding of the rise of Christianity.

Another aspect that would be in need of further reflection is the enormous social complexity that is seen in this study. While we have only begun to understand the diversity of the Judaism of the period, we are now compelled to problematize both Jewish and Gentile factions even more. In this study we have found evidence of Jews who wanted to become Gentiles, and of Gentiles who wanted to become Jews. We have found evidence of other Jews who, by becoming Jesus-believers, found a way *to cease being Jewish.* While some Gentiles originally joined the Jesus movement because of a profound interest in Judaism, other Gentiles within the same movement later *wanted to separate from Judaism and establish a non-Jewish religion.*

Within the Jesus movement we have found evidence of several interpretations of how to give concrete form to the belief that Jesus of Nazareth was the Messiah: in the Pauline version of the Jesus movement, Gentiles included in the covenant should remain Gentiles to become "one in Christ" with Jews who remained Jews and observed the torah. In James's version, the Jews should remain torah-obedient Jews, while the Gentiles should relate to the Jewish community as Jesus-believing god-fearers and be saved according to the theology of righteous Gentiles. In Ignatius' version of the Jesus movement, Jewishness had to give way to a common Gentile identity— Christianity as we know it was about to be born, and the end result, as it turned out, seems to have become the complete contradiction of the beginning.

BIBLIOGRAPHY

Ancient Sources

This bibliography follows the abbreviations in *The SBL Handbook of Style: For Ancient Near Eastern, Biblical, and Early Christian Studies*. Peabody, MA: Hendrickson, 1999.

Bibles, apocrypha, and pseudepigrapha

New Revised Standard Version Bible. Nashville: Thomas Nelson, 1990.

Lettre d'Aristée à Philocrate: introduction, texte critique, traduction et notes, index complet des mots grecs, ed. A. Pelletier. Paris: du Cerf, 1962.

Novum Testamentum Graece . . ., 27th edn, ed. B. Aland, K. Aland, J. Karavidopoulus *et al.* Stuttgart: Deutsche Bibelgesellschaft, 1993.

The Old Testament Pseudepigrapha, Volume 1: Apocalyptic Literature and Testaments, ed. J. H. Charlesworth. New York: Doubleday, 1983.

The Old Testament Pseudepigrapha, Volume 2: Expansions of the "Old Testament" and Legends, Wisdom and Philosophical Literature, Prayers, Psalms, and Odes, Fragments of Lost Judeo-Hellenistic Works, ed. J. H. Charlesworth. New York: Doubleday, 1985.

Septuaginta . . ., ed. A. Ralphs. Stuttgart: Deutsche Bibelgesellschaft, 1993 [1935].

Jewish-Hellenistic literature

Josephus

Josephus, trans. H. St. J. Thackeray *et al.*, 10 vols., Loeb Classical Library. Cambridge, MA: Harvard University Press, 1926–.

Philo

Philo, trans. F. H. Colson and G. H. Whitaker, 10 vols, Loeb Classical Library. Cambridge, MA: Harvard University Press, 1929–.

Qumran

The Dead Sea Scrolls Translated: The Qumran Texts in English, ed. F. G. Martínez. Leiden: Brill, 1994.

Rabbinic literature

Mishnah

Mishnayoth: Pointed Hebrew Text, English Translation, Introductions, Notes, Supplement, Appendix, Indexes, Addenda, Corrigenda, 2nd edn, ed. P. Blackman, 7 vols. Gateshead: Judaica Press, 1990.

Tosefta

The Tosefta: Translated from the Hebrew, ed. J. Neusner and R. S. Sarason, trans. A. J. Avery-Peck, R. Brooks *et al.*, 6 vols. Hoboken, NJ: Ktav, 1977–86.

Babylonian Talmud

The Babylonian Talmud, ed. I. Epstein, 18 vols. London: Soncino Press, 1936–52.

תלמוד בבלי. דפוס וילנא. וילנא תר״מ.

Leviticus Rabbah

Midrash Rabbah: Translated into English with Notes, Glossary and Indices, 3rd edn, ed. H. Freedman and M. Simon, 10 vols. London: Soncino Press, 1983.

ויקרא רבה, מהד׳ מ׳ מרגליות, ניו יורק, הוצאת בית המדרש לרבנים באמריקה, תשנ״ג.

Christian literature

Augustinus

The City of God Against the Pagans, trans. W. M. Green, 7 vols., Loeb Classical Library. Cambridge, MA: Harvard University Press, 1957–.

Diognetus

The Apostolic Fathers, trans. K. Lake, Vol. 2, Loeb Classical Library. Cambridge, MA: Harvard University Press, 1992 [1913].

Eusebius

The Ecclesiastical History, trans. K. Lake. 2 vols. Loeb Classical Library. Cambridge, MA: Harvard University Press, 1926–.

Ignatius

The Apostolic Fathers, trans. K. Lake, Vol. 1, Loeb Classical Library. Cambridge, MA: Harvard University Press, 1998 [1912].

John Malalas

The Chronicle of John Malalas: A Translation, ed. E. Jeffreys, M. Jeffreys, R. Scott *et al.* Melbourne: Australian Association for Byzantine Studies, 1986.

Melito of Sardis

On Pascha and Fragments: Texts and Translations, ed. S. G. Hall. Oxford: Clarendon Press, 1979.

Classical literature

Celsus

De Medicina, trans. W. G. Spencer, 3 vols, Loeb Classical Library. Cambridge, MA: Harvard University Press, 1935–.

Cicero

Cicero, trans. C. W. Keyes, 28 vols, Loeb Classical Library. Cambridge, MA: Harvard University Press, 1969–.

Dio Cassius

Dio's Roman History, trans. E. Cary, 9 vols, Loeb Classical Library. Cambridge, MA: Harvard University Press, 1914–27.

Libanius

Libanii Opera, ed. R. Foerster,13 vols. Hildesheim: Olms, 1903–.

Pliny the Younger

Letters and Panegyricus, trans. B. Radice, 2 vols, Loeb Classical Library. Cambridge, MA: Harvard University Press, 1969.

Seneca

Seneca, trans. R. M. Gummere, 10 vols, Loeb Classical Library. Cambridge, MA: Harvard University Press, 1928–.

Suetonius

Suetonius, trans. J. C. Rolfe, 2 vols, Loeb Classical Library. Cambridge, MA: Harvard University Press, 1913–.

Tacitus

Tacitus, trans. C. H. Moore and J. Jackson, 5 vols, Loeb Classical Library. Cambridge, MA: Harvard University Press, 1914–.

Papyri, ostraka and epigrapha

Reynolds, J., and R. Tannenbaum, *Jews and Godfearers at Aphrodisias: Greek Inscriptions with Commentary*. Cambridge: Cambridge Philological Society, 1987.

Corpus inscriptionum judaicarum: Jewish Inscriptions from the Third Century B.C. to the Seventh Century A.D., ed. J. Frey, Vol 1. New York: Ktav, 1975 [1936].

Corpus inscriptionum judaicarum: recueil des inscriptions juives qui vont du IIIe siècle avant Jésus-Christ au VIIe siècle de notre ère, ed. J. Frey, Vol 2, Rome: Pontificio Istituto di Archeologia Cristiana, 1952.

Corpus inscriptionum latinarum: inscriptiones urbis Romae latinae. Consilio et auctoritate Academiae Litterarum Regiae Borrussicae, ed. E. Borman, G. Henzen and C. Huelsen, Vol. 6:2. Berlin: Georgium, 1882.

Corpus papyrorum judaicarum, ed. V. Tcherikover and A. Fuks, 3 vols. Cambridge, MA: Harvard University Press, 1957–64.

Monumenta Asiae Minoris Antiqua, Vol. 6, *Monuments and Documents from Phrygia and Caria*, ed. W. H. Buckler and W. M. Calder. London: Society for the Promotion of Roman Studies, 1939.

Modern works

Abbott, W. M., ed., *The Documents of Vatican II*. New York: Guild Press, 1966.

Alexander, P. S., "'The Parting of the Ways' from the Perspective of Rabbinic Judaism," pp. 1–25 in *Jews and Christians: The Parting of Ways A.D. 70 to 135*, ed. J. D. G. Dunn. Tübingen: Mohr, 1992.

Allison, D. C., "The Eschatology of Jesus," pp. 267–302 in *The Encylopedia of Apocalypticism, Volume 1: The Origins of Apocalypticism in Judaism and Christianity*, ed. J. J. Collins. New York: Continuum, 1998.

Anderson, H., "4 Maccabees: (First Century A.D.): A New Translation and Introduction," pp. 531–64 in *The Old Testament Pseudepigrapha, Volume 2: Expansions of the "Old Testament" and Legends, Wisdom and Philosophical Literature, Prayers, Psalms, and Odes, Fragments of Lost Judeo-Hellenistic Works*, ed. J. H. Charlesworth. New York: Doubleday, 1985.

Applebaum, S., "The Legal Status of the Jewish Communities in the Diaspora," pp. 420–63 in *The Jewish People in the First Century: Historical Geography, Political History, Social, Cultural and Religious Life and Institutions*, ed. S. Safrai, M. Stern, D. Flusser *et al.* Assen: van Gorcum, 1974.

—— "The Organization of the Jewish Communities in the Diaspora," pp. 464–503 in *The Jewish People in the First Century: Historical Geography, Political History, Social, Cultural and Religious Life and Institutions*, ed. S. Safrai, M. Stern, D. Flusser *et al.* Assen: van Gorcum, 1974.

Ascough, R. S., *What Are They Saying About the Formation of Pauline Churches?* New York: Paulist Press, 1998.

—— "The Thessalonian Christian Community as a Professional Voluntary Association," *JBL*, 119, 2 (2000): 311–28.

Aufderheide, A. C., and C. Rodríguez-Martín, *The Cambridge Encyclopedia of Human Paleopathology*. Cambridge: Cambridge University Press, 1998.

Aune, D. E., "Orthodoxy in First Century Judaism? A Response to N. J. McEleney," *JSJ*, 7, 1 (1976): 1–10.

—— *Revelation 1–5*. Dallas: Word Books, 1997.

Barclay, J. M. G., *Obeying the Truth: Paul's Ethics in Galatians*. Minneapolis: Fortress Press, 1988.

—— "Deviance and Apostasy: Some Applications of Deviance Theory to First-Century Judaism and Christianity," pp. 114–27 in *Modelling Early Christianity: Social Scientific Studies of the New Testament in Its Context*, ed. P. F. Esler. London: Routledge, 1995.

—— *Jews in the Mediterranean Diaspora: From Alexander to Trajan (323 BCE–117 CE)*. Edinburgh: T. & T. Clark, 1996.

—— "Who Was Considered an Apostate in the Jewish Diaspora?," pp. 80–98 in *Tolerance and Intolerance in Early Judaism and Christianity*, ed. G. N. Stanton and G. G. Stroumsa. Cambridge: Cambridge University Press, 1998.

Baron, S. W., *A Social and Religious History of the Jews: Ancient Times, Volume 1, To the Beginning of the Christian Era*, 2nd edn. New York: Columbia University Press, 1958 [1937].

Barrett, C. K., "Jews and Judaizers in the Epistles of Ignatius," pp. 220–44 in *Jews, Greeks and Christians: Religious Cultures in Late Antiquity: Essays in Honor of William David Davies*, ed. R. Hamerton-Kelly and R. Scroggs. Leiden: Brill, 1976.

—— "The Apostolic Decree of Acts 15.29," *ABR*, 35 (1987): 50–9.

—— "Paul: Councils and Controversies," pp. 42–74 in *Conflicts and Challenges in Early Christianity*, ed. D. A. Hagner. Harrisburg, PA: Trinity Press, 1999.

Bauckham, R., "The Parting of the Ways: What Happened and Why," *ST*, 47, 2 (1993): 135–51.

Beck, R., "The Mysteries of the Mithras," pp. 176–85 in *Voluntary Associations in the Graeco-Roman World*, ed. J. S. Kloppenborg and S. G. Wilson. London: Routledge, 1996.

Beckford, J. A., "'Start Together and Finish Together': Shifts in the Premises and Paradigms Underlying the Scientific Study of Religion," *JSSR*, 39, 4 (2000): 481–95.

Berger, P. L., *The Sacred Canopy: Elements of a Sociological Theory of Religion*. Garden City, NY: Doubleday, 1969 [1967].

Berger, P. L., and T. Luckmann, *The Social Construction of Reality: A Treatise in the Sociology of Knowledge*. London: Penguin, 1991 [1966].

Betz, H. D., *Galatians: A Commentary on Paul's Letter to the Churches in Galatia*. Philadelphia: Fortress Press, 1979.

Betz, O., "The Essenes," pp. 444–70 in *The Cambridge History of Judaism, Vol. 3: The Early Roman Period*, ed. W. Horbury, W. D. Davies and J. Sturdy. Cambridge: Cambridge University Press, 1999.

Bilde, P., *Flavius Josephus between Jerusalem and Rome: His Life, his Works and their Importance*. Sheffield: JSOT Press, 1988.

Binder, D. D., *Into the Temple Courts: The Place of the Synagogue in the Second Temple Period*. Atlanta: Society of Biblical Literature, 1999.

Blasi, A. J., *Early Christianity as a Social Movement*. New York: Peter Lang, 1988.

Boardman, J., "Symposion *Furniture*," pp. 122–31 in *Sympotica: A Symposium on the Symposion*, ed. O. Murray. Oxford: Clarendon Press, 1990.

Boccaccini, G., *Middle Judaism: Jewish Thought, 300 B.C.E. to 200 C.E.* Minneapolis, MN: Fortress Press, 1991.

Bockmuehl, M., "The Noachide Commandments and the New Testament Ethics with Special Reference to Acts 15 and Pauline Halakhah," *RB*, 102, 1 (1995): 72–101.

—— "Antioch and James the Just," pp. 155–98 in *James the Just and Christian Origins*, ed. B. Chilton and C. A. Evans. Leiden: Brill, 1999.

Boers, H., *The Justification of the Gentiles: Paul's Letter to the Galatians and Romans*. Peabody, MA: Hendrickson, 1994.

Borgen, P., *Early Christianity and Hellenistic Judaism*. Edinburgh: T. & T. Clark, 1996.

Bradley, K., "The Roman Family at Dinner," pp. 36–55 in *Meals in a Social Context: Aspects of the Communal Meal in the Hellenistic and Roman World*, ed. I. Nielsen and H. S. Nielsen. Aarhus: Aarhus University Press, 1998.

Brim, O. G., and J. Kagan, eds. *Constancy and Change in Human Development*. Cambridge, MA: Harvard University Press, 1980.

Brooten, B. J., "The Jews of Ancient Antioch," pp. 29–37 in *Antioch: The Lost*

Ancient City, ed. C. Kondoleon. Princeton, NJ: Princeton University Press, 2000.

Brown, R. E., and J. P. Meier, *Antioch and Rome: New Testament Cradles of Catholic Christianity*. New York: Paulist Press, 1983.

Bruce, F. F., *The Acts of the Apostles: The Greek Text with Introduction and Commentary*. Grand Rapids, MI: Eerdmans, 1975 [1951].

—— *The Epistle to the Galatians*. Exeter: Paternoster, 1982.

—— "The Apostolic Decree of Acts 15," pp. 115–24 in *Studien zum Text und zur Ethik des Neuen Testaments: Festschrift zum 80. Geburtstag von Heinrich Greeven*, ed. W. Schrage. Berlin: de Gruyter, 1986.

Bruce, S., *Choice and Religion: A Critique of Rational Choice Theory*. Oxford: Oxford University Press, 1999.

—— "A Critique of Rational Choice Theory," pp. 28–38 in *Religions and Social Transitions*, ed. E. Helander. Helsinki: Helsinki University Press, 1999.

Bruit-Zaidman, L., and P. Schmitt-Pantel, *Religion in the Ancient Greek City*. Cambridge: Cambridge University Press, 1992 [1989, in French].

Burkert, W., "The Meaning and Function of the Temple in Classical Greece," pp. 27–47 in *Temple in Society*, ed. M. V. Fox. Winona Lake, AR: Eisenbrauns, 1988.

—— "Oriental Symposia: Contrasts and Parallels," pp. 7–24 in *Dining in a Classical Context*, ed. W. J. Slater. Ann Arbor, MI: University of Michigan Press, 1991.

Byrskog, S., *Jesus the Only Teacher: Didactic Authority and Transmission in Ancient Israel, Ancient Judaism and the Matthean Community*. Stockholm: Almqvist & Wiksell, 1994.

Callan, T., "The Background of the Apostolic Decree (Acts 15:20,29; 21:25)," *CBQ*, 55 (1993): 284–97.

Cameron, A., *Circus Factions: Blues and Greens at Rome and Byzantinium*. Oxford: Clarendon Press, 1976.

Carlbom, A., "Sverige—ett främmande moraliskt rum," *Invandrare och Minoriteter*, 24, 1 (1997): 12–15.

Carlebach, A., "Rabbinic References to Fiscus Judaicus," *JQR*, 66 (1975–6): 57–61.

Catchpole, D. R., "Paul, James and the Apostolic Decree," *NTS*, 23 (1977): 428–44.

Charlesworth, J. H., *The Pseudepigrapha and Modern Research with a Supplement*. Chico, CA: Scholars Press, 1981 [1976].

—— "Refreshing Developments in Italian Research," foreword to G. Boccaccini, *Middle Judaism: Jewish Thought 300 B.C.E. to 200 C.E.* Minneapolis, MN: Fortress Press, 1991.

Chilton, B., *A Feast of Meanings: Eucharistic Theologies from Jesus through Johannine Circles*. Leiden: Brill, 1994.

Cohen, S. J. D., "Respect for Judaism by Gentiles According to Josephus," *HTR*, 80, 4 (1987): 409–30.

——*From the Maccabees to the Mishnah*. Philadelphia: Westminster Press, 1989 [1987].

——*The Beginnings of Jewishness: Boundaries, Varieties, Uncertainties*. Berkeley, CA: University of California Press, 1999.

——"The Temple and the Synagogue," pp. 298–325 in *The Cambridge History of Judaism, Volume 3: The Early Roman Period*, ed. W. Horbury, W. D. Davies and J. Sturdy. Cambridge: Cambridge University Press, 1999.

Collins, A. Y., "Insiders and Outsiders in the Book of Revelation and its Social Context," pp. 187–218 in *"To See Ourselves as Others See Us": Christians, Jews, "Others" in Late Antiquity*, ed. J. Neusner and E. S. Frerichs. Chico, CA: Scholars Press, 1985.

——"Vilification and Self-Definition in the Book of Revelation," pp. 308–20 in *Christians Among Jews and Gentiles: Essays in Honor of Krister Stendahl on His Sixty-fifth Birthday*, ed. G. W. E. Nicklesburg and G. W. MacRae. Philadelphia, PA: Fortress Press, 1986.

Colpe, C., "Syncretism," pp. 218–27 in *The Encyclopedia of Religion, Volume 14*, ed. M. Eliade. New York: Macmillan, 1987.

Conzelmann, H., *Acts of the Apostles: A Commentary on the Acts of the Apostles*. Philadelphia: Fortress Press, 1987.

Coser, L. A., *The Functions of Social Conflict*. New York: Free Press, 1968 [1956].

Cotter, W., "The Collegia and Roman Law: State Restrictions on Voluntary Associations, 64 BCE–200 CE," pp. 74–89 in *Voluntary Associations in the Graeco-Roman World*, ed. J. S. Kloppenborg and S. G. Wilson. London: Routledge, 1996.

Cotterell, P., and M. Turner, *Linguistics and Biblical Interpretation*. Downers Grove, IL: InterVarsity Press, 1989.

Croke, B., "Malalas, the Man and His Work," pp. 1–25 in *Studies in John Malalas*, ed. E. Jeffreys, B. Croke and R. Scott. Sydney: Australian Association for Byzantine Studies, 1990.

d'Anjou, L., *Social Movements and Cultural Change: The First Abolition Campaign Revisited*. New York: de Gruyter, 1996.

d'Arms, J. H., "Heavy Drinking and Drunkenness in the Roman World: Four Questions for Historians," pp. 304–17 in *In vino veritas*, ed. O. Murray and M. Tecuşan. London: British School at Rome *et al.*, 1995.

Dalby, A., *Siren Feasts: A History of Food and Gastronomy in Greece*. London: Routledge, 1995.

Davies, W. D., *Paul and Rabbinic Judaism: Some Rabbinic Elements in Pauline Theology*. London: SPCK, 1948.

——"Jewish and Pauline Studies," *NTS*, 24 (1978): 4–39.

Demand, N., *Birth, Death, and Motherhood in Classical Greece*. Baltimore: Johns Hopkins University Press, 1994.

Descamps, S., "Tyche of Antioch," pp. 118–19 in *Antioch: The Lost Ancient City*, ed. C. Kondoleon. Princeton, NJ: Princeton University Press, 2000.

Donaldson, T. L., "Proselytes or 'Righteous Gentiles'? The Status of Gentiles in Eschatological Pilgrimage Patterns of Thought," *JSP*, 7 (1990): 3–27.

Downey, G., "The Size of the Population of Antioch," *TAPA*, 89 (1958): 84–91.

—— *A History of Antioch in Syria from Seleucus to the Arab Conquest*. Princeton, NJ: Princeton University Press, 1961.

Dunbain, K. M. D., "Ut Greco more biberetur: Greeks and Romans on the Dining Couch," pp. 81–101 in *Meals in a Social Context: Aspects of the Communal Meal in the Hellenistic and Roman World*, ed. I. Nielsen and H. S. Nielsen. Aarhus: Aarhus University Press, 1998.

Dunn, J. D. G., "The Incident at Antioch (Gal. 2:11–18)," *JSNT*, 18 (1983): 3–57.

—— *The Partings of the Ways: Between Christianity and Judaism and their Significance for the Character of Christianity*. London: SCM Press, 1991.

—— "What was the Issue between Paul and 'Those of Circumcision'?" Pages 295–317 in *Paulus und das antike Judentum: Tübingen–Durham-Symposium im Gedenken an den 50. Todestag Adolf Schlatters (19. Mai 1938)*, ed. M. Hengel and U. Heckel. Tübingen: Mohr, 1991.

—— *A Commentary on the Epistle to the Galatians*. London: A. & C. Black, 1993.

—— "Was Paul Against the Law? The Law in Galatians and Romans: A Test-Case of Text in Context," pp. 455–75 in *Texts and Contexts: Biblical Texts in Their Textual and Situational Contexts: Essays in Honor of Lars Hartman*, ed. T. Fornberg and D. Hellholm. Oslo: Scandinavian University Press, 1995.

Eberts, H. W., "Plurality and Ethnicity in Early Christian Mission," *Sociology of Religion*, 58, 4 (1997): 305–21.

Eissfeldt, O., *The Old Testament: An Introduction including the Apocrypha and Pseudepigrapha, and also the Works of Similar Type from Qumran: The History of the Formation of the Old Testament*. Oxford: Blackwell, 1966 [1965].

Ekroth, G., *The Sacrificial Rituals of Greek Hero-Cults in the Archaic to the Early Hellenistic Periods*. Stockholm: Stockholm University Press, 1999.

Eriksson, A., *Traditions as Rhetorical Proof: Pauline Argumentation in 1 Corinthians*. Stockholm: Almqvist & Wiksell, 1998.

Esler, P. F., *The First Christians in their Social Worlds: Social-Scientific Approaches to New Testament Interpretation*. London: Routledge, 1994.

—— "Making and Breaking an Agreement Mediterranean Style: A New Reading of Galatians 2:1–14," *BibInt*, 3, 3 (1995): 285–314.

—— *Community and Gospel in Luke–Acts: The Social and Political Motivations of Lucan Theology*. Cambridge: Cambridge University Press, 1996 [1987].

—— *Galatians*. London: Routledge, 1998.

—— "Models in New Testament Interpretation; A Reply to David Horrell," *JSNT*, 78 (2000): 107–13.

Farmer, W. R., "The Post-Sectarian Character of Matthew and its Post-War Setting in Antioch of Syria," *PRSt*, 3 (1976): 237–47.

—— "James the Lord's Brother, According to Paul," pp. 133–53 in *James the Just and Christian Origins*, ed. B. Chilton and C. A. Evans. Leiden: Brill, 1999.

Fee, G. D., *The First Epistle to the Corinthians*. Grand Rapids, MI: Eerdmans, 1991 [1987].

Feldman, L. H., "How Much Hellenism in Jewish Palestine?," *HUCA*, 53 (1986): 83–111.

—— "The Omnipresence of the God-Fearers," *BAR*, 12, 5 (1986): 58–63.

—— "Was Judaism a Missionary Religion in Ancient Times?," pp. 24–37 in *Jewish Assimilation, Acculturation, and Accommodation: Past Traditions, Current Issues, and Future Prospects: Proceedings of the Second Annual Symposium of the Philip M. and Ethel Klutznick Chair in Jewish Civilization held on Sunday–Monday, September 24–25, 1989*, ed. M. Mor. Lanham, MD: University Press of America, 1992.

—— *Jew and Gentile in the Ancient World: Attitudes and Interactions from Alexander to Justinian*. Princeton, NJ: Princeton University Press, 1996 [1993].

Finke, R., and R. Stark, *The Churching of America, 1776-1990: Winners and Losers in Our Religious Economy*. New Brunswick, NJ: Rutgers University Press, 1992.

Fish, S., *Is There a Text in This Class? The Authority of Interpretive Communities*. Cambridge, MA: Harvard University Press, 1980.

Fowler, R. M., *Let the Reader Understand: Reader-Response Criticism and the Gospel of Mark*. Minneapolis: Fortress Press, 1991.

France, R. T., *Matthew: Evangelist and Teacher*. Guernsey: Paternoster Press, 1992 [1989].

Fredriksen, P., *From Jesus to Christ: The Origins of the New Testament Images of Jesus*, 2nd edn. New Haven, CT: Yale Nota Bene, 2000 [1988].

—— "Judaism, the Circumcision of Gentiles, and Apocalyptic Hope: Another Look at Galatians 1 and 2," pp. 209–44 in *Recruitment, Conquest, and Conflict: Strategies in Judaism, Early Christianity, and the Greco-Roman World*, ed. P. Borgen, V. K. Robbins and D. B. Gowler. Atlanta: Scholars Press, 1998.

Frier, B. W., "More is Worse: Some Observations on the Population of the Roman Empire," pp. 139–59 in *Debating Roman Demography*, ed. W. Scheidel. Leiden: Brill, 2001.

Fung, R. Y. K., *The Epistle to the Galatians*. Grand Rapids, MI: Eerdmans, 1989 [1988].

Gabba, E., "The Growth of Anti-Judaism or the Greek Attitude Towards the Jews," pp. 614–56 in *The Cambridge History of Judaism, Volume 2: The Hellenistic Age*, ed. L. Finkelstein and W. D. Davies. Cambridge: Cambridge University Press, 1984.

Gager, J. G., *Moses in Greco-Roman Paganism*. Nashville: Abingdon, 1972.

—— *The Origins of Anti-Semitism: Attitudes Toward Judaism in Pagan and Christian Antiquity*. New York: Oxford University Press, 1985.

—— "Jews, Gentiles, and Synagogues in the Book of Acts," pp. 91–9 in

Christians Among Jews and Gentiles: Essays in Honor of Krister Stendahl on His Sixty-Fifth Birthday, ed. G. W. E. Nicklesburg and G. W. MacRae. Philadelphia: Fortress Press, 1986.

—— "Messiahs and Their Followers," pp. 37–46 in *Toward the Millennium: Messianic Expectations From the Bible to Waco*, ed. P. Schäfer and M. Cohen. Leiden: Brill, 1998.

—— *Reinventing Paul*. Oxford: Oxford University Press, 2000.

Gaston, L., "Judaism of the Uncircumcised in Ignatius and Related Writers," pp. 33–44 in *Anti-Judaism in Early Christianity: Volume 2: Separation and Polemic*, ed. S. G. Wilson. Waterloo, Ont.: Wilfrid Laurier University Press, 1986.

—— *Paul and the Torah*. Vancouver: University of British Columbia Press, 1990 [1987].

Gilbert, M., "Wisdom Literature: 4 Maccabees," pp. 316–19 in *The Literature of the Jewish People in the Period of the Second Temple and the Talmud: Jewish Writings of the Second Temple Period, II: Jewish Writings of the Second Temple Period: Apocrypha, Pseudepigrapha, Qumran Sectarian Writings, Philo, Josephus*, ed. M. E. Stone. Assen: Gorcum, 1974.

Gilman, S. L., "Decircumcision: The First Aesthetic Surgery." *Modern Judaism*, 17, 3 (1997): 201–10.

Goodman, M., "Nerva, the Fiscus Judaicus and Jewish Identity," *JRS*, 79 (1989): 40–4.

—— "Kosher Olive Oil in Antiquity," pp. 227–45 in *A Tribute to Geza Vermes: Essays on Jewish and Christian Literature and History*, ed. P. R. Davies and R. T. White. Sheffield: JSOT Press, 1990.

—— "Diaspora Reactions to the Destruction of the Temple," pp. 27–38 in *Jews and Christians: The Parting of Ways A.D. 70 to 135*, ed. J. D. G. Dunn. Tübingen: Mohr, 1992.

—— *Mission and Conversion: Proselytizing in the Religious History of the Roman Empire*. London: Clarendon Press, 1994.

Goodwin, W. E., "Uncircumcision: A Technique for Plastic Reconstruction of a Prepuce after Circumcision." *Journal of Urology*, 144 (1990): 1203–5.

Gordon, M. M., *Assimilation in American Life: The Role of Race, Religion, and National Origins*. New York: Oxford University Press, 1973 [1964].

Goulder, M. D., "Ignatius' 'Docetists'," *VC*, 53 (1999): 16–30.

Grabbe, L. L., *Judaism from Cyrus to Hadrian*. London: SCM Press, 1994 [1992].

Grant, M., *A Social History of Greece and Rome*. New York: Macmillan, 1992.

Guettel-Cole, S., "The Uses of Water in Greek Sanctuaries," pp. 161–5 in *Early Cult Practice*, ed. R. Hägg, N. Marinatos and G. C. Nordquist. Stockholm: Svenska Institutet i Athen, 1988.

Guidoboni, E., A. Comastri and G. Traina, *Catalogue of Ancient Earthquakes in the Mediterranean Area up to the 10th Century*. Rome: Istituto Nazionale di Geofisica, 1994.

Haddad, G., *Aspects of Social Life in Antioch in the Hellenistic-Roman Period*. Chicago: University of Chicago Press, 1949.

Haenchen, E., *The Acts of the Apostles: A Commentary*. Oxford: Blackwell, 1971.

Hall, R. G., "Epispasm and the Dating of Ancient Jewish Writings," *JSP*, 2 (1988): 71–86.

—— "Historical Inference and Rhetorical Effect: Another Look at Galatians 1 and 2," pp. 308–20 in *Persuasive Artistry: Studies in Rhetoric in Honor of Georg A. Kennedy*, ed. D. F. Watson. Sheffield: JSOT Press, 1991.

—— "Epispasm: Circumcision in Reverse," *BRev*, 8 (1992): 52–7.

Hallbäck, G., "Jerusalem og Antiokia i Gal. 2," *DTT*, 53 (1990): 300–16.

Hamberg, E. M., "World-Views and Value Systems Among Immigrants: Long-Term Stability or Change? A Study of Hungarian Immigrants in Sweden." *Sociale Wetenschappen*, 38, 4 (1995): 85–108.

—— "International Migration and Religious Change," pp. 23–37 in *Towards a New Understanding of Conversion*, ed. U. Görman. Lund: Teologiska Institutionen, 1999.

—— "Migration and Religious Change," pp. 71–86 in *Religion and Social Transitions*, ed. E. Helander. Helsinki: Helsinki University Press, 1999.

—— *Livsåskådningar religion och värderingar i en invandrargrupp: en studie av sverigeungrare*. Stockholm: CEIFO, 2000.

Hansen, M. H., "The *Polis* as a Citizen-State," pp. 7–29 in *The Ancient Greek City-State: Symposium on the Occasion of the 250th Anniversary of the Royal Danish Academy of Sciences and Letters, July, 1–4 1992*, ed. M. H. Hansen. Copenhagen: Munksgaard, 1993.

Harris, H. A., *Greek Athletics and the Jews*. Cardiff: University of Wales Press, 1976.

Hart, S., "The Cultural Dimension of Social Movements: A Theoretical Reassessment and Literature Review," *Sociology of Religion*, 57, 1 (1996): 87–100.

Hedner-Zetterholm, K., *Portrait of a Villain: Laban the Aramean in Rabbinic Literature*. Leuven: Peeters, 2002.

—— "The Jewish Communities of Ancient Rome," pp. 131–40 in *The Synagogue of Ancient Rome: Interdisciplinary Studies*, ed. B. Olsson, D. Mitternacht and O. Brandt. Stockholm: Paul Åström, 2001.

Hengel, M., *Judaism and Hellenism: Studies in their Encounter in Palestine During the Early Hellenistic Period*, 2 vols. London: SCM Press, 1974.

—— "The Interpretation of Judaism and Hellenism in the Pre-Maccabean Period," pp. 167–228 in *The Cambridge History of Judaism, Volume 2: The Hellenistic Age*, ed. L. Finkelstein and W. D. Davies. Cambridge: Cambridge University Press, 1984.

Hengel, M., and C. K. Barrett, *Conflicts and Challenges in Early Christianity*, ed. D. A. Hagner. Harrisburg, PA: Trinity Press, 1999.

Hengel, M., and A. M. Schwemer, *Paul Between Damascus and Antioch: The Unknown Years*. London: SCM Press, 1997.

Herford, R. T., *Judaism in the New Testament*. London: Lindsey, 1928.

Hidal, S., "The Jews as the Roman Authors Saw Them," pp. 141–4 in *The*

Synagogue of Ancient Rome: Interdisciplinary Studies, ed. B. Olsson, D. Mitternacht and O. Brandt. Stockholm: Paul Åström, 2001.

Hill, C. C., *Hellenists and Hebrews: Reappraising Division Within the Earliest Church*. Minneapolis: Fortress Press, 1992.

Hillers, D. R., *Micah: A Commentary on the Book of the Prophet Micah*. Philadelphia: Fortress Press, 1984.

Hoenig, S. B., "Oil and Pagan Defilement," *JQR*, 61 (1970–71): 63–75.

Hoffman, L. A., *Covenant of Blood: Circumcision and Gender in Rabbinic Judaism*. Chicago: University of Chicago Press, 1996.

Holmberg, B., *Paul and Power: The Structure of Authority in the Primitive Church as Reflected in the Pauline Epistles*. Lund: Almqvist & Wiksell, 1978.

—— "Sociologiska perspektiv på Gal 2:11 – 14(21)," *SEÅ*, 55 (1990): 71–92.

——*Sociology and the New Testament: An Appraisal*. Minneapolis: Fortress Press, 1990.

—— "Jewish *Versus* Christian Identity in the Early Church," *RB*, 105, 3 (1998): 397–425.

—— "The Life in the Diaspora Synagogues: An Evaluation," pp. 219–32 in *The Ancient Synagogue from its Origins until 200 C.E.: Papers Presented at an International Conference at Lund University, October 14–17, 2001*, ed. B. Olsson and M. Zetterholm. Stockholm: Almqvist & Wiksell, 2003.

Holmstrand, J., *Markers and Meaning in Paul: An Analysis of 1 Thessalonians, Philippians and Galatians*. Stockholm: Almqvist & Wiksell, 1997.

Hopkins, K., *Death and Renewal*. Cambridge: Cambridge University Press, 1985 [1983].

—— "Graveyards for Historians," pp. 113–26 in *La mort les morts et l'au-delà dans le monde romain: actes du colloque de Caen 20–22 novembre 1985*, ed. F. Hinard. Caen: Université de Caen, 1987.

Horbury, W., "The Temple Tax," pp. 265–86 in *Jesus and the Politics of His Day*, ed. E. Bammel and C. F. D. Moule. Cambridge: Cambridge University Press, 1984.

——*Jewish Messianism and the Cult of Christ*. London: SCM Press, 1998.

—— "Women in the Synagogue," pp. 358–401 in *The Cambridge History of Judaism, Volume 3: The Early Roman Period*, ed. W. Horbury, W. D. Davies and J. Sturdy. Cambridge: Cambridge University Press, 1999.

Horrell, D. G., "Models and Methods in Social-Scientific Interpretation: A Response to Philip Esler." *JSNT* 78 (2000): 83–105.

Horsley, R. A., *Galilee: History, Politics, People*. Valley Forge, PA: Trinity Press, 1995.

Hospers, J., *An Introduction to Philosophical Analysis*, 3rd edn. London: Routledge, 1992 [1990].

Hübner, R. M., "Thesen zur Echtheit und Datierung der sieben Briefe des Ignatius von Antiochien," *ZAC*, 1, 1 (1997): 44–72.

Humphrey, J. H., *Roman Circuses: Arenas for Chariot Racing*. London: Batsford, 1986.

Hunt, L., "Charles Tilly's Collective Action," pp. 244–75 in *Vision and Method in Historical Sociology*, ed. T. Skocpol. Cambridge: Cambridge University Press, 1989 [1984].

Hurd, J. C., *The Origin of 1 Corinthians*. Macon, GA: Mercer University Press, 1983 [1965].

Iannaccone, L. R., "Sacrifice and Stigma: Reducing Free-Riding in Cults, Communes, and Other Collectives," *Journal of Political History*, 100, 21 (1992): 271–91.

—— "Why Strict Churches Are Strong," *American Journal of Sociology*, 99, 5 (1994): 1180–211.

Inglehart, R., *Culture Shift in Advanced Industrial Society*. Princeton, NJ: Princeton University Press, 1990.

Iser, W., *The Act of Reading: A Theory of Aesthetic Response*. Baltimore: Johns Hopkins University Press, 1991.

Jeremias, J., *Jesus' Promise to the Nations*. Philadelphia: Fortress Press, 1982 [1958, in German].

Kajanto, I., *On the Problem of the Average Duration of Life in the Roman Empire*. Helsinki: Suomalainen Tiedeakatemia, 1968.

Kasher, A., *The Jews in Hellenistic and Roman Egypt: The Struggle for Equal Rights*. Tübingen: Mohr, 1985 [1978, in Hebrew].

Keresztes, P., "The Jews, the Christians, and Emperor Domitian," *VC*, 27 (1973): 1–28.

Kerkeslager, A., "Maintaining Jewish Identity in the Greek Gymnasium: A 'Jewish Load' in *CPJ* 3.519 (= P. Shub. 37 = P. Berol. 13406)," *JSJ*, 28, 1 (1997): 12–33.

Kieffer, R., *Foi et justification à Antioche: interprétation d'un conflit (Ga 2, 14–21)*. Paris: Cerf, 1982.

Kloppenborg, J. S., "Edwin Hatch, Churches and Collegia," pp. 212–38 in *Origins and Method: Towards a new Understanding of Judaism and Christianity: Essays in Honour of John C. Hurd*, ed. B. H. McLean and J. C. Hurd. Sheffield: JSOT Press, 1993.

—— "Collegia and *Thiasoi*: Issues in Function, Taxonomy and Membership," pp. 16–30 in *Voluntary Associations in the Graeco-Roman World*, ed. J. S. Kloppenborg and S. G. Wilson. London: Routledge, 1996.

Kniss, F., "Ideas and Symbols as Resources in Intrareligious Conflict: The Case of American Mennonites." *Sociology of Religion*, 57, 1 (1996): 7–23.

Koester, H., *Introduction to the New Testament, 1: History, Culture and Religion of the Hellenistic Age*. Philadelphia: Fortress Press, 1982 [1980, in German].

—— *Introduction to the New Testament, 2: History and Literature of Early Christianity*. Philadelphia: Fortress Press, 1982 [1980, in German].

Kondoleon, C., ed., *Antioch: The Lost Ancient City*. Princeton, NJ: Princeton University Press, 2000.

—— "The City of Antioch: An Introduction," pp. 3–11 in *Antioch: The Lost Ancient City*, ed. C. Kondoleon. Princeton, NJ: Princeton University Press, 2000.

Kraabel, A. T., "The Roman Diaspora: Six Questionable Assumptions," *JJS*, 33 (1982): 445–64.

—— "The Disappearance of the 'God-Fearers'," pp. 119–30 in *Diaspora Jews and Judaism: Essays in Honor of, and in Dialogue with, A. Thomas Kraabel*, ed. J. A. Overman and R. S. MacLennan. Atlanta: Scholars Press, 1992.

—— "Social Systems of Six Diaspora Synagogues," pp. 257–67 in *Diaspora Jews and Judaism: Essays in Honor of, and in Dialogue with, A. Thomas Kraabel*, ed. J. A. Overman and R. S. MacLennan. Atlanta: Scholars Press, 1992.

—— "Unity and Diversity among Diaspora Synagogues," pp. 21–31 in *Diaspora Jews and Judaism: Essays in Honor of, and in Dialogue with, A. Thomas Kraabel*, ed. J. A. Overman and R. S. MacLennan. Atlanta: Scholars Press, 1992.

Kraabel, A. T., and R. S. MacLennan, "The God-Fearers—A Literary and Theological Invention," pp. 131–43 in *Diaspora Jews and Judaism: Essays in Honor of, and in Dialogue with, A. Thomas Kraabel*, ed. J. A. Overman and R. S. MacLennan. Atlanta: Scholars Press, 1992.

Kraeling, C. H., "The Jewish Community at Antioch," *JBL*, 51 (1932): 130–60.

Krauss, S., "Antioche," *Revue des études juives*, 89 (1902): 27–49.

Kuhn, K. G., "προσήλυτος," pp. 516–35 in *Theological Dictionary of the New Testament*, 6, ed. G. Kittel and G. Friedrich. Grand Rapids, MI: Eerdmans, 1980 [1968].

Lambrecht, J., "University and Diversity in Galatians 1–2," pp. 177–92 in *Pauline Studies: Collected Essays*. Leuven: Leuven University Press, 1994 [1989].

Lane, W. L., "Social Perspectives on Roman Christianity during the Formative Years from Nero to Nerva: Romans, Hebrews, *1 Clement*," pp. 196–244 in *Judaism and Christianity in First-Century Rome*, ed. K. P. Donfried and P. Richardson. Grand Rapids, MI: Eerdmans, 1998.

Lapide, P., and P. Stuhlmacher, *Paul: Rabbi and Apostle*. Augsburg: Augsburg Publishing House, 1984 [1981, in German].

Legarth, P. V., *Guds tempel: tempelsymbolisme og kristologi hos Ignatius af Antiokia*. Århus: Kolon, 1992

Levine, L. I., "The Second Temple Synagogue: The Formative Years," pp. 7–31 in *The Synagogue in Late Antiquity*, ed. L. I. Levine. Philadelphia: American Schools of Oriental Research, 1987.

—— *Judaism and Hellenism in Antiquity: Conflict or Confluence?* Seattle: University of Washington Press, 1998.

—— *The Ancient Synagogue: The First Thousand Years*. New Haven, CT: Yale University Press, 2000.

—— "The First-Century Synagogue: New Perspectives," *STK*, 77 (2001): 22–30.

Levinskaya, I., *The Book of Acts in its First Century Setting, Volume 5: The Book of Acts in its Diaspora Setting*. Grand Rapids, MI: Eerdmans, 1996.

Lieu, J., *Image and Reality: The Jews in the World of the Christians in the Second Century*. Edinburgh: T. & T. Clark, 1996.

Lofland, J., *Social Movement Organizations: Guide to Research on Insurgent Realities*. New York: de Gruyter, 1996.

Lohse, E., "Synagogue of Satan and Church of God: Jews and Christians in the Book of Revelation," *SEÅ*, 58 (1993): 105–23.

Longenecker, R. N., *Galatians*. Dallas: Word Books, 1990.

Lüderitz, G., "What is the Politeuma?" Pages 183–225 in *Studies in Early Jewish Epigraphy*, ed. P. W. van der Horst and J. W. van Henten. Leiden: Brill, 1994.

Lührmann, D., *Galatians*. Minneapolis: Fortress Press, 1992 [1978].

Maas, M., "People and Identity in Roman Antioch," pp. 13–21 in *Antioch: The Lost Ancient City*, ed. C. Kondoleon. Princeton, NJ: Princeton University Press, 2000.

McAdam, D., J. D. McCarthy, and M. N. Zald, "Social Movements," pp. 695–737 in *Handbook of Sociology*, ed. N. J. Smelser. Newbury Park, CA: Sage, 1988.

McEleney, N. J., "Conversion, Circumcision and the Law," *NTS*, 20 (1974): 319–41.

McGuire, M. B., *Religion: The Social Context*. 3rd edn. Belmont, CA: Wadsworth, 1992.

McKnight, S., *A Light Among the Gentiles: Jewish Missionary Activity in the Second Temple Period*. Minneapolis: Fortress Press, 1991.

MacMullen, R., *Enemies of the Roman Order: Treason, Unrest, and Alienation in the Empire*. Cambridge: Cambridge University Press, 1966.

Manchester, K., "The Palaeopathology of Urban Infections," pp. 8–14 in *Death in Towns: Urban Responses to the Dying and the Dead, 100–1600*, ed. S. Bassett. London: Leicester University Press, 1995 [1992].

Mandell, S., "Who Paid the Temple Tax when the Jews Were under Roman Rule?," *HTR*, 77, 2 (1984): 223–32.

Marshall, I. H., *The Acts of the Apostles: An Introduction and Commentary*. Leicester: InterVarsity Press, 1984 [1980].

Martin, L. H., *Hellenistic Religions: An Introduction*. New York: Oxford University Press, 1986.

Martyn, J. L., *Galatians: A New Translation with Introduction and Commentary*. New York: Doubleday, 1997.

Meeks, W. A., *The First Urban Christians: The Social World of the Apostle Paul*. New Haven, CT: Yale University Press, 1983.

Meeks, W. A., and R. L. Wilken, *Jews and Christians in Antioch in the First Four Centuries of the Common Era*. Atlanta: Scholars Press, 1978.

Meier, J. P., *Law and History in Matthew's Gospel: A Redactional Study of Mt. 5:17–48*. Rome: Biblical Institute Press, 1976.

—— *A Marginal Jew: Rethinking the Historical Jesus, Volume 1: The Roots of the Problem and the Person*. New York: Doubleday, 1991.

—— "Matthew and Ignatius: A Response to William R. Schoedel," pp. 178–86 in *Social History of the Matthean Community: Cross-Disciplinary Approaches*, ed. D. L. Balch. Minneapolis: Fortress Press, 1991.

——*A Marginal Jew: Rethinking the Historical Jesus, Volume 2: Mentor, Message, and Miracles*. New York: Doubleday, 1994.

Metcalf, W. E., "The Mint of Antioch," pp. 105–11 in *Antioch: The Lost Ancient City*, ed. C. Kondoleon. Princeton, NJ: Princeton University Press, 2000.

Meyer, P., "Romans 10:4 and the 'End of the Law'," pp. 59–78 in *The Divine Helmsman: Studies on God's Control of Human Events, Presented to Lou H. Silberman*, ed. J. L. Crenshaw and S. Sandmel. New York: Ktav, 1980.

Millar, F., "The Greek City in the Roman Period," pp. 7–29 in *The Ancient Greek City-State: Symposium on the Occasion of the 250th Anniversary of the Royal Danish Academy of Sciences and Letters, July, 1–4 1992*, ed. M. H. Hansen. Copenhagen: Munksgaard, 1993.

——*The Roman Near East, 31 BC – AD 337*. Cambridge, MA: Harvard University Press, 1993.

Mitternacht, D., *Forum für Sprachlose: eine kommunikationspsychologische und epistolärrhetorische Untersuchung des Galaterbriefs*. Stockholm: Almqvist & Wiksell, 1999.

——"Foolish Galatians?—A Recipient-Oriented Assessment of Paul's Letter," pp. 408–33 in *The Galatians Debate: Contemporary Issues in Rhetorical and Historical Interpretation*, ed. M. D. Nanos. Peabody, MA: Hendrickson, 2002.

Montefiore, C. G., *Judaism and St Paul: Two Essays*. London: Goshen, 1914.

Moore, G. F., "Christian Writers on Judaism," *HTR*, 14 (1921): 197–254.

Morris, I., "The Early Polis as City and State," pp. 25–57 in *City and Country in the Ancient World*, ed. J. Rich and A. Wallace-Hadrill. London: Routledge, 1991.

Munck, J., *The Acts of the Apostles: Introduction, Translation and Notes*. New York: Doubleday, 1986 [1967].

Nanos, M. D., *The Mystery of Romans: The Jewish Context of Paul's Letter*. Minneapolis: Fortress Press, 1996.

——*The Irony of Galatians: Pauls' Letter in First Century Context*. Philadelphia: Fortress Press, 2001.

——"What Was at Stake in Peter's 'Eating with Gentiles' at Antioch?," pp. 282–318 in *The Galatians Debate: Contemporary Issues in Rhetorical and Historical Interpretation*, ed. M. D. Nanos. Peabody, MA: Hendrickson, 2002.

Niehoff, M. R., "Philo's Views on Paganism," pp. 135–58 in *Tolerance and Intolerance in Early Judaism and Christianity*, ed. G. N. Stanton and G. G. Stroumsa. Cambridge: Cambridge University Press, 1998.

Nielsen, I., "Royal Banquets: The Development of Royal Banquets and Banqueting Halls from Alexander to the Tetrarchs," pp. 102–33 in *Meals in a Social Context: Aspects of the Communal Meal in the Hellenistic and Roman World*, ed. I. Nielsen and H. S. Nielsen. Aarhus: Aarhus University Press, 1998.

Nixon, L., and S. Price, "The Size and Resources of Greek Cities," pp. 137–70 in *The Greek City: From Homer to Alexander*, ed. O. Murray and S. Price. Oxford: Clarendon Press, 1991 [1990].

Nolland, J., "Uncircumcised Proselytes?," *JSJ*, 12, 2 (1981): 173–94.

Norris, F. W., "Isis, Sarapis and Demeter in Antioch of Syria," *HTR*, 75, 2 (1982): 189–207.

—— "Antioch-on-the-Orontes as a Religious Center, I. Paganism before Constantine," pp. 2322–79 in *Aufstieg und Niedergang der Römischen Welt: Geschichte und Kultur Roms im Spiegel der neueren Forschung, Teil II: Principat, Band 18: Religion (Heidentum): die religiösen Verhältnisse in den Provinzen (forts.)) 4. Teilband*. Berlin: de Gruyter, 1990.

—— "Artifacts from Antioch," pp. 248–58 in *Social History of the Matthean Community: Cross-Disciplinary Approaches*, ed. D. L. Balch. Minneapolis: Fortress Press, 1991.

Novak, D., *The Image of the Non-Jew in Judaism*. New York: Edwin Mellen Press, 1983.

Noy, D., "The Sixth Hour is the Mealtime for Scholars: Jewish Meals in the Roman World," pp. 134–44 in *Meals in a Social Context: Aspects of the Communal Meal in the Hellenistic and Roman World*, ed. I. Nielsen and H. S. Nielsen. Aarhus: Aarhus University Press, 1998.

Obermann, J., "The Sepulchre of the Maccabean Martyrs," *JBL*, 50 (1931): 250–65.

Oberschall, A., *Social Movements: Ideologies, Interests, and Identities*. New Brunswick, NJ: Transactions, 1993.

Oppenheimer, A., "Terumot and Ma'serot," pp. 1025–7 in *Encyclopaedia Judaica, 15*, ed. C. Roth and G. Wigoder. Jerusalem: Keter, 1978 [1972].

Overman, J. A., *Matthew's Gospel and Formative Judaism: The Social World of the Matthean Community*. Minneapolis: Fortress Press, 1990.

—— "The God-Fearers: Some Neglected Features," pp. 145–52 in *Diaspora Jews and Judaism: Essays in Honor of, and in Dialogue with, A. Thomas Kraabel*, ed. J. A. Overman and R. S. MacLennan. Atlanta: Scholars Press, 1992.

Paget, J. C., "Jewish Proselytism at the Time of Christian Origins: Chimera or Reality?," *JSNT*, 62 (1996): 65–103.

Painter, J., *Just James: The Brother of Jesus in History and Tradition*. Minneapolis: Fortress Press, 1999 [1997].

Parkes, J., *The Conflict of the Church and the Synagogue. A Study in the Origins of Antisemitism*. New York: Athaneum, 1934.

Patterson, J. R., "Patronage, *Collegia* and Burial in Imperial Rome," pp. 15–27 in *Death in Towns: Urban Responses to the Dying and the Dead, 100–1600*, ed. S. Bassett. London: Leicester University Press, 1995 [1992].

Pearson, B. A., "Christians and Jews in First-Century Alexandria," pp. 206–16 in *Christians among Jews and Gentiles*, ed. G. W. E. Nickelsburg and G. W. MacRae. Philadelphia: Fortress Press, 1986.

Petersen, W., *Population*. New York: Macmillan, 1966.

Pettersson, T., and O. Riis, *Scandinavian Values: Religion and Morality in the Nordic Countries*. Stockholm: Almqvist & Wiksell, 1994.

Porter, S. E., "Paul of Tarsus and His Letters," pp. 533–85 in *Handbook of Classical Rhetoric in the Hellenistic Period, 330 B.C. – A.D. 400*, ed. S. E. Porter. Leiden: Brill, 1997.

Porton, G. G., "Diversity in Postbiblical Judaism," pp. 57–80 in *Early Judaism and its Modern Interpreters*, ed. R. A. Kraft and G. W. E. Nicklesburg. Philadelphia: Fortress Press, 1986.

Price, S., *Religions of the Ancient Greeks*. Cambridge: Cambridge University Press, 2000 [1999].

Purvis, J. D., "The Samaritans," pp. 591–613 in *The Cambridge History of Judaism, Volume 2: The Hellenistic Age*, ed. L. Finkelstein and W. D. Davies. Cambridge: Cambridge University Press, 1984.

Quasten, J., *Patrology, Volume 1*. Brussels: Spectrum, 1950.

Quine, W. V., and J. S. Ullian, *The Web of Belief*, 2nd edn. New York: McGraw-Hill, 1978.

Rajak, T., "The Hasmoneans and the Uses of Hellenism," pp. 261–80 in *A Tribute to Geza Vermes: Essays on Jewish and Christian Literature and History*, ed. P. R. Davies and R. T. White. Sheffield: JSOT Press, 1990.

—— "The Jewish Community and its Boundaries," pp. 9–28 in *The Jews Among Pagans and Christians*, ed. J. Lieu, J. North and T. Rajak. London: Routledge, 1994.

—— "The Synagogue Within the Greco-Roman City," pp. 161–73 in *Jews, Christians and Polytheists in the Ancient Synagogue: Cultural Interaction During the Greco-Roman Period*, ed. S. Fine. London: Routledge, 1999.

—— *The Jewish Dialogue with Greece and Rome: Studies in Cultural and Social Interaction*. Leiden: Brill, 2001.

Rajak, T., and D. Noy, "*Archisynagogoi*: Office, Title and Social Status in the Greco-Jewish Synagogue," *JRS*, 83 (1993): 75–93.

Repschinski, B., *The Controversy Stories in the Gospel of Matthew: Their Redaction, Form and Relevance for the Relationship Between the Matthean Community and Formative Judaism*. Göttingen: Vandenhoeck, 2000.

Rex, J., "Religion and Ethnicity in the Metropolis," pp. 17–26 in *Religion and Ethnicity: Minorities and Social Change in the Metropolis*, ed. R. Barot. Kampen: Kok Pharos, 1993.

Reynolds, J., and R. Tannenbaum, *Jews and Godfearers at Aphrodisias: Greek Inscriptions with Commentary*. Cambridge: Cambridge Philological Society, 1987.

Rhodes, P. J., "The Greek *Poleis*: Demes, Cities and Leagues," pp. 161–81 in *The Ancient Greek City-State: Symposium on the Occasion of the 250th Anniversary of the Royal Danish Academy of Sciences and Letters, July, 1–4 1992*, ed. M. H. Hansen. Copenhagen: Munksgaard, 1993.

Richardson, P., "Early Synagogues as Collegia in the Diaspora and Palestine," pp. 90–109 in *Voluntary Associations in the Graeco-Roman World*, ed. J. S. Kloppenborg and S. G. Wilson. London: Routledge, 1996.

——"Augustan-Era Synagogues in Rome," pp. 17–29 in *Judaism and Christianity in First-Century Rome*, ed. K. P. Donfried and P. Richardson. Grand Rapids, MI: Eerdmans, 1998.

——"An Architectural Case for Synagogues as Associations," pp. 90–117 in *The Ancient Synagogue from its Origins until 200 C.E.: Papers Presented at an International Conference at Lund University, October 14–17, 2001*, ed. B. Olsson and M. Zetterholm. Stockholm: Almqvist & Wiksell, 2003.

Roberts, C., and K. Manchester, *The Archaeology of Disease*, 2nd edn. Ithaca, NY: Cornell University Press, 1997 [1995].

Rosivach, V. J., *The System of Public Sacrifice in Fourth-Century Athens*. Atlanta: Scholars Press, 1994.

Rosner, F., "Hemophilia in the Talmud and Rabbinic Writings." *Annals of Internal Medicine*, 70, 4 (1969): 833–7.

Rubin, J. P., "Celsus' Decircumcision Operation: Medical and Historical Implications," *Urology*, 16, 1 (1980): 121–4.

Runesson, A., *The Origins of the Synagogue: A Socio-Historical Study*. Stockholm: Almqvist & Wiksell, 2001.

——"Water and Worship: Ostia and the Ritual Bath in the Diaspora Synagogue," pp. 115–29 in *The Synagogue of Ancient Rome: Interdisciplinary Studies*, ed. B. Olsson, D. Mitternacht and O. Brandt. Stockholm: Paul Åström, 2001.

Russell, J., "Household Furnishings," pp. 79–89 in *Antioch: The Lost Ancient City*, ed. C. Kondoleon. Princeton, NJ: Princeton University Press, 2000.

Rutgers, L. V., "Diaspora Synagogues: Synagogue Archaeology in the Greco-Roman World," pp. 67–95 in *Sacred Realm: The Emergence of the Synagogue in the Ancient World*, ed. S. Fine. Oxford: Oxford University Press, 1996.

——*The Hidden Heritage of Diaspora Judaism*, 2nd edn. Leuven: Peeters, 1998.

——"The Importance of Scripture in the Conflict Between Jews and Christians: The Example of Antioch," pp. 287–303 in *The Use of Sacred Books in the Ancient World*, ed. L. V. Rutgers, P. W. van der Horst, H. W. Havelaar *et al.* Leuven: Peeters, 1998.

——"Roman Policy Toward the Jews: Expulsions from the City of Rome During the First Century C.E.," pp. 93–116 in *Judaism and Christianity in First-Century Rome*, ed. K. P. Donfried and P. Richardson. Grand Rapids, MI: Eerdmans, 1998.

Safrai, S., "Jewish Self-Government," pp. 377–419 in *The Jewish People in the First Century: Historical Geography, Political History, Social, Cultural and Religious Life and Institutions*, ed. S. Safrai, M. Stern, D. Flusser *et al.* Assen: van Gorcum, 1974.

——"Relations between the Diaspora and the Land of Israel," pp. 184–215 in *The Jewish People in the First Century: Historical Geography, Political History, Social, Cultural and Religious Life and Institutions*, ed. S. Safrai, M. Stern, D. Flusser *et al.* Assen: van Gorcum, 1974.

——"Elisha ben Avuya," pp. 668–70 in *Encyclopaedia Judaica*, ed. C. Roth and G. Wigoder. Jerusalem: Keter, 1978 [1972].

Sanders, E. P., "The Covenant as a Soteriological Category and the Nature of Salvation in Palestinian and Hellenistic Judaism," pp. 11–44 in *Jews, Greeks and Christians: Religious Cultures in Late Antiquity: Essays in Honor of William David Davies, George Washington Ivey Professor of Advanced Studies and Resarch in Christian Origins, Duke University*, ed. R. Hamerton-Kelly and R. Scroggs. Leiden: Brill, 1976.

——*Paul and Palestinian Judaism: A Comparison of Patterns of Religion.* Minneapolis: Fortress Press, 1977.

——*Jesus and Judaism.* Philadelphia: Fortress Press, 1985.

——*Paul, the Law, and the Jewish People.* Minneapolis: Fortress Press, 1985 [1983].

—— "Jewish Associations with Gentiles and Galatians 2:11–14," pp. 170–88 in *The Conversation Continues: Studies in Paul and John in Honour of J. Louis Martyn*, ed. R. T. Fortna and B. R. Gaventa. Nashville: Abingdon Press, 1990.

——*Judaism: Practice and Belief, 63 BCE–66 CE.* London: SCM Press, 1994.

—— "Common Judaism and the Synagogue in the First Century," pp. 1–17 in *Jews, Christians and Polytheists in the Ancient Synagogue: Cultural Interaction During the Greco-Roman Period*, ed. S. Fine. London: Routledge, 1999.

Sanders, J. T., *Schismatics, Sectarians, Dissidents, Deviants: The First One Hundred Years of Jewish–Christian Relations.* London: SCM Press, 1993.

—— "Did Early Christianity Succeed Because of Jewish Conversions?," *Social Compass*, 46, 4 (1999): 493–505.

——*Charisma, Converts, Competitors: Societal and Sociological Factors in the Success of Early Christianity.* London: SCM Press, 2000.

Schäfer, P., *The History of the Jews in Antiquity.* Luxembourg: Harwood, 1995 [1983, in German].

——*Judeophobia: Attitudes toward the Jews in the Ancient World.* Cambridge, MA: Harvard University Press, 1997.

—— "Diversity and Interactions: Messiahs in Early Judaism," pp. 15–35 in *Toward the Millennium: Messianic Expectations From the Bible to Waco*, ed. P. Schäfer and M. Cohen. Leiden: Brill, 1998.

Schatkin, M., "The Maccabean Martyrs," *VC*, 28 (1974): 97–113.

Scheidel, W., "Progress and Problems in Roman Demography," pp. 1–81 in *Debating Roman Demography*, ed. W. Scheidel. Leiden: Brill, 2001.

Schiffauer, W., "Migration and Religiousness," pp. 146–58 in *The New Islamic Presence in Western Europe*, ed. T. Gerholm and Y. G. Lithman. London: Mansell, 1990 [1988].

Schmidt, K. L., "ἐκκλησία," pp. 501–36 in *Theological Dictionary of the New Testament*, 3, ed. G. Kittel and G. W. Bromiley. Grand Rapids, MI: Eerdmans, 1979 [1966].

Schmitt-Pantel, P., "Collective Activities and the Political in the Greek City," pp. 199–213 in *The Greek City: From Homer to Alexander*, ed. O. Murray and S. Price. Oxford: Clarendon Press, 1991 [1990].

Schoedel, W. R., "Theological Norms and Social Perspectives in Ignatius of Antioch," pp. 30–56 in *Jewish and Christian Self-Definition: The Shaping of Christianity in the Second and Third Centuries*, ed. E. P. Sanders. London: SCM Press, 1980.

——*Ignatius of Antioch: A Commentary on the Letters of Ignatius of Antioch*. Philadelphia: Fortress Press, 1985.

—— "Ignatius and the Reception of the Gospel of Matthew in Antioch," pp. 129–77 in *Social History of the Matthean Community: Cross-Disciplinary Approaches*, ed. D. L. Balch. Minneapolis: Fortress Press, 1991.

Schrage, W., "συναγωγή," pp. 798–841 in *Theological Dictionary of the New Testament*, 6, ed. G. Kittel and G. Friedrich. Grand Rapids, MI: Eerdmans, 1980 [1971].

Scroggs, R., "The Sociological Interpretation of the New Testament: The Present State of Research," *NTS*, 26 (1980): 164–79.

Segal, A. F., *Rebecca's Children: Judaism and Christianity in the Roman World*. Cambridge, MA: Harvard University Press, 1986.

——*Paul the Convert: The Apostolate and Apostasy of Saul the Pharisee*. New Haven, CT: Yale University Press, 1990.

—— "Matthew's Jewish Voice," pp. 3–37 in *Social History of the Matthean Community: Cross-Disciplinary Approaches*, ed. D. L. Balch. Minneapolis: Fortress Press, 1991.

Seland, T., "Philo and the Associations of Alexandria," pp. 110–27 in *Voluntary Associations in the Graeco-Roman World*, ed. J. S. Kloppenborg and S. G. Wilson. London: Routledge, 1996.

——*Paulus i Polis: Paulus' sosiale verden som forståelsebakgrunn for hans forkynnelse*. Volda: Høgskulen i Volda, 1998.

Senior, D., *What Are They Saying About Matthew?* New York: Paulist Press, 1996.

Shaffir, W., "Boundaries of Self-Presentation Among the Hasidim: A Study in Identity Maintenance," pp. 31–68 in *New World Hasidim: Ethnographic Studies of Hasidic Jews in America*, ed. J. S. Belcove-Shalin. Albany: State University of New York, 1995.

Sigal, P., and L. Sigal, *Judaism: The Evolution of a Faith*. Grand Rapids, MI: Eerdmans, 1988 [1986, in German].

Smallwood, M. E., "Domitian's Attitude Toward the Jews and Judaism," *CP*, 51, 1 (1956): 1–13.

——*Philonis Alexandrini Legatio ad Gaium: Edited with an Introduction, Translation and Commentary*, 2nd edn. Leiden: Brill, 1970 [1st edn 1961].

—— *The Jews under Roman Rule From Pompey to Diocletian: A Study in Political Relations*. Leiden: Brill, 1981.

Sourvinou-Inwood, C., "What is *Polis* Religion?," pp. 295–322 in *The Greek City: From Homer to Alexander*, ed. O. Murray and S. Price. Oxford: Clarendon Press, 1991 [1990].

Stambaugh, J., and D. Balch, *The Social World of the First Christians*. London: SPCK, 1992.

Stanton, G., "Other Early Christian Writings: 'Didache', Ignatius,

'Barnabas', Justin Martyr," pp. 174–90 in *Early Christian Thought in its Jewish Context*, ed. J. Barclay and J. Sweet. Cambridge: Cambridge University Press, 1996.

Stark, R., "German and German-American Religiousness: Approximating a Crucial Experiment," *JSSR*, 36, 2 (1997): 182–93.

—— *The Rise of Christianity: How the Obscure, Marginal Jesus Movement Became the Dominant Religious Force in the Western World in a Few Centuries*. San Francisco: HarperCollins, 1997.

Stark, R., and R. Finke, *Acts of Faith: Explaining the Human Side of Religion*. Berkeley: University of California Press, 2000.

Stegemann, E. W., and W. Stegemann, *The Jesus Movement: A Social History of its First Century*. Edinburgh: T. & T. Clark, 1999 [1995, in German].

Steinberg, M., *As a Driven Leaf*. New York: Behrman, 1939.

Stendahl, K., *Paul Among Jews and Gentiles, and other Essays*. Philadelphia: Fortress Press, 1976.

Stern, M., "The Jewish Diaspora," pp. 117–83 in *The Jewish People in the First Century: Historical Geography, Political History, Social, Cultural and Religious Life and Institutions*, ed. S. Safrai, M. Stern, D. Flusser *et al*. Assen: van Gorcum, 1974.

—— *Greek and Latin Authors on Jews and Judaism: Edited with Introductions, Translations and Commentary, Vols. 1–3*. Jerusalem: Israel Academy of Sciences and Humanities, 1974–84.

Strathmann, H., "πολιτεία," pp. 516–35 in *Theological Dictionary of the New Testament*, 6, ed. G. Kittel and G. Friedrich. Grand Rapids, MI: Eerdmans, 1980 [1968].

Stroumsa, G. G., "From Anti-Judaism to Antisemitism in Early Christianity?" Pages 1–26 in *Contra Iudaeos: Ancient and Medival Polemics between Christians and Jews*, ed. O. Limor and G. G. Stroumsa. Tübingen: Mohr, 1996.

Sumney, J. L., "Those Who 'Ignorantly Deny Him': The Opponents of Ignatius of Antioch," *JECS*, 3, 3 (1993): 299–324.

Svartvik, J., *Mark and Mission: Mk 7:1–23 in its Narrative and Historical Contexts*. Stockholm: Almqvist & Wiksell, 2000.

Takács, S. A., "Pagan Cults at Antioch," pp. 198–200 in *Antioch: The Lost Ancient City*, ed. C. Kondoleon. Princeton, NJ: Princeton University Press, 2000.

Tannehill, R. C., "The Disciples in Mark: The Function of a Narrative Role," *JR*, 57 (1977): 386–405.

Taylor, J., "Why Were the Disciples First Called 'Christians' at Antioch? (Acts 11:26)," *RB*, 101, 1 (1994): 75–94.

—— "The Jerusalem Decree (Acts 15:20, 29 and 21:25) and the Incident at Antioch (Gal. 2:11–14)," *NTS*, 47 (2001): 372–80.

Taylor, N. H., *Paul, Antioch and Jerusalem: A Study in Relationships and Authority in Earliest Christianity*. Sheffield: Sheffield Academic Press, 1992.

—— "The Social Nature of Conversion in the Early Christian World," pp.

128–36 in *Modelling Early Christianity: Social Scientific Studies of the New Testament in its Context*, ed. P. F. Esler. London: Routledge, 1995.

Tcherikover, V., *Hellenistic Civilisations and the Jews*. Peabody, MA: Hendrickson, 1999 [1959].

Tcherikover, V. A., and A. Fuks, eds, *Corpus Papyrorum Judaicarum, Volume 1*. Cambridge, MA: Harvard University Press, 1957.

——*Corpus Papyrorum Judaicarum, Volume 2*. Cambridge, MA: Harvard University Press, 1960.

Tellbe, M., *Paul between Synagogue and State: Christians, Jews, and Civic Authorities in 1 Thessalonians, Romans, and Philippians*. Stockholm: Almqvist & Wiksell, 2001.

Theissen, G., *The Religion of the Earliest Churches: Creating a Symbolic World*. Minneapolis: Fortress Press, 1999.

Thompson, L. A., "Domitian and the Jewish Tax," *Historia*, 31 (1982): 329–42.

Tilly, C., *From Mobilization to Revolution*. New York: Random House, 1978.

Tomson, P. J., *Paul and the Jewish Law: Halakha in the Letters of the Apostle to the Gentiles*. Assen and Maastricht: van Gorcum, 1990.

Trevett, C., *A Study of Ignatius of Antioch in Syria and Asia*. Lewiston, NY: Edwin Mellen Press, 1992.

Troiani, L., "The πολιτεία of Israel in the Graeco-Roman Age," pp. 11–22 in *Josephus and the History of the Greco-Roman Period: Essays in Memory of Morton Smith*, ed. F. Parente and J. Sievers. Leiden: Brill, 1994.

Tushnet, L., "Uncircumsicion," *Medical Times*, 93, 6 (1965): 588–93.

van Henten, J. W., *The Maccabean Martyrs as Saviours of the Jewish People: A Study of 2 and 4 Maccabees*. Leiden: Brill, 1997.

Waardenburg, J., "The Institutionalization of Islam in the Netherlands, 1961–86," pp. 239–62 in *The New Islamic Presence in Western Europe*, ed. T. Gerholm and Y. G. Lithman. London: Mansell, 1990 [1988].

Walker-Ramisch, S., "Graeco-Roman Voluntary Associations and the Damascus Document: A Sociological Analysis," pp. 128–45 in *Voluntary Associations in the Graeco-Roman World*, ed. J. S. Kloppenborg and S. G. Wilson. London: Routledge, 1996.

Wallace, R., and W. Williams, *The Three Worlds of Paul of Tarsus*. London: Routledge, 1998.

Walser, G., *The Greek of the Ancient Synagogue: An Investigation on the Greek of the Septuagint, Pseudepigrapha and the New Testament*. Stockholm: Almqvist & Wiksell, 2001.

Wechsler, A., *Geschichtsbild und Apostelstreit: eine forschungsgeschichtliche und exegetische Studie über den antiochenischen Zwischenfall (Gal 2,11–14)*. Berlin: de Gruyter, 1991.

Whittaker, M., *Jews and Christians: Graeco-Roman Views*. Cambridge: Cambridge University Press, 1984.

Williams, M. H., "Domitian, the Jews and the 'Judaizers'—A Simple Matter of Cupiditas and Maiestas?," *Historia*, 39 (1990): 196–211.

—— "The Structure of Roman Jewry Re-Considered: Were the Synagogues of Ancient Rome Entirely Homogeneous?," *ZPE*, 104 (1994): 129–41.

Winslow, D. F., "The Maccabean Martyrs: Early Christian Attitudes," *Judaism*, 23, 89 (1974): 78–86.

Winter, B. W., "The Imperial Cult," pp. 93–103 in *The Book of Acts in its First Century Setting, Volume 2: The Book of Acts in Its Graeco-Roman Setting*, ed. D. W. J. Gill and C. Gempf. Grand Rapids, MI: Eerdmans, 1994.

Witherington, B., *The Acts of the Apostles: A Socio-Rhetorical Commentary*. Grand Rapids, MI: Eerdmans, 1998.

—— *Grace in Galatia: A Commentary on St Paul's Letter to the Galatians*. Edinburgh: T. & T. Clark, 1998.

Wright, N. T., *The Climax of the Covenant: Christ and the Law in Pauline Theology*. Minneapolis: Fortress Press, 1992.

Yegül, F., "Baths and Bathing in Roman Antioch," pp. 146–51 in *Antioch: The Lost Ancient City*, ed. C. Kondoleon. Princeton, NJ: Princeton University Press, 2000.

Zetterholm, M., "A Covenant for Gentiles? Covenantal Nomism and the Incident at Antioch," pp. 168–88 in *The Ancient Synagogue from its Origins until 200 C.E.: Papers Presented at an International Conference at Lund University, October 14–17, 2001*, ed. B. Olsson and M. Zetterholm. Stockholm: Almqvist & Wiksell, 2003.

INDEX OF PASSAGES

INDEX OF PASSAGES

INDEX OF SUBJECTS